R. Gupta's®

Sainik School

PREVIOUS YEARS' PAPERS (SOLVED)

WITH EXPLANATORY ANSWERS

For Class VI

by
RPH Editorial Board

2021
EDITION

Ramesh Publishing House, New Delhi

Published by
O.P. Gupta *for* Ramesh Publishing House

Admin. Office
12-H, New Daryaganj Road, Opp. Officers' Mess,
New Delhi-110002 ☏ 23261567, 23275224, 23275124

E-mail: info@rameshpublishinghouse.com
Website: www.rameshpublishinghouse.com

Showroom
● Balaji Market, Nai Sarak, Delhi-6 ☏ 23253720, 23282525
● 4457, Nai Sarak, Delhi-6, ☏ 23918938

Book Code: R-1655

ISBN: 978-93-5012-441-3

HSN Code: 49011010

CONTENTS

R. Gupta's® Useful Books For
Sainik School/ACC / RIMC / NTSE / JNV Exams

RAMESH PUBLISHING HOUSE

12-H, New Darya Ganj Road, Opp. Officers' Mess, New Delhi-110002

For Online Shopping: www.rameshpublishinghouse.com

All India Sainik School Entrance Exam, 2020*
(CLASS-VI)

PAPER-I : MATHEMATICS, GK AND LANGUAGE

Section-A : Mathematics

1. Find the difference between the greatest and the least number that can be written using the digits 6, 2, 7, 4, 3 each only once.
   A. 52965
   B. 53965
   C. 52956
   D. 52659

2. Estimate the product 5980 × 428 by rounding off each number to the nearest hundreds.
   A. 236000
   B. 240000
   C. 2400000
   D. 3000000

3. Three numbers are in the ratio of 3 : 4 : 5 and their LCM is 2400. Their HCF is:
   A. 120
   B. 60
   C. 80
   D. 40

4. Leela reads 25 pages of a book containing 100 pages. Lalita read $\frac{2}{5}$ of the same book. Who read less and by how much?
   A. Leela, 15 pages
   B. Lalita, 16 pages
   C. Leela, 20 pages
   D. Lalita, 20 pages

5. $\left(\frac{\sqrt{625}}{11} \times \frac{14}{\sqrt{25}} \times \frac{11}{\sqrt{196}} \right)$ is equal to
   A. 5
   B. 6
   C. 8
   D. 11

6. Naveen bought 3 m 20 cm cloth for his shirt and 2 m 5 cm cloth for his trousers. Find the total length of cloth bought by him.
   A. 5.7 m
   B. 5.25 m
   C. 4.25 m
   D. 5.00 m

7. The least common multiple of 3, 4 and 9 is:
   A. 36
   B. 12
   C. 27
   D. 45

8. An aeroplane covers a certain distance at a speed of 240 km/h in 5 hours. To cover the same distance in $1\frac{2}{3}$ hours, it must travel at a speed of?
   A. 300 km/h
   B. 360 km/h
   C. 600 km/h
   D. 720 km/h

9. 'A' can lay railway track between two given stations in 16 days and 'B' can do the same job in 12 days. With the help of 'C', they did the job in 4 days only. Then, 'C' alone can do the job in how many days?
   A. $9\frac{1}{5}$ days
   B. $9\frac{2}{5}$ days
   C. $9\frac{3}{5}$ days
   D. $9\frac{4}{5}$ days

10. In the figure, find the ratio of Number of triangles to the number of circles inside the rectangle and Number of squares to all the figures inside the rectangle. 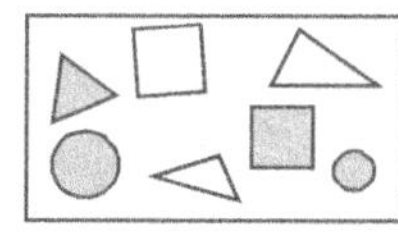
    A. $\frac{3}{2}, \frac{2}{7}$
    B. $\frac{3}{7}, \frac{2}{7}$
    C. $\frac{2}{7}, \frac{2}{7}$
    D. 3, 2

11. Ram, Rahul and Rohit shared a bag of marbles. The bag contained 272 marbles. How many marbles were left over after the friends shared them equally?
    A. 90
    B. 91
    C. 6
    D. 2

12. Cost of 4 dozens of bananas is ₹ 60. How many bananas can be purchased for ₹ 12.50?
A. 10   B. 15
C. 12   D. 18

13. The average weight of 16 boys in a class is 50.25 kg and that of the remaining 8 boys is 45.15 kg. Find the average weight of all the boys in the class.
A. 47.55 kg   B. 48 kg
C. 48.55 kg   D. 49.25 kg

14. Manju runs around a rectangular park of length 35 m and breadth 20 m. Meenu runs around a square park of side 30 m. Who covers less distance any by how much, if Meenu takes 4 rounds and Manju takes 3 rounds completely.
A. Meenu, 150 m   B. Manju, 120 m
C. Manju, 150 m   D. Meenu, 120 m

15. A photo frame is in the shape of quadrilateral with one diagonal longer than the other. Which of the following is the possible shape of the photo frame?
A. Square   B. Rectangle
C. Rhombus   D. None of these

16. The product of a non-zero whole number and its successor is always:
A. Divisible by 3   B. An odd number
C. A prime number   D. An even number

17. A sum fetched a total simple interest of ₹ 4016.25 at the rate of 9% in 5 years. What is the sum?
A. ₹ 4462   B. ₹ 8032
C. ₹ 8900   D. ₹ 8925

18. Find the angle measure between the hands of the clock when time shows 6 PM.
A. 90°   B. 45°
C. 180°   D. 270°

19. Find the volume of a cube of side 6 cm:
A. 216 cm³   B. 360 cm³
C. 72 cm³   D. 108 cm³

20. Write Roman numerical CDXXXIX in Arabic numeral.
A. 439   B. 449
C. 529   D. 539

21. The product of two numbers is 1296. If one number is 16 times the other, find the smaller number.
A. 12   B. 16
C. 4   D. 9

22. The measure of an angle is $\frac{3}{4}$ of 60°. What is the measure of its complementary angle?
A. 30°   B. 60°
C. 45°   D. 20°

23. Subtract the difference of 8.362 and 7.942 from the sum of 5.675 and 1.327.
A. 6.582   B. 4.348
C. 3.982   D. 4.384

24. Find the perimeter of the figure:

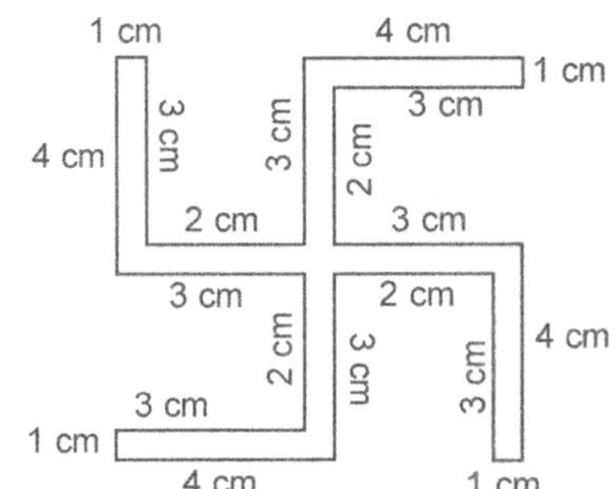

A. 51 cm   B. 52 cm
C. 53 cm   D. 54 cm

25. How much time will it take for an amount of ₹ 450 to yield ₹ 81 as interest at 4.5% per annum of simple interest?
A. 3 years   B. 4 years
C. 6 years   D. 5 years

26. In a triangle, if the second angle is 2 times the first angle and the third angle is 3 times the first angle, find the angles of the triangle.
A. 30°, 60°, 90°   B. 15°, 30°, 45°
C. 45°, 45°, 90°   D. 20°, 40°, 120°

27. The area of a circle is 616 cm². Find its diameter. $\left(\pi = \frac{22}{7} \right)$
A. 28 cm   B. 14 cm
C. 56 cm   D. 32 cm

28. Find the quotient when 53.016 is divided by 24.
A. 2.29
B. 2.209
C. 2.292
D. 2.029

29. A rectangular path of 60 m length and 3 m width is covered by square tiles of side 25 cm. Find the number of tiles used to make this path?
A. 2250
B. 1440
C. 2880
D. 1200

30. What is the value of A in 475 + 64% of 950 = 900 + A.
A. 183
B. 233
C. 1983
D. None of the above

31. What will be HCF of 216, 288 and 720?
A. 12
B. 24
C. 84
D. 72

32. Solve $(106 \times 106 - 94 \times 94) = ?$
A. 2400
B. 2000
C. 1904
D. 1906

33. If $\dfrac{2}{3}$ of 70% of 600 when subtracted from a number is 320, what is the number?
A. 300
B. 600
C. 720
D. 500

34. A mobile phone is sold for ₹ 1650 after purchasing it for ₹ 1500. What is the percentage of profit?
A. 10
B. 15
C. 20
D. 16

35. In the first test of mathematics a student gets 18 marks out of 25. In the second test of same weightage he got 22 marks. What percentage of marks did he get more in the second test?
A. 4%
B. 8%
C. 16%
D. None of the above

36. Average of 20 results is 18. If 3 is subtracted from each result, then what will be the new average?
A. 21
B. 15
C. 16
D. 17

37. Solve $\dfrac{\dfrac{7}{3} \times \dfrac{2}{3} \div \dfrac{3}{5}}{2 + 1\dfrac{2}{3}}$:
A. $\dfrac{99}{70}$
B. $\dfrac{70}{99}$
C. $\dfrac{33}{30}$
D. $\dfrac{70}{27}$

38. If 90.0675 is divided by 15, then quotient is:
A. 6.0045
B. 6.0450
C. 60.0450
D. 0.6045

39. How many seconds are there in 24 hours?
A. 30
B. 60
C. 3600
D. 86400

40. $\sqrt{1089 \div 121}$ value is:
A. 3
B. 13
C. 33
D. 53

41. If angles A, B and C in a triangle ABC are $3x$, $5x$ and $8x + 4$ respectively, then find all the three angles.
A. 33, 55, 92
B. 70, 75, 35
C. 90, 75, 15
D. 90, 95, 100

42. What are Prime factors of 37800?
A. $2 \times 2 \times 3 \times 3 \times 5 \times 5 \times 7 \times 7$
B. $2 \times 2 \times 2 \times 3 \times 3 \times 3 \times 5 \times 5 \times 7$
C. $8 \times 27 \times 25 \times 7$
D. $2 \times 4 \times 25 \times 27 \times 7$

43. (10% of 3.75 + 15% of 7.25) convert into decimal:
A. 1.4625
B. 14.625
C. 1.4652
D. 14.652

44. Which sequence correctly matches these angles with their measures.

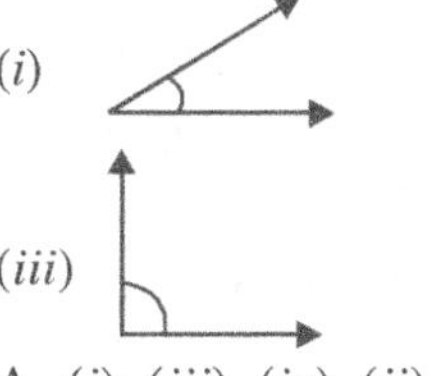

A. (*i*), (*iii*), (*iv*), (*ii*)
B. (*i*), (*ii*), (*iii*), (*iv*)
C. (*iv*), (*iii*), (*ii*), (*i*)
D. (*i*), (*iv*), (*iii*), (*ii*)

45. I am a prime number. If you subtract 2 from me, I become divisible by 7.
- A. 29
- B. 19
- C. 31
- D. 23

Directions (Qs. No. 46 to 50): *The following table has to be consulted.*

Name of the city	Temp. at 3 AM (°C)	Temp. at 3 PM (°C)
Chennai	21.1	29.9
Mumbai	19.0	35.1
Thiruvananthapuram	21.6	33.5
Kolkata	13.1	26.5
Bhopal	9.8	25.9
Srinagar	1.3	8.1
Guwahati	12.8	24.8
Jaipur	10.2	23.2

46. Which place had the highest temperature at 3 AM?
- A. Chennai
- B. Thiruvananthapuram
- C. Srinagar
- D. Jaipur

47. Which place is the coolest at 3 PM?
- A. Kolkata
- B. Srinagar
- C. Mumbai
- D. Bhopal

48. How much higher is the temperature in Mumbai from that of Srinagar at 3 PM?
- A. 8.1
- B. 35.1
- C. 27
- D. 29

49. How many degrees will the temperature at 3 AM need to rise for it to reach 40 degree celsius in Thiruvananthapuram.
- A. 6.5
- B. 18.4
- C. 21.6
- D. 33.5

50. How much lower is the temperature of Kolkata from that in Chennai at both times (3 AM and 3 PM)?
- A. 8° and 3.3°
- B. 3° and 8°
- C. 8° and 8°
- D. 3.3° and 3.3°

Section–B : General Knowledge

51. Black Soil is also known as?
- A. Regur Soil
- B. Red Soil
- C. Laterite Soil
- D. Mountain Soil

52. P.V. Sindhu is associated with which sports?
- A. Badminton
- B. Cricket
- C. Football
- D. Hockey

53. The Space Programme of Govt. of India is looked after by:
- A. ISBT
- B. NTRO
- C. NABARD
- D. ISRO

54. Bhakranangal Project is built on the river?
- A. Sutlej
- B. Mahanadi
- C. Godavari
- D. Cauvery

55. Who is known as a 'Iron Man' of India?
- A. Jawahar Lal Nehru
- B. Mahatma Gandhi
- C. Sardar Vallabhbhai Patel
- D. Subhash Chandra Bose

56. The longest river in South India is?
- A. Mahanadi
- B. Indus
- C. Saraswati
- D. Godavari

57. Which planet is known as a morning star as well as evening star?
- A. Mars
- B. Venus
- C. Mercury
- D. Earth

58. Which Article of constitution provides Indian Citizen 'Right to Equality'?
- A. Article 12
- B. Article 13
- C. Article 17
- D. Article 14

59. 'Narora' nuclear power plant is located in the state of?
- A. Maharashtra
- B. Tamil Nadu
- C. Uttar Pradesh
- D. West Bengal

60. Which of the following diseases spreads through contaminated food and water?
- A. Malaria
- B. Cholera
- C. Dengue
- D. Filaria

61. Which is biggest desert in the World?
A. Kalhari Desert B. Atakama Desert
C. Sahara Desert D. Gobi Desert

62. Manas national park is located in the state of?
A. Assam B. Arunachal Pradesh
C. Himachal Pradesh D. Andhra Pradesh

63. Which of these grows from the roots?
A. Potato B. Ginger
C. Carrot D. Sweet Potato

64. Sahyadris is also known as?
A. Aravali B. Western Ghats
C. Himadri D. Eastern Ghats

65. The gas filled in a weather balloons is:
A. Neon B. Helium
C. Argon D. Oxygen

66. Growing children need more of:
A. Carbohydrates B. Vitamins
C. Proteins D. Fats

67. Which gas is dissolved under pressure in soft drinks?
A. Oxygen B. Carbon dioxide
C. Nitrogen D. Hydrogen

68. Who is the lowest ranked Air Force Officer among these?
A. Wing Commander B. Group Captain
C. Flying officer D. Flight lieutenant

69. Which of the following is a national festival?
A. Baisakhi B. Republic day
C. Pongal D. Chhath puja

70. Dr. Amartya Sen won Nobel Prize in which field?
A. Economics B. Peace
C. Chemistry D. Literature

71. The imaginary line drawn half way between North Pole and South Pole is called:
A. Tropic of Cancer B. Equator
C. Arctic Circle D. Antarctic Circle

72. The largest island in the world is:
A. Australia B. New Zealand
C. Greenland D. Mozambique

73. The coldest place in world, lying in the south frigid zone is
A. Greenland B. Antarctica
C. Australia D. New Zealand

74. Who invented telephone in 1876?
A. Alexander Graham Bell
B. James Hickey
C. Guglielmo Macron
D. Logie Baird

75. 'Ghoomar' is a popular folk dance of which of the following states?
A. Rajasthan B. Madhya Pradesh
C. Odisha D. Uttar Pradesh

Section-C : Language

Directions (Qs. No. 76 to 80): *Read the following passage and answer the questions:*

Midas, the king, was a greedy person. He loved gold more than anything in the world. He had lots of wealth but he was never really a happy person.

One day God Bacchus came to Midas. Midas had once helped god Bacchus and in return Bacchus offered him a gift. "What shall I give you to make you happy," God asked him, Midas thought for a while and then said, "Please give me the power to turn everything I touch into gold." Bacchus laughed and said. "Your wish is granted. As soon as the Sun rises tomorrow, you will have the golden touch."

The next morning Midas woke up, and he had his golden touch. He touched his bed, the chairs, doors, windows and all became gold.

Suddenly, he felt very hungry. He sat at the table but as soon as the food touched his lips. It turned into gold. So did the water, it seemed he could no longer eat or drink. After some time, his daughter came to him, when he put his hand on her, she became a gold statue. In the end, Midas became very sad and prayed God Bacchus to take away the golden touch from him.

76. What kind of man was Midas?
A. a greedy person B. a great miser
C. a brave man D. wise man

77. Who came to Midas one day?
   A. God Jesus   B. God Bacchus
   C. God Zeus   D. God

78. Why did Bacchus offer him a gift?
   A. because he had helped God once
   B. because he had pleased Bacchus
   C. because he had annoyed Bacchus
   D. because he cared for Bacchus

79. What was Midas' wish?
   A. To become rich
   B. To turn anything into gold
   C. To turn his daughter a golden doll
   D. To become powerful

80. Who turned into gold statue when Midas touched?
   A. daughter   B. son
   C. uncle   D. aunt

Rearrange the following words/phrases to make meaningful sentences. Choose the correct sequence.

81. it (a)/ life is (b)/ what we (c)/ make (d)
   A. abcd   B. cdab
   C. dabc   D. bcda

82. gold (a)/ is not (b)/ glitters (c)/ all that (d)
   A. abcd   B. cdba
   C. dabc   D. dcba

83. playing (a)/ in the (b)/ park (c)/ children are (d)
   A. abcd   B. bcda
   C. dabc   D. cdab

Fill in the blanks with the appropriate option.

84. Either work hard ______ give up studies.
   A. nor   B. or
   C. and   D. but

85. He is afraid ______ the dog.
   A. on   B. of
   C. in   D. by

86. He ______ tea every morning.
   A. drinks   B. is drinking
   C. drank   D. drunk

87. The child has been missing ______ yesterday.
   A. for   B. of
   C. by   D. since

Do as directed.

88. John is my ______ brother. (Find out the correct adjective)
   A. elder   B. bigger
   C. old   D. young

89. French is ______ easy language. (Select the correct article)
   A. a   B. an
   C. the   D. none

90. Ashok ______ him yesterday. (Write the correct from of the verb)
   A. meet   B. met
   C. will meet   D. is meeting

Choose the most appropriate option.

91. Which word means nearly the same as 'sufficient'?
   A. infinite   B. adequate
   C. merry   D. surplus

92. Which word is the opposite of 'simple'.
   A. complex   B. easy
   C. obey   D. show

93. A list of books in a library.
   A. monologue   B. dialogue
   C. catalogue   D. diary

94. Find the feminine gender of 'horse'.
   A. mare   B. doe
   C. ewe   D. ram

95. Choose the word which means the opposite of 'RISE'.
   A. fall   B. smooth
   C. pride   D. rash

96. Choose the word which means same as 'GRIEF'.
   A. cheerful   B. sorrow
   C. happy   D. injury

97. One who does not believe in existence of God.
   A. theist   B. pacifist
   C. ascetic   D. atheist

98. The match has been postponed ______ it has been raining outside. (Supply Conjunction)
   A. so   B. because
   C. therefore   D. and

99. This is the boy _______ parents have died. (Supply correct Pronoun)
A. whose   B. who
C. whom   D. his

100. He doesn't help the poor, _______ ? (Use Question Tag)
A. did he   B. does he
C. doesn't   D. do he

PAPER–II : INTELLIGENCE TEST

101. If CATTLE is related to HERD then SHEEP is related to _______.

CATTLE : HERD :: SHEEP : ?
A. FLOCK   B. SWARM
C. SHOAL   D. MOB

102. Choose the alternative that has the same relationship to 09 as 07 has with 56.

07 : 56 :: 09 : ?
A. 54   B. 81
C. 72   D. 99

103. Choose the alternative that will continue the number series below:

5, 11, 17, 23, ?
A. 31   B. 29
C. 28   D. 35

104. If you fold the transparent paper along the dotted line in Figure 'X' which alternative figure from A, B, C and D would you get?

(X)

A.   B.

C.   D.

105. Choose the word which is least like the other words in the group.
A. BAKE   B. PEEL
C. FRY   D. ROAST

106. Which of the following diagrams indicate the best relation between India, Haryana and World?

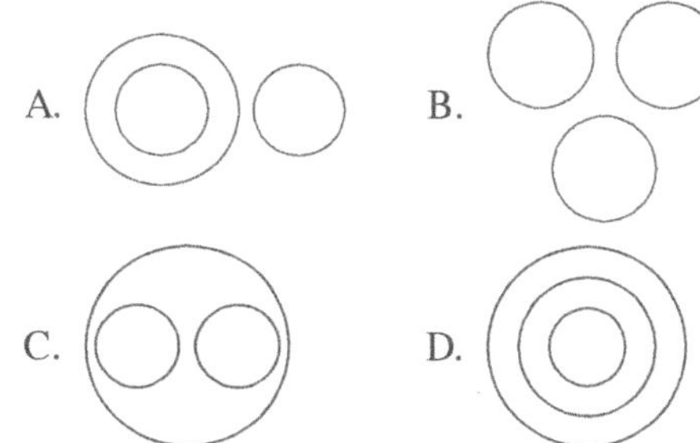

A.   B.

C.   D.

107. Choose the word which is least like the other words in the group.
A. VIRGO   B. PISCES
C. CANCER   D. ORION

108. If STATEMENT is coded as TNEMETATS then POLITICAL will be coded as:
A. LACITILOP   B. LCATILIOP
C. OPILITACL   D. LACITIPOL

109. Figure 'X' is embedded in any one of the four alternative, figures (*a*), (*b*), (*c*) and (*d*). Find the alternative which contains figure 'X' as its part.

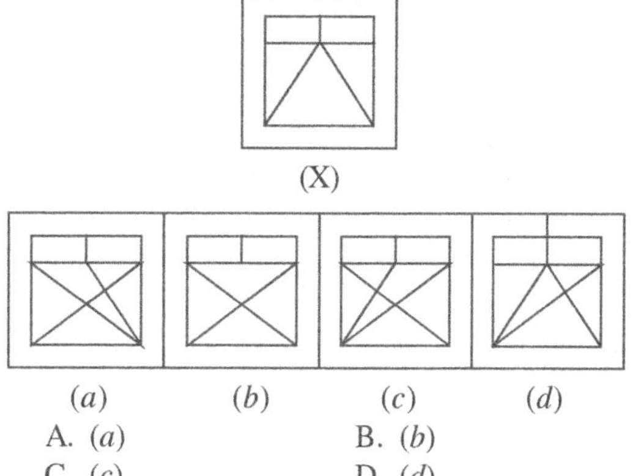

(X)

(*a*)   (*b*)   (*c*)   (*d*)

A. (*a*)   B. (*b*)
C. (*c*)   D. (*d*)

110. If 'A' means add, 'B' means subtract, 'C' means multiply and 'D' means divide, then what would be the answer of the equation?

15 D 5 C 2 A 3 =
A. 13
B. 11
C. 03
D. 09

111. Five men (*a*), (*b*), (*c*), (*d*) and (*e*) read a newspaper. The one who reads first gives it to (*c*). The one who reads last had taken from (*a*), (*e*) was not the first or last to read. There were two readers between (*b*) and (*a*). Who read the newspaper last?
A. (*a*)
B. (*b*)
C. (*c*)
D. (*d*)

112. Choose the alternative that has the same relationship to 16 as 12 has with 168.

12 : 168 :: 16 : ?
A. 232
B. 256
C. 224
D. 208

113. If you fold the transparent paper along the dotted line Figure 'X' which alternative figure would you get?

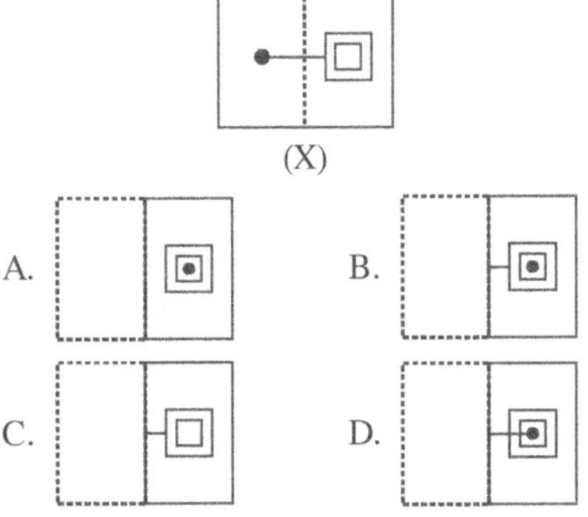

(X)

A.
B.
C.
D.

114. If in a certain code DEAF is written as 3587 and FILE is written as 7465 then IDEAL will be written as?
A. 43568
B. 43586
C. 63548
D. 48536

115. Choose the word which is least like the other words in the group.
A. PLASTIC
B. WOOL
C. PAPER
D. WOOD

116. If we arrange the given words in alphabetical order, which word would come at last place, choose the correct alternative?
A. ROBBER
B. RANDOM
C. RESTRICT
D. RESTAURANT

117. Choose the alternative that will continue the number series below:

11, 13, 17, 19, 23, 25, ?
A. 27
B. 29
C. 31
D. 33

118. Choose the correct alternative that has the same relation to BMJ as HSY is to EPV.

BMJ : ? :: EPV : HSY
A. DRM
B. YJG
C. EPM
D. EON

119. Which of the following diagrams indicates the best relation between Flower, Lotus and Rose?

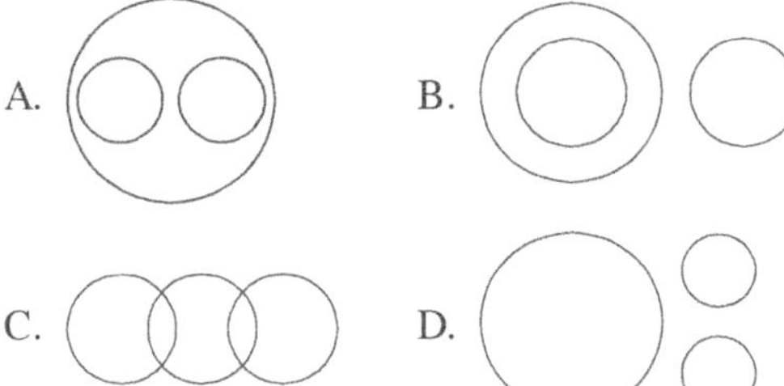

A.
B.
C.
D.

120. Choose the alternative that has the same relationship to 11 as 49 has with 07.

07 : 49 :: 11 : ?
A. 111
B. 90
C. 81
D. 121

121. Choose the word which is least like the other words in the group.
A. GREEN
B. PINK
C. INDIGO
D. VIOLET

122. If X is the brother of the son of Y's son, how is X related to Y?
A. Son
B. Brother
C. Grandson
D. Cousin

123. Area of rectangle is 48 m². If the length is 6 m then breadth = ______.
A. 13 m
B. 6 m
C. 10 m
D. 8 m

124. The priest told the devotee, "The temple bell is rung at regular intervals of 45 minutes. The last bell was rung 5 minutes ago. The next bell is due to be rung at 7 : 45 AM." At what time did the priest give this information to the devotee?

A. 7:00 AM   B. 7:05 AM
C. 6:55 AM   D. 7:40 AM

125. If in a certain code MBS is coded as ODU then BRL will be coded as?
A. DTN   B. DUN
C. CSM   D. CTN

ANSWERS

1	2	3	4	5	6	7	8	9	10
A	C	D	A	A	B	A	D	C	A
11	**12**	**13**	**14**	**15**	**16**	**17**	**18**	**19**	**20**
D	A	C	C	C	D	D	C	A	A
21	**22**	**23**	**24**	**25**	**26**	**27**	**28**	**29**	**30**
D	C	A	B	B	A	A	B	C	A
31	**32**	**33**	**34**	**35**	**36**	**37**	**38**	**39**	**40**
D	A	B	A	C	B	B	A	D	A
41	**42**	**43**	**44**	**45**	**46**	**47**	**48**	**49**	**50**
A	B	A	A	D	B	B	C	B	A
51	**52**	**53**	**54**	**55**	**56**	**57**	**58**	**59**	**60**
A	A	D	A	C	D	B	D	C	B
61	**62**	**63**	**64**	**65**	**66**	**67**	**68**	**69**	**70**
C	A	C	B	B	C	B	C	B	A
71	**72**	**73**	**74**	**75**	**76**	**77**	**78**	**79**	**80**
B	C	B	A	A	A	B	A	B	A
81	**82**	**83**	**84**	**85**	**86**	**87**	**88**	**89**	**90**
D	D	C	B	B	A	D	A	B	B
91	**92**	**93**	**94**	**95**	**96**	**97**	**98**	**99**	**100**
B	A	C	A	A	B	D	B	A	B
101	**102**	**103**	**104**	**105**	**106**	**107**	**108**	**109**	**110**
A	C	B	D	B	D	D	A	D	D
111	**112**	**113**	**114**	**115**	**116**	**117**	**118**	**119**	**120**
D	C	D	B	A	A	B	C	A	D
121	**122**	**123**	**124**	**125**					
B	C	D	B	A					

EXPLANATORY ANSWERS

1. Using the digits 6, 2, 7, 4, 3 each only once
Greatest number = 76432
Least number = 23467
∴ Difference = greatest number – least number
= 76432 – 23467
= 52965

2. 5980 × 428 = 2559440
In option (C) 2400000, the nearest hundreds.

3. Let three numbers are $3x$, $4x$, $5x$
Then LCM = $60x$ (LCM of $3x$, $4x$ and $5x$)
$\Rightarrow$ $2400 = 60x \Rightarrow x = 40$

$\therefore$ Three numbers are 3 × 40, 4 × 40, 5 × 40

$\therefore$ HCF = 40   [HCF = least common]

4. The number of pages of a book = 100

Lalita reads pages = $\dfrac{2}{5}$ of a book

$$= \dfrac{2}{5} \times 100 = 40$$

and Leela reads pages = 25

$\therefore$ Lalita reads pages – Leela reads pages

$$= 40 - 25 = 15$$

Here, Leela reads 15 pages less than Lalita.

5. $\dfrac{\sqrt{625}}{11} \times \dfrac{14}{\sqrt{25}} \times \dfrac{11}{\sqrt{196}}$

$$= \dfrac{25}{11} \times \dfrac{14}{5} \times \dfrac{11}{14}$$

$$\left[\sqrt{625} = 25, \sqrt{25} = 5, \sqrt{196} = 14 \right]$$

$$= \dfrac{25}{5} = 5$$

6. The total length of cloth = 3m 20 cm + 2 m 5 cm

$$= 5 \text{ m } 25 \text{ cm}$$
$$= 5.25 \text{ m}$$

$$25 \text{ cm} = \dfrac{25}{100} \text{m} = 5.25 \text{ m}$$

7. $3 = 3 \times 1$

         $4 = 2 \times 2 = 2^2$

         $9 = 3 \times 3 = 3^2$

      LCM $= 2^2 \times 3^2$

         $= 4 \times 9 = 36.$

8. Speed of an aeroplane = 240 km/h

and   time = 5 hours

         [distance = speed × time]

$\therefore$ distance cover = 240 × 5 = 1200 km

Now, to cover the same distance in $1\dfrac{2}{3}$ hours

$\therefore$ Speed $= \dfrac{\text{Distance}}{\text{time}}$

$$= \dfrac{1200}{1\dfrac{2}{3}} = \dfrac{1200}{\dfrac{5}{3}}$$

$$= 1200 \times \dfrac{3}{5} = 24 \times 3 = 720 \text{ km/h}$$

$\therefore$ Speed = 720 km/h.

9. As, A can lay railway track in 16 days

So, A can lay railway track in 1 day = $\dfrac{1}{16}$

and B can lay railway track in 12 days

So, B can lay railway track in 1 day = $\dfrac{1}{12}$

Let C can lay railway track in x days

Then C can lay railway track in 1 day = $\dfrac{1}{x}$

$\therefore$ By question,

$$\dfrac{1}{16} + \dfrac{1}{12} + \dfrac{1}{x} = \dfrac{1}{4}$$

$\Rightarrow$ $\dfrac{3+4}{48} + \dfrac{1}{x} = \dfrac{1}{4}$

$\Rightarrow$ $\dfrac{7}{48} + \dfrac{1}{x} = \dfrac{1}{4}$

$\Rightarrow$ $\dfrac{1}{x} = \dfrac{1}{4} - \dfrac{7}{48}$

$$= \dfrac{12-7}{48} = \dfrac{5}{48}$$

$\Rightarrow$ $\dfrac{1}{x} = \dfrac{5}{48}$

$\Rightarrow$ $x = \dfrac{48}{5} = 9\dfrac{3}{5}$ days

Hence, (C) alone can do the job in $9\dfrac{3}{5}$ days.

10. The number of triangles inside the rectangle

$$= 3$$

and the number of circles inside the rectangle

$$= 2$$

$\therefore$ Ratio of the number of triangles and circles

$$= \dfrac{3}{2}$$

and the number of squares inside the rectangle

$$= 2$$

and, the number of all the figures inside the rectangle = 7

∴ Ratio of the number of squares and all figures = $\dfrac{2}{7}$

Hence, ratio is $\dfrac{3}{2}, \dfrac{2}{7}$

11. The number of Marbles in a bag = 272

∵ Ram, Rahul and Rohit shared then equally

∴

$$3 \, \big|\, \underline{272} \, \big|\, 90$$
$$\underline{-270}$$
$$2$$

∴ 272 = 3 × 90 + 2, Here, 272 – 30 × 90 = 2

∴ Marbles were left after share = 2.

12. ₹ 60 cost = 4 dozens of bananas

= 4 × 12 bananas

∵ ₹ 60 cost = 48 bananas

∴ ₹ 1 cost = $\dfrac{48}{60}$ bananas

∴ ₹ 12.50 cost = $\dfrac{48}{60} \times 1250$ bananas

$$= \dfrac{48}{6000} \times 12.50 = \dfrac{48}{600} \times 125$$

$$= \dfrac{4}{50} \times 125 = \dfrac{4}{2} \times 5$$

$$= 2 \times 5 = 10 \text{ bananas.}$$

Hence, 10 bananas can be purchased for ₹ 12.50.

13. As, the average weight of 16 boys = 50.25 kg

So, the total weight of 16 boys = 16 × 50.25 kg

and, the average weight of 8 boys = 45.15 kg

∴ The total weight of 8 boys = 8 × 45.15 kg

∴ The average weight of all the boys in the class

$$= \dfrac{\text{The total weight of all the boys}}{\text{The total number of all the boys}}$$

$$= \dfrac{16 \times 50.25 + 8 \times 45.15}{24}$$

$$= \dfrac{804.00 + 361.20}{24}$$

$$= \dfrac{1165.20}{24} = 48.55 \text{ kg.}$$

14. A rectangular park,

Length = 35 m

Breadth = 20 m

∴ Perimeter = 2(l + b)

= 2(35 + 20)

= 2 × 55 = 110 m

∴ Manju takes 3 rounds a rectangular park

∴ Manju covers distance = 3 × perimeter

= 3 × 110 m

= 330 m

And, A square park

Length of side = 30 m

∴ Perimeter = 4 × side = 4 × 30 = 120 m

Meenu takes 4 rounds a square park

∴ Meenu covers distance = 4 × perimeter

= 4 × 120 m = 480 m

Hence, Manju covers less distance by

= 480 – 330 m = 150 m.

15. A quadrilateral with one diagonal longer then the other.

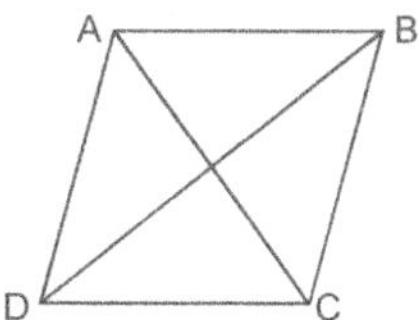

∴ Quadrilateral is a rhombus

Here, in figure

BD > AC, and all sides equal.

17. ∵ Simple interest = ₹ 4016.25

$r = 9\%$, $t = 5$ years ∴ $p = ?$

∴

$$\text{S.I.} = \dfrac{p \times t \times r}{100}$$

$$\Rightarrow 4016.25 = \dfrac{p \times 5 \times 9}{100}$$

∴

$$p = \dfrac{4016.25 \times 100}{5 \times 9}$$

∴

$$p = \dfrac{401625}{5 \times 9} = \dfrac{80325}{9} = 8925$$

Hence, p = sum = ₹ 8925.

18. The angle measure between the hands of the clock when time show 12 AM = 360°

and the angle measure between the hands in 12 hours = 360°

∴ 1 hour = $\dfrac{360°}{12} = 30°$

∴ 6 hours = 30° × 6 = 180°

$\therefore$ The angle measures between the hands when time shows 6 PM = 180°.

19. A side of cube = 6 cm

$\therefore$ The volume of a cube
$$= (\text{side})^3 = (6 \text{ cm})^3 = 216 \text{ cm}^3.$$

20. Roman numeral CDXXXIX
Arabic numeral 439.

21. Let the smaller number = x
Then, one number = $16\,x$

$\therefore \quad x \times 16x = 1296$

$\Rightarrow \quad 16x^2 = 1296$

$\Rightarrow \quad x^2 = \dfrac{1296}{16} = \dfrac{162}{2} = 81$

$\Rightarrow \quad x^2 = 81$

$\Rightarrow \quad x = \sqrt{81}$

$\Rightarrow \quad x = 9$

Hence, smaller number = $x = 9$.

22. The measure of an angle
$$= \frac{3}{4} \times 60 = 45°$$

$\therefore$ Complementary of 45° = 90 − 45° = 45°.

23. $(5.675 + 1.327) − (8.362 − 7.942)$
$$= 7.002 − 0.42 = 6.582.$$

24. The perimeter of one part of figure

$$= AB + BC + CD + DE + EF$$
$$= (2 + 3 + 1 + 4 + 3) \text{ cm}$$
$$= 13 \text{ cm}$$

$\therefore$ The perimeter of the figure
$$= 4 \times 13 \text{ cm} = 52 \text{ cm}.$$

25. Here, p = ₹ 450, r = 4.5%,
Simple interest = ₹ 81

$\therefore \qquad \text{time} = \dfrac{\text{S.I.} \times 100}{p \times r}$

$$= \frac{81 \times 100}{450 \times 4.5} = \frac{81 \times 1000}{450 \times 45}$$

$$= \frac{9 \times 100}{45 \times 5} = \frac{1 \times 20}{5} = 4 \text{ years.}$$

26. Let the first angle is $x°$ in a triangle
Then, the second angle = $2x$
and, the third angle = $3x$
As, sum of the angles in a triangle is 180°
So, $x° + 2x° + 3x° = 180°$

$\Rightarrow \qquad 6x° = 180°$

$\Rightarrow \qquad x° = \dfrac{180°}{6} = 30°$

$\Rightarrow \qquad x° = 30°$

$\therefore$ angles are $x = 30°$, $2x = 60°$, $3x = 90°$

27. The area of a circle = 616 cm²

$\therefore \qquad \pi r^2 = 616 \text{ cm}^2$

$\Rightarrow \qquad \dfrac{22}{7} r^2 = 616 \text{ cm}^2$

$$r^2 = \frac{616}{\dfrac{22}{7}} = \frac{616}{22} \times 7 = 28 \times 7$$

$\Rightarrow \qquad r^2 = 28 \times 7 = 4 \times 7 \times 7$

$\Rightarrow \qquad r^2 = (2 \times 7)^2$

$\Rightarrow \qquad r = 2 \times 7 = 14 \text{ cm}$

$\therefore$ Diameter = $2r$ = 2 × 14 cm = 28 cm.

28. 53.016 is divide by 24

$\therefore \quad \dfrac{53.016}{24} = 2.209$

$\therefore$ quotient = 2.209

```
24 | 53.016 | 2.209
     −48
     ─────
      50
     −48
     ─────
      216
     −216
     ─────
        ×
```

29. A rectangular path
length = 60 m = 60 × 100 = 6000 cm
and width = 3 m = 3 × 100 = 300 cm

$\therefore$ Area of path = $l \times b$ = 6000 × 300 cm²
$$= 18,00,000 \text{ cm}^2$$

and, Side of square tile = 25 cm
Area of tiles = $(\text{side})^2$
$$= (25)^2 = 625 \text{ cm}^2$$

The number of tiles used to make this path

13

$$= \frac{\text{area of park}}{\text{area of tile}}$$

$$= \frac{18,00,000}{625} = \frac{72,000}{25}$$

$$= \frac{720 \times 100}{25} = 720 \times 4 = 2880$$

Hence, the number of tiles = 2880.

30. 475 + 64% of 950 = 900 + A

$$\Rightarrow 475 + 950 \times \frac{64}{100} = 900 + A$$

$$\Rightarrow 475 + 950 \times \frac{16}{25} = 900 + A$$

$$\Rightarrow 475 + 38 \times 16 = 900 + A$$

$\Rightarrow 475 + 608 = 900 + A$

$\Rightarrow \quad 1083 = 900 + A$

$\Rightarrow \qquad A = 1083 - 900$

$\Rightarrow \qquad A = 183$

31. HCF of 216, 288 and 720

$$\begin{array}{r|r|l} 216 & 288 & 1 \\ & -216 & \\ \hline & 72 \end{array} \begin{array}{r|l} 720 & 10 \\ -720 & \\ \hline \times \end{array}$$

$$\text{HCF} = 72$$

32. $106 \times 106 - 94 \times 94 = 11236 - 8836 = 2400$

33. Let the number = x

Then, $x - \dfrac{2}{3}$ of 70% of 600 = 320

$$\Rightarrow x - \frac{2}{3} \times \frac{70}{100} \times 600 = 320$$

$$\Rightarrow x - \frac{2}{3} \times 70 \times 6 = 320$$

$\Rightarrow x - 2 \times 70 \times 2 = 320$

$\Rightarrow \ x - 280 = 320$

$\Rightarrow \qquad x = 280 + 320$

$\Rightarrow \qquad x = 600$

Hence, the number of $x = 600$

34. Here, Selling price of a mobile phone = ₹ 1650
and Cost price = ₹ 1500

$\therefore \qquad$ Profit = S.P. – C.P.

$$= 1650 - 1500 = ₹\ 150$$

Now, the percentage of profit = $\dfrac{\text{Profit} \times 100}{\text{Cost price}}$

$$= \frac{150 \times 100}{1500} = \frac{150}{15} = 10\%$$

35. In the first test, 18 marks out of 25

$\therefore$ Percentage = $\dfrac{18}{25} \times 100 = 72\%$

And, in the second test, he got 22 marks of 25

$\therefore$ Percentage = $\dfrac{22}{25} \times 100 = 88\%$

$\therefore$ In second test he get more mark

$$= 88 - 72 = 16\%$$

36. Average of 20 results is 18

$\therefore$ All results = 20 × 18 = 360

If 3 is subtracted from each result

Then, new results = 360 – 60 = 300

$\therefore$ The new average = $\dfrac{300}{20} = 15$

37. $$\dfrac{\dfrac{7}{3} \times \dfrac{2}{3} \div \dfrac{3}{5}}{2 + 1\dfrac{2}{3}} = \dfrac{\dfrac{7}{3} \times \dfrac{2}{3} \times \dfrac{5}{3}}{2 + \dfrac{5}{3}}$$

$$= \dfrac{\dfrac{70}{27}}{\dfrac{6+5}{3}}$$

$$= \frac{70}{27} \times \frac{3}{11} = \frac{70}{99}$$

38. If 90.0675 is divided by 15

Then, $\dfrac{90.0675}{15} = 6.0045,$

$$\begin{array}{r|l|l} 15 & 90.0675 & 6.0045 \\ & -90 & \\ \hline & 067 & \\ & -60 & \\ \hline & 75 & \\ & -75 & \\ \hline & \times & \end{array}$$

Hence, quotient = 6.0045

39. 24 hours = 24 × 60 min.

$$= 24 \times 60 \times 60 \text{ sec.}$$

$$= 24 \times 3600 \text{ sec.}$$

$$= 86400 \text{ sec.}$$

40. $\sqrt{1089 \div 21} = \sqrt{\dfrac{1089}{121}} = \dfrac{33}{11} = 3$

41. The sum of all angles of a triangle is 180°

$\angle A + \angle B + \angle C = 180°$

$\Rightarrow 3x + 5x + 8x + 4 = 180°$

$\Rightarrow 16x + 4° = 180°$

$\Rightarrow 16x = 180° - 4° = 176°$

$\Rightarrow x = \dfrac{176°}{16} = 11°$

Hence, all the three angles are

$\angle A = 3x = 33°,$

$\angle B = 5x = 55°,$

$\angle C = 8x + 4 = 92°$

i.e., 33°, 55°, 92°

42.

2	37800
2	18900
2	9450
3	4725
3	1575
3	525
5	175
5	35
	7

Therefore, prime factor of 37800

$= 2 \times 2 \times 2 \times 3 \times 3 \times 3 \times 5 \times 5 \times 7$

43. 10% of 3.75 + 15% of 7.25

$= \dfrac{10}{100} \times 3.75 + \dfrac{15}{100} \times 7.25$

$= \dfrac{1}{100} \times 3.75 + 0.15 \times 7.25$

$= 0.1 \times 3.75 \times + 1.0875$

$= 0.375 + 1.0875$

$= 1.4625$

44. (*i*) 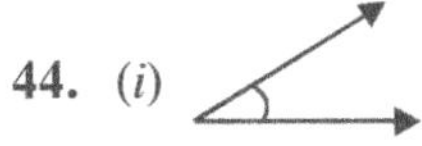

(*iii*) 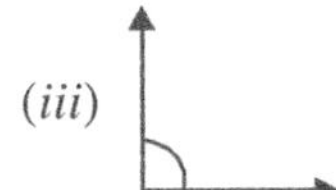

(*iv*) 

(*ii*)

45. $23 - 2 = 21,\ \dfrac{21}{7} = 3$

46. 21.6°C = Thiruvananthapuram had the highest temperature at 3AM.

47. Srinagar is the coolest at 3 PM = 8.1°C.

48. The temperature in Mumbai from that of Srinagar at 3 PM = 35.1° – 8.1°C = 27°C.

49. The temperature at 3 PM need to rise 40°C in Thiruvananthapuram = 45°C – 21.6° = 18.4°.

50. At 3 AM → Chennai – Kolkata

$= 21.1°C – 13.1°C = 8°C$

At 3 PM → Chennai – Kolkata

$= 29.9°C – 26.6°C = 3.3°C$

101. CATTLE : HERO :: SHEEP : ?

As, group of CATTLE is related to HERO

So, group of SHEEP is related to FLOCK.

102. 07 : 56 :: 09 : ?

Here, $07 \times 8 = 56$

Similarly, $09 \times 8 = 72$

103.

$5 \underset{+6}{\quad} 11 \underset{+6}{\quad} 17 \underset{+6}{\quad} 23 \underset{+6}{\quad} ?$

$5 + 6 = 11,$

$11 + 6 = 17,$

$17 + 6 = 23,$

$23 + 6 = 29$

106. Haryana is an unit of India and India is an unit of world.

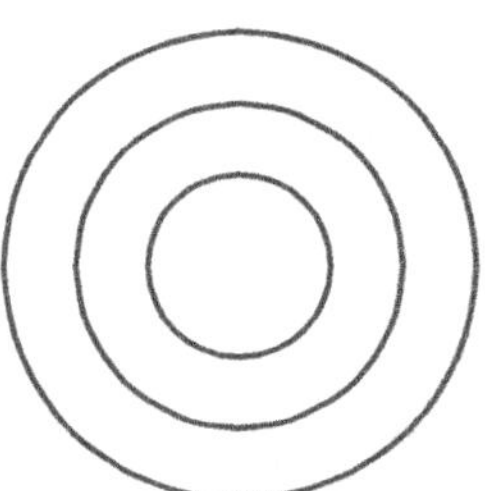

So, diagram idicate the best relation.

107. All expect Orion are Zodiac signs while orion is a constellaiton.

108. 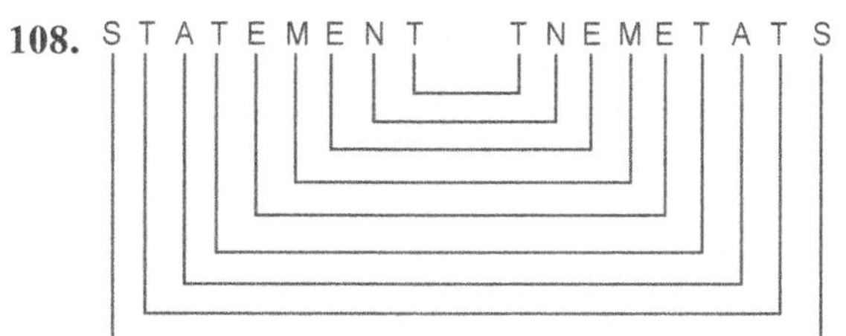

Similarly,

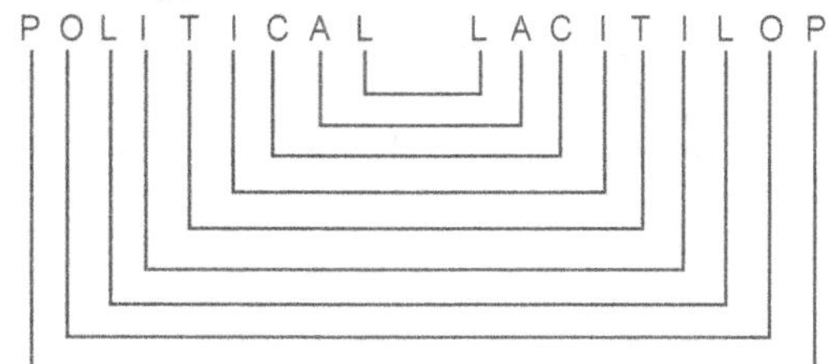

The letters of the word are written backward.

110. $15 \; D \; 5 \; C \; 2 \; A \; 3 = 15 \div 5 \times 2 + 3$
$= 3 \times 2 + 3 = 6 + 3 = 9$

111. Five men (a), (b) (c), (d) and (e) read a newspaper.

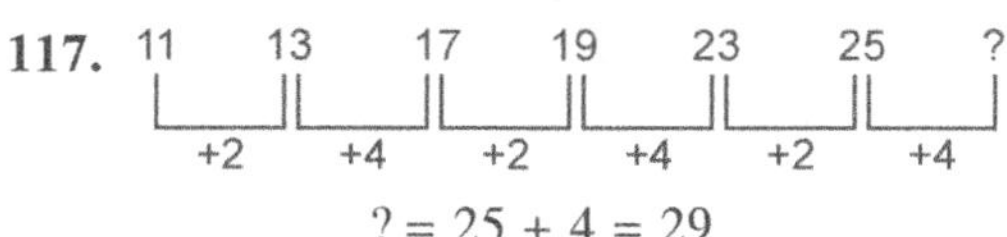

(d) reads the newspaper last.

112. $12 : 168 :: 16 : ?$
As, $12 \times 14 = 168$
So, $16 \times 14 = 224$

114. Code DEAF is written as 3587
and FILE is written as 7465
$\therefore$ IDEAL will be written as 43586
As, I = 4, D = 3, E = 5, A = 8, L = 6

116. We arrange the given words in alphabetical order.
RANDOM ← RESTAURANT ← RESTRICT ← ROBBER

117. 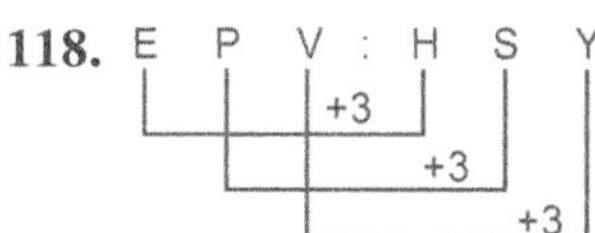

$? = 25 + 4 = 29$

118. E P V : H S Y

Similarly,

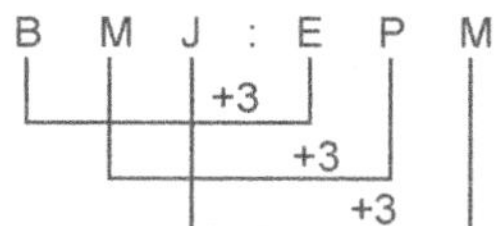

The word is coded by moving the letters two steps forward.

119. As, Lotus and Rose are flower
So, the diagram indicate the best relation between Flower, Lotus and Rose

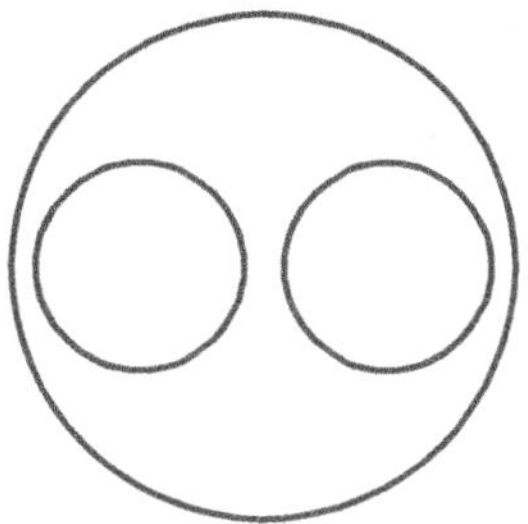

120. $07 : 49 :: 11 : ?$
Here, $(07)^2 = 49$
Similarly, $(11)^2 = 121$

121. PINK colours is not in 7 colour

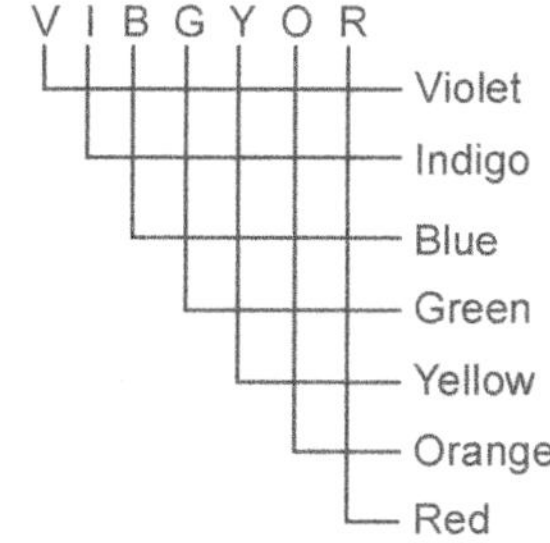

122. A is the son of Y,
B is the son of Y's son,
B is the grandson of Y
X is the brother of B

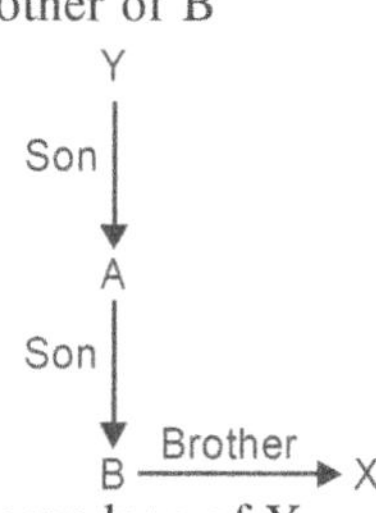

Here, X is grandson of Y

123. Area of rectangle $= 48$ m^2, $l = 6$ m

$\Rightarrow \quad l \times b = 48$ m^2

$\Rightarrow \quad 6 \times b = 48$

$\Rightarrow \qquad b = \dfrac{48}{6} = 8$ m

$\Rightarrow \qquad b = 8$ m

$\therefore \quad$ Breadth $= 8$ m

124. Regular intervals $= 45$ minutes

The next bell be rung at 7 : 45 AM

The last bell was rung 5 minutes ago

$\therefore$ Present time $= 7 : 05$ AM

125. 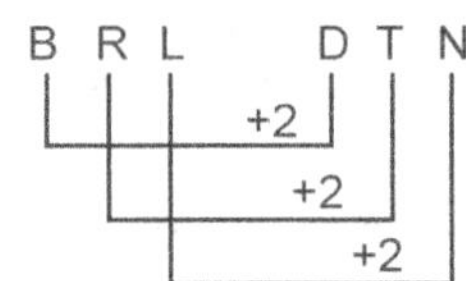

Similarly,

The coded letters are moved two steps forward.

All India Sainik School Entrance Exam, 2019*
(CLASS-VI)

PAPER-I : MATHEMATICS, GK AND LANGUAGE

Section-A : Mathematics

1. A student multiplied 7236 by 65 instead of multiplying by 56. By how much was his answer greater than the correct answer?
   A. 87555
   B. 65124
   C. 72360
   D. 65000

2. Simplify: $1 \div \left\{ \dfrac{1}{2} + \dfrac{1}{3} + \dfrac{1}{6} \div \left(\dfrac{3}{4} - \dfrac{1}{3} \right) \right\}$

   A. $\dfrac{30}{37}$
   B. $\dfrac{37}{30}$
   C. $\dfrac{15}{37}$
   D. $\dfrac{15}{30}$

3. Find the perimeter of the following figure
   A. 15 cm
   B. 15 cm^2
   C. 16 cm
   D. 25 cm^2

4. A floor is 5 m long and 4 m wide. A square carpet of side 3 m is laid on the floor. Find the area of the floor that is not carpeted.
   A. 21 m^2
   B. 29 m^2
   C. 11 m^2
   D. 21 cm^2

5. Find out the smallest number which is divisible by 6, 12, 18
   A. 360
   B. 180
   C. 120
   D. 60

6. Which of the following measures of angles given can be those of a isosceles triangle?
   A. 90, 45
   B. 60, 30
   C. 120, 40
   D. 90, 50

7. The length of a rectangle is 5 cm more than its breadth. If the perimeter of the rectangle is 50 cm than what is the area?
   A. 150 cm^2
   B. 250 cm^2
   C. 900 cm^2
   D. 800 cm^2

8. 12 persons can finish a piece of work in 15 days. In how many days will the same work be completed by 20 persons?
   A. 15 days
   B. 9 days
   C. 30 days
   D. 20 days

9. The LCM of two prime numbers is
   A. difference
   B. product
   C. sum
   D. none of the above

10. In a School of 1000 students, 330 come by bus, 400 come walking and the remaining are dropped by parents. What is the percentage of students that do not ride the bus to school?
    A. 67%
    B. 27%
    C. 50%
    D. 33%

11. A train from Station A to Station B covers a distance of 616 km at a uniform speed of 112 km/hr. It Halts at Station. B for 1 hour before starting back. How much time will it take to complete the journey and reach back to Station A (i.e. from A to B and back)?
    A. 11 hours
    B. 12 hours 45 minutes
    C. 12 hours
    D. 5 hours 30 minutes

12. A table was sold at 16% loss for ₹ 3360. Find the cost price of the table

---

A. ₹ 4000   B. ₹ 3392
C. ₹ 3600   D. ₹ 4296

13. There are 17 rooms in a school, every room has two fans and four LED bulbs. How many switches are required for the school if every fan requires a switch and one switch is required for every two bulbs?
A. 34   B. 68
C. 102   D. 17

14. The product of two decimal numbers is 12.194. If one of them is 4.69, what the other number is?
A. 7.6   B. 2.6
C. 9.8   D. 4.8

15. Rahul purchases a chair for ₹ 600 and uses ₹ 200 for repairs. If he sells it for ₹ 1000 then he has:
A. no profit no loss
B. 25% loss
C. 25% profit
D. cannot be calculated

16. The temperature dropped 15 degree celsius in the last 30 days. If the rate of temperature drop remains the same, how many degrees will the temperature drop in the next ten days?
A. 10 degrees   B. 5 degrees
C. 20 degrees   D. 15 degrees

17. From a basket of mangoes when counted in twos there was one extra, counted in threes there were two extra, counted in fours there were three extra, counted in fives there were four extra, counted in sixes there were five extra. But counted in sevens there were no extra. At least how many mangoes were there in the basket?
A. 119   B. 110
C. 111   D. 126

18. Which of the following two digit number when added to 27 gets reversed?
A. 27   B. 24
C. 47   D. 70

19. The ratio of income to expenditure of Radha is 7:5. If she saves ₹ 2000 a month, what is her annual income?
A. ₹ 144000   B. ₹ 60000
C. ₹ 95000   D. ₹ 84000

20. The ratio of the length to breadth of a rectangular lawn is 3 : 5. It costs ₹ 3200 to fence it at the rate of ₹ 2 a meter. What would be the cost of developing the lawn at the rate of ₹ 10 per square meter?
A. ₹ 18,00,000   B. ₹ 15,00,000
C. ₹ 19,00,000   D. ₹ 21,00,000

21. A, B and C divide an amount amongst themselves in the ratio of 4 : 7 : 9 respectively. If B's share in the amount is ₹ 2989, what is the total amount?
A. ₹ 9820   B. ₹ 8540
C. ₹ 2720   D. ₹ 8640

22. The average age of a class of 40 students is 18 years. When the teachers age is also included to calculate the average age becomes 19 years. What is the teacher's age?
A. 59 years   B. 69 years
C. 49 years   D. 39 years

23. What is the greatest number which when divides 3026 and 5053 leaves remainders 11 and 13 respectively?
A. 15   B. 30
C. 45   D. 60

24. Ravi purchased a chair at ₹ 500 and sold it at ₹ 550. What was his gain or loss percent?
A. 10%   B. 20%
C. 30%   D. 40%

25. A certain distance is being covered in 28 hours by walking with a speed of 5 km/h. If the speed is increased by 2 km/h then in how much time the same distance will be covered?
A. 30 hours   B. 15 hours
C. 20 hours   D. 25 hours

26. A piece of wire $\dfrac{7}{8}$ meter long broke into two pieces. One piece was $\dfrac{1}{4}$ meter long. How long is the other piece?
A. $\dfrac{4}{8}$ m   B. $\dfrac{5}{8}$ m
C. $\dfrac{6}{8}$ m   D. $\dfrac{7}{8}$ m

27. What is the missing number in the sequence 2, 5, 10, 14, 18, 23, 26, 32 ..... ?
A. 33
B. 34
C. 36
D. 37

28. 30 men can do a piece of work in 16 days. In how many days 8 men can do the same work?
A. 30 days
B. 40 days
C. 50 days
D. 60 days

29. Ram, Shyam and Mohan runs at speed of 75, 50 and 30 m/minute respectively. After how much time will they meet together for the first time running with the same speed?
A. 5 hours
B. 2 hours
C. 3 hours
D. $\dfrac{5}{2}$ hours

30. Represent 26 kg 5 gram using concept of decimals.
A. 26.05 kg
B. 26.005 kg
C. 26.5 kg
D. 26.0005 kg

31. At what rate, a sum of ₹ 6000 will amounts to ₹ 7800 in 5 years?
A. 3%
B. 4%
C. 5%
D. 6%

32. What will be the depth of a cubical pond whose volume is 729 m^3?
A. 9 m
B. 6 m
C. 8 m
D. 5 m

33. Evaluate:
$3 \times 7 + 4 - 6 \div 3 - 7 + 45 \div 5 \times 4 + 49$
A. 101
B. 103
C. 99
D. 35

34. In what time a train whose length is 100 m moving with a speed of 60 km/h crosses a platform whose length is 150 m?
A. 15s
B. 14s
C. 18s
D. 20s

35. Ashu takes 12 days to complete the work. Pranav takes 10 days to complete the same work. Ashu, Pranav and Ramu take 5 days to complete the same work. How many days will Ramu take to complete the same work?
A. 70 days
B. 90 days
C. 60 days
D. 50 days

36. The LCM of two numbers is 28 times of their HCF. The sum of their LCM and HCF is 1740. If one number is 240 then what is the other number?
A. 420
B. 460
C. 500
D. 380

37. Four clocks rings at the time interval of 6s, 8s, 12s and 18s respectively. If they ring together at 12 am then how many times will they ring together within the time span of 6 minutes?
A. 6 times
B. 4 times
C. 7 times
D. 5 times

38. What is the least multiple of 23 which when divided by 18, 21 and 24 leaves remainders 7, 10 and 13 respectively?
A. 1240
B. 3013
C. 2364
D. 7628

39. A milkman has two cans of milk containing 75 litres and 45 litres of milk respectively. What will be the measure of largest vessel that can measure the milk of the two cans exactly?
A. 12 litres
B. 18 litres
C. 15 litres
D. 10 litres

40. A table was purchased at ₹ 1000 and was sold at ₹ 800. What was gain or loss% in this transaction?
A. 5%
B. 10%
C. 20%
D. 30%

41. The average weight of 6 boys gets increased by 5 kg if a boy with weight 20 kg is replaced by a new boy. What is the weight of new boy?
A. 41 kg
B. 50 kg
C. 65 kg
D. 49 kg

42. A man covers a distance of 40 km. He covers first 10 km at 10 km/h, second 10 km at 20 km/h, third 10 km at 30 km/h and last 10 km at 40 km/h. What is the average speed of man?
A. 18.2 km/h
B. 19.2 km/h
C. 19.0 km/h
D. 16.2 km/h

43. If area of rectangular garden of 5 m breadth is 300 sq. m, then what will be the length of garden?

A. 60 m   B. 70 m
C. 80 m   D. 90 m

44. If the square of a number is added to the square of 28 the result is 1808. What is the number?
A. 66   B. 50
C. 32   D. 16

45. Cost of a dozen pens is ₹ 180 and cost of 8 ball pens is ₹ 56. The ratio of the cost of a pen to the cost of a ball pen is
A. 15:7   B. 180:56
C. 1:1   D. 8:15

46. A truck requires 108 litres of diesel for covering a distance of 594 km. How much diesel will be required by the truck to cover a distance of 1650 km?
A. 3000 litres   B. 108 litres
C. 300 litres   D. 165 litres

47. Find the simple interest on ₹ 5000 at the rate of $7\frac{1}{2}\%$ for a period of 3 years
A. ₹ 5000   B. ₹ 6125
C. ₹ 2000   D. ₹ 1125

48. The angles of a triangle are in the ratio of 1:2:3. Find the values of the angles
A. 30, 60, 90   B. 15, 45, 120
C. 60, 60, 60   D. 45, 45, 90

49. One number exceeds another number by 36. The sum of numbers is 48 then the numbers are
A. 40, 08   B. 36, 12
C. 42, 06   D. 32, 16

50. At which one of the following times is the angle between the hands of a clock exactly one straight angle?
A. 12 AM   B. 12 PM
C. 9.15 AM   D. 6 AM

Section-B : General Knowledge

51. Out of the following list of Param Vir Chakra (PVC) Awardees who was awarded with PVC during Kargil War?
A. Lt Col Ardeshir Burzorji Tarapore
B. 2/Lt Arun Khetarpal
C. Capt Vikram Batra
D. Maj Somnath Sharma

52. Which state among the following has adopted Sanskrit as its one of the official languages?
A. Himachal Pradesh
B. Uttrakhand
C. Rajasthan
D. Uttar Pradesh

53. Who is the current Vice-President of India?
A. Shri Narendra Modi
B. Shri Venkaiah Naidu
C. Shri Arun Jaitley
D. Shri Ram Nath Kovind

54. A medical practitioner specializing in children and their diseases
A. Geologist   B. Paediatrician
C. Cardiologist   D. Neurologist

55. A group of stars is called a
A. Solar system   B. Constellations
C. Planets   D. Comets

56. Which gas when solidified is commonly known as Dry ice?
A. Carbon monoxide
B. Nitrous oxide
C. Carbon dioxide
D. Hydrogen peroxide

57. The members of the Rajya Sabha can have a maximum tenure of how long?
A. Five years   B. Six years
C. Seven years   D. Two years

58. P Gopichand is associated with which Sport?
A. Badminton   B. Cricket
C. Football   D. Hockey

59. Which of the following company does not sell mobiles?
A. Apple   B. BSNL
C. HP   D. Sony

60. A vehicle capable of travelling over land and water is called

A. Hovercraft   B. Rovercraft
C. Mowercraft   D. Car

61. The space programme of Government of India is looked after
A. ISBT   B. NTRO
C. NABARD   D. ISRO

62. The Motto of the Indian Navy is
A. Sarvatra Sarvottam Suraksha
B. Sham No Varunah
C. Valour and Wisdom
D. Nabhah Sparsham Deeptam

63. Which is the largest gland in human body?
A. salivary gland   B. lungs
C. liver   D. stomach

64. Who has written 'Sare Jahan Se Achchha'?
A. Rabindra Nath Tagore
B. Bankim Chandra Chatterjee
C. Muhammad Iqbal
D. Subash Chandra Bose

65. Which is the deepest ocean?
A. Indian Ocean   B. Arctic Ocean
C. Antarctic Ocean   D. Pacific Ocean

66. Who fixes the salaries and the allowances of the Speaker of Lok Sabha?
A. Council of Ministers
B. Presient
C. Parliament
D. Judge of Supreme Court

67. Which article of constitution provides Indian citizen 'Right To Equality'?
A. Article 12   B. Article 13
C. Article 17   D. Article 14

68. 1024 Kilobytes is equal to:
A. 8 Bits
B. 1 Megabyte (MB)
C. 1 Gigabyte (GB)
D. 1 Byte

69. Hirakund dam is built on the river:
A. Cauvery   B. Mahanadi
C. Krishna   D. Sutlej

70. Deficiency of Iodine causes:
A. Goitre   B. Malaria
C. Cataract   D. Scurvy

71. Who is known as 'Iron man' of India?
A. Jawaharlal Nehru
B. Mahatma Gandhi
C. Sardar Patel
D. Subhas Chandra Bose

72. Which among of the following is not an Indian Sport?
A. Kabbadi   B. Kho-Kho
C. Hockey   D. Rugby

73. Those who study things that were made and used in the past these people are called ....
A. Biologist   B. Archaeologist
C. Geologist   D. Doctor

74. What is the ratio of width to the length of National Flag of India?
A. 4:5   B. 2:3
C. 1:1   D. 5:6

75. Where is Wagah-Border located?
A. Longewala, Rajasthan
B. Moreh, Manipur
C. Rann of Kutch, Gujarat
D. Amritsar, Punjab

Section-C : Language

Choose the most appropriate option given against each question.

76. Which word means nearly the same as "scream"?
A. find   B. stop
C. sell   D. shout

77. Which word means nearly the same as "happy"
A. conditions   B. disgusted
C. content   D. ambitious

Choose the appropriate option to complete the sentences

78. The men are working. Their .... are at home.
A. wife   B. husbands
C. husband   D. wives

79. Rahul works less .... than Mohan.
A. carefully   B. more careful
C. careful   D. careful as

80. It .... all day long yesterday.
    A. was rained   B. raining
    C. rained   D. has rained

Rearrange the following words/groups of words to make meaningful sentences. Choose the correct sequence given in the options.

81. (A) quite happy / (B) i was / (C) the first prize / (D) to receive.
    A. BADC   B. ABCD
    C. DCBA   D. BACD

82. (A) protect / (B) we must / (C) natural resources / (D) our.
    A. ABCD   B. BADC
    C. ACDB   D. DCAB

Choose the appropriate option to fill in the blanks:

83. One who leads an austere life
    A. Ruler   B. Auditor
    C. Ascetic   D. Carpenter

84. A person who presents a radio/television programme.
    A. Director   B. Actress
    C. Actor   D. Anchor

85. Pick the opposite gender of 'Lad'
    A. Lass   B. Queen
    C. Woman   D. Dame

86. Choose the opposite gender of 'Fox'
    A. Filly   B. Goose
    C. Witch   D. Vixen

Do as directed:

87. .... always stood third in her class (supply the correct pronoun)
    A. You   B. They
    C. He   D. She

88. All the candidates should bring .... own pen (supply the correct pronoun)
    A. Everyone   B. They
    C. Nobody   D. Their

89. Experience is the .... teacher (supply the correct adjective)
    A. Better   B. Good
    C. Best   D. Great

90. .... a beautiful scene it is ! (pick up the correct adverb)
    A. What   B. How
    C. Always   D. Never

91. Did you apply .... this post? (Supply the correct preposition)
    A. To   B. At
    C. For   D. Of

92. You should take care .... your health (supply the correct preposition)
    A. Of   B. In
    C. At   D. To

93. He is rich .... he is not happy (supply the correct conjunction)
    A. Yet   B. Though
    C. Because   D. But

94. Work hard .... you will fail (supply the correct conjunction)
    A. Or   B. Still
    C. Because   D. Either

95. The child .... for two hours (select the correct form of verb)
    A. Has been sleeping
    B. Have been sleeping
    C. Has slept
    D. Will sleep

Directions (Qs. No. 96 to 100): *Read the following passage and answer the questions:*

From far out in space, Earth looks like a blue ball. Since water covers three-fourths of the Earth's surface, blue is the colour we see most. The continents look brown, like small islands floating in the huge, blue sea. White clouds wrap around the Earth like a light blanket. The Earth is shaped like a sphere, or a ball. It is 25,000 miles around! It would take more than a year to walk around the whole planet. A spaceship can fly around the widest part of the sphere in only 90 minutes.

Even though spaceships have travelled to the Moon, people cannot visit the Moon without special suits. The Moon has no air or water. Plants and animals can't live there either. Astronauts first landed on the Moon in 1969. After that, there were six more trips to the Moon. They brought back Moon rocks, which scientists are still studying. There are holes, or craters, all over the Moon's surface. Scientists believe that meteorites smashed into the Moon millions of years ago and formed the craters.

The Sun is the closest star to Earth. A star is a hot ball of burning gas. The Sun looks very big because it is so close. But the Sun is just a medium-sized star. Billions of far-away stars are much bigger than our Sun. The burning gases from the Sun are so hot that they warm the Earth from 93 million miles away! Even though the Sun is always glowing, the night here on Earth is dark. That's because the Earth rotates, or turns around, every 24 hours. During the day, the Earth faces the Sun. Then we see light. During the night, the Earth turns away from the Sun. Then it faces the darkness of space. Each day we learn more about the Earth, the Moon, and the Sun.

96. Why is blue the colour we see most when looking at Earth from outer space?
A. Because most of the Earth is covered in land.
B. Because the Sun's rays make the Earth look blue.
C. Because most of the Earth is covered in water.
D. Because clouds wrap around the Earth.

97. What does 'formed' mean?
A. hit B. made
C. broke D. stopped

98. What causes daylight on Earth?
A. The full Moon causes daylight.
B. Daylight is caused by the Earth facing away from the Sun.
C. The heat of the Sun's rays causes daylight.
D. Daylight is caused by the Earth facing toward the Sun.

99. Which of the following sentences BEST describes the Sun?
A. The Sun looks small because it is so far from Earth.
B. The Sun is a ball of burning gases that gives the Earth heat and light.
C. The Sun is a small star.
D. The Sun is not as hot as it looks.

100. Why did the astronauts bring rocks back from the Moon?
A. Because they didn't know if they would return to the Moon ever again.
B. Because they wanted to prove that they went to the Moon.
C. Because they wanted to remember how the Moon looked.
D. Because they wanted to study them and learn more about the Moon.

PAPER-II : INTELLIGENCE TEST

101. If you see the problem figure in the mirror, which figure out of the four figures A, B, C and D will be the mirror image of figure 'X'.

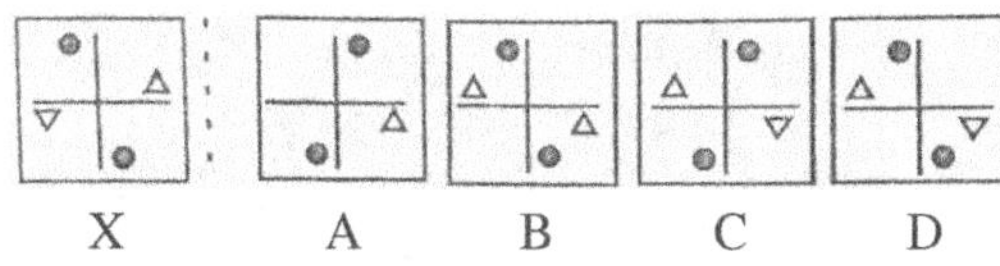

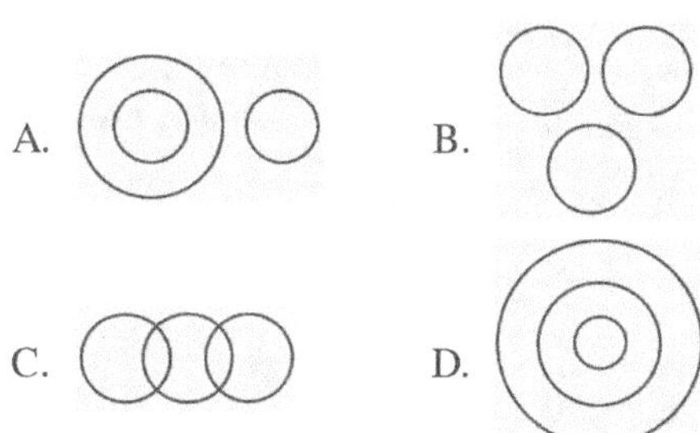

102. Choose the word which is least like the other words in the group.
A. PICTURE B. POSTER
C. BOOK D. SCENERY

103. Which of the following diagram indicates the best relation between Travellers, Train and Bus?

104. If CAR is to PETROL then TELEVISION is to ....
A. ANTENNA
B. TRANSMISSION
C. ENTERTAINMENT
D. ELECTRICITY

105. Which figure among the four figures A, B, C and D would replace the question mark in figure 'X'?

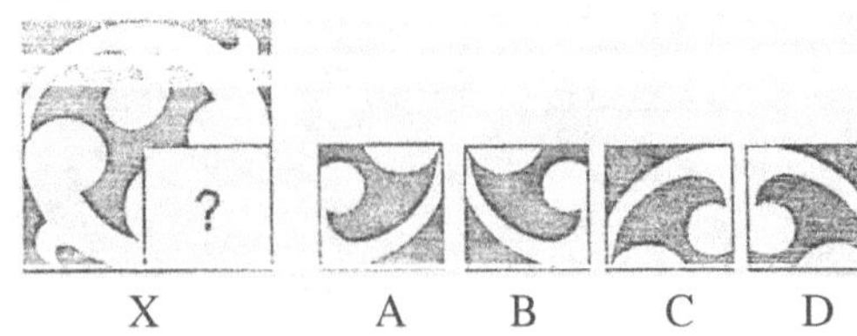

X   A   B   C   D

106. A class of boys stands in a single line. One boy is nineteenth in order from both the ends. How many boys are there in the class?
A. 27   B. 37
C. 38   D. 39

107. If you fold the transparent paper along the dotted line Figure 'X' which alternative figure from A, B, C and D would you get?

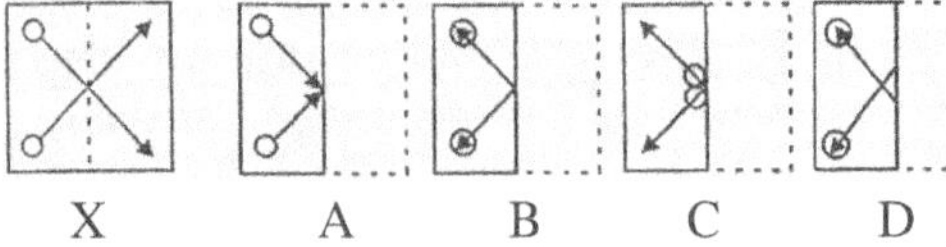

X   A   B   C   D

108. If SCHOOL is to EDUCATION then BANK is to .... ?
A. ATM   B. CHEQUE
C. LOAN   D. LOCKER

109. If the given word is seen in mirror, which alternative would resemble its mirror image?

SHARE

A. ƎЯAHƧ   B. ƎЯAHƧ
C. ƎЯHAƧ   D. ƎƧAHƧ

110. Choose the alternative that resembles the water image of the given alpha-numeric series below:

HR2642O

A. O2642ЯH   B. HЯ2642O
C. O2642ЯH   D. HЯ2642O

111. Choose the word which is least like the other words in the group.
A. EARTH   B. SUN
C. MERCURY   D. JUPITER

112. Which figure among the four alternatives A, B, C and D would replace the question mark in figure X?

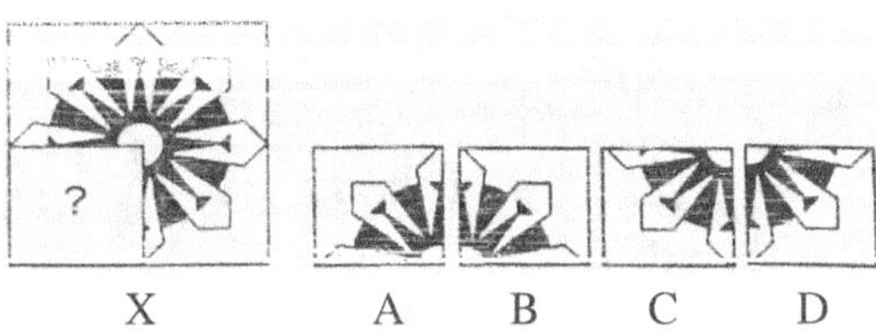

X   A   B   C   D

113. If all directions are rotated clockwise by 90° angle *i.e.*, North is changed to West, East to North and to on, then what will come in place of North West?
A. SOUTH – WEST
B. NORTH – EAST
C. SOUTH – EAST
D. EAST – WEST

114. Choose the word which can be formed from the given word:
INFRASTRUCTURE
A. RUPTURE   B. SCULPTURE
C. FRACTURE   D. VULTURE

115. If you see the problem figure in the mirror along the dotted line, which figure out of the four figures A, B, C and D will be the mirror image of figure 'X'.

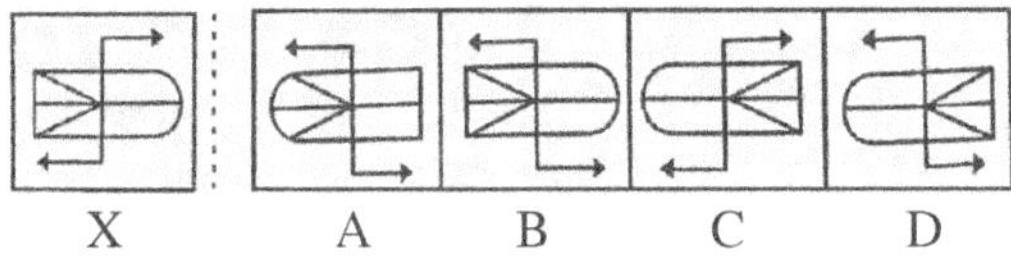

X   A   B   C   D

116. Choose the word which is least like the other words in the group.
A. STUDENT
B. LAWYER
C. MECHANIC
D. ENGINEER

117. If you see the problem figure 'X' in the mirror, which figure out of the four figures A, B, C and D will be the mirror image of it.

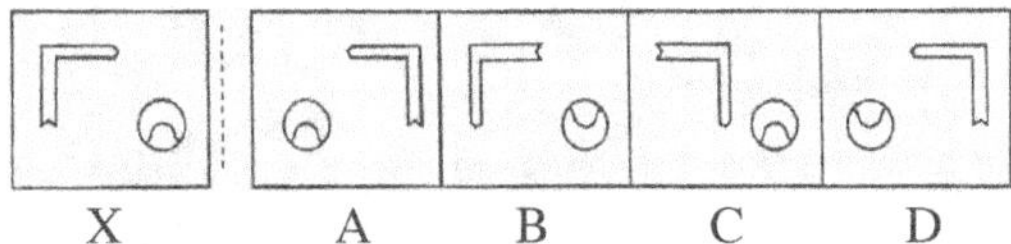

X   A   B   C   D

118. If '+' means '÷', '÷' means '–', '–' means '×' and '×' means '+', then what would be the answer of the equation?
$$12 + 6 \div 3 - 2 \times 8 = ?$$

A. –2   B. 2
C. 4   D. 8

119. Figure 'X' is embedded in any one of the four alternative figures A, B, C or D. Find the alternative which contains figure 'X' as its part.

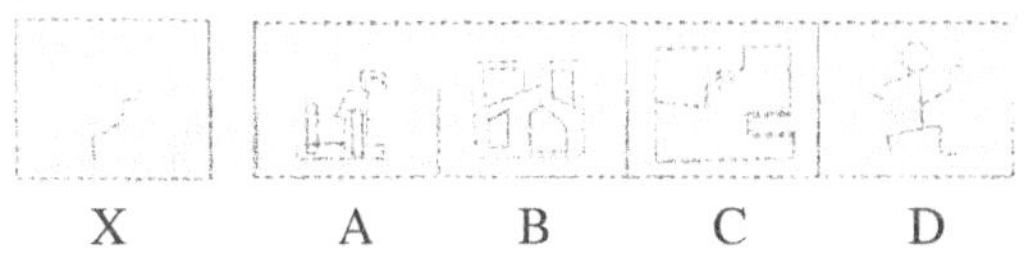

    X   A   B   C   D

120. If '÷' means '×', '×' means '+' , '+' means '–' and '–' means '÷', then what would be the answer of the equation?

$$16 × 3 + 5 – 2 ÷ 4 = ?$$

A. 9   B. 10
C. 19   D. None of these

121. Nitin ranks eighteenth from the top in a class of 49 students. What is his rank from the last?
A. 18   B. 19
C. 31   D. 32

122. Which figure among the four alternatives A, B, C and D would replace the question mark in figure 'X'?

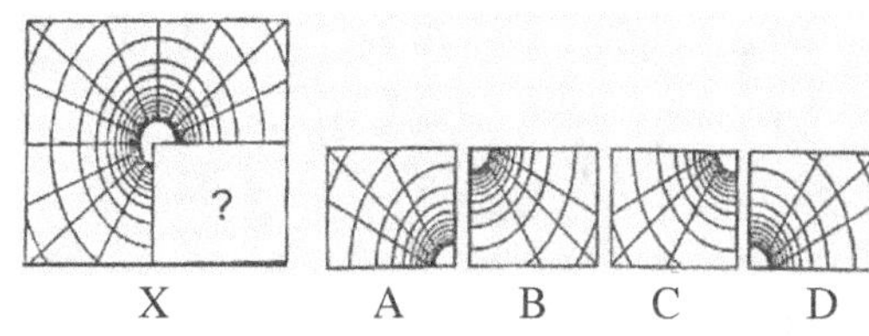

    X   A   B   C   D

123. Find out the figure which does not belong to the group of other figures.

    A   B   C   D

124. Find the missing number in the number series given below:

06, 11, 21, 36, 56, ...?

A. 42   B. 51
C. 81   D. 91

125. Find the missing number that has same relation to 26 as 37 has to 19.

19 : 37 : : 26 : ?

A. 52   B. 51
C. 46   D. 43

ANSWERS

1	2	3	4	5	6	7	8	9	10
B	A	A	C	B	A	A	B	B	A

11	12	13	14	15	16	17	18	19	20
C	A	B	B	C	B	A	C	D	B

21	22	23	24	25	26	27	28	29	30
B	A	C	A	C	B	B	D	D	B

31	32	33	34	35	36	37	38	39	40
D	A	A	A	C	A	C	B	C	C

41	42	43	44	45	46	47	48	49	50
B	B	A	C	A	C	D	A	C	C

51	52	53	54	55	56	57	58	59	60
C	B	B	B	B	C	B	A	B	A

61	62	63	64	65	66	67	68	69	70
D	B	C	C	D	C	D	B	B	A

71	72	73	74	75	76	77	78	79	80
C	D	B	B	D	D	C	D	A	C
81	**82**	**83**	**84**	**85**	**86**	**87**	**88**	**89**	**90**
A	B	C	D	A	D	D	D	C	A
91	**92**	**93**	**94**	**95**	**96**	**97**	**98**	**99**	**100**
C	A	D	A	A	C	B	D	B	D
101	**102**	**103**	**104**	**105**	**106**	**107**	**108**	**109**	**110**
C	C	C	D	A	B	B	C	A	D
111	**112**	**113**	**114**	**115**	**116**	**117**	**118**	**119**	**120**
B	C	A	C	D	A	A	C	D	A
121	**122**	**123**	**124**	**125**					
D	B	C	C	B					

EXPLANATORY ANSWERS

1. This answer greater than the correct answer
$$= 7236 \times 65 - 7236 \times 56$$
$$= 7236 (65 - 56)$$
$$= 7236 \times 9 = 65124.$$

2. $1 \div \left\{ \dfrac{1}{2} + \dfrac{1}{3} + \dfrac{1}{6} \div \left(\dfrac{3}{4} - \dfrac{1}{3} \right) \right\}$

According to BODMAS rule

$$= 1 \div \left\{ \frac{1}{2} + \frac{1}{3} + \frac{1}{6} \div \frac{5}{12} \right\}$$

$$= 1 \div \left\{ \frac{1}{2} + \frac{1}{3} + \frac{1}{6} \times \frac{12}{5} \right\}$$

$$= 1 \div \left\{ \frac{1}{2} + \frac{1}{3} + \frac{2}{5} \right\}$$

$$= 1 \div \left\{ \frac{15 + 10 + 12}{30} \right\} = 1 \div \left\{ \frac{37}{30} \right\} = \frac{30}{37}$$

3. 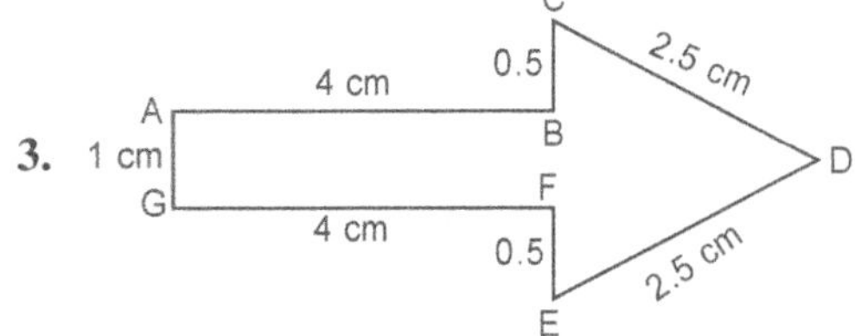

The perimeter of the figure
$$= AB + BC + CD + DE + EF + FG + GA$$
$$= 4 + 0.5 + 2.5 + 2.5 + 0.5 + 4 + 1$$
$$= 15 \text{ cm.}$$

4. 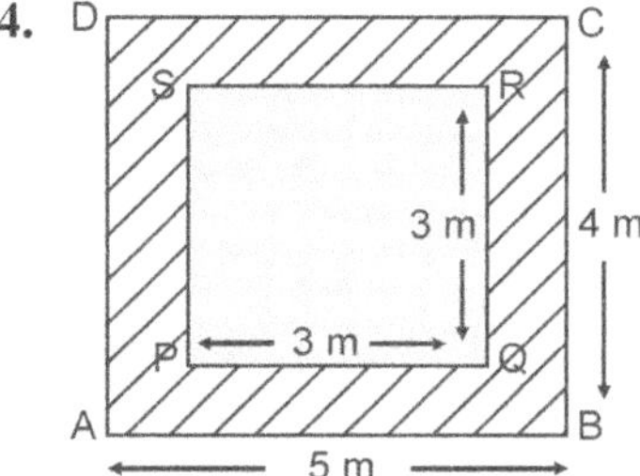

∴ The area of the floor that is not carpeted
= Area of Rectangle ABCD – Area of square PQRS
$$= l \times b - a^2$$
$$= 5 \times 4 - (3)^2$$
$$= 20 - 9 = 11 \text{ m}^2.$$

5. Required smallest No. which is divisible by
6, 12, 18 = LCM (6, 12, 18)
$$= 2 \times 2 \times 3 \times 3 = 36.$$
The answer will be multiple of 36, in the given option 180 is the smallest number.

2	6, 12, 18
2	3, 6, 9
3	3, 3, 9
3	1, 1, 3
	1, 1, 1

6. $\because$ In Isosceles Triangle, two angles are same
Check the option
(a) 90, 45,   *i.e.*, $\angle A = 90°$, $\angle B = 45°$
$$\angle C = 180 - (90 + 45)$$
$$= 180 - 135 = 45°$$
$\because \qquad\qquad \angle B = \angle C$
$\therefore$ Option (A) is the correct answer.

7. Let the breadth of the rectangle $= x$
Then, the length of the rectangle $(l) = x + 5$
Perimeter of the rectangle $= 50$ cm
$$2(l + b) = 50$$
$$l + b = 25$$
$$x + x + 5 = 25$$
$$2x + 5 = 25$$
$$2x = 20$$
$$x = 10$$
$\therefore$ Breadth $(b) = 10$ cm
Length $(l) = 10 + 5 = 15$ cm
$\therefore \qquad$ Area $= l \times b$
$$= 10 \times 15 = 150 \text{ cm}^2.$$

8. $\because \qquad\qquad W_1 = W_2$
$\therefore \qquad M_1 \times D_1 = M_2 \times D_2$
$$12 \times 15 = 20 \times D_2$$
$\therefore \qquad D_2 = \dfrac{12 \times 15}{20} = 9$ days

Hence option (B) is the correct answer.

10. No. of students who do not ride the bus
$$= 1000 - 330 = 670$$
$\therefore$ Required percentage $= \dfrac{\text{No. of students who do not ride the bus}}{\text{Total student}} \times 100$
$$= \dfrac{670}{1000} \times 100$$
$$= 67\%.$$

11.

$$\xleftarrow{\hspace{1cm}} \text{616 km} \xrightarrow{\hspace{1cm}}$$

Station A $\qquad$ 112 km/hr $\qquad$ Station B

Total time taken $= \dfrac{\text{Distance AB}}{\text{Speed}} + 1\text{h} + \dfrac{\text{Distance BA}}{\text{Speed}}$

$$= \dfrac{616}{112} + 1 + \dfrac{616}{112}$$

$$\left[\because \text{ Time} = \dfrac{\text{Distance}}{\text{Speed}}\right]$$

$$= 5.5 \text{ h} + 1 \text{ h} + 5.5 \text{ h}$$
$$= 12 \text{ h}.$$

12. $\because \qquad \%$ Loss $= \dfrac{CP - SP}{CP} \times 100$
$$16 = \dfrac{CP - 3360}{CP} \times 100$$
$$16 \text{ CP} = 100 \text{ CP} - 336000$$
$$84 \text{ CP} = 336000$$
$$CP = \dfrac{336000}{84} = ₹ \, 4000.$$

14. $4.69 \times$ Other No. $= 12.194$
$\therefore \qquad$ Other No. $= \dfrac{12.194 \times 1000}{4.69 \times 1000}$
$$= \dfrac{12194}{4690} = 2.6.$$

15. Total cost price of the chair $= ₹ \, 600 + ₹ \, 200$
$$= ₹ \, 800$$
Selling price of the chair $= ₹ \, 1000$
$\because \qquad\qquad SP > CP \rightarrow$ Profit
Required profit $\% = \dfrac{SP - CP}{CP} \times 100$
$$= \dfrac{1000 - 800}{800} \times 100$$
$$= \dfrac{200 \times 100}{800}$$
$$= 25\% \text{ profit}$$

16. Temperature dropped in 30 days $= 15°C$
Temperature dropped in 1 day
$$= \dfrac{15}{30} = \dfrac{1}{2} °C/day$$

Temperature drop in the next 10 days

$$= \frac{1}{2} \times 10 = 5°C.$$

17. No. of mangoes in the basket 1

Which gives remainder 1 when divide by 2

Which gives remainder 2 when divide by 3

Which gives remainder 3 when divide by 4

Which gives remainder 4 when divide by 5

Which gives remainder 5 when divide by 6

Which gives remainder 0 when divide by 7

Check from the option

(A)

$$2)\overline{119}(59$$
$$\underline{10}$$
$$\overline{19}$$
$$\underline{18}$$
$$\overline{1}$$

$$3)\overline{119}(39$$
$$\underline{9}$$
$$\overline{29}$$
$$\underline{27}$$
$$\overline{2}$$

$$4)\overline{119}(29$$
$$\underline{8}$$
$$\overline{39}$$
$$\underline{36}$$
$$\overline{3}$$

$$5)\overline{119}(23$$
$$\underline{10}$$
$$\overline{19}$$
$$\underline{15}$$
$$\overline{4}$$

$$6)\overline{119}(19$$
$$\underline{6}$$
$$\overline{59}$$
$$\underline{54}$$
$$\overline{5}$$

$$7)\overline{119}(17$$
$$\underline{7}$$
$$\overline{49}$$
$$\underline{49}$$
$$\overline{\times}$$

So, no. of mangoes will be 119.

18. Check the option

A. $27 + 27 = 54$ (✗)

B. $24 + 27 = 51$ (✗)

C. $47 + 27 = 74$ (✓)

Hence (C) is the correct option.

19. Let Radha income and expenditure are $7x$ and $5x$ respectively.

Then, Saving = Income – Expenditure

$$7x - 5x = 2000$$
$$2x = 2000$$
$$x = 1000$$

$\therefore$ Monthly income of Radha = $7x$

$$= 7 \times 1000 = 7000$$

Annual income of Radha = 12×7000

$$= 84000.$$

20. Let the length and breadth of rectangular lawn are $3x$ and $5x$ respectively

The perimeter of the lawn $2(l + b) = \dfrac{₹\,3200}{2}$

$$2(l + b) = 1600$$
$$2(3x + 5x) = 1600$$
$$16x = 1600$$
$$x = 100$$

$\therefore$ Length of the lawn = $3x$

$$= 3 \times 100 = 300 \text{ m}$$

Breadth of the lawn = $5x$

$$= 5 \times 100 = 500 \text{ m}$$

Area of the lawn = $l \times b$

$$= 300 \times 500$$
$$= 150000 \text{ m}^2$$

$\therefore$ Cost of developing the lawn

$$= 150000 \times 10$$
$$= 1500000.$$

21. Let the share of A, B and C are $4x$, $7x$ and $9x$ respectively

Given that

B's share = ₹ 2989

$$7x = 2989$$
$$x = 427$$

$\therefore$ Total amount = $4x + 7x + 9x = 20x$

$$= 20 \times 427$$
$$= ₹\ 8540.$$

22. Required teacher's age = $41 \times 19 - 40 \times 18$

$$= 779 - 720$$
$$= 59 \text{ years}$$

$$\left[\because \text{Average Age} = \frac{\text{Total sum of age}}{\text{Total no. of student}} \right].$$

23. Required greatest no.

= HCF ($|3026 - 11|$, $|5053 - 13|$)

= HCF (3015, 5040) = 45

3	3015
3	1005
5	335
	67

2	5040
2	2520
2	1260
2	630
3	315
3	105
5	35
	7

$3015 = 3 \times 3 \times 5 \times 67$

$5040 = 2 \times 2 \times 2 \times 2 \times 3 \times 3 \times 5$

HCF (3015, 50, 40) = $3 \times 3 \times 5$ = 45.

24. Cost price of the chair = ₹ 500

Selling price of the chair = ₹ 550

$\because$ SP > CP $\rightarrow$ Profit

$$\text{\% Profit} = \frac{SP - CP}{CP} \times 100$$

$$= \frac{550 - 500}{500} \times 100$$

$$= \frac{50}{500} \times 100 = 10\%$$

25. $\because$ Distance = Speed $\times$ Time

$$= 5 \times 28 = 140 \text{ km}$$

New speed = 5 + 2 = 7 km/h

$\therefore$ $$\text{Time} = \frac{\text{Distance}}{\text{Speed}}$$

$$\text{Time} = \frac{140}{7} = 20 \text{ h.}$$

26. Length of other piece = $\dfrac{7}{8} - \dfrac{1}{4}$

$$= \frac{7 - 2}{8} = \frac{5}{8} \text{ meter.}$$

27.

2   5   10   14   18   23   26   32   34

+8   +8   +8   +8

+9   +9   +9

28. $\because$ $\qquad$ $W_1 = W_2$

$\therefore$ $\qquad$ $M_1 \times D_1 = M_2 \times D_2$

$$30 \times 16 = 8 \times D_2$$

$$D_2 = \frac{30 \times 16}{8}$$

$$D_2 = 60 \text{ days.}$$

29. Required time = LCM (75, 50, 30)

2	75, 50, 30
3	75, 25, 15
5	25, 25, 5
5	5, 5, 1
	1, 1, 1

$$= 2 \times 3 \times 5 \times 5$$

$$= 150 \text{ min}$$

$$= \frac{5}{2} \text{ hour.}$$

30. $\because$ $\qquad$ 1 kg = 1000 gm

$\therefore$ 26 kg 5 gram = $26 \text{ kg} + \dfrac{5}{1000} \text{ kg}$

$$= 26 + 0.005$$

$$= 26.005 \text{ kg.}$$

31. $\because$ $\qquad$ SI = Amount – Principle

$$= 7800 - 6000$$

$$= ₹ 1800$$

$\because$ $\qquad$ $$SI = \frac{P \times r \times t}{100}$$

$$1800 = \frac{6000 \times r \times 5}{100}$$

$$r = \frac{1800 \times 100}{6000 \times 5}$$

$$r = 6\%.$$

32. $\because$ Volume of cube = a^3

$\therefore$ $\qquad$ $a^3 = 729$

$$a = 9 \text{ m}$$

$\because$ Depth of a cubical pond = 9 m.

33. $3 \times 7 + 4 - 6 \div 3 - 7 + 45 \div 5 \times 4 + 49$

According to BODMAS rule

$= 3 \times 7 + 4 - 2 - 7 + 9 \times 4 + 49$

$= 21 + 4 - 2 - 7 + 36 + 49$

$= 110 - 9 = 101.$

34. Require time $= \dfrac{\text{Distance}}{\text{Speed}}$

$= \dfrac{\text{Length of train} + \text{Length of platform}}{\text{Speed of train}}$

$= \dfrac{100 + 150}{60 \times \dfrac{5}{18}} \qquad \left[\because 1 \text{ km/h} = \dfrac{5}{18} \text{m/s} \right]$

$= \dfrac{250 \times 18}{60 \times 5} = 15 \text{ sec.}$

35. Ashu's 1 day work $= \dfrac{1}{12}$

Pranav's 1 day work $= \dfrac{1}{10}$

Ashu, Pranav and Ramu's 1 day work $= \dfrac{1}{5}$

$\therefore$ Ramu's one day work $= \dfrac{1}{5} - \left(\dfrac{1}{12} + \dfrac{1}{10} \right)$

$= \dfrac{12 - 5 - 6}{60}$

$= \dfrac{1}{60}$

$\therefore$ Ramu complete the work $= 60$ days.

36. Given that

$\quad$ LCM $(a, b) = 28 \times$ HCF $(a, b) \qquad ...(1)$

$\because \quad$ LCM $(a, b) +$ HCF (a, b)

$\qquad\qquad = 1740 \qquad ...(2)$

From equations (1) and (2)

$\quad$ 28 HCF $(a, b) +$ HCF $(a, b) = 1740$

$\qquad\qquad$ 29 HCF $(a, b) = 1740$

$\qquad\qquad$ HCF $(a, b) = 60$

$\qquad\qquad$ LCM $(a, b) = 28 \times 60$

$\qquad\qquad\qquad\qquad = 1680$

$\because$ We know that

$\quad$ LCM $(a, b) \times$ HCF $(a, b) = a \times b$

$\qquad$ $60 \times 1680 = 240 \times b$

$\therefore \qquad$ Second no. $b = \dfrac{60 \times 1680}{240}$

$\qquad\qquad\qquad = 420.$

37. Clock rings again after LCM $(6, 8, 12, 18)$ second

$\quad$ LCM $(6, 8, 12, 18) = 2 \times 2 \times 2 \times 3 \times 3$

$\qquad\qquad\qquad = 72$

2	6, 8, 12, 18
2	3, 4, 6, 9
2	3, 2, 3, 9
3	3, 1, 3, 9
3	1, 1, 1, 3
	1, 1, 1, 1

$\therefore$ In 6 minutes clock rings $= \dfrac{6 \times 60}{72} = 6$

$\qquad\qquad\qquad = 6 + 1 \text{ (In starting)}$

$\qquad\qquad\qquad = 7 \text{ times.}$

38. LCM $(18, 21, 24) = 2 \times 2 \times 2 \times 3 \times 3 \times 7$

$\qquad\qquad\qquad = 504$

Common remainder $\Rightarrow 18 - 7 = 11$

$\qquad\qquad\qquad \Rightarrow 21 - 10 = 11$

$\qquad\qquad\qquad \Rightarrow 24 - 13 = 11$

2	18, 21, 24
2	9, 21, 12
2	9, 21, 6
3	9, 21, 3
3	3, 7, 1
7	1, 7, 1
	1, 1, 1

In each case, remainder is equal i.e. 11

$\therefore$ We have to find of multiple 504, which is divisible by 23 after subtracting 11

$504 \times 1 - 11 = 493 \quad (\times)$

$504 \times 2 - 11 = 997 \quad (\times)$

$504 \times 3 - 11 = 1501 \quad (\times)$

$504 \times 4 - 11 = 2005 \quad (\times)$

$504 \times 5 - 11 = 2509 \quad (\times)$

$504 \times 6 - 11 = 3013 \quad (\checkmark)$

$\therefore$ 3013 is the required No.

39. Required largest vessel = HCF (75, 45)

$$= 3 \times 5$$
$$= 15 \text{ litres.}$$

3	75
5	25
5	5
	1

3	45
3	15
5	5
	1

$75 = ③ \times ⑤ \times 5$

$45 = ③ \times 3 \times ⑤$

40. Cost price of the table = ₹ 1000

Selling price of the table = ₹ 800

$\therefore \qquad \text{SP} < \text{CP} \rightarrow \text{Loss}$

$$\% \text{ Loss} = \frac{\text{CP} - \text{SP}}{\text{CP}} \times 100$$

$$= \frac{1000 - 800}{1000} \times 100$$

$$= \frac{200}{10} = 20\% \text{ Loss.}$$

41. Let the initial average = x kg

and the weight of new boy = y kg

$$6 \times x + y - 20 = 6(x + 5)$$
$$6x + y - 20 = 6x + 30$$
$$y - 20 = 30$$
$$y = 50 \text{ kg}$$

42. Average speed $= \dfrac{\text{Total distance}}{\text{Total time taken to cover the distance}}$

$$= \frac{40 \text{ km}}{\dfrac{10}{10}\text{h} + \dfrac{10}{20}\text{h} + \dfrac{10}{30}\text{h} + \dfrac{10}{40}\text{h}}$$

$$= \frac{40 \text{ km}}{1 + \dfrac{1}{2} + \dfrac{1}{3} + \dfrac{1}{4}}$$

$$= \frac{40 \times 12}{12 + 6 + 4 + 3} = \frac{40 \times 12}{25}$$

$$= \frac{480}{25} = 19.2 \text{ km/h.}$$

43. Let the length of the garden = x m

$\therefore \qquad \text{Area} = l \times b$

$$x \times 5 = 300$$

$$x = \frac{300}{5} = 60 \text{ m.}$$

44. Let the number = x

Then, according to question

$$x^2 + (28)^2 = 1808$$
$$x^2 + 784 = 1808$$
$$x^2 = 1808 - 784$$
$$x^2 = 1024$$
$$x = \sqrt[2]{1024}$$
$$x = 32.$$

	32
3	1029
	9
62	124
2	124
	$\times$

45. The cost of a dozen (12) pens = ₹ 180

The cost of a pen $= \dfrac{180}{12} = ₹ 15$

The cost of 8 ball pens = ₹ 56

The cost of 1 ball pen $= ₹ \dfrac{56}{8} = ₹ 7$

Required ratio = 15 : 7.

46. Diesel requires for covering 594 km distance

$$= 108 \text{ litres}$$

Diesel requires for covering 1 km distance

$$= \frac{108}{594} \text{ lit/km}$$

Diesel requires for covering 1650 km distance

$$= \frac{108}{594} \times 1650$$

$$= 300 \text{ litre.}$$

47. $\qquad \text{SI} = \dfrac{P \times r \times t}{100}$

$$= \frac{5000 \times \dfrac{15}{2} \times 3}{100}$$

$$= \frac{5000 \times 15 \times 3}{200}$$

$$= \frac{225000}{200} = ₹\ 1125$$

48. Let the angles of triangle are $x°$, $2x°$ and $3x°$ respectively

Then, the sum of three angles of a triangle
$$= 180°$$
$$x + 2x + 3x = 180°$$
$$6x = 180°$$
$$x = 30°$$

Then angles are 30°, 60° and 90°.

49. Let the numbers are x and y

Then, $\quad x - y = 36 \qquad ...(1)$

$\qquad x + y = 48 \qquad ...(2)$

Equation (1) + equation (2)
$$2x = 36 + 48$$
$$2x = 84$$
$$x = 42$$

$x = 42$ put in equation (1)
$$42 - y = 36$$
$$y = 42 - 36 = 6$$
$$\therefore \text{ Numbers are 42 and 6.}$$

50. At 9 : 15

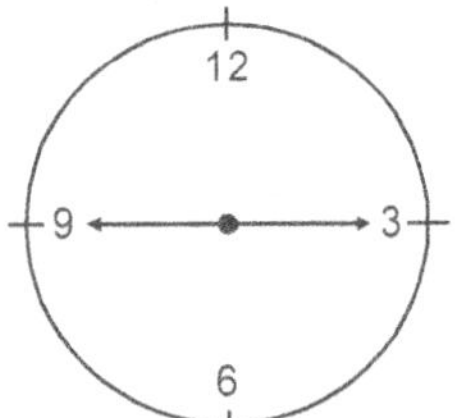

103.

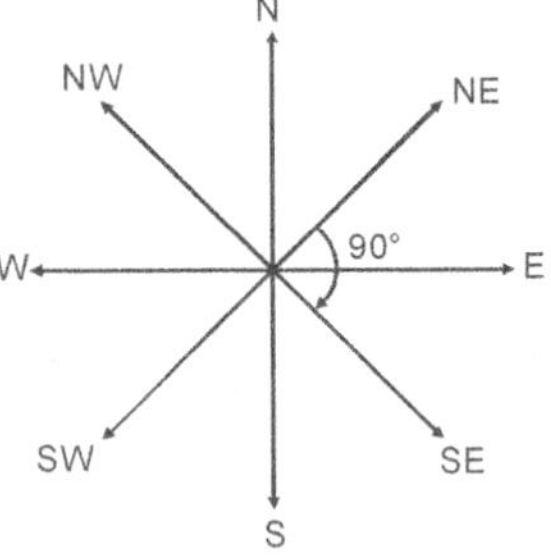

106. 37 is a prime number.

111. Sun is a star, all others are planet.

113.

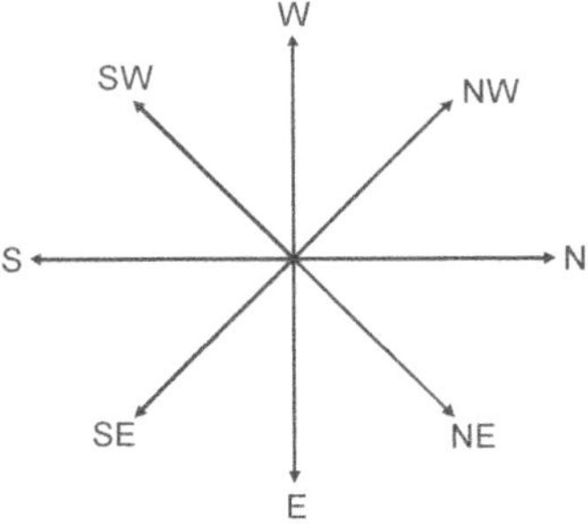

After rotation 90° clockwise

118. $12 + 6 \div 3 - 2 \times 8$

$= 12 \div 6 - 3 \times 2 + 8$

According to BODMAS rule
$$= 2 - 3 \times 2 + 8$$
$$= 2 - 6 + 8$$
$$= 10 - 6 = 4.$$

120. $16 \times 3 + 5 - 2 \div 4$

$= 16 + 3 - 5 \div 2 \times 4$

According to BODMAS rule
$$= 16 + 3 - \frac{5}{2} \times 4$$
$$= 16 + 3 - 5 \times 2$$
$$= 16 + 3 - 10$$
$$= 19 - 10 = 9.$$

121. $\quad$ Total student $= L + R - 1$
$$49 = 18 + L - 1$$
$$L = 49 - 17$$
$$L = 32.$$

124.

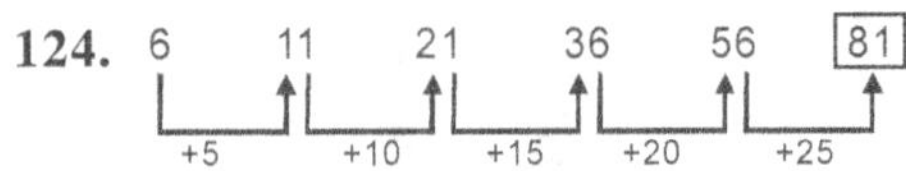

125. $\quad$ 19 : 37 :: 26 : 51

All India Sainik School Entrance Exam., 2018*

(CLASS-VI)

PAPER-I : MATHEMATICS, GK AND LANGUAGE

Section-A : Mathematics

1. The greatest 8-digits number with given digits 5, 8, 7, 5, 2, 0, 6, and 1 is
   A. 88765210
   B. 87765210
   C. 88765521
   D. 87655210

2. Choose the correct option if numbers 52806, 52086, 52860, 52800 and 58260 are arranged in ascending order
   A. 52086, 52806, 52860, 52800, 58260
   B. 52800, 52860, 52086, 58260, 52806
   C. 52086, 52800, 52806, 52860, 58260
   D. 52800, 52806, 52860, 52086, 58260

3. A number that must be subtracted from 925564 to make it equal to the sum of 234251 and 352421 will be
   A. 238892
   B. 338882
   C. 338892
   D. 337892

4. The product of 10101×25 is
   A. 252725
   B. 252525
   C. 25025025
   D. 272725

5. The average age of 3 sisters is 15. If the ages of 2 sisters are 12 years and 15 years, the age of the third sister is
   A. 21 years
   B. 17 years
   C. 18 years
   D. 16 years

6. $\dfrac{7}{6}$ of a leap year = ... week
   A. 427
   B. 35
   C. 61
   D. 13

7. Write Roman numerals CDXLIX in Arabic numerals
   A. 569
   B. 449
   C. 549
   D. 469

8. Value of $(700 \div 10) - \{(12 \times 8) \div (34 - 10)\}$ is
   A. 69
   B. 68
   C. 67
   D. 66

9. $2 = $ .... %
   A. 200
   B. 0.02
   C. $\dfrac{2}{100}$
   D. 20

10. Vicky bought a bicycle for ₹ 3,000.00 and sold it for ₹ 2,700.00. What was his loss or gain per cent?
    A. 10% loss
    B. 10% gain
    C. 11.11% gain
    D. 11.11% loss

11. A train leaves Hyderabad at 01:15 PM on Friday and reaches Chennai at 07:30 AM on Saturday. The duration of the journey is
    A. 18 hrs 30 min
    B. 17 hrs 45 min
    C. 18 hrs 15 min
    D. 17 hrs 15 min

12. Karishma bought two necklace for ₹ 1,39,500.00. She sold one of them for ₹ 75,000.00 and the other one for ₹ 80,000.00. How much money did she gain?
    A. ₹ 25,500.00
    B. ₹ 15,500.00
    C. ₹ 20,500.00
    D. ₹ 15,000.00

13. A tall office building has 85 floors. Each floor has 48 windows. Each window is to be decorated with 64 tiny bulbs. How many bulbs would be needed to decorate all the windows?
    A. 261120
    B. 273920
    C. 456960
    D. 209920

14. The smallest 5-digit number that is divisible by 19 is

A. 10019   B. 10013
C. 10032   D. 10000

15. The greatest number that divides 38 and 68 leaving 8 as remainder in each case is
A. 10   B. 15
C. 60   D. 30

16. The decimal notation of 10 kg 2 dag 6 g is
A. 10.260 kg   B. 10.206 kg
C. 10.026 kg   D. 10.006 kg

17. Which of the following pair of angles are supplementary?
A. 46° and 44°   B. 113° and 67°
C. 245° and 115°   D. 90° and 180°

18. The perimeter of the rectangle and square are same. Length and breadth of the rectangle are 10 cm and 8 cm respectively. What is the area of the square?
A. 114 sq. cm   B. 36 sq.cm
C. 81 sq.cm   D. 64 sq.cm

19. Which of the following measures of three angles can be those of a triangle?
A. 52°, 69°, 79°   B. 30°, 69°, 71°
C. 132°, 169°, 59°   D. 32°, 69°, 79°

20. Which statement is true?
A. All hexagons are triangles because they have at least 3 sides.
B. All octagons are polygons because they have at least 3 sides.
C. All parallelograms are rectangles because they have 2 sets of parallel sides.
D. All rhombus are squares because they have 4 sides that are all the same length.

21. The fraction equivalent to 1.25 is:
A. $1\dfrac{1}{4}$ B. $12\dfrac{1}{2}$
C. $1\dfrac{1}{8}$ D. $12\dfrac{1}{4}$

22. The sum of two numbers is 11009. If one of them is 9999, the other number is
A. 1010   B. 1110
C. 2110   D. 21008

23. Simplify : $6 \div 6 + 6 \times 6 - 6$
A. 1   B. 7
C. 31   D. 36

24. Simplify: $1\dfrac{1}{24} - 1 + \dfrac{7}{36}$
A. $\dfrac{17}{72}$ B. $1\dfrac{17}{72}$
C. $\dfrac{7}{60}$ D. $\dfrac{5}{60}$

25. Sara poured $1\dfrac{1}{8}$ cups of lemonade each in 5 glasses. What was the total amount of lemonade Sara poured in 5 glasses?
A. $3\dfrac{7}{8}$ cups   B. $5\dfrac{1}{8}$ cups
C. $5\dfrac{5}{8}$ cups   D. $6\dfrac{1}{8}$ cups

26. Ritu has $\dfrac{1}{4}$ of a sack of rice. She divides the rice equally into 7 bags. What fraction of the full sack of rice is in each bag?
A. $\dfrac{1}{28}$ B. $\dfrac{1}{7}$
C. $\dfrac{2}{11}$ D. $\dfrac{11}{28}$

27. $1 + 0 + \dfrac{9}{100} + \dfrac{3}{1000} =$
A. 1.093   B. 1.903
C. 1.93   D. 1.0093

28. Which two quadrilaterals have both 2 pairs of parallel sides and 2 acute angles?

A. 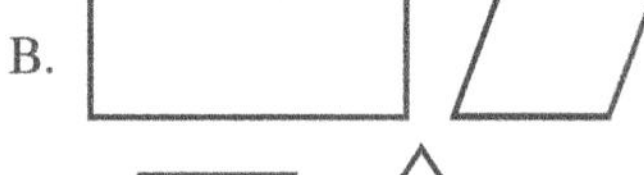

B. 

C. 

D.

29. What is the sum of 20.08, 20.008, 20.088 and 20.888?
A. 81.064   B. 81.604
C. 80.064   D. 80.888

30. Round off 37504 to the nearest hundreds
A. 37500   B. 37000
C. 38000   D. 30000

31. A train is running at a speed of 75 kms/hour. How much time will it take to cover a distance of 350 kms?
A. 4 hrs   B. 5 hrs
C. 4 hrs 30 min   D. 4 hrs 40 min

32. A block of wood is in the form of a cube, its edge is 4 m. How many rectangular pieces of dimension 20 cm × 10 cm × 5 cm can be cut from the block?
A. 640   B. 64
C. 6400   D. 64000

33. In how many years, a sum of ₹ 500 at 5% per annum will amount to ₹ 600?
A. 3 years   B. 4 years
C. 5 years   D. 6 years

34. The average of four numbers is 30. If the sum of first three numbers is 85, the fourth number is:
A. 35   B. 25
C. 45   D. 55

35. What percent of 10 km is 10 m?
A. 0.1%   B. 1.0%
C. 10.0%   D. 40.0%

36. The number of square tiles, of side 15 cm, required for flooring a room of size 3.6 m × 4.5 m, will be:
A. 720   B. 360
C. 10800   D. 5400

37. The smallest odd number formed by using the digits 1, 2, 3, 4, and 5 is:
A. 12345   B. 12435
C. 12453   D. 12534

38. Which of the following numbers are arranged in ascending order?
A. $\frac{1}{3}, \frac{1}{2}, 0.25$ B. $0.25, \frac{1}{2}, \frac{1}{3}$
C. $0.25, \frac{1}{3}, \frac{1}{2}$ D. $\frac{1}{2}, \frac{1}{3}, 0.25$

39. A boat is flowing in still water at the speed of 18 km/hour. The speed of boat in m/sec is:
A. 50 m/sec   B. 72 m/sec
C. 7.2 m/sec   D. 5 m/sec

40. The value of 200°F in degree Celsius is .... [Use C = 5/9 (F–32)]
A. 80.3°C   B. 93.3°C
C. 100.3°C   D. 105.3°C

41. Find the difference between the number 36490 and the number obtained by interchanging the places of 6 and 9:
A. 2970   B. 3030
C. 2070   D. 2790

42. Convert (3.75 of 5% + 7.25 of 10%) into decimals:
A. 0.9152   B. 0.9521
C. 0.9125   D. 09527

43. What is the next row of numbers?
28	84	112
38	114	152
48	144	192

A. 58   174   232
B. 58   184   244
C. 68   204   272
D. 68   214   292

44. A boy runs around a rectangular field of length 40 m and breadth 25 m. How much distance will he run if he takes 4 rounds of that field.
A. 4000 m   B. 260 m
C. 520 m   D. 400 m

45. A room is 15 m long and 10 m broad. Find the cost of carpeting its floor if 1 sq cm of carpet costs ₹ 2.00.
A. ₹ 300   B. ₹ 300000
C. ₹ 30000   D. ₹ 3000000

46. The cost of a pack of 15 balls is ₹ 300 and a pack of 12 shuttle cock is ₹ 96. If Raghu bought 1 ball and 1 shuttle cock, how much would he pay to shopkeeper?
A. ₹ 24   B. ₹ 22
C. ₹ 26   D. ₹ 28

47. The greatest number which divides 624 and 936 exactly is 312. Find the smallest number which is divisible by 624 and 936?
A. 1820   B. 1872
C. 1272   D. 1864

48. A person purchased an old bicycle for ₹ 450 and spends ₹ 50 on its maintenance. If he sold the old bicycle for ₹ 600 then his profit percentage is

A. 15%   B. 18%

C. 20%   D. 25%

49. Find the area of figure given below:

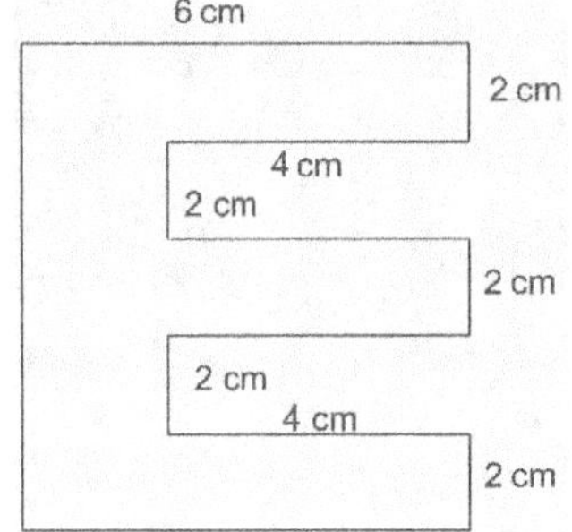

A. 56 sq cm

B. 48 sq cm

C. 44 sq cm

D. 60 sq cm

50. Amar spent $\frac{3}{8}$ of his time studying Science. He spent $\frac{2}{5}$ as much time studying English as Science. What fraction of Amar's study time was spent studying English?

A. $\frac{1}{40}$ B. $\frac{3}{20}$

C. $\frac{31}{40}$ D. $\frac{15}{16}$

Section-B : General Knowledge

51. Which feature helps a coconut fruit to float in water?

A. a fibrous outer covering

B. a spongy part

C. presence of hook

D. presence of spine

52. Which of the following is a non-communicable disease?

A. chickenpox   B. beriberi

C. common cold   D. measles

53. The rabies virus is carried by

A. cockroaches   B. hens

C. dogs   D. rabbits

54. Milk turning sour is a

A. physical change   B. reversible change

C. chemical change   D. none of these

55. The wearing off or carrying away of soil by the action of water or wind is called

A. storm   B. flood

C. soil erosion   D. deforestation

56. Whales and dolphins are classified as

A. fishes   B. reptiles

C. mammals   D. amphibians

57. The working of the internal organs of our body is controlled by this system

A. reproductive   B. circulatory

C. respiratory   D. nervous

58. A person might faint if his heart does not send enough blood to his

A. feet   B. liver

C. kidneys   D. brain

59. The upward push of water on a floating object is called

A. buoyant force   B. volume

C. density   D. pressure

60. The first artificial satellite launched by India in 1975 was

A. Sputnic 1   B. Aryabhatta

C. Charaka   D. Insat

61. Those who study earthquakes are called

A. geologist   B. seismologists

C. astronomers   D. astrologers

62. Which of the following gas is not a greenhouse gas?

A. carbon dioxide B. oxygen

C. methane   D. CFC

63. The model of the earth is called a
A. circle   B. sphere
C. globe   D. marble

64. Agriculture cannot be practiced on mountains on a large scale as they
A. are thinly populated
B. have a shortage of land
C. have a thin soil cover
D. have unsuitable climate

65. The condition of the atmosphere at a given place and time is called
A. season   B. climate
C. altitude   D. weather

66. The highway of Central Africa is another name for
A. River Nile   B. River Congo
C. River Zimbani   D. River Kwango

67. Most of the grasslands of the world are found in the
A. Tropical Zone   B. Temperate Zone
C. Torrid Zone   D. Frigid Zone

68. Any sound louder than 90 decibels can cause
A. asthma
B. digestive problems
C. typhoid
D. loss of hearing

69. Aligarh Muslim University is associated with
A. Rabindranath Tagore
B. Tansen
C. Kalidas
D. Syed Ahmad Khan

70. The English Government introduced the policy of divide and rule to
A. educate Indian
B. encourage nationalism
C. reform Indians
D. suppress nationalism

71. Purna Swaraj means
A. non-cooperation
B. civil disobedience
C. boycott
D. complete Independence

72. The Lok Sabha can have a maximum of
A. 12 members   B. 552 members
C. 238 members   D. 543 members

73. The League of Nations was formed to prevent
A. destruction   B. loss of lives
C. droughts   D. another world war

74. The world has been made smaller due to
A. wheels
B. steam engines
C. fast means of transport
D. cars

75. Internet is a source of information on
A. documentaries   B. e-mail
C. any topic   D. a few topic

Section-C : Language

Read the following passage and answer the questions.

HORACE DENBY

Everyone thought that Horace Denby was a good and honest citizen. He was about fifty years old and unmarried, and he lived with a housekeeper who worried over his health. In fact, he was usually very well and happy, except for attacks of hay fever in summer. He made expensive locks and was successful enough at his business to have two helpers. Yes, Horace Denby was good and respectable – but not completely honest.

Fifteen years ago, Horace had served his first and only sentence in prison for stealing jewels. The priest at the prison had liked Horace – everyone did – and had tried to help him to live an honest life. But Horace did not want to become honest. He only wanted to make sure that his dishonesty never got him into trouble again.

76. Horace Denby was ....
A. old   B. unmarried
C. handicapped   D. both A & B

77. .... worried about the health of Horace.
A. his wife   B. the priest
C. his housekeeper   D. Horace

78. For stealing jewels, Horace was sent to prison ....
- A. only once
- B. twice
- C. thrice
- D. never

79. The profession of Horace was ....
- A. businessman
- B. thief
- C. housekeeper
- D. locksmith

80. Choose the word which means the opposite of <u>EXPENSIVE</u>.
- A. cheap
- B. luxurious
- C. costly
- D. heavy

81. Choose the word which means almost same as <u>UNMARRIED</u>.
- A. handsome
- B. widow
- C. young
- D. bachelor

Choose the most appropriate option given against each question.

82. A herd of cows or ....
- A. birds
- B. elephant
- C. sheep
- D. horse

83. This is my book and that is ....
- A. yours
- B. your
- C. our
- D. ours

84. Rajan's father and Rohan's father .... businessmen.
- A. are
- B. have
- C. is
- D. has

85. My friends .... been asking for the party photographs.
- A. do
- B. does
- C. have
- D. has

86. Rakesh .... his mother tongue very fluently.
- A. speak
- B. speaking
- C. speaks
- D. None of these

87. Ankit and his family .... in Europe for three weeks.
- A. have been travelling
- B. have travelling
- C. been travelling
- D. have travelled

88. Bharti .... yoga classes these days.
- A. attending
- B. has attending
- C. is attending
- D. has been attending

89. My house is .... as yours.
- A. big
- B. as big
- C. bigger
- D. biggest

90. This is the .... comics I have ever read.
- A. most interesting
- B. more interesting
- C. less interesting
- D. None of these

Select one word from the options for the given definition.

91. A book or work of art whose author is unknown:
- A. anonymous
- B. playwright
- C. novelist
- D. poet

92. A person who believes in the existence of God:
- A. atheist
- B. theist
- C. agnostic
- D. pacifist

Select the most appropriate option for question tag.

93. I have completed my homework, ... ?
- A. have I
- B. has I
- C. do I
- D. haven't I

94. He does not do his work sincerely, ... ?
- A. does he
- B. did he
- C. doesn't he
- D. do he

Rearrange the following words/groups of words to make meaningful sentences. Choose the correct sequence given in the options.

95. (A) and grandpa / (B) my grandma / (C) too much / (D) love each other
- A. BDAC
- B. BACD
- C. DBCA
- D. BADC

96. (A) was very pretty / (B) in her childhood / (C) my grandma / (D) and beautiful
- A. CBAD
- B. ADBC
- C. CADB
- D. CDAB

Mark the option with the correct spelling of the given words:

97.
- A. address
- B. adres
- C. adress
- D. addres

98. A. appresiation   B. appreciation
     C. appreciason   D. apreciation

Choose the appropriate option to fill in the blanks:

99. 'Books' is for 'book', ... is for 'ship'.

     A. sheeps   B. ships
     C. shepherds   D. sheep

100. 'Kids' is for 'kid', ... is for 'child'
     A. childs   B. child
     C. children   D. None of these

PAPER-II : INTELLIGENCE TEST

101. Find the missing number in the number series given below:

     20, 30, 42, ?
     A. 64   B. 56
     C. 62   D. 54

102. Victory is to Joy as .... is to Sorrow.
     A. Defeat   B. Depression
     C. Loneliness   D. Cry

103. Find the missing number that has same relation to 289 as 13 has to 169.
     169 : 13 : : 289 : ?
     A. 19   B. 17
     C. 27   D. 23

104. If TRAIN is written as WUDLQ then BUS would be written as ....
     A. EXU   B. DWU
     C. EXV   D. VXE

105. If FLOW is related to RIVER then STAGNANT is related to ....
     A. Pool   B. Rain
     C. Stream   D. Canal

106. Choose the word which is least like the other words in the group?
     A. Ladder   B. Staircase
     C. Bridge   D. Escalator

107. If we arrange the given words in alphabetical order, which word would come at the second place, choose the correct alternative?
     A. Plane   B. Plain
     C. Plenty   D. Player

108. Choose the alternative that resembles the water image of the given word below:

     A1M3b
     A. ∀1W3P   B. ∀NW3P
     C. ∀1W3P   D. ∀1M3P

109. Choose the word which is least like the other words in the group.
     A. Eyes   B. Ear
     C. Hand   D. Scarf

110. Choose the alternative that will continue the number series below:

     2, 3, 5, 7, 11, 13 ?
     A. 15   B. 19
     C. 17   D. 21

111. Which of the following diagram indicates the best relation between Country, Nepal and India?

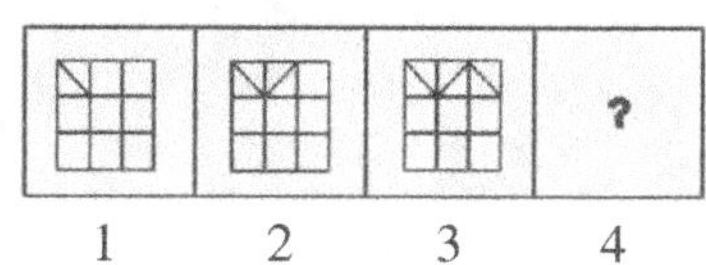

112. Choose the alternative that will continue the number series below:

     5, 11, 19, 29, ?, 55
     A. 39   B. 41
     C. 37   D. 43

113. A FISH is to GILLS then a MAN is to ....
     A. Ear   B. Eye
     C. Lungs   D. Nose

114. Which figure among the five alternatives A, B, C, D and E would replace the question mark in figure '4'?

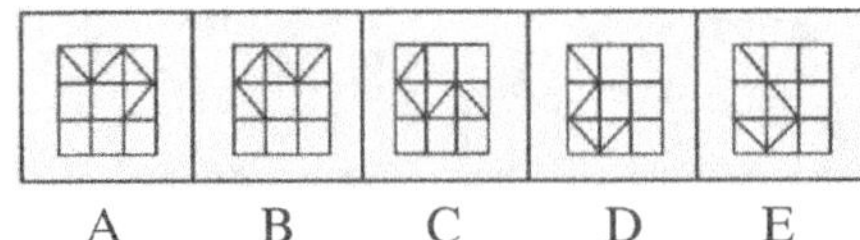

A	B	C	D	E

115. Choose the word which is least like the other words in the group.
A. Sun B. Planets
C. Stars D. Satellites

116. If Maya is the only daughter of Richa's grandmother's brother, how is Maya's daughter related to Richa?
A. Niece B. Cousin
C. Aunt D. Mother

117. O, P, Q, R, S and T are standing on a bench according to their height. P is taller than O but shorter than S. Only S is taller than T. R is shorter than P but taller than Q. Who is the shortest?
A. O B. Q
C. P D. Cannot be said

118. If '+' means '÷', '×' means '−', '÷' means '+' and '−' means '×', then what would be the answer of the equation?

$$16 ÷ 8 × 6 − 2 + 12 = ?$$

A. 22 B. 24
C. 23 D. 20

119. Count the number of triangles present in the given figure.

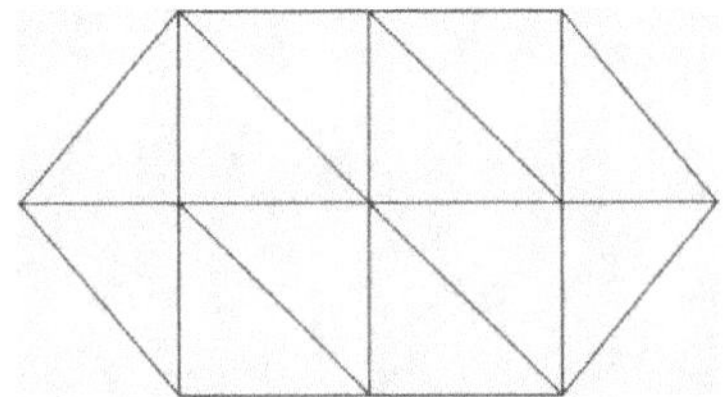

120. If DOG is to RABIES then MOSQUITO is to .... ?
A. Plague B. Death
C. Malaria D. Sting

121. It is 3 O'clock in a watch and it is rotated by 10 degree in a manner such that if the minute hand points towards the North–East, then hour hand will point towards which direction?
A. South
B. South-West
C. North-West
D. South-East

122. LOVE is to HATE then FRIEND is to ....?
A. Trust B. Companion
C. Enemy D. Despire

123. If the given alpha-numeric series is seen in mirror, which alternative would resemble its mirror image?

ANS43Q12

A. ꓯИƧ4ƐОГƐ B. ƧГꓩƐ4ƧИꓯ
C. ƧИꓯƐ4ꓩƧƐ D. ГƧWꓱ4ƐꓯИƧ

124. Given that A and B are a married couple. If X and Y are brothers and X is the brother of A. How is Y related to B?
A. Brother-in-law B. Brother
C. Cousin D. None of these

125. If '+' means '−', '−' means '×'; '×' means '÷' and '÷' means '+', then what would be the answer of the equation?

$$15 × 5 ÷ 10 + 5 − 3 = ?$$

A. 9.5 B. 0
C. −2 D. 24

ANSWERS

1	2	3	4	5	6	7	8	9	10
D	C	C	B	C	C	B	D	A	A

11	12	13	14	15	16	17	18	19	20
C	B	A	B	B	C	B	C	D	B

21	22	23	24	25	26	27	28	29	30
A	A	C	A	C	A	A	C	A	A

31	32	33	34	35	36	37	38	39	40
D	D	B	A	A	A	A	C	D	B

41	42	43	44	45	46	47	48	49	50
A	C	A	C	D	D	B	C	C	B

51	52	53	54	55	56	57	58	59	60
A	B	C	C	C	C	D	D	A	B

61	62	63	64	65	66	67	68	69	70
B	B	C	C	D	B	B	D	D	D

71	72	73	74	75	76	77	78	79	80
D	B	D	C	C	D	C	A	D	A

81	82	83	84	85	86	87	88	89	90
D	C	A	A	C	C	A	C	B	A

91	92	93	94	95	96	97	98	99	100
A	B	D	A	D	C	A	B	B	C

101	102	103	104	105	106	107	108	109	110
B	A	B	C	A	C	A	C	D	C

111	112	113	114	115	116	117	118	119	120
A	B	C	A	C	B	D	C	A	C

121	122	123	124	125
D	C	B	A	C

EXPLANATORY ANSWERS

1. The greatest 8-digits number with given digits 5, 8, 7, 5, 2, 0, 6 and 1

$$= 87655210.$$

2. 52806, 52086, 52860, 52800, and 58260 are given numbers.

52086, 52800, 52806, 52860 and 58260 are in ascending order.

3. Sum of 234251 and 352421 = 586672

$$925564 - 586672 = 338892$$

Hence, 338892 that must be subtracted from 925564 to make it equal to the sum of 234251 and 352421.

4. $10101 \times 25 = 252525$

$$
\begin{array}{r}
10101 \\
25 \\
\hline
50505 \\
20202 \\
\hline
252525
\end{array}
$$

5. Total age of 3 sisters = 3×15

$$= 45 \text{ years}$$

Sum of two sisters = $12 + 15$

$$= 27 \text{ years}$$

$\therefore$ Age of the third sister = $45 - 27$

$$= 18 \text{ years.}$$

6. $\dfrac{7}{6} \times 366$ days $= 7 \times 61$ days

$$= 427 \text{ days}$$

$$= \dfrac{427}{7} \text{ week}$$

$$= 61 \text{ week.}$$

7. The value of Roman numerals CDXLIX in Arabic numerals

$$= 400 + 40 + 9$$
$$= 449.$$

8. $(700 \div 10) - \{(12 \times 8) \div (34 - 10)\}$

$$= 70 - \{96 \div 24\}$$
$$= 70 - 4 = 66$$

9. $\qquad 2 = 200\%$

$$\left[\because 200\% = \dfrac{200}{100} = 2\right]$$

10. $\qquad$ C.P. = ₹ 3000

$$\text{S.P.} = ₹ 2700$$

$$\text{Loss} = 3000 - 2700 = ₹ 300$$

$$\text{Loss \%} = \dfrac{300}{3000} \times 100 = 10\%.$$

11. Duration of the Journey = 12 hrs + 6.15 hrs

$$= 18 \text{ hrs } 15 \text{ min.}$$

12. $\qquad$ C.P. = ₹ 1,39,500

$$\text{S.P.} = ₹ 75,000 + ₹ 80,000$$

$$= ₹ 1,55,000$$

$$\text{Gain} = ₹ 1,55,000 - ₹ 1,39,500$$

$$= ₹ 15,500.$$

13. Required no. of bulbs

$$= 85 \times 48 \times 64$$
$$= 4080 \times 64 = 261120.$$

15. $38 - 8 = 30$ and $68 - 8 = 60$

HCF of 30 and 60 = 30

Hence, the required number = 30.

16. 10 kg + 2 dag + 6 g

$$= \left(10 + \dfrac{2}{100} + \dfrac{6}{1000}\right) \text{ kg} = 10.026 \text{ kg.}$$

18. Perimeter of rectangle $= 2(l + b)$

$$= 2(10 + 8) = 36 \text{ cm.}$$

According to the question,

Perimeter of rectangle = Perimeter of square

$$\therefore \qquad \text{Side of square} = \dfrac{36}{4} = 9 \text{ cm}$$

Area of the square $= 9 \times 9 = 81 \text{ cm}^2.$

19. Sum of three angles of a triangle $= 180°$

(A) $\quad 52° + 69° + 79° = 200°$

(B) $\quad 30° + 69° + 71° = 170°$

(C) $132° + 169° + 59° = 360°$

(D) $\quad 32° + 69° + 79° = 180°$

Hence, option (D) is correct.

21. $\qquad 1.25 = \dfrac{125}{100} = \dfrac{5}{4} = 1\dfrac{1}{4}.$

22. Sum of two numbers = 11009

One number = 9999

$$\therefore \text{ Other number} = \begin{array}{r} 11009 \\ -9999 \\ \hline 1010 \end{array}$$

Hence, other number = 1010.

23. $6 \div 6 + 6 \times 6 - 6$

$$= 1 + 36 - 6 = 37 - 6 = 31.$$

24. $1\dfrac{1}{24} - 1 + \dfrac{7}{36}$

$$\Rightarrow \quad \dfrac{25}{24} - 1 + \dfrac{7}{36}$$

$$= \dfrac{75 - 72 + 14}{72} = \dfrac{17}{72}.$$

25. Total amount of lemonade Sara poured in 5 glasses

$$= 1\dfrac{1}{8} \times 5 = \dfrac{9}{8} \times 5$$

$$= \dfrac{45}{8} = 5\dfrac{5}{8} \text{ Cups.}$$

26. Required rice in each bag $= \dfrac{1}{4} \div 7$

$$= \dfrac{1}{4} \times \dfrac{1}{7} = \dfrac{1}{28}.$$

27. $1 + 0 + \dfrac{9}{100} + \dfrac{3}{1000} = 1.093.$

29.

$$\begin{array}{r} 20.088 \\ 20.08 \\ 20.008 \\ 20.888 \\ \hline 81.064 \end{array}$$

Hence, required sum = 81.064.

30. Round off 37504 to the nearest hundreds
$$= 37500.$$

31. $\because \qquad \text{Speed} = \dfrac{\text{Distance}}{\text{Time}}$

$\therefore \qquad \text{Time} = \dfrac{\text{Distance}}{\text{Speed}}$

$$= \dfrac{350}{75} = \dfrac{14}{3} \text{ hrs.}$$

$$= 4\dfrac{2}{3} \text{ hrs} = 4 \text{ hrs } 40 \text{ minutes.}$$

32. Number of rectangular pieces

$$= \dfrac{\text{Volume of cube}}{\text{Volume of rectangular pieces}}$$

$$= \dfrac{400 \times 400 \times 400}{20 \times 10 \times 5}$$

$$= \dfrac{64000000}{1000} = 64000.$$

33. $P = ₹ \ 500$

$A = ₹ \ 600$

$S.I. = A - P$

$$= 600 - 500 = ₹ \ 100$$

$$\text{Time} = \dfrac{S.I. \times 100}{P \times r}$$

$$= \dfrac{100 \times 100}{500 \times 5} = 4 \text{ years.}$$

34. Total numbers of 4 numbers
$$= 4 \times 30 = 120$$

Sum of first-three numbers = 85

$\therefore$ The fourth number $= 120 - 85 = 35$

35. Let $x\%$ of 10000 m = 10 m

$\Rightarrow \qquad \dfrac{x}{100} \times 10000 = 10$

$\Rightarrow \qquad 100x = 10$

$\Rightarrow \qquad x = \dfrac{10}{100} = \dfrac{1}{10}\% = 0.1\%.$

36. Number of square tiles

$$= \dfrac{360 \times 450}{15 \times 15} = 720.$$

37. The smallest odd number formed by using the digits 1, 2, 3, 4 and 5 = 12345.

38. (A) $\dfrac{1}{3}, \dfrac{1}{2}, \dfrac{25}{100}$

$\Rightarrow \dfrac{1}{3}, \dfrac{1}{2}, \dfrac{1}{4}$ are not in ascending order

(B) $\dfrac{1}{4}, \dfrac{1}{2}, \dfrac{1}{3}$ are not in ascending order

(C) $\dfrac{1}{4}, \dfrac{1}{3}, \dfrac{1}{2}$ are in ascending order

(D) $\dfrac{1}{2}, \dfrac{1}{3}, \dfrac{1}{4}$ are not in ascending order

Hence, option (C) is correct.

39. $18 \text{ km/hr} = 18 \times \dfrac{5}{18} \text{ m/s} = 5 \text{ m/s}$

Hence, the speed of boat = 5 m/s.

40. $C = \dfrac{5}{9}(F - 32)$

$$= \dfrac{5}{9}(200 - 32)$$

$$= \dfrac{5}{9} \times 168 = \dfrac{5}{3} \times 56$$

$$= \dfrac{280}{3} = 93.3°C$$

Hence, the value of 200°F in degree Celsius
$$= 93.3°C.$$

41.

$$\begin{array}{r} \text{Difference} = \quad 39460 \\ -36490 \\ \hline 2970 \end{array}$$

42. $\dfrac{375}{100} \times \dfrac{5}{100} + \dfrac{725}{100} \times \dfrac{10}{100}$

$= \dfrac{1875}{10000} + \dfrac{7250}{10000} = \dfrac{9125}{10000} = 0.9125.$

43.

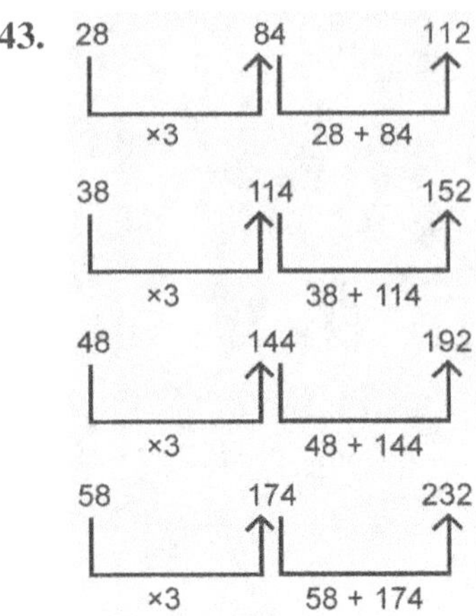

Hence, the next row of numbers is 58 174 232.

44. Perimeter of rectangular field
$$= 2(l + b) = 2(40 + 25) = 130 \text{ m}$$
In 1 round distance = 130 m
In 4 rounds distance = 130×4 m = 520 m.

45. Area of the room $= l \times b$
$$= 1500 \times 1000 \text{ cm}^2$$
$$= 1500000 \text{ m}^2$$
Cost of 1 cm^2 = ₹ 2
Cost of 1500000 cm^2 = ₹ 3000000
∴ Cost of carpeting its floor = 3000000

46. Cost of 15 balls = ₹ 300

Cost of 1 ball = ₹ $\dfrac{300}{15}$ = ₹ 20

Cost of 12 shuttle = ₹ 96

Cost of 1 shuttle = ₹ $\dfrac{96}{12}$ = ₹ 8

∴ Cost of 1 ball and 1 shuttle
$$= ₹\ 20 + ₹\ 8 = ₹\ 28.$$

47. HCF × LCM = 1st no. × 2nd no.
$$312 \times \text{LCM} = 624 \times 936$$
∴ LCM $= \dfrac{624 \times 936}{312}$

$= 2 \times 936 = 1872$
Hence, required smallest number = 1872.

48. Total C.P. = ₹ 450 + ₹ 50 = ₹ 500
Total S.P. = ₹ 600
Profit = S.P. – C.P.
$$= 600 - 500 = ₹\ 100$$

Profit % $= \dfrac{\text{Profit}}{\text{CP}} \times 100$

$= \dfrac{100}{500} \times 100 = 20\%.$

49. Area of the given figure
$$= 10 \times 6 - 4 \times 2 - 4 \times 2$$
$$= 60 - 16 = 44 \text{ cm}^2.$$

50. Let total time spent by Amar in study = x hrs.

Time spent on Science $= \dfrac{3x}{8}$

Time spent on English $= \dfrac{3x}{8} \times \dfrac{2}{5} = \dfrac{3x}{20}$

Hence, $\dfrac{3}{20}$ of Amar's study time was spent studying English.

101. 20, 30, 42, ?
$$20 + 10 = 30$$
$$30 + 12 = 42$$
$$42 + 14 = 56$$

103. $(13)^2 = 169$
$(17)^2 = 289$

110. 2, 3, 5, 7, 11, 13 are prime numbers.
Hence, next prime number is 17.

112.
$5 + 6 = 11$	$11 + 8 = 19$
$19 + 10 = 29$	$29 + 12 = 41$
$41 + 14 = 55.$	

118. $16 \div 8 \times 6 - 2 + 12 = ?$
$$16 + 8 - 6 \times 2 \div 12$$
$$= 16 + 8 - 6 \times 2 \times \dfrac{1}{12}$$
$$= 16 + 8 - 1 = 24 - 1 = 23.$$

125. $15 \times 5 \div 10 + 5 - 3 = ?$
$$= 15 \div 5 + 10 - 5 \times 3$$
$$= 15 \times \dfrac{1}{5} + 10 - 5 \times 3$$
$$= 3 + 10 - 15 = 13 - 15 = -2.$$

All India Sainik School Entrance Exam., 2017
(CLASS-VI)

PAPER-I : MATHEMATICS AND LANGUAGE ABILITY

Part-A : Mathematics

Section-I

(Each question carries two marks)

1. Form the smallest and greatest 6-digit numerals by repeating any 2 digits from 7, 9, 5, 4.

2. Find the square root of 7921.

3. If a man can do a work in 32 days, in how many days will 24 men complete the same work?

4. Find the simple interest, if P = ₹ 400, R = 3.65% per annum and time = 150 days.

5. Round 48,540 and 23,467 to the nearest 1000 and find the difference.

6. Express 804.291 kg as decagrams.

7. Find the smallest number which when divided by 12 and 20 leaves no remainder.

8. Sonali and Priya are classmates. Sonali completed her homework in $\frac{5}{6}$ of an hour and Priya in $\frac{3}{4}$ of an hour. Who was faster?

9. Simplify $6\frac{3}{10} - 2\frac{3}{4} - 1\frac{2}{5}$

10. Two angles of a quadrilateral are each 90° and remaining two angles are such that one is 3 times the other. Find these two angles.

Section-II

(Each question carries three marks)

11. Find the ratio of 90 cm to 1.5 m.

12. Arrange the following in descending order:
$$\frac{3}{7}, \frac{3}{11}, \frac{3}{5}, \frac{3}{2} \text{ and } \frac{3}{17}.$$

13. The number of girl students in each class of a co-educational middle school is depicted by the pictograph:

Classes	Number of girl students	👧 - 4 Girls
I	👧👧👧👧👧👧	
II	👧👧👧👧◖	
III	👧👧👧👧◖	
IV	👧👧👧◖	
V	👧👧◖	
VI	👧👧👧👧	
VII	👧👧◖	
VIII	👧◖	

Observe this pictograph and answer the following questions:

(*a*) Which class has the maximum number of girl students?

(*b*) Is the number of girls in Class V less than the number of girls in Class III?

(*c*) How many girls are there in Class VII?

14. Akhilesh runs a coffee shop and sells 51 cups of coffee in 6 hours. If this is three-fourths of the total number of cups he sells in the whole day, find out the number of cups he sells in a day.

15. Simplify $4\dfrac{6}{8} - \left\{3\dfrac{1}{3} + \left(2\dfrac{1}{2} - 1\dfrac{1}{4}\right)\right\}$.

16. Find the greatest number which divides 149 and 101 leaving remainder 5 in each case.

17. Mrs. Singhal deposited ₹ 10,000 in a Post Office Saving at an interest of 3% per annum. How much amount will she receive at the end of 4th month?

18. Suppose your watch gains 4 seconds every 8 hours. How many seconds will it gain in a week?

19. A fruit seller had 2,00,000 apples. He packed them in boxes. Each box contains 176 apples. How many boxes were used and how many apples were left over?

20. Find the average of all prime numbers between 60 and 80.

Section-III

(Each question carries five marks)

21. Bob wants to cover the floor of a room 3 m wide and 4 m long by squared tiles. If each square tile is of side 0.5 m, then find the number of tiles required to cover the floor of the room.

22. Name the types of following triangles:
(*a*) Triangle with lengths of sides 7 cm, 8 cm and 9 cm.
(*b*) Δ ABC with AB = 8.7 cm, AC = 7 cm and BC = 6 cm.
(*c*) Δ PQR such that PQ = QR = PR = 5 cm.
(*d*) Δ DEF with m∠D = 90°.
(*e*) Δ XYZ with m∠Y = 90° and XY = YZ.

23. Find the smallest 4 digit number such that when it is divided by 12, 18, 21 and 28, it leaves remainder 3 in each case.

24. How much time will a 171 m long train take to cross 229 m long bridge, if it is running at a speed of 45 km/h?

25. Divide rupees 4000 among A, B, C, so that their shares may be in the ratio of 5 : 7 : 8.

26. Find the number of cubical boxes of cubical side 3 cm which can be accommodated in a carton of dimension 15 cm × 9 cm × 12 cm?

27. Fill in the blanks:
(*a*) There are only .... symbols in Roman numerals.
(*b*) The predecessor of the smallest 8 digit number is ....
(*c*) $\dfrac{4}{7} X$ .... = 84
(*d*) Length of a Rectangle $= \dfrac{?}{\text{Breadth}}$
(*e*) .... is the smallest prime number.

28. A crockery dealer ordered for 50 pieces of China tea sets for ₹ 18,000. When the goods arrived, he found that two tea sets were damaged. At what price per set should he sell the remaining tea sets to earn a total profit of ₹ 1200?

29. Vina's father baked a rectangular cake. In the evening $\dfrac{5}{6}$ of the cake was left. Vina ate half of it. What fraction of the cake did Vina eat?

30. (*a*) The product of two numbers is 2925. If LCM is 195, find HCF.
(*b*) Sohan bought rice at ₹ 4800.75 per quintal. Due to a fall in prices he could sell it as ₹ 4600.75 per quintal only. Find his total loss if he has bought 13.5 quintals rice.

ANSWERS

1. Greatest number = 997754
Smallest number = 445579.

2.

```
   8 | 7921 | 89
       64
   ---------
  169 | 1521
        1521
   ---------
        ×
```
∴ Square root of 7921 = 89.

3. ∵ 1 man can do a work in 32 days
∴ 24 men can do this work $\dfrac{32}{24} = \dfrac{4}{3}$ days
$= 1\dfrac{1}{3}$ days.

4. S.I. $= \dfrac{P \times r \times t}{100} = \dfrac{400 \times 365 \times 150}{100 \times 100 \times 365} = ₹\ 6$

Hence, Simple interest $= ₹\ 6$.

5.
$$48540 = 49000$$
$$23467 = 23000$$
Required difference $= 49000 - 23000$
$$= 26000.$$

6. 804.291 kg $= \dfrac{804291}{1000}$ kg

$\qquad = \dfrac{804291}{1000} \times 100$ deca gram

$\qquad = 80429.1$ deca grams.

7. LCM of 12 and 20 $= 60$

Hence, the smallest number which when divided by 12 and 20 leaves no. remainder is 60.

8. Time taken by Sonali to complete her home work $= 60 \times \dfrac{5}{6}$ minutes $= 50$ min.

Time taken by Priya to complete her home work $= 60 \times \dfrac{3}{4}$ minutes $= 45$ min.

Hence, Priya is faster than Sonali.

9. $6\dfrac{3}{10} - 2\dfrac{3}{4} - 1\dfrac{2}{5} = \dfrac{63}{10} - \dfrac{11}{4} - \dfrac{7}{5}$

$= \dfrac{126 - 55 - 28}{20} = \dfrac{126 - 83}{20} = \dfrac{43}{20} = 2\dfrac{3}{20}.$

10. Let remaining two angles are $x°$ and $3x°$

$x° + 3x° + 90° + 90° = 360°$

$\Rightarrow \quad 4x = 360 - 180 = 180$

$\Rightarrow \quad x = \dfrac{180}{4} = 45°$

$3x = 3 \times 45 = 135°$

Hence, remaining two angles are 45° and 135°.

11. The ratio of 90 cm : 1.5 m

$= \dfrac{90}{150} = \dfrac{3}{5} = 3 : 5$

12. Arrange in descending order of the following:

$\dfrac{3}{7}, \dfrac{3}{11}, \dfrac{3}{5}, \dfrac{3}{2}$ and $\dfrac{3}{17}$

$\dfrac{3}{2}, \dfrac{3}{5}, \dfrac{3}{7}, \dfrac{3}{11}, \dfrac{3}{17}$ are in descending order.

13. (*a*) The maximum number of girl students in class I $= 6 \times 4 = 24$ girls.

(*b*) The number of girls in class V less than the number of girls in class III.

In V class, no. of girls $= 10$

In III class, no. of girls $= 5 \times 4 = 20$.

(*c*) Number of girls in class VII $= 4 \times 3 = 12$.

14. Let, x cups he sells in a day

According to the question,

$\dfrac{3}{4}$ of $x = 51 \quad \Rightarrow \quad x = \dfrac{4 \times 51}{3} = 68.$

15. $4\dfrac{6}{8} - \left\{ 3\dfrac{1}{3} + \left(2\dfrac{1}{2} - 1\dfrac{1}{4} \right) \right\}$

$= \dfrac{38}{8} - \left\{ \dfrac{10}{3} + \left(\dfrac{5}{2} - \dfrac{5}{4} \right) \right\}$

$= \dfrac{38}{8} - \left\{ \dfrac{10}{3} + \left(\dfrac{10 - 5}{4} \right) \right\} = \dfrac{38}{8} - \left\{ \dfrac{10}{3} + \dfrac{5}{4} \right\}$

$= \dfrac{38}{8} - \left\{ \dfrac{40 + 15}{12} \right\} = \dfrac{38}{8} - \dfrac{55}{12} = \dfrac{114 - 110}{24}$

$= \dfrac{4}{24} = \dfrac{1}{6}.$

16.
$$149 - 5 = 144$$
$$101 - 5 = 96$$
HCF of 144 and 96 $= 48$

Hence, required greatest no. $= 48$.

17. $\qquad$ S.I. $= \dfrac{P \times r \times t}{100}$

$\qquad = \dfrac{10000 \times 3 \times 4}{100 \times 12} = ₹\ 100$

Amount $= 10000 + 100 = 10100$

Hence, she will receive ₹ 10100 at the end of 4th month.

18. In 8 hrs watch gains 4 seconds

In 24 hrs watch gains 12 seconds

In 1 day watch gains 12 seconds

In 7 days watch gains 12×7 seconds

$\qquad \qquad = 84$ seconds.

19. $200000 \div 176$ then we get

quotient $= 1136$, remainder $= 64$

Hence, no. of boxes $= 1136$ and 64 apples were left.

20. 61, 67, 71, 73 and 79 are prime numbers between 60 and 80

Average of all prime numbers

$$= \frac{61+67+71+73+79}{5} = \frac{351}{5} = 70.2$$

21. Required no. of tiles $= \dfrac{3 \times 4}{0.5 \times 0.5}$

$$= \frac{3 \times 4 \times 10 \times 10}{5 \times 5} = 48.$$

22. (a) Triangle with lengths of sides 7 cm, 8 cm and 9 cm is scalene triangle.

(b) $\triangle$ABC with AB = 8.7 cm, AC = 7 cm and BC = 6 cm is scalene triangle.

(c) In $\triangle$PQR where PQ = QR = PR = 5 cm This type of triangle is equilateral triangle.

(d) In $\triangle$DEF, $\angle$D = 90° This type of triangle is right triangle.

(e) In $\triangle$XYZ, $\angle$Y = 90° and XY = YZ This type of triangle is isosceles right triangle.

23. LCM of 12, 18, 21 and 28 = 252

The smallest 4 digit number = 1000

$\therefore$ 252 k + 3 is the smallest number of 4 digit number

$\therefore$ 252 × 4 + 3 = 1008 + 3 = 1011

Hence, the required no. = 1011.

24. Speed = 45 km/hr $= \dfrac{45 \times 1000}{60 \times 60} = \dfrac{25}{2}$ m/s

Distance = 171 m + 229 m = 400 m

Time taken $= \dfrac{400}{\dfrac{25}{2}} = \dfrac{400 \times 2}{25}$ seconds

$$= 16 \times 2 \text{ seconds}$$
$$= 32 \text{ seconds.}$$

25. A : B : C = 5 : 7 : 8

A's share $= \dfrac{5}{20} \times 4000 = ₹ 1000$

B's share $= \dfrac{7}{20} \times 4000 = ₹ 1400$

C's share $= \dfrac{8}{20} \times 4000 = ₹ 1600.$

26. No. of cubical boxes $= \dfrac{15 \times 9 \times 12}{3 \times 3 \times 3}$

$$= 5 \times 3 \times 4 = 60.$$

27. (a) There are only seven symbols in Roman numerals. [IVXLCDM]

(b) The predecessor of the smallest 8 digit number is 9999999.

(c) $\dfrac{4}{7} \times 147 = 84$

(d) Lenght of a rectangle $= \dfrac{\text{Area}}{\text{Breadth}}$

(e) 2 is the smallest prime number.

28. Cost price of 48 China tea sets = ₹ 18000

Cost of each China tea set $= \dfrac{18000}{48} = ₹ 375$

Selling price of 48 China tea sets
$$= 18000 + 1200 = ₹ 19200$$

Selling price of each China tea set

$$= \frac{19200}{48} = ₹ 400.$$

29. Portion of the cake left in the evening

$$= \frac{5}{6} \text{ portion.}$$

Portion of the cake ate by Vina $= \dfrac{1}{2}$ of $\dfrac{5}{6}$

$$= \frac{5}{6} \times \frac{1}{2} = \frac{5}{12}$$

30. (a) HCF $= \dfrac{\text{Product of two numbers}}{\text{LCM}}$

$$= \frac{2925}{195} = 15.$$

(b) Cost of 1 quintal rice = ₹ 4800.75

Selling price of 1 quintal rice = ₹ 4600.75

Loss per quintal = ₹ 200

Loss for 13.5 quintal = ₹ 200 × 13.5

$$= ₹ 200 \times \frac{135}{10}$$

$$= ₹ 2700.$$

PART-B : LANGUAGE ABILITY

1. Write 15 sentences on any *one* of the following topics: **(15)**
   Importance of Cleanliness or A Journey by Bus.

2. Read the following passage carefully and answer the questions that follow: **(15)**

   The Sahara Desert covers large parts of Africa. The desert is covered with sand dunes or sand seas. The desert also has several deeply dissected mountains and mountain ranges along with many volcanic mountains. Most of the rivers and streams that are found in Sahara are seasonal or intermittent, except the Nile river, which crosses the desert from its origins in central Africa to empty into Mediterranean.

   The central part of the Sahara is very dry, with little vegetation. The northern and southern reaches of the desert, along with the highlands, have areas of sparse grasslands and desert shrub, with trees and taller shrubs at places where moisture collects.

   (a) What is the meaning of word "seasonal"?
   (b) "The desert is covered by sand dunes or sand seas". What is the meaning of sand sea in the paragraph?
   (c) "The central part of Sahara is very dry, with little vegetation". What does it mean?
   (d) Give the meaning of "sparse".
   (e) What is the meaning of vegetation in paragraph?

3. Make your own sentences using the underlined words in the following paragraph. **(5 × 2 = 10)**

   Do you **support** a football or hockey team? Perhaps you follow the **success** of your national cricket team. You know every game has its own importance and follows its own **discipline.** To become a good player of any game you need to have **regular** practice of that game. Learinng basic skills of the game is very **essential.**
   (a) ....
   (b) ....

(c) ....
(d) ....
(e) ....

4. Form meaningful sentences by rearranging the words in proper order: **(5 × 2 = 10)**
   (a) crying/she had/as/lost her/Manju was/pencil
   (b) at that hospital/Anil said that/was a doctor/his father
   (c) environmental/of everybody/protection/is responsibility/the
   (d) the/knocking/who/at/door/is
   (e) early to bed/good habit/and early to rise/is a

5. Give one word for the following: **(5 × 1 = 5)**
   (a) A person who carries our luggage
      ....
   (b) A person who spends money extravagantly
      ....
   (c) Young one of a horse
      ....
   (d) Happening once in two years
      ....
   (e) One who makes wooden furninture
      ....

6. Choose the correct word given in the brackets and fill in the blanks: **(5 × 2 = 10)**
   (a) Cleanliness is next to ....
      (God, Goddess, Godliness)
   (b) My father tells me to .... daily.
      (Play, played, playing)
   (c) Yesterday, a cyclone .... a small town near the beach. (hit/has hit)
   (d) I like .... blue candle the best.
      (a, an, the)
   (e) There is .... eucalyptus tree beside the house. (a, an, the)

7. Use the given word in separate sentences of your own to show the difference in the meaning of the words of the pair given below:
   (5 × 2 = 10)
   (a) Early, Yearly   (b) Greatness, Grateful
   (c) Pray, Prey   (d) Break, Brake
   (e) Lose, Loose

8. Give the Antonym (opposite) of the following words: **(5 × 1 = 5)**
   (*a*) Risky　　　　(*b*) Doubtful
   (*c*) Negligent　　(*d*) Deep
   (*e*) Differ

9. Change each of the following as directed: **(5 × 2 = 10)**
   (*a*) The news is too good to be true.
   　　　　　　　　(Remove "too")
   ....
   (*b*) She is your mother.
   　　　　(Change into interrogative)
   ....
   (*c*) Fire destroyed the town.
   　　　　　　　(Change the Voice)
   ....
   (*d*) He said, 'I am very thirsty'
   　　　　(Change into indirect speech)
   ....
   (*e*) Raju is not as bad as Gaurav.
   (Rewrite using comparative form of "good")
   ....

10. Imagine your name is Akash and you live at House No. 23, Dr Kalam Road, Jayanagar, Bangalore. Your sister, Deepika who lives at Shanti Nivas, Linking Road, Mumbai, has sent you a Rakhi on Rakshbandhan. Write a letter of thanks to her. **(10)**

$$\boxed{\text{ANSWERS}}$$

1.　　　　**Importance of Cleanliness**

It is rightly said, "Cleanliness is next only to godliness." Cleanliness is to our body what godliness is to our soul and mind. For the purity of our mind we should have noble thoughts. Similarly, for our good health, we must observe cleanliness in letter and spirit. Moreover, an unclean person or thing is very unsightly, unpleasant and a mere nuisance. Who wants to look at a filthy dog or a pig rolling in a heap of dung, though everybody would like the sight of a dancing peacock or a hopping sparrow? We should bathe daily and put on fresh well-washed clothes. We should keep our books neat and clean and our house spick and span. There should be no puddles which breed mosquitos and flies near our home as they are a source of many obnoxious diseases. Similarly, we should keep our roads, parks and village or town clean. Throwing of heaps of rubbish here and there or spitting everywhere can cause several diseases to ourselves and to others. Similarly, food should be fresh and covered and free from the approach of flies. Let the children be taught the habit of cleanliness from their very early life.

2. (*a*) Seasonal means relating to or characteristic of a particular season of the year.
   (*b*) Sand sea means a vast expanse of sand.
   (*c*) It means there is scarcity of water and plant in the central part of Sahara.
   (*d*) Sparse means thinly dispersed.
   (*e*) Vegetation means plants collectively.

3. (*a*) We must support the good cause.
   (*b*) Success depends upon you efforts.
   (*c*) We must follow the rules of discipline.
   (*d*) We must be regular in exercise.
   (*e*) It is essential to clear the test.

4. (*a*) Manju was crying as she had lost her pencil.
   (*b*) Anil said that his father was a doctor at that hospital.
   (*c*) The environmental protection is responsibility of everybody.
   (*d*) Who is knocking at the door?
   (*e*) Early to bed and early to rise is a good habit.

5. (*a*) Porter　　　　(*b*) Spendthrift
   (*c*) Colt　　　　　(*d*) Biennial
   (*e*) Carpenter

6. (*a*) Godliness　　(*b*) Play
   (*c*) hit　　　　　(*d*) the
   (*e*) a

7. (*a*) We must get up early in the morning.
   　　You have to pay the maintenance charges yearly.
   (*b*) Every one know him for this greatness.
   　　We are grateful to our teachers.
   (*c*) We pray to God every morning.
   　　The deer was an easy prey for the tiger.
   (*d*) Never break the rules of discipline.
   　　You must apply the brakes of your bicycle.
   (*e*) Never lose your temper.
   　　The brakes of your bicycle are loose.

8. (*a*) Safe   (*b*) Sure
   (*c*) Careful   (*d*) Shallow
   (*e*) Agree

9. (*a*) The news is so good that it cannot be true.
   (*b*) Is she your mother?
   (*c*) The town was destroyed in fire.
   (*d*) He told that he was very thirsty.
   (*e*) Raju is better than Gaurav.

10. House No. 23,
Dr Kalam Road,
Jayanagar, Bangalore.

August 7, 20....

My Dear Sister,

Hope this letter of mine will find you in good health and happiness. I received the precious Rakhi sent by you today. It looks really beautiful in my hand.

Thank you very much for the lovely Rakhi. I am sending you a small gift and hope you will like it.

Hope we will be together on the next Raksha Bandhan.

Love to Arpan and Regards to dear Jijaji.

Yours affectionately
AKASH

Postage

To
   Ms Deepika,
   Shanti Niwas,
   Linking Road,
Mumbai

PAPER-II : INTELLIGENCE TEST*

Directions (Qs. 1-6) : *In each of the following series determine the order of the letters/numbers. Then from the given options select the one which will complete the given series.*

1. B D G K ? V
   (*a*) N   (*b*) P
   (*c*) Q   (*d*) M

2. dfe, jih, mln, ?, vut
   (*a*) oqp   (*b*) psr
   (*c*) prq   (*d*) rsp

3. QPO, SRQ, UTS, WVU, (?)
   (*a*) XVZ   (*b*) ZYA
   (*c*) YXW   (*d*) VWX

4. 4, 9, 19, 34, 54, ?, 109
   (*a*) 89   (*b*) 84
   (*c*) 74   (*d*) 79

5. 7776, 1296, 216, 36, 6, ?
   (*a*) 6   (*b*) 0
   (*c*) 3   (*d*) 1

6. 3, 15, 90, 630, 5040, ?
   (*a*) 35280   (*b*) 40320
   (*c*) 45360   (*d*) 10080

Directions (Qs. 7 and 8): *In the following questions select the right option which indicates the correct code for the word or letter given in the question.*

7. If BAD is coded as 7, HIS as 9, LOW will be coded as :
   (*a*) 50   (*b*) 8
   (*c*) 23   (*d*) 5

8. In a certain code LIBERATE is written as 56403170, TRIBAL will be written in the same code as :
   (*a*) 734615   (*b*) 736415
   (*c*) 136475   (*d*) 034615

9. Reena walked from A and B in the East 10 feet. Then she turned to the right and walked 3 feet. Again she turned to the right and walked 14 feet. How far is she from A?
   (*a*) 4 feet   (*b*) 5 feet
   (*c*) 24 feet   (*d*) 27 feet

10. Amit started walking positioning his back towards the sun. After some time, he turned left, then turned right and towards the left again. In which direction is he going now?
   (*a*) North or South   (*b*) East or West
   (*c*) North or West   (*d*) South or West

11. Pointing to a man, a lady said, "His brother's father is my grandfather's only son." How is the lady related to the man?
   (*a*) Mother   (*b*) Sister
   (*c*) Daughter   (*d*) Aunt

---

* Memory Based

12. Vidya is the wife of Gopi and Gopi is the brother of Akhil. Akhil is the uncle of Vijay. What is Vijay's relation with Vidya?
  (*a*) Son
  (*b*) Nephew
  (*c*) Brother-in-law
  (*d*) Brother

Directions (Qs. 13-17) : *In the questions given below one term is missing. Based on the relationship of the two given words/letters/numbers find the missing term from the given options.*

13. ACE : FGH : : LNP : ?
  (*a*) QRS
  (*b*) PQR
  (*c*) QST
  (*d*) MOQ

14. EIGHTY : GIEYTH : : OUTPUT : ?
  (*a*) UTOPTU
  (*b*) UOTUPT
  (*c*) TUOUTP
  (*d*) TUOTUP

15. 23 : 53 : : 8 : ?
  (*a*) 66
  (*b*) 57
  (*c*) 27
  (*d*) 19

16. PEARL : NECKLACE : : FLOWER : ?
  (*a*) Plant
  (*b*) Garden
  (*c*) Petal
  (*d*) Bouquet

17. ALPHABET : WORD : : WORD : ?
  (*a*) Sound
  (*b*) Music
  (*c*) Sentence
  (*d*) Dictionary

Directions (Qs. 18–24) : *In each of the following questions, there are four options. Three options are alike in certain manner. Only one option does not fit in. Choose the one which is different from the rest.*

18. (*a*) 18
  (*b*) 12
  (*c*) 30
  (*d*) 20

19. (*a*) 336
  (*b*) 213
  (*c*) 436
  (*d*) 819

20. (*a*) 28751
  (*b*) 52638
  (*c*) 85362
  (*d*) 63852

21. (*a*) AEHJ
  (*b*) EIJK
  (*c*) DHKM
  (*d*) CGJL

22. (*a*) Rabbit
  (*b*) Crocodile
  (*c*) Earthworm
  (*d*) Snail

23. (*a*) Tree
  (*b*) Leaf
  (*c*) Bush
  (*d*) Herb

24. (*a*) Doctor
  (*b*) Teacher
  (*c*) Engineer
  (*d*) Diver

25. How many 7's are there in the following series which are preceded by 6 which is not preceded by 8?

8 7 6 7 8 6 7 5 6 7 9 8 6 1 6 7 7 6 8 8 6 9 7 6 8 7

  (*a*) 2
  (*b*) 3
  (*c*) 4
  (*d*) Only 1

26. If "+" means "÷"; "×" means "–"; "÷" means "×" and "–" means "+", what will be the value of the following expression?
$$9 + 3 \div 4 - 8 \times 2 = ?$$
  (*a*) $6\dfrac{3}{4}$
  (*b*) $-1\dfrac{3}{4}$
  (*c*) $-6\dfrac{1}{4}$
  (*d*) 18

27. If "–" means "÷"; "+" means "×"; "÷" means "–" and "×" means "+", then which of the following must be true?
  (*a*) $1 \div 2 + 3 \times 6 - 8 = 12$
  (*b*) $2 + 3 - 5 \times 8 \div 4 = 7$
  (*c*) $5 + 6 \times 8 - 2 \div 3 = 31$
  (*d*) $6 \div 1 + 2 - 8 \times 4 = 31$

28. If Thursday was the day after the day before yesterday five days ago, what is the least number of days ago when Sunday was three days before the day after tomorrow?
  (*a*) Two days ago
  (*b*) Three days ago
  (*c*) Four days ago
  (*d*) Five days ago

29. If the fifth day of a month is Friday, which of the following will be the Seventh day from 10th of that month?
  (*a*) Tuesday
  (*b*) Monday
  (*c*) Wednesday
  (*d*) Thursday

30. In a certain language 'mu mit es' means 'who is she' and 'elb mu es' means 'where is she'. What is the code for 'where' in this language?
  (*a*) es
  (*b*) elb
  (*c*) mu
  (*d*) mit

31. In a certain code language '069' means 'grapes are sweet', '476' means 'very sweet fruit' and '509' means 'grapes are ripe'. Which of the following digits means 'ripe' in that language?
  (*a*) 0
  (*b*) 5
  (*c*) 9
  (*d*) 7

32. If the odd numbers between 20 to 40 are arranged in a row, what will be the 6th number from the right?

(*a*) 27   (*b*) 31
(*c*) 33   (*d*) 29

Directions (Qs. 33–35) : *In each of the following questions, three out of four alternatives contain alphabet placed in a particular form. Find the one that does not belong to the group.*

33. (*a*) PEAR   (*b*) TORE
(*c*) REAP   (*d*) TEAR

34. (*a*) QePFoLA   (*b*) OrDFkV
(*c*) TuMBiN   (*d*) XZaWoB

35. (*a*) KQ14   (*b*) AY13
(*c*) MR11   (*d*) GW15

Directions (Qs. 36-40): *There are two sets of figure given. There is a definite relationship between first two. Establish a similar relationship between third and fourth by selecting a suitable figure from answer that would replace the question mark.*

36. Question Figures

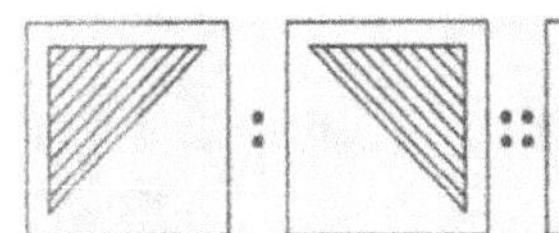 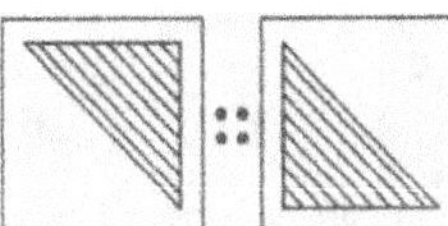 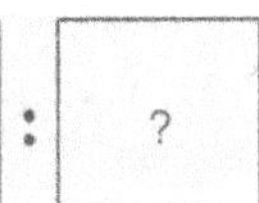

Answer Figures

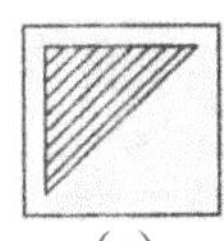 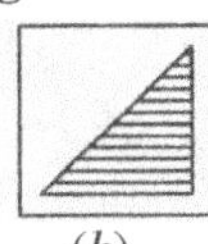 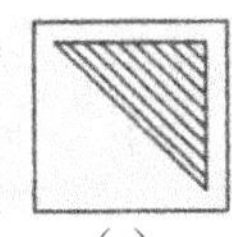 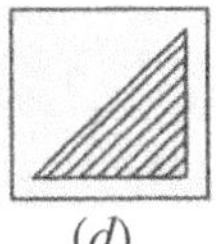

(*a*)   (*b*)   (*c*)   (*d*)

37. Question Figures

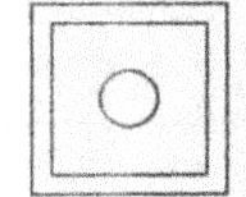  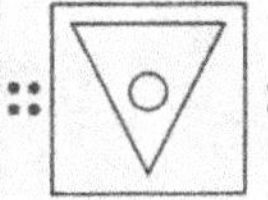 

Answer Figures

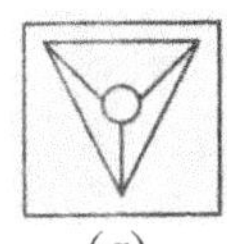 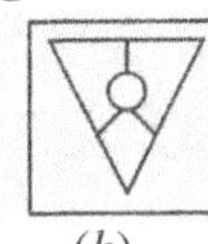 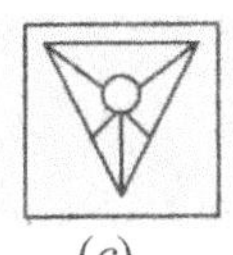 

(*a*)   (*b*)   (*c*)   (*d*)

38. Question Figures

 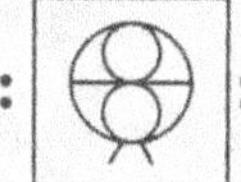 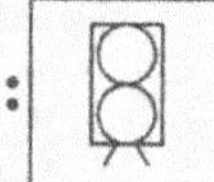 

Answer Figures

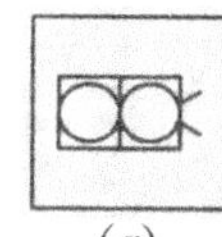 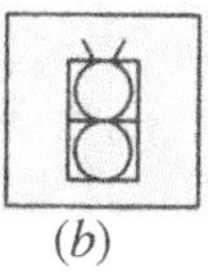 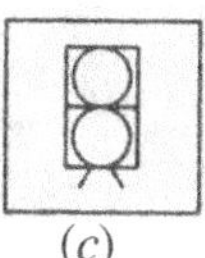 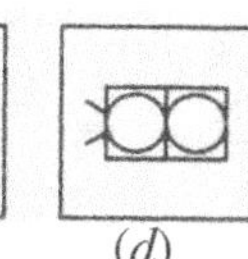

(*a*)   (*b*)   (*c*)   (*d*)

39. Question Figures

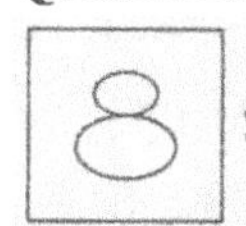 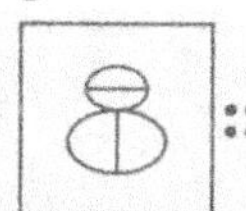 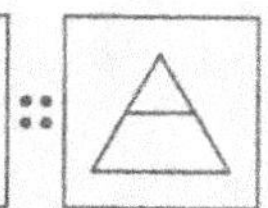 

Answer Figures

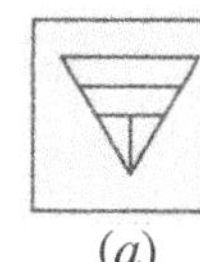 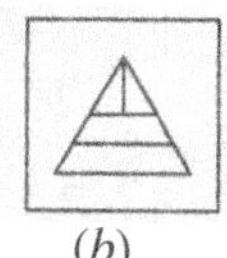 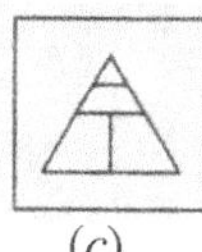 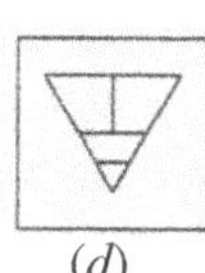

(*a*)   (*b*)   (*c*)   (*d*)

40. Question Figures

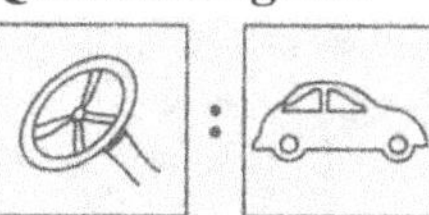  

Answer Figures

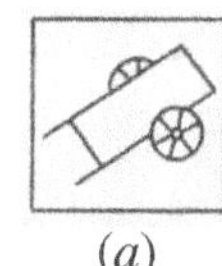   

(*a*)   (*b*)   (*c*)   (*d*)

Directions (Qs. 41-45): *In each of the following questions, there are three figures and the space for the fourth figure is left blank. The problem figures are in a series. Find out one figure from among the answer figures which occupies the blank space for the fourth figure and completes the series. Indicate your answer in the answer sheet.*

41. Problem Figures

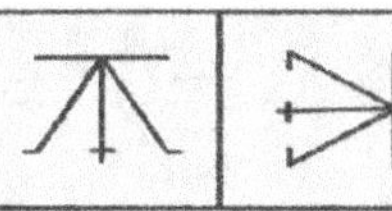 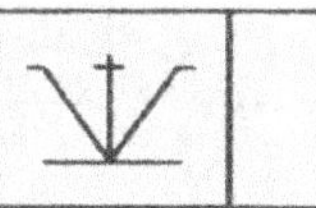 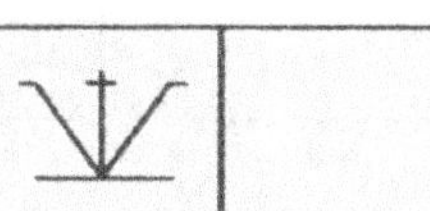

Answer Figures

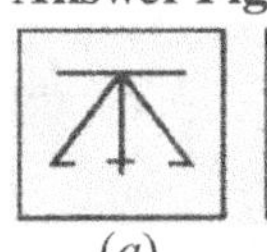 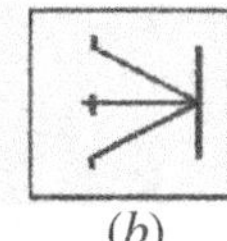 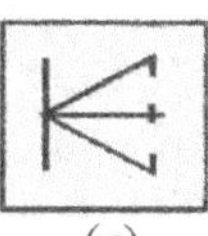 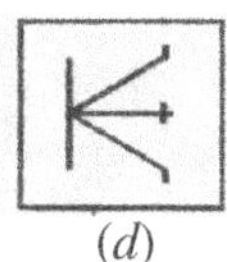

(*a*)   (*b*)   (*c*)   (*d*)

42. Problem Figures

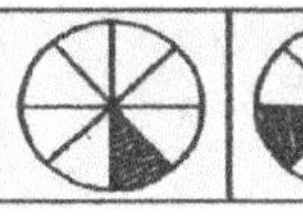 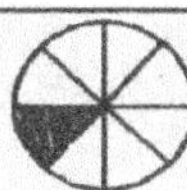 

Answer Figures

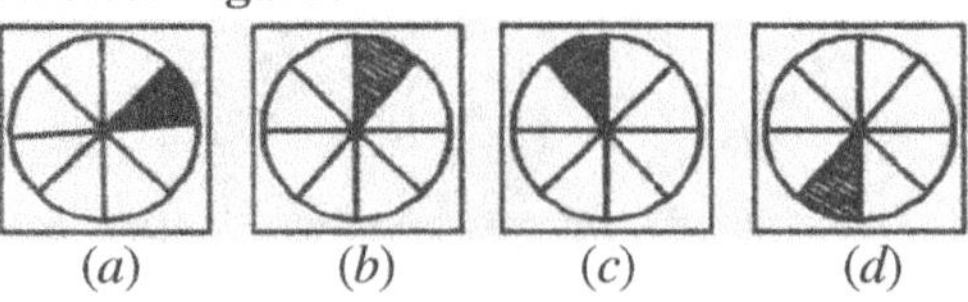

(a) *(b)* *(c)* *(d)*

43. Problem Figures

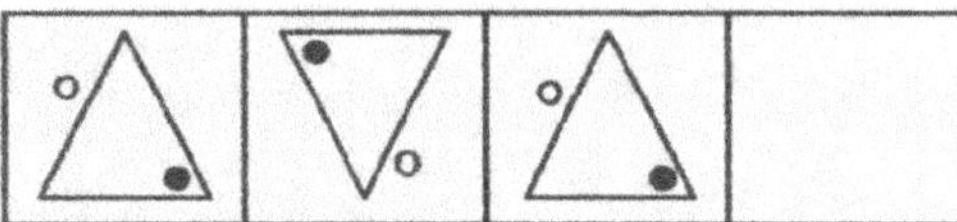

Answer Figures

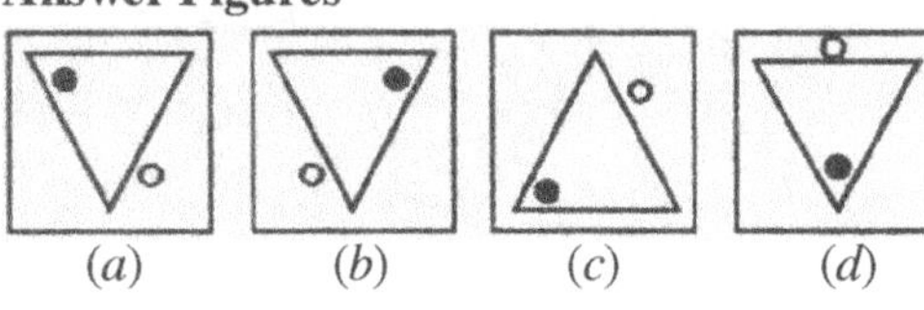

(a) *(b)* *(c)* *(d)*

44. Problem Figures

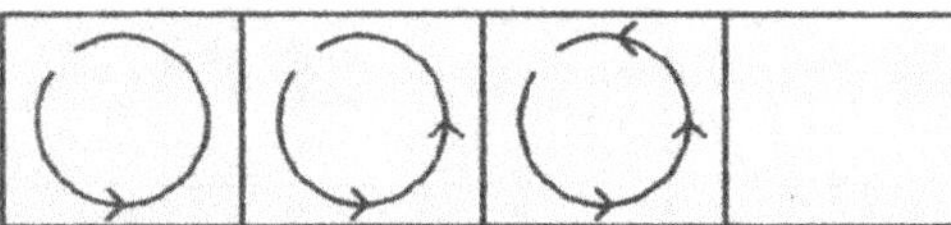

Answer Figures

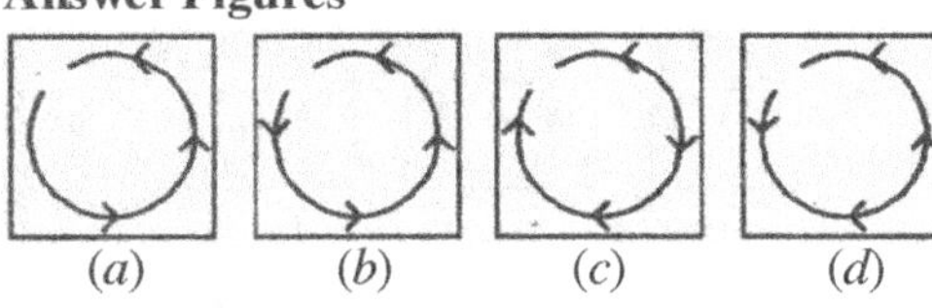

(a) *(b)* *(c)* *(d)*

45. Problem Figures

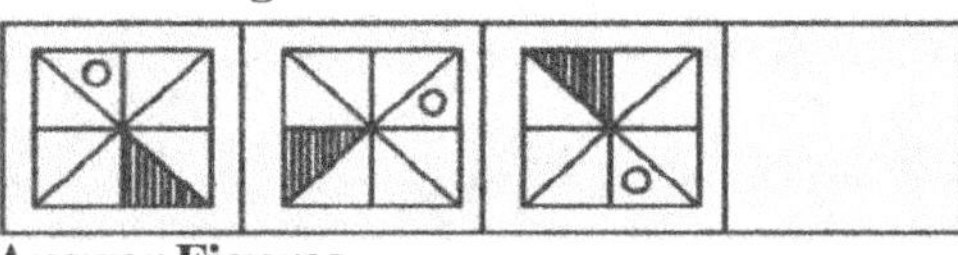

Answer Figures

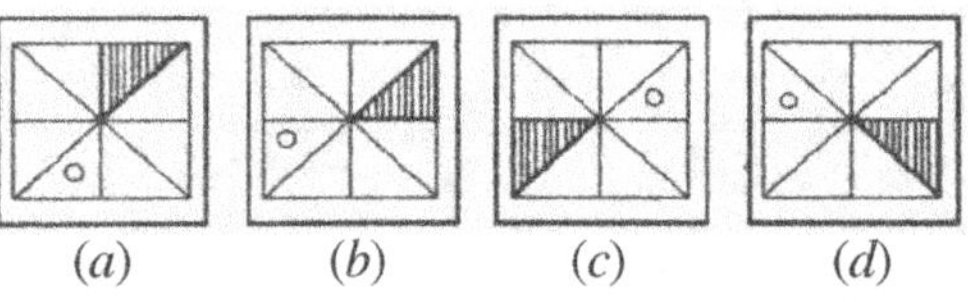

(a) *(b)* *(c)* *(d)*

Directions (Qs. 46-50) : *There is a problem figure on the left-hand side, a part of which is missing. Observe the answer figures (a), (b), (c) and (d) on the right-hand side and find out the answer figure which, without changing the direction, fits in the missing part of the problem figure in order to complete the pattern in the problem figure. Indicate your answer by letter of the answer figure chosen by you in the box against the number corresponding to the questions in the answer sheet.*

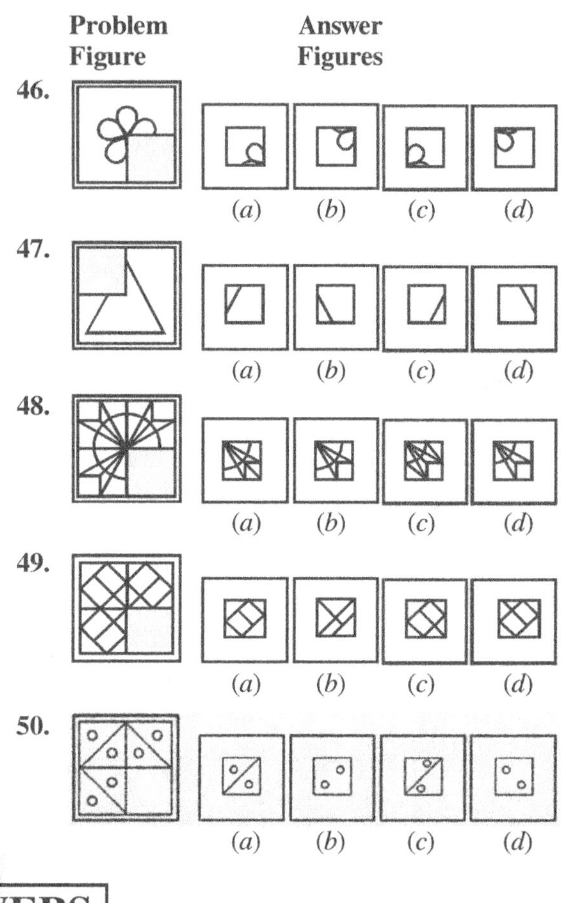

ANSWERS

1	2	3	4	5	6	7	8	9	10
(b)	*(c)*	*(c)*	*(d)*	*(d)*	*(c)*	*(d)*	*(b)*	*(b)*	*(a)*

11	12	13	14	15	16	17	18	19	20
(b)	*(b)*	*(a)*	*(d)*	*(d)*	*(d)*	*(c)*	*(a)*	*(c)*	*(a)*

21	22	23	24	25	26	27	28	29	30
(b)	*(a)*	*(b)*	*(d)*	*(b)*	*(d)*	*(c)*	*(a)*	*(c)*	*(b)*

31	32	33	34	35	36	37	38	39	40
(b)	(d)	(b)	(b)	(c)	(d)	(a)	(c)	(c)	(b)

41	42	43	44	45	46	47	48	49	50
(c)	(a)	(a)	(b)	(b)	(d)	(c)	(b)	(d)	(a)

EXPLANATORY ANSWERS

1. The difference between the letters increases at each step after beginning with two.

2.

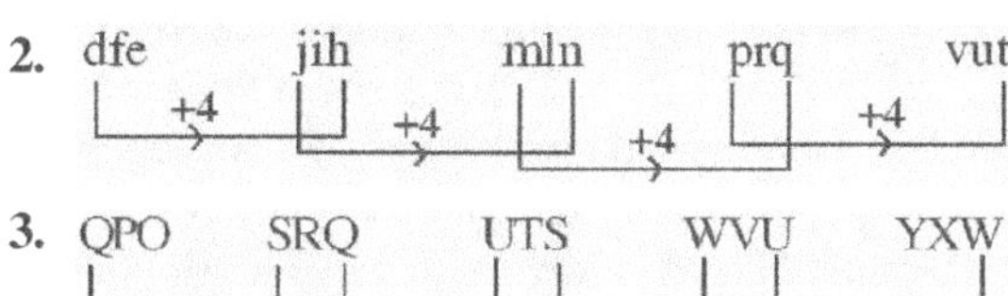

3. QPO   SRQ   UTS   WVU   YXW

6. The sequence in the series is $\times 5, \times 6, \times 7, \times 8, \times 9$.

$$3 \quad 15 \quad 90 \quad 630 \quad 5040 \quad 45360$$
$$\times 5 \quad \times 6 \quad \times 7 \quad \times 8 \quad \times 9$$

7. The coded number is the sum of number digits signifying the position of the alphabet in the natural order.

B   A   D
↓   ↓   ↓
2nd 1st 4th   *i.e.,* $2 + 1 + 4 = 7$

Similarly,

H   I   S
↓   ↓   ↓
8th 9th 19th   *i.e.,* $8 + 9 + 19 = 36$
further, $3 + 6 = 9$

Also,

L   O   W
↓   ↓   ↓
12th 15th 23rd   *i.e.,* $12 + 15 + 23 = 50$
further, $5 + 0 = 0$

8. The letters of the word TRIBAL are picked from LIBERATE. So will be the coded numbers.

L I B E R A T E → given word
5 6 4 0 3 1 7 0 → codes

Similarly,

T R I B A L → word to be coded
7 3 6 4 1 5 → answer codes

9.

Required distance = AD

$$= \sqrt{3^2 + (14 - 10)^2}$$
$$= \sqrt{9 + 16} = \sqrt{25} = 5 \text{ ft}$$

11.

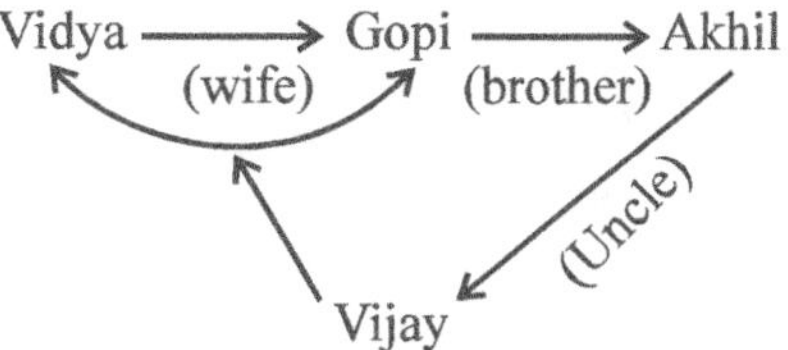

Man's brother's father is also the lady's father as he is the only son of lady's grandfather. So, the lady is man's sister.

12. The relationship chart based on problem is:

Vidya —→ Gopi —→ Akhil
(wife) (brother)
(Uncle)
Vijay

Vidya is wife of Gopi who is brother of Akhil. So, Vidya is sister-in-law of Akhil. If Akhil is uncle of Vijay then Gopi will naturally be the uncle of Vijay as it is not specified that any of the mentioned persons are Vijay's parents. Now, when Vijay is Gopi's nephew then he will also be Vidya's nephew.

13. The three letters are moved 5, 4, and 3 steps forward respectively.

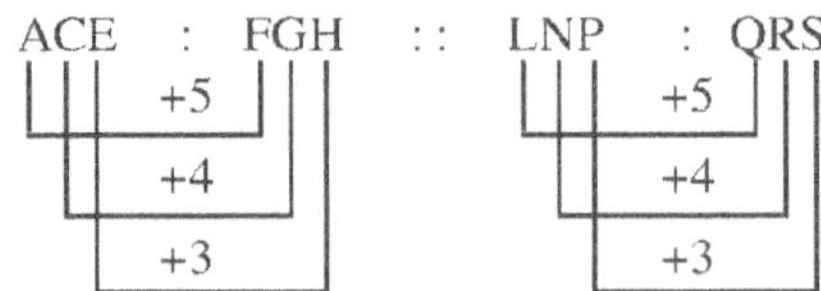

14. The word is divided into two sections and the letters are written backwards.

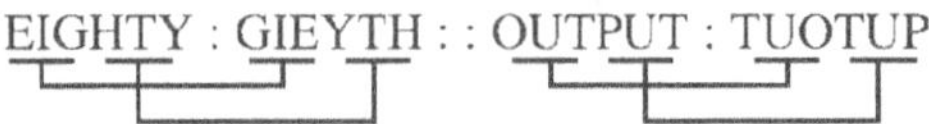

15. All the numbers are prime numbers.

18. The other numbers are $3^2 + 3 = 12$, $5^2 + 5 = 30$, $4^2 + 4 = 20$, $6^2 + 6 = 42$

19. In all other numbers the digit on the right is the sum of two digits on the left.

20. 28751 is an odd number.

21. In all other groups, there is a gap of 3 letters between first and second, 2 letters between second and third and 1 letter between third and fourth.

22. All others are crawling animals.

23. All others are types of vegetation.

25. $\underset{1}{\underline{876}}\,786\,\underset{2}{\underline{756}}\,798\,616\,\underset{3}{\underline{776}}\,886\,976\,87$

26. $9 \div 3 \times 4 + 8 - 2$
$12 + 8 - 2 = 18$

27. (a) $1 - 2 \times 3 + 6 \div 8 = 12$

$\dfrac{-17}{4} = 12$

(b) $2 \times 3 \div 5 + 8 - 4 = 7$

$\dfrac{26}{5} = 7$

(c) $5 \times 6 + 8 \div 2 - 3 = 31$
$31 = 31$

(d) $6 - 1 \times 2 \div 8 + 4 = 31$

$\dfrac{-39}{4} = 31$

28. Day after the day-before-yesterday five days ago is the 6th day which is Thursday. And so, the 3rd day will be Sunday. Three days before the day-after-tomorrow is Yesterday which is the 1st day of the five days. So, two days ago was Sunday.

29. Seventh day from 10th is 17th.
5th day is Friday. Next Friday is on 12th
$17 - 12 = 5$, 5 days ahead of Friday will be Wednesday. So, 17th is Wednesday.

30.

Code	Sentence
1. *mu* mit *es*	who *is she*
2. **elb** *mu* es	**where** *is she*

The code words 'mu' and 'es' are repeated in Ist and IInd sentence. The only code left is 'elb' which means 'where'.

31.

Code	Sentence
1. *069*	*grapes are* sweet
2. *476*	very sweet fruit
3. **509**	*grapes are* **ripe**

The code numbers '0' and '9' are repeated in 1st and 3rd sentences. The only code remaining is '5' which stands for 'ripe'.

32. 21, 23, 25, 27, 29, 31, 33, 35, 37, 39
6th

33. All other groups contain E, A and R.

34. In all other groups, the small letters are vowels.

36. Second image is the mirror image of (vertically placed mirror along y-axis) first image.

37. Centre figure is get connected to vertices in next image.

38. A common tangent line passes through the intersection point of two circles.

39. A horizontal line and vertical line comes in picture in upper and lower portion of the figure respectively.

41. In every next figure the main design rotates 90° clockwise and two small lines move in and out.

42. In every next figure the shaded portion of the circle moves ahead two steps clockwise.

43. The first and third figures are similar. Hence, the answer figure will be similar to the second figure.

44. In every next figure an arrow-head is added in the anticlockwise direction.

45. In every next figure the circle and the shaded part is moving two steps clockwise.

Previous Paper (Solved)

All India Sainik School Entrance Exam., 2016

(CLASS-VI)

PAPER-I : MATHEMATICS AND LANGUAGE ABILITY

Time : 2 Hrs.   Max. Marks : 200

Part-A : Mathematics

Section-I

(Each question carries two marks.)

1. Estimate the difference of 879 and 338 to the nearest hundred.

2. Write 15 m as a percentage of 1000 km.

3. Find LCM of 120, 210 and 225.

4. Arrange $\dfrac{1}{3}, \dfrac{3}{10}, \dfrac{5}{6}, \dfrac{2}{5}$ in ascending order.

5. Find the sum of $1\dfrac{3}{5}$ and $2\dfrac{7}{10}$.

6. An aeroplane covers 1020 kms in an hour. How much distance will it cover in $4\dfrac{1}{6}$ hours.

7. Convert 131°F into Celsius scale.

8. Convert 2222 hours into days and hours.

9. One of the two equal angles of an Isosceles triangle measures 55°. Find the measure of all the angles of triangle.

10. Find the radius of a circle whose circumference is 79.2 cm. Given that $\pi = \dfrac{22}{7}$.

Section-II

(Each question carries three marks.)

11. Find the square numbers lying between 75 and 225.

12. Simplify: $125 - 25 \times 125 \div 25 + 25$.

13. Sudha scored 23 marks out of 30 in maths and 29 marks out of 50 in Hindi. In which subject did she perform better and by what percentage?

14. Find the HCF of 902, 1394 and 3321.

15. Jubaida took a loan of ₹ 4000 on 12% annual interest. After 3 years how much money she will have to return?

16. Find the square root of

   (a) $6\dfrac{9}{36}$ (b) $5\dfrac{41}{16}$

17. A baby elephant drinks around 12 litre of milk every day. How much milk will it drink in two years?

18. John plans to tile his kitchen floor with square tiles. Each side of the tile is 10 cm. His kitchen is 2.2 M long and 1.8 M wide. How many tiles will John need?

19. There are 24 Laddoos in 1 kg. How many Laddoos will be there in 8 kg? If 16 Laddoos can be packed in 1 box, how many boxes are needed to pack all the laddoos?

20. Find the mean of first ten even numbers.

Section-III

(Each question carries five marks.)

21. Annual Income of Rohan is ₹ 6,00,000. He spends ₹ 99,250 on food, ₹ 36,750 on clothes and ₹ 1,11,500 on other expenditures annually. What is his annual saving? What % of his income does he save in a year?

13

22. (*a*) Find the value of following angles:
(*i*) $\angle$ BOC   (*ii*) $\angle$ COD

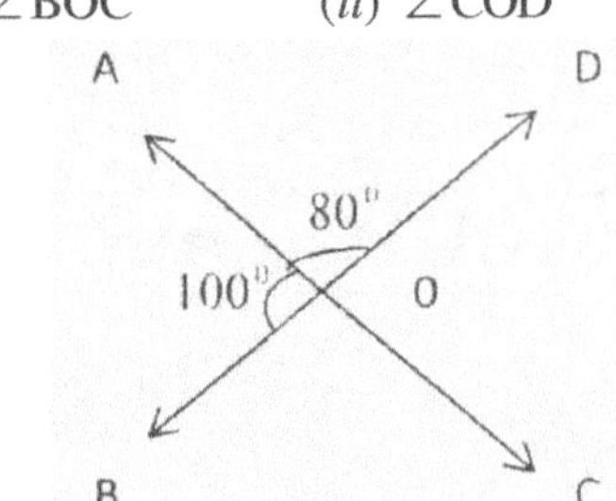

(*b*) Find HCF of 20 and 70 by prime factorization method.

23. Simplify:

$$0.2\left[3.5 - 0.3\left\{2.5 + 1.3\left(3.6 + 1.4\right)\right\}\right]$$

24. Find out perimeter and area of the given diagram.

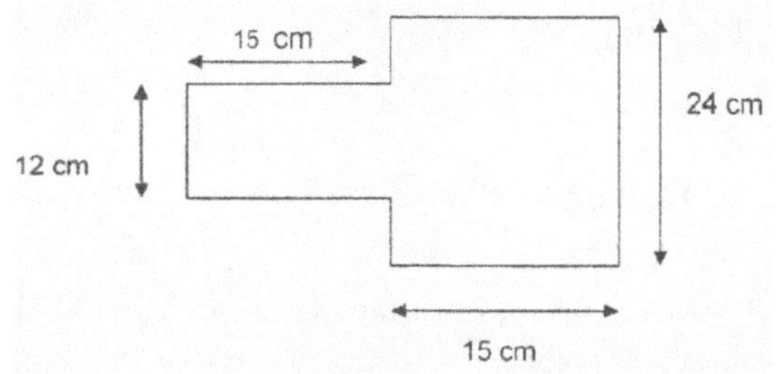

25. How many stones of 0.50 m^2 can be fixed in a court yard of length 15 m and width 10 m. if cost of fixing one stone is ₹ 2.50, what will be the expenditure on fixing stones in the courtyard?

26. An alloy contains 15% Carbon, 25% Zinc and rest is Copper. In 60 Kg alloy, find the quantity of each metal.

27. Fill in the blanks:

(*a*) $\dfrac{6}{21} = \dfrac{?}{7}$ (*b*) $.01 = \dfrac{1}{?}$

(*c*) Largest 7 digit number is ....

(*d*) Radius $= \dfrac{\text{Diameter}}{?}$

(*e*) In 75897, place value of 8 is ....

28. The denominator of a fraction is greater than its numerator by 3 . If 3 is subtracted from the numerator and 2 is added to its denominator, the new number become $\dfrac{1}{5}$. Find the original number.

29. Out of 40 students of a class, 60% passed in first division, 30% in second division and remaining in third division. Find out the number of students in each category?

30. (*a*) A shopkeeper sells a box costing ₹ 900 giving 15% discount. Find out the sale price of the box?

(*b*) The HCF and LCM of two number is 18 and 252 respectively. If one number is 126 find out another number?

EXPLANATORY ANSWERS

1. $879 - 338 = 541$
$= 500$ (Nearest hundred).

2. $15 = 1000 \times 1000 \times \dfrac{x}{100}$

$\Rightarrow \quad 15 = 10000x$

$\Rightarrow \quad x = \dfrac{15}{10000} = 0.0015\%.$

3.

2	120,	210,	225
3	60,	105,	225
5	20,	35,	75
	4,	7,	15

L.C.M. $= 2 \times 3 \times 5 \times 4 \times 7 \times 15$
$= 12600.$

4. $\dfrac{1}{3}, \dfrac{3}{10}, \dfrac{5}{6}$ and $\dfrac{2}{5} = \dfrac{10, 9, 25, 12}{30}$

$\therefore \dfrac{3}{10}, \dfrac{1}{3}, \dfrac{2}{5}, \dfrac{5}{6}$ are in ascending order.

5. $1\dfrac{3}{5} + 2\dfrac{7}{10} = \dfrac{8}{5} + \dfrac{27}{10} = \dfrac{16 + 27}{10} = \dfrac{43}{10} = 4\dfrac{3}{10}.$

6. $\because$ In 1 hour aeroplane covers 1020 km

$\therefore$ In $\dfrac{25}{6}$ hours aeroplane will cover

$= 1020 \times \dfrac{25}{6}$ km

$= 170 \times 25$ km $= 4250$ km.

7. $\because \qquad \dfrac{C}{5} = \dfrac{F-32}{9}$

$\Rightarrow \qquad \dfrac{C}{5} = \dfrac{131-32}{9} = \dfrac{99}{9}$

$\Rightarrow \qquad \dfrac{C}{5} = 11$

$\Rightarrow \qquad C = 55°C$

Hence, $131°F = 55°C$.

8. $\dfrac{2222}{24} = 92, \quad \dfrac{14}{24} \times 24 = 92$ days 14 hours.

9. Let, third angle $= x°$

$\qquad \angle A + \angle B + \angle C = 180°$

$\Rightarrow \quad 55° + 55° + x° = 180°$

$\Rightarrow \qquad x + 110° = 180°$

$\Rightarrow \qquad\qquad x = 70°$

$\therefore \quad \angle A = 55°, \angle B = 55°, \angle C = 70°$.

10. $\qquad C = 2\pi r$

$\Rightarrow \qquad 79.2 = 2 \times \dfrac{22}{7} \times r$

$\Rightarrow \qquad r = \dfrac{79.2 \times 7}{2 \times 22} = 1.8 \times 7 = 12.6$

Hence, radius of the circle $= 12.6$ cm.

11. The square numbers 81, 100, 121, 144, 169, 196 are lying between 75 and 225.

12. $125 - 25 \times 125 \div 25 + 25$

$= 125 - 25 \times 5 + 25$

$= 125 - 125 + 25 = 25$.

13. % of Maths $= \dfrac{23}{30} \times 100 = \dfrac{230}{3} = 76.6\%$

% of Hindi $= \dfrac{29}{50} \times 100 = 58\%$

Maths is better than Hindi

Difference $= 76.6\% - 58\% = 18.6\%$.

14.
```
          1
    902)1394(
        902   1
       492)902(
           492   1
          410)492(
              410   5
             82)410(
                410
                 ×
```

Hence required H.C.F. = 41.

15. $\qquad P = ₹\ 4000$

$\qquad r = 12\%$

$\qquad t = 3$ years

$\text{S.I.} = \dfrac{P \times r \times t}{100} = \dfrac{4000 \times 12 \times 3}{100} = 1440$

$A = P + \text{S.I.}$

$\quad = 4000 + 1440 = ₹\ 5440$

Hence, Jubaida will have to return ₹ 5440 after 3 years.

16. (a) $\sqrt{6\dfrac{9}{36}} = \sqrt{\dfrac{225}{36}} = \dfrac{15}{6} = \dfrac{5}{2} = 2.5$.

(b) $\sqrt{5\dfrac{41}{16}} = \sqrt{\dfrac{121}{16}} = \dfrac{11}{4} = 2.75$.

17. In 1 day baby elephant drinks $12l$ of milk

In 730 days baby elephant drink

$= 12 \times 730\ l$ of milk $= 8760\ l$ of milk.

18. Area of the kitchen floor $= 220 \times 180$ cm^2

Area of each tile $= 10 \times 10$ cm^2

$\therefore \quad$ No. of tiles $= \dfrac{220 \times 180}{10 \times 10}$

$\qquad\qquad = 22 \times 18 = 396$.

19. In 1 kg = 24 Laddoos

In 8 kg = $24 \times 8 = 192$ Laddoos

Required no. of boxes $= \dfrac{192}{16} = 12$.

20. Mean $= \dfrac{2+4+6+8+10+12+14+16+18+20}{10}$

$= \dfrac{110}{10} = 11$

Hence, mean of first ten even numbers = 11.

21.

$\qquad$ Annual income $= ₹\ 600000$

$\qquad$ Annual expenditure $= ₹\ 99250$

$\qquad\qquad\qquad ₹\ 36750$

$\qquad\qquad\qquad ₹\ 111500$

$\qquad\qquad\qquad \overline{₹\ 247500}$

Annual saving = ₹ 6000000 − ₹ 247500

= ₹ 352500

% Saving = $\dfrac{352500}{600000} \times 100 = \dfrac{705}{12} = 58.75\%$.

22. (a)

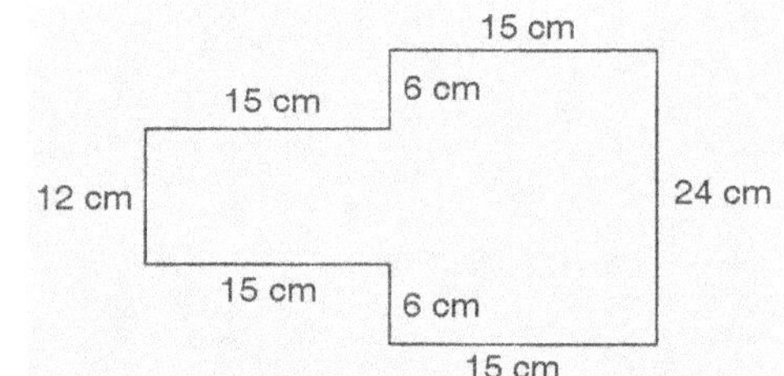

∵ AC and BD intersect at O

(i) ∠BOC = ∠AOD = 80°

(Vertically opp. angles)

(ii) ∠COD = ∠AOB = 100°

(Vertically opp. angles)

(b) 20 = 2 × 2 × 5

70 = 2 × 5 × 7

∴ H.C.F. = 2 × 5 = 10.

23. $0.2\big[3.5 - 0.3\{2.5 + 1.3(3.6 + 1.4)\}\big]$

$= 0.2\big[3.5 - 0.3\{2.5 + 1.3(5)\}\big]$

$= 0.2\big[3.5 - 0.3\{2.5 + 6.5\}\big]$

$= 0.2\big[3.5 - 0.3\{9\}\big]$

$= 0.2[3.5 - 2.7] = 0.2\,[.8] = 0.16.$

24.

Perimeter = 12 + 15 + 6 + 15 + 24 + 15

+ 6 + 15 = 108 cm

Area of the given figure

= 12 × 15 + 15 × 24

= 180 + 360 = 540 cm².

25. No. of stones = $\dfrac{15 \times 10 \times 100}{50} = 300$

∵ Cost of 1 stone = ₹ 2.50

∴ Cost of 300 stones = $\dfrac{250}{100} \times 300 = ₹\ 750.$

26. Carbon = 15%

$= \dfrac{15}{100} \times 60$ kg

= 9 kg

Zinc = $\dfrac{25}{100} \times 60$ kg

= 15 kg

Copper = $\dfrac{60}{100} \times 60 = 36$ kg.

27. (a) $\dfrac{6}{21} = \dfrac{\boxed{2}}{7}$

(b) $.01 = \dfrac{1}{\boxed{100}}$

(c) Largest 7 digit number = 9999999

(d) Radius = $\dfrac{\text{Diameter}}{\boxed{2}}$

(e) In 75897, place value of 8 = 800.

28. Let, numerator = x

∴ Denominator = $x + 3$

∴ Fraction = $\dfrac{x}{x+3}$

According to the question,

$$\dfrac{x-3}{x+3+2} = \dfrac{1}{5}$$

$\Rightarrow$ $\dfrac{x-3}{x+5} = \dfrac{1}{5}$

$\Rightarrow$ $5x - 15 = x + 5$

$\Rightarrow$ $4x = 20 \Rightarrow x = 5$

∴ Fraction = $\dfrac{x}{x+3} = \dfrac{5}{8}.$

29. No of students in first division

= 60% of 40

$= \dfrac{60}{100} \times 40 = 24$

No. of students in second division

= 30% of 40

$= \dfrac{30}{100} \times 40 = 12$

No. of students in third division

= 10% of 40

$= \dfrac{10}{100} \times 40 = 4.$

30. (*a*) Discount = 15% of x

$$= \frac{15}{100} \times x = \frac{3x}{20}$$

$$\text{S.P.} = x - \frac{3x}{20} = \frac{17x}{20}$$

When M.P. ₹ x then S.P. $= \dfrac{17x}{20}$

When M.P. ₹ 900 then S.P. $= \dfrac{17x}{20 \times x} \times 900$

$$= 17 \times 45$$
$$= ₹ 765$$

Hence, the sale price of the box = ₹ 765.

(*b*) ∵ H.C.F. × L.C.M. = First no. × 2nd no.

$$\therefore \quad \text{2nd number} = \frac{\text{H.C.F.} \times \text{L.C.M.}}{\text{First number}}$$

$$= \frac{18 \times 252}{126} = 36$$

Hence, another number = 36.

PART-B : LANGUAGE ABILITY

1. Write 15 sentences on anyone of the following topics: **(15)**
My Friend or Aim of my life

2. Read the following passage carefully and answer the questions that follow:
(5 × 3 = 15)

Florence Nightingale was born on the 15th May, 1820 at Florence in Italy and her parents called her after the name of the city where she was born. Her main ambition was to be a nurse and so she gave up all thoughts of marriage and personal happiness. She spent years visiting hospital after hospital. Day and night she visited every bed in the hospital to see that no patient was neglected and that all were as comfortable as possible. However hard she might have worked all day, every night she would take her lamp and move from bed to bed. 'The Lady with the Lamp' the soldiers called her and that is the name by which the world has remembered her ever since.

(*a*) Where was Florence Nightingale born?

(*b*) Why her parents named her Florence Nightingale?

(*c*) Why Florence Nightingale was called 'The Lady with the Lamp'?

(*d*) Give opposite of 'comfortable'?

(*e*) What did she do every night with a lamp in her hand?

3. Make a sentence of your own for each underlined word given in the following passage. (Do not copy any sentence from the given paragraph.) **(5 × 2 = 10)**

People who live in regions **covered** with forests and surrounded by hills generally believe that the **desert** is a vast **stretch** of dry, hot and sandy land. But those who have studied it, find the desert quite beautiful. It is not entirely **uninhabited** either. A **variety** of people, animals and plants make the desert their home.

(*a*) ....

(*b*) ....

(*c*) ....

(*d*) ....

(*e*) ....

4. Form meaningful sentences by rearranging the words in proper order: **(5 × 2 = 10)**

(*a*) a good/exercise/swimming/is

(*b*) Middle East/india/to/the/exporting/is/onions

(*c*) was/John/drinking /tea

(*d*) man/a strong /Sardar Patel/was

(*e*) named/Diamond/had/Newton/little dog/a

5. Give one word for the following: **(5 × 1 = 5)**

(*a*) One who knows everything

....

(*b*) A building in which monks live

....

(*c*) A person whose profession is to keep accounts ....

(*d*) All the customs and beliefs of a society ....

(*e*) Eater of flesh ....

6. Choose the correct article (a, an or the) and fill in the blanks. **(5 × 2 = 10)**

(*a*) Here is .... book I borrowed from you yesterday.

(*b*) Jordan drives .... Mazda.

(*c*) He goes to .... Delhi Golf Course on Sundays.

(*d*) James works as .... electrician.

(*e*) Raman sang .... song.

7. Use the given word in separate sentences of your own to show the difference in the meaning of the words of the pair given below: **(5 × 2 = 10)**

(*a*) Principal, Principle   (*b*) Cattle, Kettle

(*c*) Whether, Weather   (*d*) Idle, Idol

(*e*) Floor, Flour

8. Change each of the following as directed: **(5 × 2 = 10)**

(*a*) I met an old man.

(Change into Future Continuous)

....

(*b*) The driver stopped the train.

(Change into Passive Voice)

....

(*c*) The Sky grew dark.

(Change into negative sentence)

....

(*d*) Mr Verma teaches us grammar.

(Change into interrogative sentence)

....

(*e*) Peter said, "Imran will not be playing the match."

(Change into indirect sentence)

....

9. Give the Antonym (opposite) of the following words: **(5 × 1 = 5)**

(*a*) Arrest   (*b*) Boon

(*c*) Heaven   (*d*) Grateful

(*e*) Bravery

10. Write a letter to the Principal requesting him to organize an educational tour to Shimla. **(10)**

EXPLANATORY ANSWERS

1.   **Aim of my life**

It is rightly said that the chief aim of education is to broaden the horizon of human mind. But we know that in the modern world, we also have to make a living by taking up some profession. I have decided to become a teacher as I grow up. It is rightly said that a teacher is a nation builder. By becoming a teacher, I want to kill two birds with one stone. On the one hand, I want to make a decent living. The teachers are well-paid these days. They also command a high respect in society. On the other hand, my aim is to serve the society at large. I want to inculcate great moral values of life in the minds of young children. This I'll do while blending matter-of-fact and imaginative elements in my teaching. Fortunately, I'm a brilliant student and I hope I'll achieve my aim in life. Morever, both my father and mother are teachers and they are my good guides and a source of great inspiration to me.

2. (*a*) Florence Nightingale was born at Florence in Italy.

(*b*) Her parents named her Florence Nightingale after the name of the city where she was born.

(*c*) She was named so because she used to visit every bed in the hospital with a lamp.

(*d*) Uncomfortable.

(*e*) She moved with a lamp in her hand to see that all the patients were properly cared.

3. (*a*) She covered her face with a scarf.

(*b*) The camel is called the ship of the desert.

(*c*) There is a barren stretch of land in the village.

(*d*) The place is almost uninhabited.

(*e*) The student gave a variety of reasons to study at Sainik School.

4. (*a*) Swimming is a good exercise.

(*b*) India is exporting onions to the Middle East.

(*c*) John was drinking tea.

(*d*) Sardar Patel was a strong man.

(*e*) Newton had a little dog named Diamond.

5. (*a*) Omniscient   (*b*) Monastery

(*c*) Accountant   (*d*) Traditions

(*e*) Carnivorous

6. (*a*) the   (*b*) a

(*c*) the   (*d*) an

(*e*) a

7. (*a*) Who is the principal of your school? What is the principle of your life?

(*b*) He was grazing the cattle in the field. He poured tea from the kettle.

(*c*) She asked me whether I was going to school.
The weather is cozy now-a-days.

(*d*) Never sit idle, do something.
He was selected the Indian Idol last year.

(*e*) You must clean the floor everyday.
He grinds the wheat to make flour.

8. (*a*) I shall have been meeting an old man.
(*b*) The train was stopped (by the driver).
(*c*) The sky did not grow bright.
(*d*) Does Mr. Verma teach us grammar?
(*e*) Peter told that Imran would not be playing the match.

9. (*a*) Release   (*b*) Bane
(*c*) Hell   (*d*) Thankless
(*e*) Cowardice

10. Dated ....
To

The Principal
Sainik School
New Delhi

Respected Sir,

I am a new student of class VI in your school. Our class teacher has told us that every year on school organises an educational tour to some far off place. I request you to organise a tour to Shimla this year. Shimla is a famous tourist spot. It is popular for its scenic beauty. There is a lot for students to learn in Shimla about the mother nature.

I hope you will accept my request.

Thanking you   Yours Obediently
XYZ.

PAPER-II : INTELLIGENCE TEST*

Time : 40 Minutes.   **Max. Marks : 100**

Directions (Qs. 1 to 6): *In the following questions, select the number(s)/letters from the given options for completing the given series.*

1. 27, 28, 25, 25, 23, 22, 21, ?
(*a*) 20   (*b*) 21
(*c*) 19   (*d*) 18

2. 80, 63, 72, 72, 64, 81, 56, ?
(*a*) 96   (*b*) 98
(*c*) 89   (*d*) 90

3. 0, 5, 22, 57, ?, 205
(*a*) 198   (*b*) 116
(*c*) 172   (*d*) 92

4. R K F ? B
(*a*) D   (*b*) C
(*c*) E   (*d*) B

5. LAZ, NEX, PIV, ?
(*a*) SLS   (*b*) QNS
(*c*) RMT   (*d*) RMS

6. -bbcaa-bcaa-bc-a-bca
(*a*) bacab   (*b*) abbab
(*c*) abcba   (*d*) bcaab

7. In a certain code LIBERATE is written as 56403170, TRIBAL will be written in the same code as:
(*a*) 734615   (*b*) 736415
(*c*) 136475   (*d*) 034615

8. In a certain language, (a) 'FOR' stands for 'old is gold'; (b) 'ROT' stands for 'gold is pure'; (c) 'ROM' stands for 'gold is costly'. How will 'pure old gold is costly' be written?
(*a*) TFROM   (*b*) FOTRM
(*c*) FTORM   (*d*) TOMRF

9. Facing the West direction, Priya jogs for 20 m, turns left and goes further 40 m. She turns left again and jogs for 20 m. Then she turns right to go 20 m to reach the park. How far is the park from her starting point and in which direction?
(*a*) 20 m South   (*b*) 40 m West
(*c*) 60 m South   (*d*) 100 m East

10. Pointing to a woman in the photograph a man said, "She is the daughter of my grandmother's only son. How is the woman related to the man?
(*a*) Mother   (*b*) Daughter
(*c*) Sister-in-law   (*d*) Sister

11. If the following words are arranged in natural order, what will come in the last place in ascending order?
1. Captain

---
* Memory Based

2. Brigadier
3. Major
4. Lieutenant-General
5. Lieutenant
(*a*) Lieutenant-General (*b*) Brigadier
(*c*) Captain (*d*) Major

12. What would be the proper order of the following :
   1. Decameter   2. Meter
   3. Kilometer   4. Centimeter
   5. Milimeter
   (*a*) 1 4 3 2 5   (*b*) 5 4 1 2 3
   (*c*) 5 4 3 2 1   (*d*) 5 4 2 1 3

Directions (Qs. 13-17) : *In the questions given below one term is missing. Based on the relationship of the two given words/numbers find the missing term from the given options.*

13. Physicist : Physics : : ? : Anatomy
   (*a*) Botany   (*b*) Botanist
   (*c*) Body   (*d*) Biologist

14. Frequently : Always : : Selden : ?
   (*a*) Often   (*b*) Rarely
   (*c*) Occasionally   (*d*) Never

15. RRS : XMW : : ITB : ?
   (*a*) PNE   (*b*) NOG
   (*c*) RSW   (*d*) OOF

16. BYDW : FVHT : : GQIO : ?
   (*a*) JLNP   (*b*) QSTR
   (*c*) KMOL   (*d*) KNML

17. Which number will come in the place of question mark?
   25 : 81 : : 36 : ?
   (*a*) 121   (*b*) 93
   (*c*) 65   (*d*) 103

Directions (Qs. 18-24): *In each of the following questions, there are four options. Three numbers/words in these options, are alike in certain manner. Only one number/word does not fit in. Choose the one which is different from the rest.*

18. (*a*) Tutor   (*b*) Principal
   (*c*) Pupil   (*d*) Professor

19. (*a*) Pond   (*b*) River
   (*c*) Stream   (*d*) Brook

20. (*a*) Quotation   (*b*) Duty
   (*c*) Tax   (*d*) Octroi

21. (*a*) 3215   (*b*) 9309
   (*c*) 4721   (*d*) 2850

22. (*a*) 24   (*b*) 90
   (*c*) 54   (*d*) 36

23. (*a*) 3730   (*b*) 6820
   (*c*) 5568   (*d*) 4604

24. (*a*) 2587   (*b*) 7628
   (*c*) 8726   (*d*) 2867

25. In the following list of numerals, how many 3s are followed by 3, but NOT preceded by 3?
   2 4 6 3 3 1 5 7 8 3 3 3 4 6 2 3 3 3 3 9 7 2 3
   (*a*) 1   (*b*) 2
   (*c*) 3   (*d*) 4

26. If the + and × signs of the following equations are inter-changed, which will be the correct equation?
   (*a*) $7 \times 5 + 3 = 20$ (*b*) $4 + 9 \times 1 = 42$
   (*c*) $6 \times 5 + 8 = 46$ (*d*) $2 + 11 \times 4 = 28$

27. If '+' stands for multiplication, '×' stands for addition, '÷' stands for subtraction and '–' stands for division, then what will be the result of the following equation?
   $7 \times 4 \div 10 \times 2 + 5 = ?$
   (*a*) 7   (*b*) 0
   (*c*) 11   (*d*) 15

28. If the day before yesterday was Thursday, when will Sunday be?
   (*a*) Tomorrow
   (*b*) Day after tomorrow
   (*c*) Today
   (*d*) Two days after today

29. If the seventh day of a month is three (3) days earlier than Friday, what day will it be on the nineteenth day of the month?
   (*a*) Sunday   (*b*) Monday
   (*c*) Wednesday   (*d*) Friday

Directions (Qs. 30 and 31): *In the following questions select the right option which indicates the correct code for the word or letter given in the question.*

30. If 'w' is coded as 'a', 's' as 'r' and 'r' as 'w', how will 'answer' be written?

   (*a*) wnsaes   (*b*) anraew

   (*c*) anrwas   (*d*) wnraes

31. In certain military code, SYSTEM is written as SYSMET, and NEARER as AENRER, what will be the code for FRACTION?

   (*a*) CRAFNOIT   (*b*) FRCAITNO

   (*c*) CARFNOIT   (*d*) FRACNOIT

32. A and B are two brothers. C is sister of B. D is sister of E. E is son of A. Who is D's uncle?

   (*a*) D   (*b*) E

   (*c*) B   (*d*) C

Directions (Qs. 33-35) : *In each of the following series determine the order of the letters. Then from the given options select the one which will complete the given series.*

33. B A F E J I P O ? U

   (*a*) V   (*b*) T

   (*c*) S   (*d*) Q

34. V R O K ? D

   (*a*) L   (*b*) I

   (*c*) H   (*d*) J

35. CFI, IKM, OPQ, ?

   (*a*) UUU   (*b*) UST

   (*c*) VUS   (*d*) TUV

Directions (Qs. 36-40): *The second figure in the first unit of the Problem Figures bears a certain relationship to the first figure. Similarly, one of the figures in the Answer Figures bears the same relationship to the first figure in the second unit of the Problem Figures. Locate the figure which would fit the question mark.*

36. Problem Figures

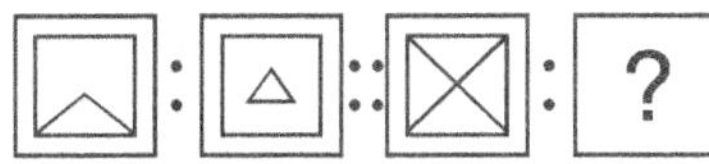

Answers Figures

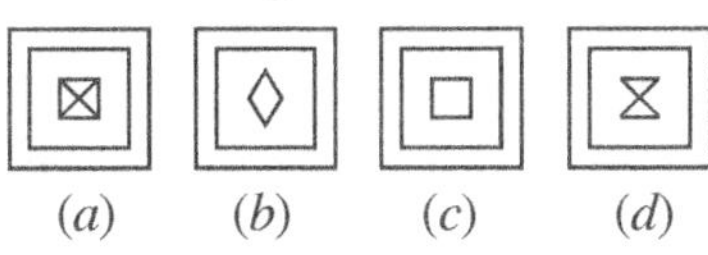

   (*a*)   (*b*)   (*c*)   (*d*)

37. Problem Figures

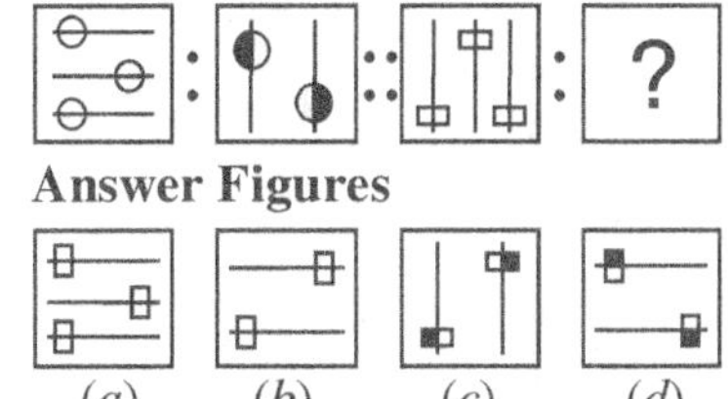

Answer Figures

   (*a*)   (*b*)   (*c*)   (*d*)

38. Problem Figures

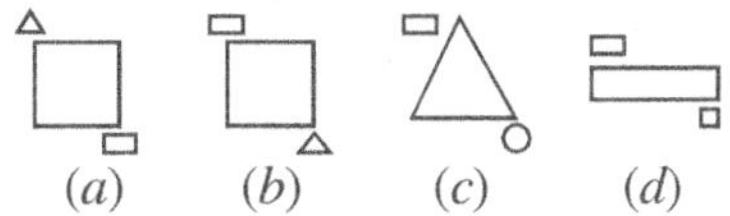

Answer Figures

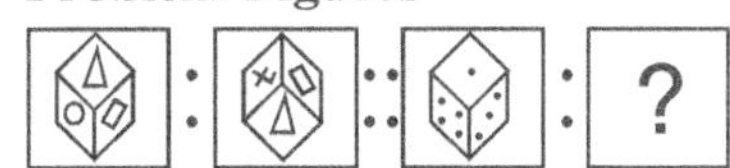

   (*a*)   (*b*)   (*c*)   (*d*)

39. Problem Figures

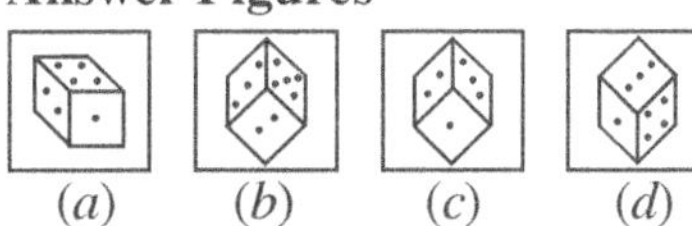

Answer Figures

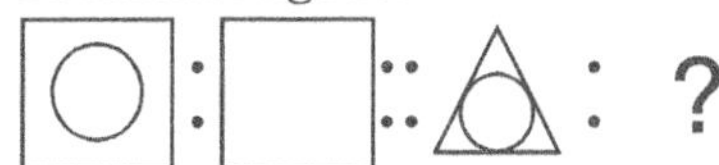

   (*a*)   (*b*)   (*c*)   (*d*)

40. Problem Figures

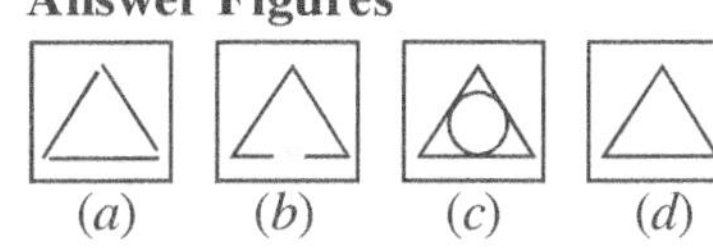

Answer Figures

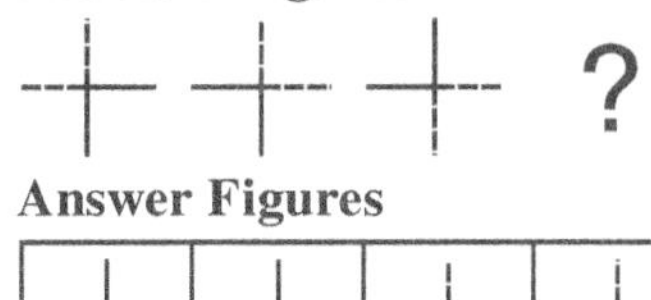

   (*a*)   (*b*)   (*c*)   (*d*)

Direction (Qs. 41-45): *Each of the following questions consist of problem figures followed by answer figures. Select a figure from amongst the answer figures which will continue the same series or pattern as established by the problem figures.*

41. Problem Figures

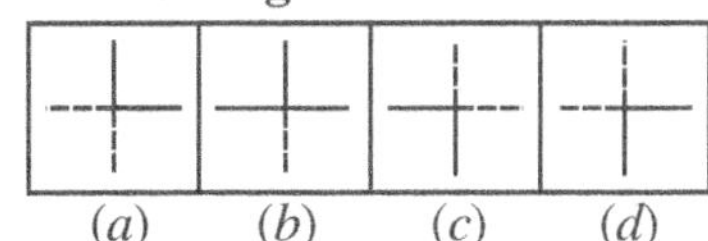

Answer Figures

   (*a*)   (*b*)   (*c*)   (*d*)

42. Problem Figures

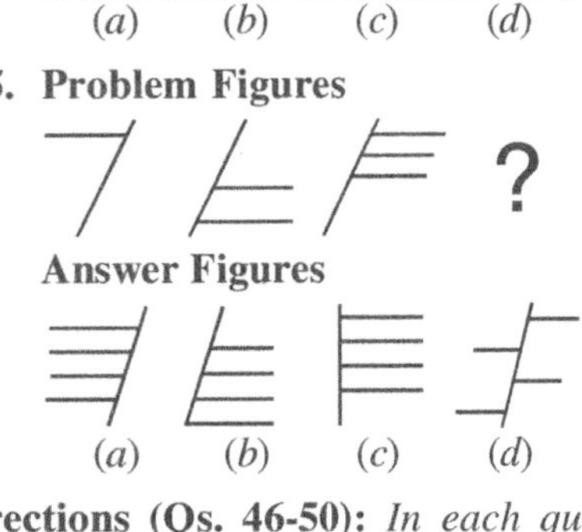

Answer Figures

(a)   (b)   (c)   (d)

43. Problem Figures

Answer Figures

(a)   (b)   (c)   (d)

44. Problem Figures

Answer Figures

(a)   (b)   (c)   (d)

45. Problem Figures

Answer Figures

(a)   (b)   (c)   (d)

Directions (Qs. 46-50): *In each question, which one of the alternative figures will complete the given figure pattern?*

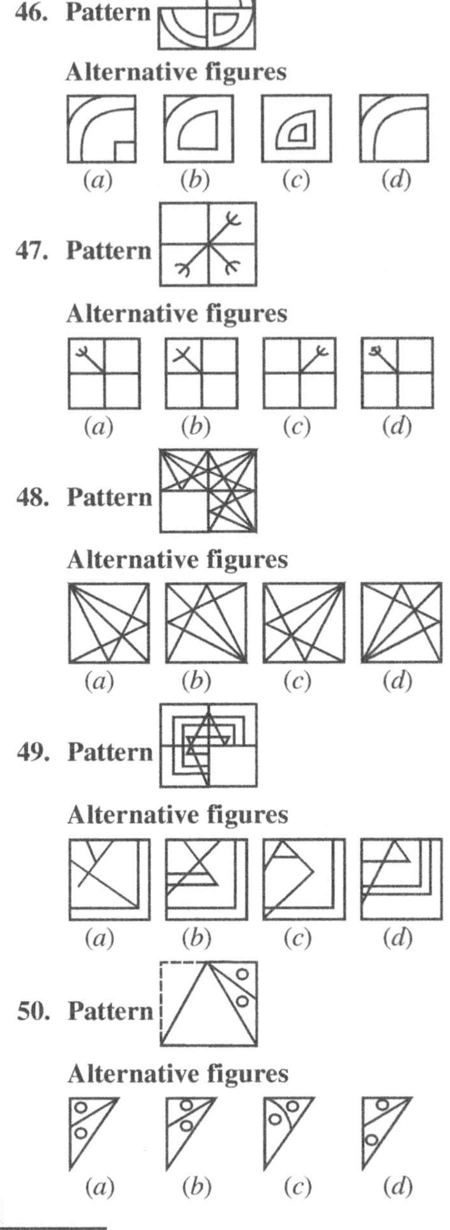

46. Pattern

Alternative figures

(a)   (b)   (c)   (d)

47. Pattern

Alternative figures

(a)   (b)   (c)   (d)

48. Pattern

Alternative figures

(a)   (b)   (c)   (d)

49. Pattern

Alternative figures

(a)   (b)   (c)   (d)

50. Pattern

Alternative figures

(a)   (b)   (c)   (d)

ANSWERS

1	2	3	4	5	6	7	8	9	10
(c)	(d)	(b)	(b)	(c)	(b)	(b)	(a)	(c)	(d)

11	12	13	14	15	16	17	18	19	20
(a)	(d)	(d)	(d)	(d)	(d)	(a)	(c)	(a)	(a)

21	22	23	24	25	26	27	28	29	30
(b)	(a)	(b)	(a)	(c)	(c)	(c)	(a)	(a)	(b)
31	32	33	34	35	36	37	38	39	40
(c)	(c)	(a)	(c)	(a)	(d)	(d)	(a)	(c)	(d)
41	42	43	44	45	46	47	48	49	50
(a)	(a)	(d)	(c)	(a)	(b)	(a)	(d)	(d)	(a)

SOME SELECTED EXPLANATORY ANSWERS

3. The series follows this sequence : cube of natural numbers starting from 1 minus odd numbers starting from 1.

$$0 \quad 5 \quad 22 \quad 57 \quad 116 \quad 205$$
$$\downarrow \quad \downarrow \quad \downarrow \quad \downarrow \quad \downarrow \quad \downarrow$$
$$1^3{-}1 \quad 2^3{-}3 \quad 3^3{-}5 \quad 4^3{-}7 \quad 5^3{-}9 \quad 6^3{-}11$$

4. The difference between the letters is reduced by two at each step.

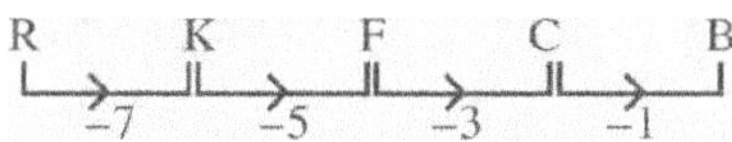

6. The series is abbca, abbca, abbca, abbca.

7. The letters of the word TRIBAL are picked from LIBERATE. So will be the coded numbers.

L I B E R A T E → given word
5 6 4 0 3 1 7 0 → codes

Similarly,

T R I B A L → word to be coded
7 3 6 4 1 5 → answer codes

9. (40 + 20) = 60 metres South

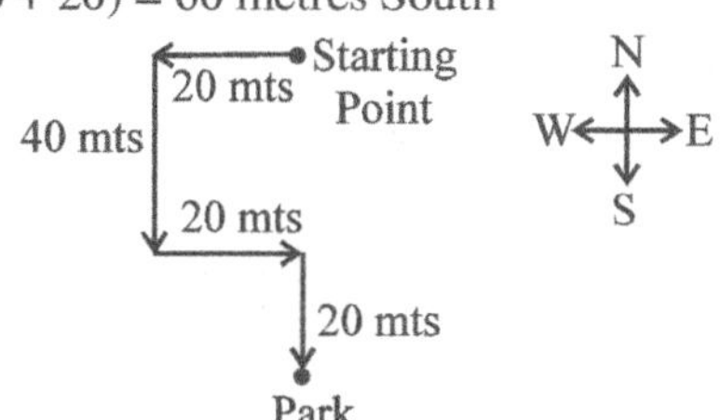

10.

'My grandmother's only son' is the father of the man, and 'daughter of my grandmother's only son' is the sister of the man.

11. The arrangement of ranks in ascending order is— Lieutenant, Captain, Major, Brigadier, **Lieutenant-General.**

12. The proper order of measurement in increasing order is—Milimeter, Centimeter, Meter, Decameter, Kilometer.

13. Physicist deals with the subject Physics and biologist with subject anatomy.

14. The related words are near opposites.

16. The letters are moved +4, −3, +4, −3 steps respectively

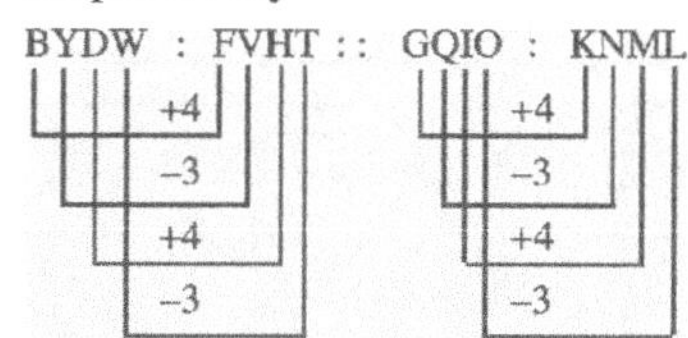

17. All the numbers are squares of different numbers.

$$25 \quad : \quad 81 \quad :: \quad 36 \quad : \quad 121$$
$$\downarrow \quad \quad \downarrow \quad \quad \downarrow \quad \quad \downarrow$$
$$5^2 \quad \quad 9^2 \quad \quad 6^2 \quad \quad 11^2$$

18. All others are instructors. Pupil learns from the instructor.

19. All others are running forms of water.

20. All others are forms of taxes.

21. In other numbers, no digit is repeated.

22. In other numbers, the sum of both the digits is 9.

23. In all other numbers, two digits are same.

24. Other numbers are made with digits 2, 6, 7 and 8.

25. 2 4 6 3 3 1 5 7 8 3 3 3 4 6 2 3 3 3 3 9 7 2 3

    ⎵₁   ⎵₂   ⎵₃

26. After interchanging the signs the equations are:
(a) 7 + 5 × 3 = 22 which is wrong

(*b*) $4 \times 9 + 1 = 37$ which is wrong
(*c*) $6 + 5 \times 8 = 46$ which is correct
(*d*) $2 \times 11 + 4 = 26$ which is wrong

27. $7 + 4 - 10 + 2 \times 5$
$7 + 4 - 10 + 10 = 11.$

28. Thursday —Day-before-yesterday
Friday —Yesterday
Saturday —Today
Sunday — Tomorrow

29. 7th day is 3 days earlier than Friday so, 10th day is Friday, so also is 17th.

$\therefore$ 19th day will be 2nd day ahead of Friday, *i.e.,* Sunday.

30. Alphabet whose codes are given

w $\rightarrow$ a
s $\rightarrow$ r
r $\rightarrow$ w

All other alphabet will remain unchanged, so, 'answer' will be coded as :

31. The word is divided into two equal parts and the letters of each part are written in reverse order.

Similarly,

32. The relationship chart based on the problem is:

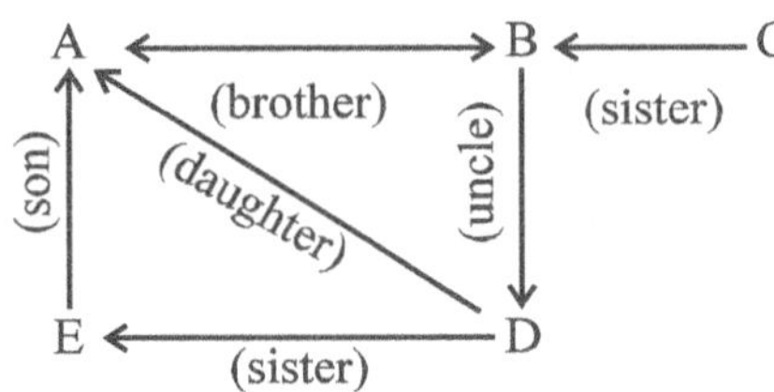

When D is sister of E, who is son of A then D is daughter of A. Brother of A is B and so, B is D's uncle.

33. Each vowel (AEIOU) is preceded by the letter that comes next to it in the natural alphabetical series.

B A   F E   J I   P O   V U

34. The letters are in reverse series and the difference is four and three alternately.

V   R   O   K   H   D
-4 -3 -4 -3 -4

35. The three alphabet in one group correspond to the alphabet in the next group in the manner +6, +5, +4 respectively, *i.e.,*

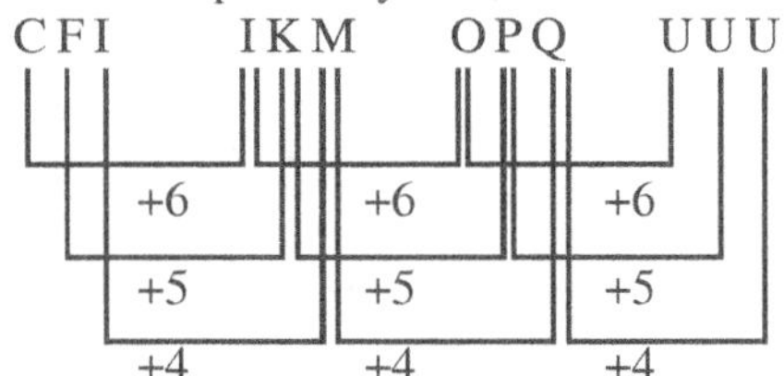

38. The element at the bottom is moved to the diagonal corner, the element in the top is enlarged and moved to the centre and element in the middle is reduced and moved to the bottom right corner.

40. The inner shape in the first figure is removed to get the second figure.

41. The cross is turned 90° clockwise at each step.

43. The complete figure is turned 90° clockwise at each step.

44. A new figure is added to the previous set of figures at each step.

46.    **47.** 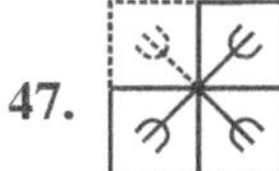

48. 

49. 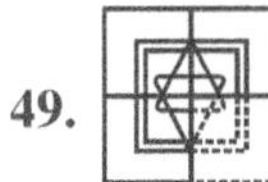

50. 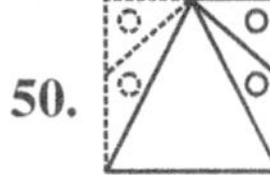

Sainik School Entrance Exam., 2015
(CLASS-VI)

PAPER-I : MATHEMATICS AND LANGUAGE

Time : 2 Hrs. **Max. Marks : 200**

Part-A : Mathematics

Section-I

(Each question carries two marks.)

1. What is the LCM of two numbers if their HCF is 2 and the product is 112?

2. Write the Hindu-Arabic numerals for MDCL.

3. John had $2\frac{1}{2}$ Cake. His friends ate $1\frac{2}{3}$ of the Cake. How much of the Cake is left?

4. The dimensions of a rectangular field are 36 m and 24 m. Find the cost of fencing of the field if cost of wire is ₹ 4.50 per meter.

5. Find the average of first 9 prime numbers.

6. Simplify : $\dfrac{\dfrac{1}{5} \div \dfrac{1}{5} \text{ of } \dfrac{1}{5}}{\dfrac{1}{5} \text{ of } \dfrac{1}{5} \div \dfrac{1}{5}}$

7. A train covers 20 m in a second. Convert the speed of train in Km/h.

8. Form the greatest and smallest 4 digit numbers with digits 9, 3, 7 and 1.

9. Mayank bought a ball for ₹ 20. He sold it for ₹ 30 and again bought it back for ₹ 40. Again he sold it for ₹ 50. Did he gain or lose? By how much did he gain or lose?

10. 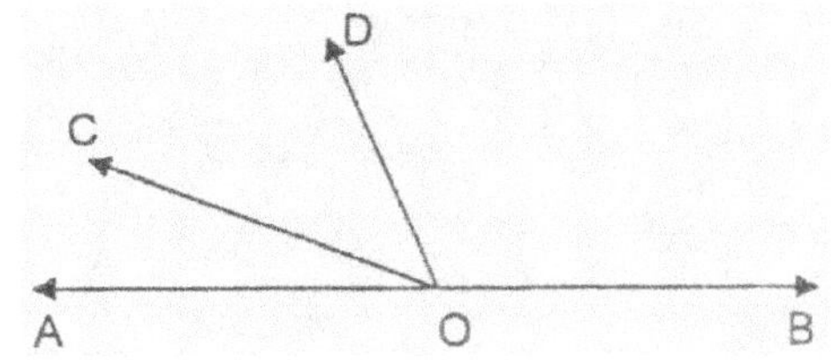

In the above figure if
$\angle AOC = x$
$\angle COD = 2x$
$\angle BOD = 3x$
Then find each angle in degree.

Section-II

(Each question carries three marks.)

11. Solve : $\dfrac{2}{7}$ of $\left[2 + \{2(11 + \overline{4-2})\}\right] - 2$

12. What percent is 200 grams of 4.5 kg?

13. If the simple interest on ₹ 12800 for a period of 2 years is ₹ 3840, then find the rate of interest per annum.

14. If the circumference of a circular park is 88 m, then find the area of the park.

15. Arrange the following in ascending order :
$\dfrac{3}{7}, \dfrac{4}{5}, \dfrac{7}{9}, \dfrac{1}{2}$ and $\dfrac{3}{5}$.

16. Mohan, a student of Class-V secured 315 marks out of 450. Find marks in percentage.

17. In the given figure, what is the value of angles BAC ($x°$) and CAD ($y°$)?

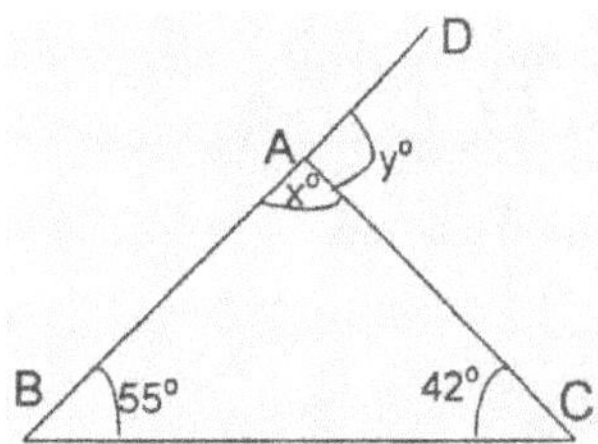

SSE(VI)-PP'15 (E)–1

18. Sachin saved ₹ 400 each in the first and second months, ₹ 800 and ₹ 600 in the third and fourth months respectively. Find average monthly saving over the four months.

19. If average (mean) of the following marks obtained by students of Class-V is 35.
26 45 37 43 49 20 x 22 and 30. Find unknown mark *i.e.* x.

20. Find : $1 - 2 + 3 - 4 + 5 - 6 + ... + 19 - 20$.

Section-III

(Each question carries five marks.)

21. A rectangle and a square have the same perimeter 100 m. Find the side of the square if the rectangle has a breadth 2 m less than that of the square. Find breadth, length and area of the rectangle.

22. Rakesh completes one round of a running track in 8 minutes and Saroj completes it in 6 minutes. How long will it take for both to arrive again at their starting point together, if they start running at the same time and maintain their speed?

23. Akshita's dad needed a loan of ₹ 20,000 to buy a new car. Mr. Das, the Bank Manager agreed to give him the loan at 3% per annum. If the loan was to be paid back after 5 years, what total amount must he return to the bank?

24. Find the value of 'x' for following figure if AB ∥ CD.

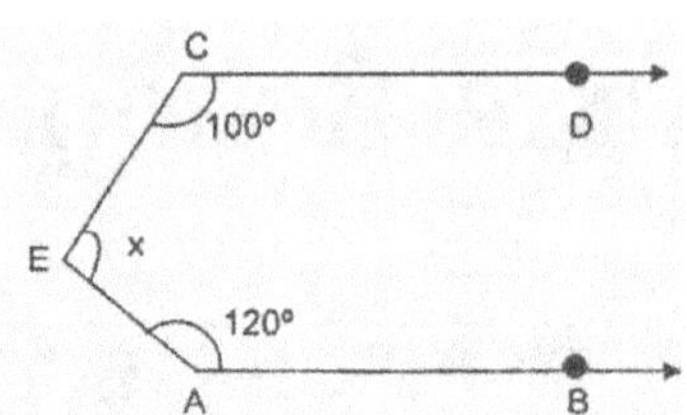

25. A Supermarket sells 19 oranges for ₹ 114, 6 Apples for ₹ 48, 22 Pomegranates for ₹ 154 and 17 Mangoes for ₹ 153. Which one of the fruits is the cheapest?

26. A rectangular grassy lawn measuring 48 m by 35 m is to be surrounded externally by a path, which is 2.5 m wide. Find the cost of leveling the path at the rate ₹ 4.50 per Sq. m.

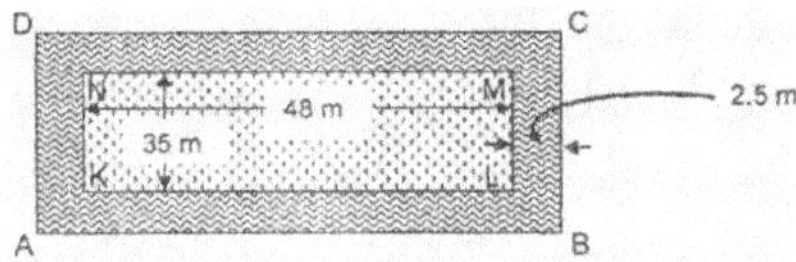

27. One number exceeds another number by 36. If sum of both number is 48. Find the numbers.

28. Find the smallest number, having four different prime factors.

29. What sum of money will produce ₹ 143 interest in $3\frac{1}{4}$ years at $2\frac{1}{2}\%$ simple interest?

30. A brick measures 20 cm by 10 cm by $7\frac{1}{2}$ cm. How many bricks will be required for a wall 25 m long, 2 m high and $\frac{3}{4}$ m thick?

EXPLANATORY ANSWERS

1. $\text{LCM} = \dfrac{\text{Product of numbers}}{\text{H.C. F.}}$

$= \dfrac{112}{2} = 56$

2. M — 1000
D — 500
C — 100
L — 50

3. Remaining Cake $= \dfrac{5}{2} - \dfrac{5}{3} = \dfrac{15 - 10}{6} = \dfrac{5}{6}$

4. Perimeter of the rectangular field $= 2(l + b)$
$= 2(36 + 24) = 120$ m.
Cost of fencing of the field
$= ₹ \dfrac{9}{2} \times 120$
$= ₹ 9 \times 60 = ₹ 540$

5. Average of first 9 prime numbers
$= \dfrac{2 + 3 + 5 + 7 + 11 + 13 + 17 + 19 + 23}{9}$
$= \dfrac{100}{9} = 11.1$

6. Simplify $\dfrac{\dfrac{1}{5} \div \dfrac{1}{5} \text{ of } \dfrac{1}{5}}{\dfrac{1}{5} \text{ of } \dfrac{1}{5} \div \dfrac{1}{5}}$

$= \dfrac{\dfrac{1}{5} \div \dfrac{1}{5} \times \dfrac{1}{5}}{\dfrac{1}{5} \times \dfrac{1}{5} \div \dfrac{1}{5}} = \dfrac{\dfrac{1}{5} \div \dfrac{1}{25}}{\dfrac{1}{25} \div \dfrac{1}{5}} = \dfrac{\dfrac{1}{5} \times \dfrac{25}{1}}{\dfrac{1}{25} \times \dfrac{5}{1}} = \dfrac{5}{\dfrac{1}{5}}$

$= \dfrac{5}{1} \times \dfrac{5}{1} = 25$

7. Speed of the train = 20 m/s

$$= 20 \times \dfrac{18}{5} \text{ km/hr}$$

$$= 72 \text{ km/hr}$$

8. The greatest number = 9731
The smallest number = 1379

9. Total CP = 20 + 40 = ₹ 60
Total SP = 30 + 50 = ₹ 80
SP > CP ∴ he got profit.
Profit = SP – CP = 80 – 60 = ₹ 20

10.

$x + 2x + 3x = 180º$
$\Rightarrow 6x = 180º \Rightarrow x = 30º$
$\angle AOC = 30º$, $\angle COD = 2 \times 30 = 60º$
$\angle BOD = 3 \times 30 = 90º$

11. $\dfrac{2}{7}$ of $\left[2 + \{2(11 + \overline{4 - 2})\} \right] - 2$

$= \dfrac{2}{7}$ of $\left[2 + \{2(11 + 2)\} \right] - 2$

$= \dfrac{2}{7}$ of $\left[2 + \{26\} \right] - 2$

$= \dfrac{2}{7}$ of $\left[28 \right] - 2$

$= \dfrac{2}{7} \times 28 - 2$

$= 8 - 2 = 6$

12. Required % $= \dfrac{200}{4500} \times 100$

$= \dfrac{40}{9} = 4.4\%$

13. Rate of interest $= \dfrac{\text{SI} \times 100}{p \times t} = \dfrac{3840 \times 100}{12800 \times 2}$

∴ $r = 15\%$

14. $C = 2\pi r$

$\Rightarrow \quad 88 = 2 \times \dfrac{22}{7} \times r$

$\Rightarrow \quad r = \dfrac{88 \times 7}{44} = 14 \text{ m.}$

Area of the circular park $= \pi r^2$

$= \dfrac{22}{7} \times 14 \times 14$

$= 22 \times 28 = 616 \text{ m}^2.$

15. $\dfrac{3}{7} = 0.4$

$\dfrac{4}{5} = 0.8$

$\dfrac{7}{9} = 0.7$

$\dfrac{1}{2} = 0.5$

$\dfrac{3}{5} = 0.6$

∴ $\dfrac{3}{7}, \dfrac{1}{2}, \dfrac{3}{5}, \dfrac{7}{9}, \dfrac{4}{5}$ are in ascending order.

16. Out of 450 marks Mohan got 315 marks.
Out of 100 marks Mohan got

$= \dfrac{315}{450} \times 100 = 70\%$

17.

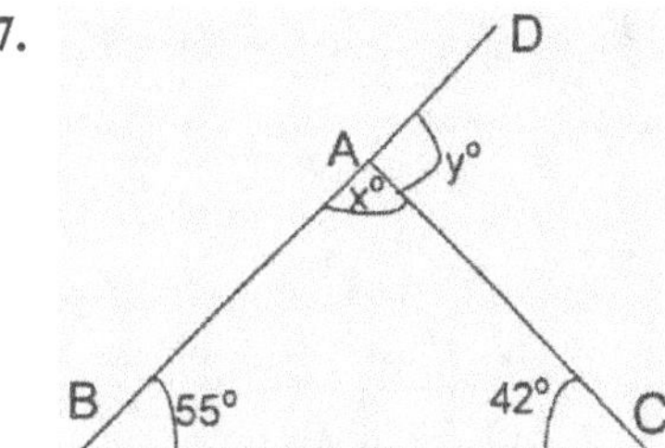

In $\triangle$ ABC,
$x + 55^\circ + 42^\circ = 180^\circ$
$\Rightarrow x = 180^\circ - 97^\circ = 83^\circ$
$x + y = 180^\circ$ (linear pair)
$\therefore y = 180^\circ - 83^\circ = 97^\circ$

18. Average monthly saving

$$= \frac{400 + 400 + 800 + 600}{4}$$

$$= \frac{2200}{4} = ₹\,550$$

19. $\dfrac{x + 26 + 45 + 37 + 43 + 49 + 20 + 22 + 30}{9} = 35$

$\Rightarrow x + 272 = 35 \times 9 = 315$
$\Rightarrow x = 315 - 272 = 43$

20. $1 + 3 + 5 + 7 + 9 + 11 + 13 + 15 + 17 + 19$
$-(2 + 4 + 6 + 8 + 10 + 12 + 14 + 16 + 18 + 20)$
$= 100 - 110 = -10$

21.

100 m	100 m
rectangle	square

$\therefore$ Perimeter of square = perimeter of rectangle
$$= 100 \text{ m}$$

$\therefore$ Side of square $= \dfrac{100}{4} = 25\,\text{m}$

Breadth of rectangle $= 25 - 2 = 23$ m
Now $\qquad 2(l + b) = 100$
$\qquad\qquad l + b = 50$
$\Rightarrow \qquad\qquad l + 23 = 50 \quad \Rightarrow \quad l = 27$ m
Length of rectangle $= 27$ m
$\therefore$ Area of rectangle $= l \times b = 27 \times 23$
$$= 621 \text{ m}^2$$

22. L.C.M. of 8 and 6 = 24

$$\begin{array}{r|ll} 2 & 8, & 6 \\ \hline & 4, & 3 \end{array}$$

L.C.M. $= 2 \times 4 \times 3 = 24$
Hence, both will arrive together after 24 min.

23. P $= ₹\,20{,}000$
$r = 3\%$
$t = 5$ years

$$A = p\left(1 + \frac{r}{100}\right)^t$$

$$= 20000\left(1 + \frac{3}{100}\right)^5$$

$$= 20000 \times \frac{103}{100} \times \frac{103}{100} \times \frac{103}{100} \times \frac{103}{100} \times \frac{103}{100}$$

$$= \frac{23184069486}{1000000} = 23184.069486$$

$\therefore$ Required total amount paid $= ₹\,23184$

24.

$\because$ AB $\parallel$ CD
$\therefore$ $\angle$FCE $= 180 - 100 = 80^\circ$
and $\angle$EAG $= 180 - 120 = 60^\circ$
$\angle$CEH $= 80^\circ$ (alternate angle)
$\angle$AEH $= 60^\circ$ (alternate angle)
$\therefore$ $x = 80^\circ + 60^\circ = 140^\circ$

25. Cost of 1 Orange $= \dfrac{114}{19} = ₹\,6$

Cost of 1 Apple $= \dfrac{48}{6} = ₹\,8$

Cost of 1 Pomegranate $= \dfrac{154}{22} = ₹\,7$

Cost of 1 Mango $= \dfrac{153}{17} = ₹\,9$

Hence, Orange is the cheapest fruit.

26. 48 m + 5 m = 53 m
35 m + 5 m = 40 m
Area without path $= 48 \times 35 = 1680$ m^2
Area with path $= 53 \times 40 = 2120$ m^2
$\therefore$ Area of path $= 2120 - 1680 = 540$ m^2

Cost of leveling the path $= 540 \times \dfrac{9}{2}$.

$= 270 \times 9 = ₹\,2430$

27. Let one number $= x$
$\therefore$ other number $= x + 36$
$\qquad\quad x + x + 36 = 48$
$\Rightarrow \qquad\qquad 2x = 48 - 36 = 12$
$\Rightarrow \qquad\qquad x = 6, \quad x + 36 = 6 + 36 = 42$
$\therefore$ Numbers are 6 and 42.

28. Required number $= 2 \times 3 \times 5 \times 7 = 210$.

29. $P = \dfrac{\text{S.I.} \times 100}{R \times T} = \dfrac{143 \times 100 \times 2 \times 4}{13 \times 5}$

$= 88 \times 20 = ₹\ 1760$

30. Volume of Wall $= l \times b \times h$

$= 2500 \times 200 \times \dfrac{3}{4} \times 100$

$= 2500 \times 150 \times 100 \text{ cm}^3$

Volume of each brick $= l \times b \times h$

$= 20 \times 10 \times \dfrac{15}{2}$

$= 1500 \text{ cm}^3$

$\therefore$ Number of bricks $= \dfrac{2500 \times 150 \times 100}{1500}$

$= 25000$

PART-B : LANGUAGE ABILITY

1. Write 15 sentences on any one of the following topics— **(15 Marks)**
   (*a*) My Favourite Sportsperson
   (*b*) Festivals of India

2. Read the following passage carefully and answer the questions that follow: **(15 Marks)**

   Ants are the most interesting of all insects because they are so like human beings in many ways. They live in families, build their own houses, and have a king and a 'queen'. Each ant has its own work to do and it does its work well. The very young ants who have just come out of their cocoons are generally the nurses. When they are older and their skins are harder, they are ready to leave the nest and do other kinds of work. Some of the ants hunt for food. Most other kinds of insects go about looking for food, but it is always for themselves alone. But the ants think of the nest. They bring in food for the queen and other workers as well as for themselves.

   (*a*) How are ants similar to human beings?
   (*b*) What jobs are done by the very young ants?
   (*c*) When do these very young ants leave the nest?
   (*d*) Which word in the passage conveys the meaning – "a cover that keeps someone safe and warm".
   (*e*) How are ants different from most other kinds of insects?

3. Make a sentence of your own for each underlined word given in the following passage. (Do not copy any sentence from the given paragraph.) **(10 Marks)**

   Laughter is indicative of joy. A man who **laughs** radiates **happiness** and wins friends. Laughter can be the best tonic. A man who cannot laugh fails to **attract** friends, loses his **health** and deprives himself of any **pleasure** of life.

   (*a*) ....
   (*b*) ....
   (*c*) ....
   (*d*) ....
   (*e*) ....

4. Rearrange the jumbled words to form meaningful sentences. **(10 Marks)**
   (*a*) newspapers/very important/day to day life/in our/have become
   (*b*) others/at/you/not/laugh/should
   (*c*) smiles/full of/tears/is/life/and
   (*d*) a/standing/the/fox/was/clever/tree/under
   (*e*) the/west/in/the/sets/sun

5. Give one word for the following: **(5 Marks)**
   (*a*) A doctor who does operations
   ....
   (*b*) A bunch of flowers
   ....
   (*c*) A person who works with machines
   ....
   (*d*) Happening once a year
   ....
   (*e*) A house or shelter for a dog
   ....

6. Choose the correct word/phrase from the brackets and fill in the blanks: **(10 Marks)**
   (*a*) He .... a new bicycle last week. (bought, have bought, had bought)

(*b*) It .... since early morning. (rained, is raining, has been raining)

(*c*) He .... TV most evening. (is watch, watches, is watching)

(*d*) I .... a lot of work today. (do, have done, had done)

(*e*) He .... fast when the accident happened. (is driving, was driving, drove)

7. Use each of the word in separate sentences of your own to show the difference in the meaning of the words of the pairs given below: **(10 Marks)**

(*a*) Dairy, Diary   (*b*) There, Their

(*c*) Tail, Tale   (*d*) Peace, Piece

(*e*) Weight, Wait

8. Write opposite words for the following: **(5 Marks)**

(*a*) Win   (*b*) Refuse

(*c*) Cruel   (*d*) Ascending

(*e*) Give

9. Change each of the following as directed: **(10 Marks)**

(*a*) It is going to rain.

(Change into Interrogative)

....

(*b*) Mr Mukherji knows Chinese.

(Change into negative)

....

(*c*) He knows me well.

(Change verb to past tense)

....

(*d*) You are very smart.

(Change into Exclamatory)

....

(*e*) The cat killed the mouse.

(Change into Passive Voice)

....

10. Your elder brother has sent you a birthday gift. Write a letter of Thanks to him. **(10 Marks)**

EXPLANATORY ANSWERS

1. (*b*)   **Festivals of India**

India is a land of festivals. The most famous festival in the Christian world is Christmas. The Mohammedans observe Id-ul-Fitr as one of their most important festivals. In India the most famous festival is the Diwali which though chiefly a Hindu festival, is celebrated by other communities also because of their beliefs. Diwali comes in October or November. The Dussehra which precedes the Diwali by twenty days is another famous festival which is celebrated all over India. Holi which comes in February or March, is also celebrated all over India, but most vehemently in North India. Baisakhi which often comes off on 13th April, marks the beginning of harvest season and advent of the Hindu new Calendar. The harvest festival of Kerala is Onam which comes off in September. In Tamil Nadu, Pongal is the harvest festival which comes off in September. There are other festivals like Pushkar Mela at Pushkar in Rajasthan. It is celebrated in November. Vishwakarma Day is celebrated by the artisans on the day next to Diwali. Desert Festival is celebrated at Jaisalmer in Rajasthan during February. Surajkund Crafts Mela is held in Haryana in the same month *i.e.* February. There are Gurpurbs celebrated by the Sikhs. Similarly there are other festivals like Lohari, Basant, etc., and social days for other communities. There are also celebrations on more or less scale on days like Purnima, Amavas, Ekadishi, etc. In Kashmir we have the famous Amarnath Yatra and "Chhari Mubarak" March.

2. (*a*) Because they live in families, build their own houses, and do work like human beings.

(*b*) The very young ants do the jobs of nurses.

(*c*) When they are older and their skins are harder, then they leave the nest.

(*d*) Cocoon.

(*e*) Ant collect food for other ants also while most other kinds of insect do it just for themselves only.

3. (*a*) Never laugh at poor and deprived poeple.

(*b*) Laughter is a sign of happiness.

(*c*) Those who laugh often, attract more friends.

(*d*) Laughter also improves the health.

(*e*) Laughter, happiness and pleasure are good for healthy life.

4. (*a*) Newspapers have become very important in our day to day life.
(*b*) You should not laugh at others.
(*c*) Life is full of tears and smiles.
(*d*) The clever fox was standing under a tree.
(*e*) The sun sets in the west.

5. (*a*) Surgeon
(*b*) Bouquet
(*c*) Engineer, Mechanic, Machinist
(*d*) Annual
(*e*) Kennel

6. (*a*) bought   (*b*) has been raining
(*c*) watches   (*d*) have done
(*e*) was driving

7. (*a*) We go to Mother Dairy to fetch milk.
I maintain a daily diary for record.
(*b*) There is a snake in the grass.
Their car broke down on the way.
(*c*) The dog was wagging its tail.
He narrated a long tale of a king.
(*d*) All religions teach us to live in peace.
I also ate a piece of cake there.

(*e*) Your body weight should be normal.
After a long wait I left the place.

8. (*a*) Lose   (*b*) Accept
(*c*) Kind   (*d*) Descending
(*e*) Take

9. (*a*) Is it going to rain?
(*b*) Mr Mukherji doesn't know Chinese.
(*c*) He knew me well.
(*d*) How smart!
(*e*) The mouse was killed by the cat.

10. Examination Hall,
TUV City
6 March, ...
My dear Brother,

I thank you very much for the watch that you have just sent as my birthday gift. It is really a beautiful watch. It keeps correct time. I will never be late for college now. My friends also like it very much.

I request you to attend my birthday party in person the next year. Don't forget to bring the kids.
Your affectionate brother,
ABC.

PAPER-II : INTELLIGENCE TEST

Time : 40 Minutes.   **Max. Marks : 100**

Directions (Qs. 1 to 5): *Out of the four choices: (A), (B), (C) and (D) given in each problem three are similar in one way. However one choice is not like the other three. Choose the choice which is different from the rest and write the answer in the answer box.*

1. (*a*) Open & Close   (*b*) Hate & Dislike
(*c*) Rise & Fall   (*d*) Go & Come

2. (*a*) R5A1T6   (*b*) B2A1D4
(*c*) C3E5A1   (*d*) H8B2D4

3. (*a*) Far and Near
(*b*) Last and First
(*c*) Distance and Fare
(*d*) High and Low

4. (*a*) You   (*b*) He
(*c*) She   (*d*) Am

5. (*a*) 699   (*b*) 789
(*c*) 773   (*d*) 798

Directions (Q. 6 to 9): *In each of the following questions, arrange the letters of each word then find fourth letter.*

6. ENKAL (A BODY PART)   ....

7. HCDNGRHAIA (A UNION TERRETORY)

      ....

8. HEPES (AN ANIMAL)   ....

9. NEGOAR (A FRUIT)   ....

10. (*a*) Lion and Roar
(*b*) Elephant and Trumpet
(*c*) Snake and Hiss
(*d*) Dogs and Cook

11. (*a*) Cow and Goat
(*b*) Horse and Mare

(c) Dog and Bitch

(d) Cock and Hen

Directions (Qs. 12 to 15): *Choose the right answer and write the answer in the answer box.*

12. Uncle is to Aunt as Cook is to
   (a) Fowl
   (b) Hen
   (c) Chicken
   (d) Duck

13. Wood is to table as .... is to coat
   (a) Shirt
   (b) Wear
   (c) Trouser
   (d) Cloth

14. Boy is to Girl as nephew is to ....
   (a) Uncle
   (b) Niece
   (c) Brother in law
   (d) Aunt

15. Fish is to Bird as submarine is to
   (a) Ship
   (b) Train
   (c) Aeroplane
   (d) Car

16. Disease : Pathology : : Planet : ?
   (a) Sun
   (b) Stars
   (c) Astrology
   (d) Astronomy

17. Waiting : Boredom : : Education : ?
   (a) Class
   (b) Enlightenment
   (c) Schooling
   (d) Cunning

18. Light : Sun : : Heat : ?
   (a) Electricity
   (b) Moon
   (c) Fire
   (d) Star

Directions (Qs. 19 to 22): *Below are given numbers/ alphabets/figures followed by 4 answer choices marked as A, B, C and D. Choose a correct answer option, which will continue the series.*

19. 246, 357, 468, 579 ....
   (a) 759
   (b) 690
   (c) 678
   (d) 459

20. A/2, 4/C, E/6 ....
   (a) 8/G
   (b) 8/K
   (c) 7/G
   (d) G/8

21. B, D, G, K ....
   (a) P
   (b) A
   (c) O
   (d) N

22. 1243, 2354, 3465, ...
   (a) 4576
   (b) 4675
   (c) 4796
   (d) 4367

23. C - 3, E - 6, G - 12, I - 24, K - 48, ?
   (a) S - 48
   (b) M - 96
   (c) L - 96
   (d) O - 48

24. 3, 6, 8, 16, 18, ...
   (a) 28
   (b) 36
   (c) 54
   (d) 34

25. KPA, LQB, MRC, NSD, ?
   (a) UOT
   (b) OTE
   (c) EOT
   (d) TOE

26. If CHAIR is coded as FKDLU, then RAID is coded as:
   (a) ULGD
   (b) ULKG
   (c) ULDG
   (d) UDLG

27. If "grey" is called "brown", "white" is called "pink", "red" is called "grey", "black" is called "red", "brown" is called "white", what is the colour of "coal"?
   (a) brown
   (b) red
   (c) black
   (d) pink

28. If $5 \times 8 = 28$, $3 \times 7 = 12$, $8 \times 6 = 35$, then find the value of 13×13?
   (a) 169
   (b) 130
   (c) 140
   (d) 144

29. If TOUR is written as 1234, CLEAR is written as 56784 and SPARE is written as 90847, find the code for CARE?
   (a) 1247
   (b) 4847
   (c) 5247
   (d) 5847

30. If RAJI has been coded as TCLK, then what would be the code for KLCT?
   (a) MENV
   (b) RAJI
   (c) MNFV
   (d) MNEV

Directions (Qs. 31 & 32): *Choose the word, which will come third in the dictionary and write the answer in answer box.*

31. (a) Battalion
   (b) Barrister
   (c) Banana
   (d) Balance

32. (a) Dear
   (b) Decide
   (c) Diagram
   (d) Departure

33. If ÷ means ×, × means +, + means – and –
means ÷. Find the value of $16 \times 3 + 5 - 2 \div 4$
(*a*) 19   (*b*) 10
(*c*) 9   (*d*) 13

34. What is common in hydrometer, lactometer
and manometer?
(*a*) They are units of measurement
(*b*) They are instruments
(*c*) They are scales
(*d*) They are equipments used in physics

35. What is common in Bauxite, Iron, Tungsten
and Monazite?
(*a*) They are all minerals
(*b*) They are all metals
(*c*) They are all chemicals
(*d*) None of these

Directions (Qs. 36-40): *In each of the following
sets of figures, select the one that is different from
the rest.*

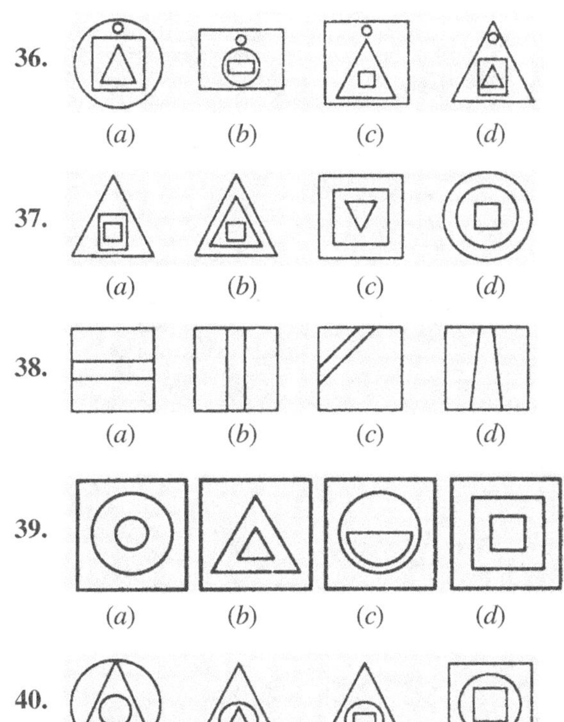

36.
(*a*)   (*b*)   (*c*)   (*d*)

37.
(*a*)   (*b*)   (*c*)   (*d*)

38.
(*a*)   (*b*)   (*c*)   (*d*)

39.
(*a*)   (*b*)   (*c*)   (*d*)

40.
(*a*)   (*b*)   (*c*)   (*d*)

Directions (Qs. 41-45): *Each of the following
questions consists of unmarked figures followed by
four figures mark (a), (b), (c) and (d). Select a figure
from the marked figures which will continue the series
established by the unmarked figures.*

41. Problem Figures

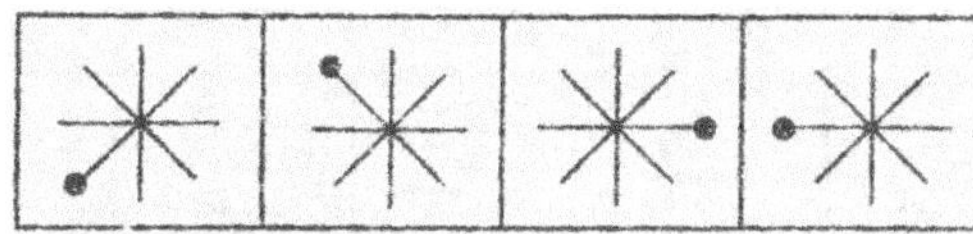

Answer Figures

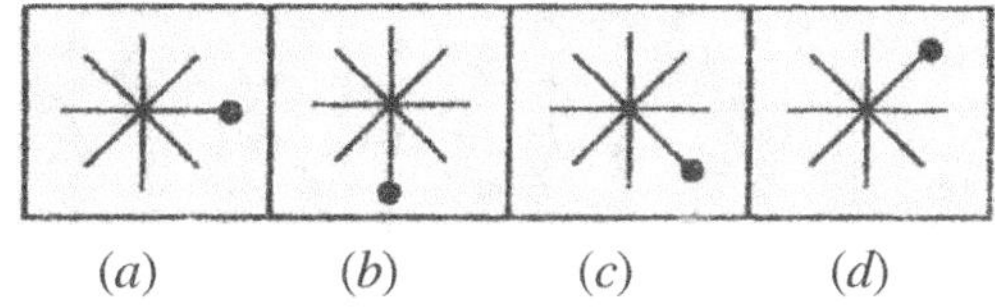

(*a*)   (*b*)   (*c*)   (*d*)

42. Problem Figures

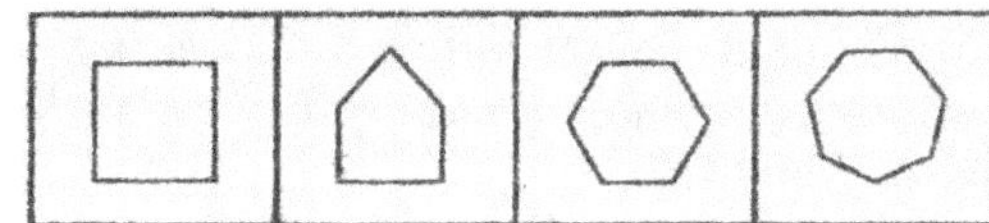

Answer Figures

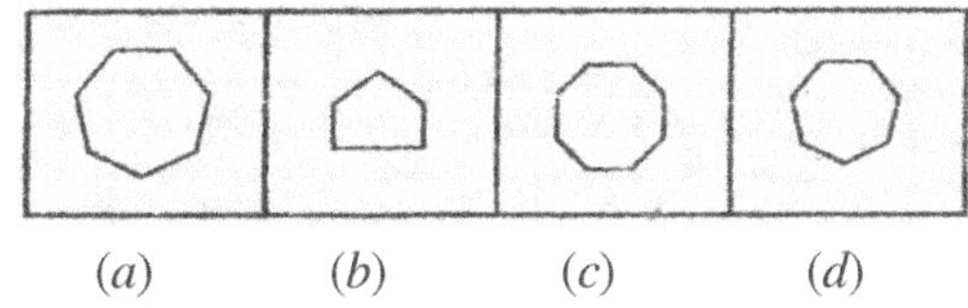

(*a*)   (*b*)   (*c*)   (*d*)

43. Problem Figures

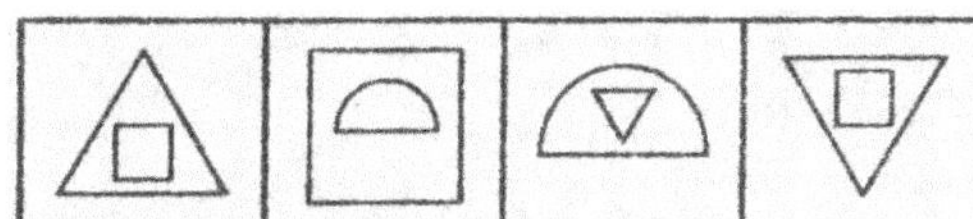

Answer Figures

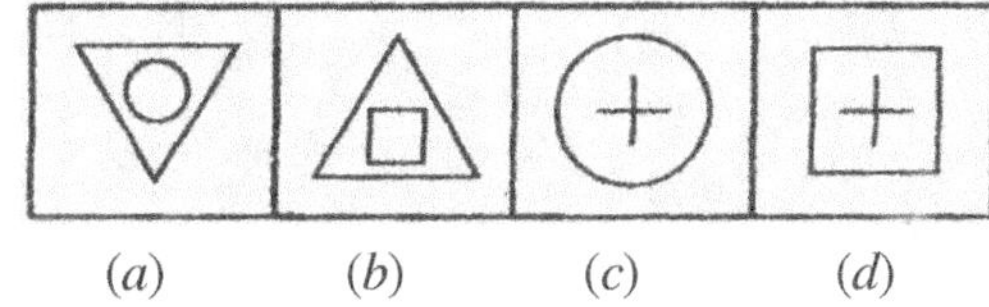

(*a*)   (*b*)   (*c*)   (*d*)

44. Problem Figures

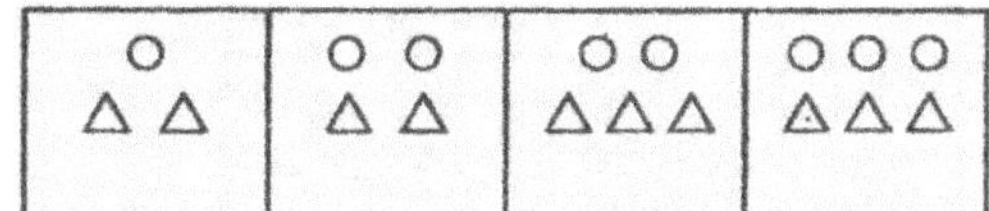

Answer Figures

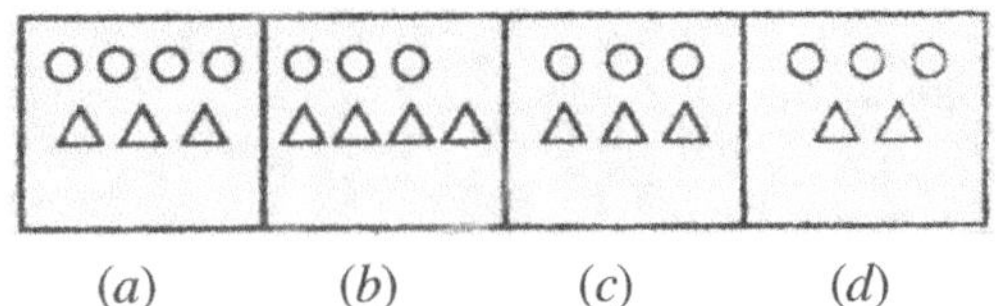

(a)   (b)   (c)   (d)

45. Problem Figures

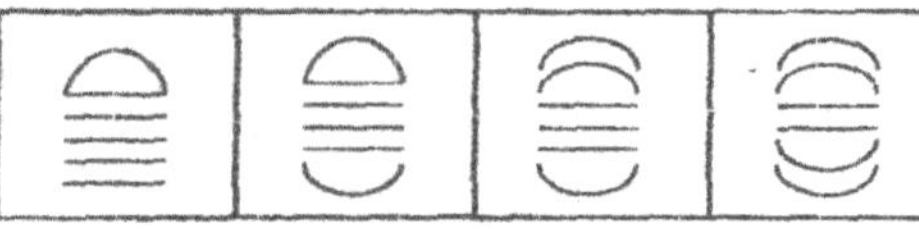

Answer Figures

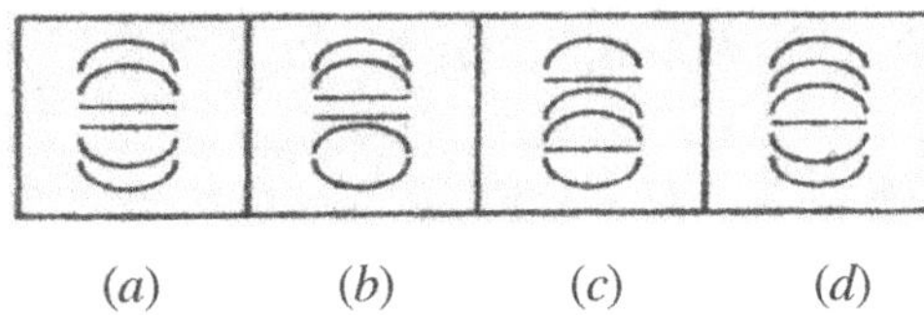

(a)   (b)   (c)   (d)

Directions (Qs. 46 to 50): *In each question, which one of the alternative figures will complete the given figure pattern?*

46. Pattern 

Alternative figures

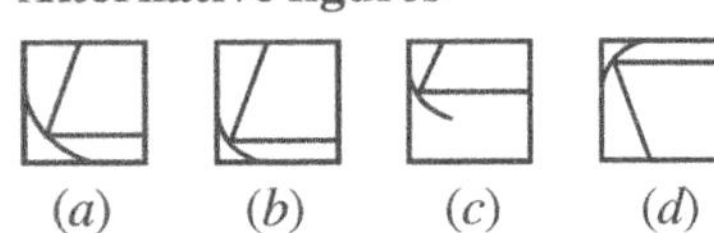

(a)   (b)   (c)   (d)

47. Pattern

Alternative figures

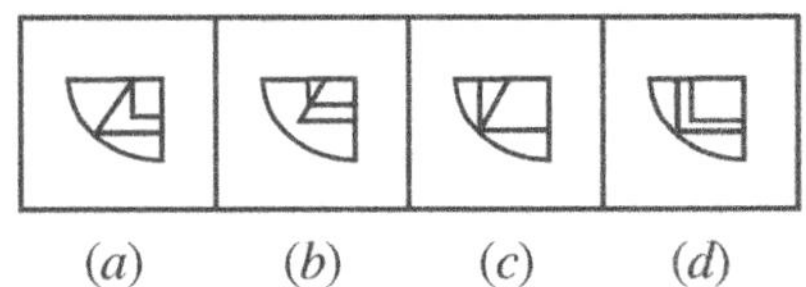

(a)   (b)   (c)   (d)

48. Pattern 

Alternative figures

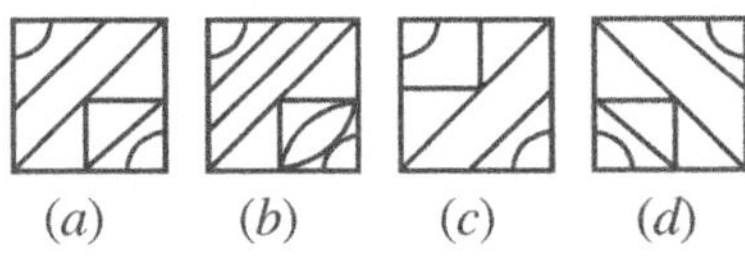

(a)   (b)   (c)   (d)

49. Pattern 

Alternative figures

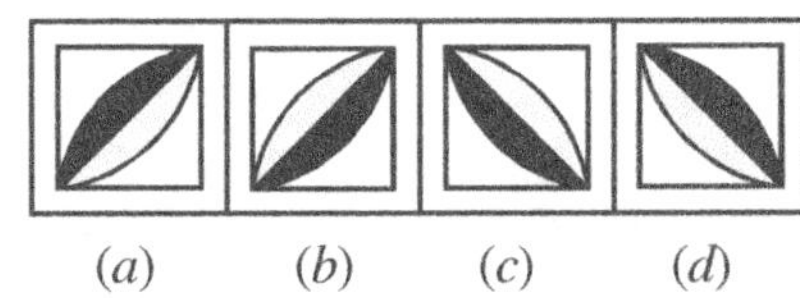

(a)   (b)   (c)   (d)

50. Pattern 

Alternative figures

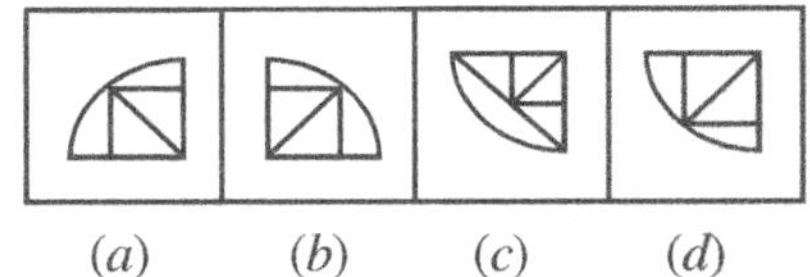

(a)   (b)   (c)   (d)

ANSWERS

1	2	3	4	5	10
(b)	(a)	(c)	(d)	(c)	(d)

11	12	13	14	15	16	17	18	19	20
(a)	(b)	(d)	(b)	(c)	(d)	(b)	(c)	(b)	(a)

21	22	23	24	25	26	27	28	29	30
(a)	(a)	(b)	(b)	(b)	(d)	(b)	(d)	(d)	(d)

31	32	33	34	35	36	37	38	39	40
(c)	(b)	(c)	(b)	(a)	(a)	(a)	(d)	(c)	(c)

41	42	43	44	45	46	47	48	49	50
(c)	(c)	(d)	(b)	(d)	(a)	(b)	(c)	(b)	(c)

SOME SELECTED EXPLANATORY ANSWERS

2. The given term is english alphabet and its position

		Latter		**Position**
B2A1D4	$\rightarrow$	A	—	1
		B	—	2
		D	—	4
C3E5A1	$\rightarrow$	C	—	3
		E	—	5
		A	—	1
H8B2D4	$\rightarrow$	H	—	8
		B	—	2
		D	—	4

Hence, worng term is R5A1T6

5. Except '773' other three numbers are divisible by '3'.

6. ENKAL $\rightarrow$ ANKLE $\rightarrow$ 4th letter is L.

7. HCDNGRHAIA $\rightarrow$ CHANDIGARH $\rightarrow$ 4th letter is N.

8. HEPES $\rightarrow$ SHEEP $\rightarrow$ 4th letter is E.

9. NEGOAR $\rightarrow$ ORANGE $\rightarrow$ 4th letter is N.

19. 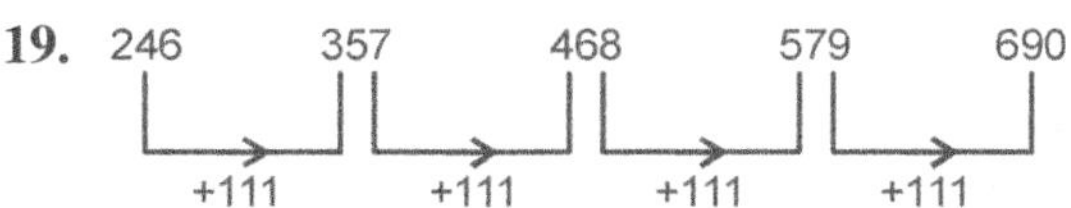

21. 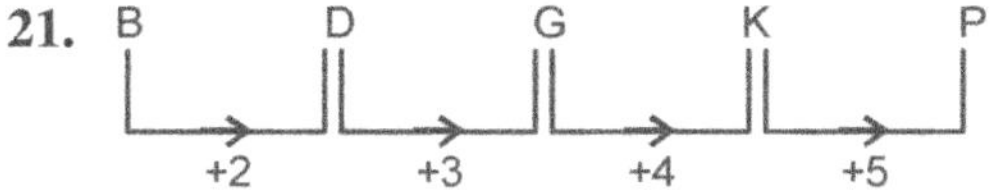

22. 

23. 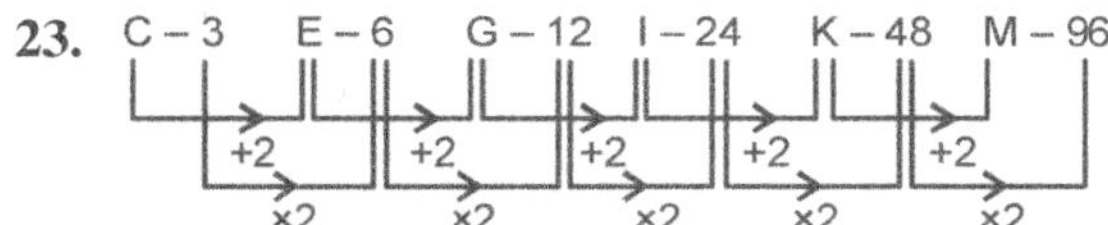

24. 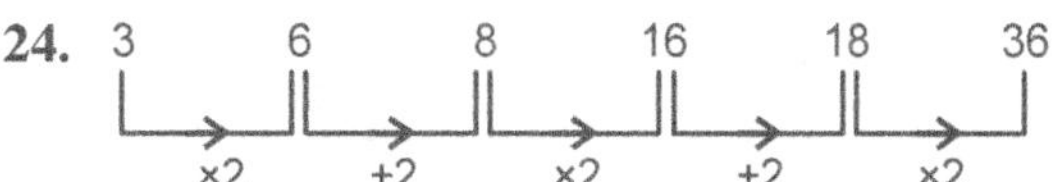

25. 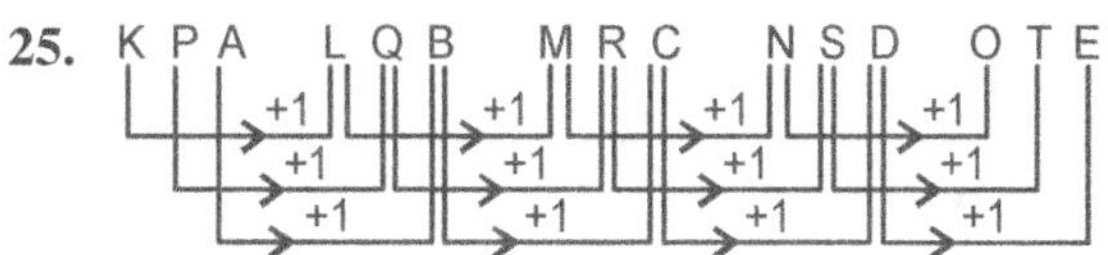

26. 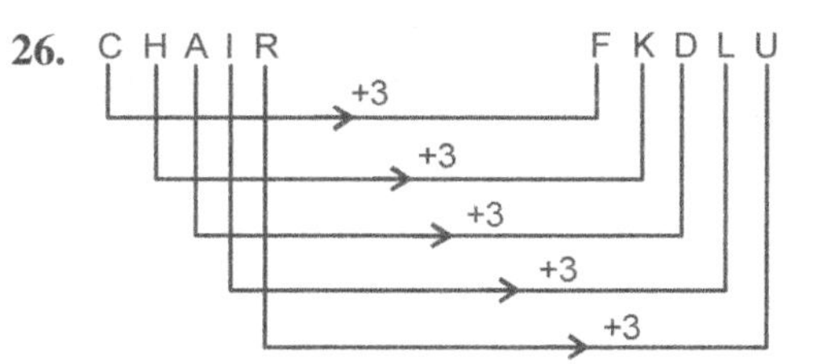

Similarly,

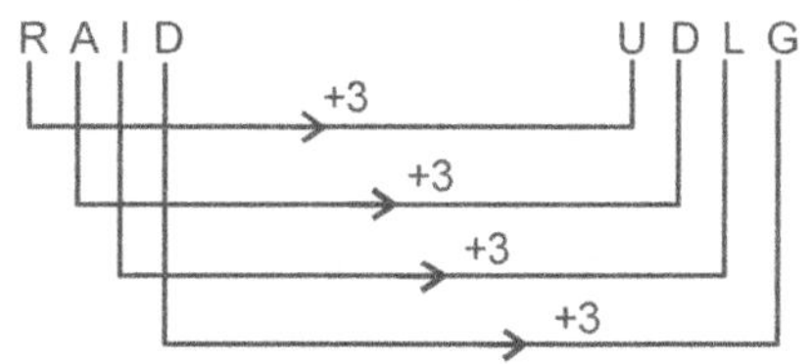

28. $5 \times 8 = (5 - 1) \times (8 - 1) = 4 \times 7 = 28$
$3 \times 7 = (3 - 1) \times (7 - 1) = 2 \times 6 = 12$
$8 \times 6 = (8 - 1) \times (6 - 1) = 7 \times 5 = 35$

Similarly,

$13 \times 13 = (13 - 1) \times (13 - 1) = 12 \times 12 = 144$

29.

Letters :	T	O	U	R	C	L	E	A	S	P
Code :	1	2	3	4	5	6	7	8	9	0

Hence, Code for 'CARE' is 5847.

30.

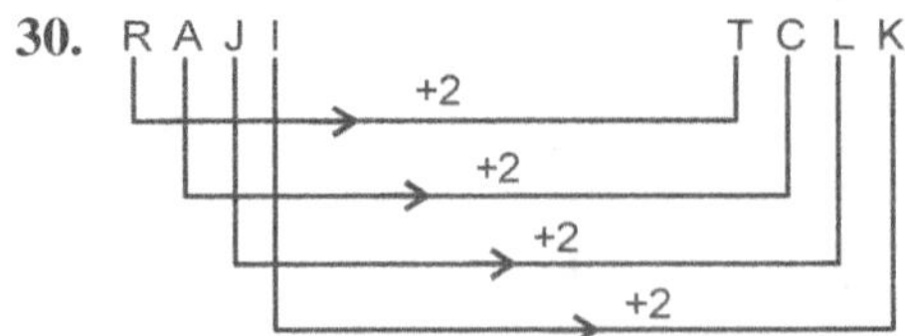

Similarly,

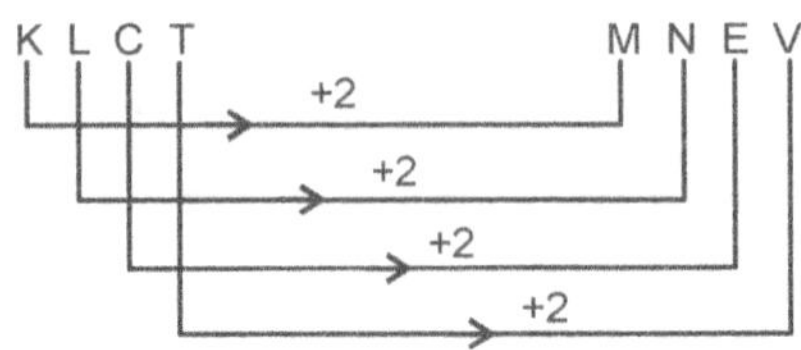

36. Except (*a*) in all others, the outer and inner figures are the same.

37. Except (*a*) in all others, the first two outer figures are same.

38. Except (*d*) all others have parallel lines inside.

39. Except (*c*) all others have similar figures inside as well as outside.

40. Except (*c*) in all others, the outer and inner figures are the same.

41. The dots move, two, three, four, five steps respectively in a clockwise direction.

42. The number of sides in each figure increases by one in each next figure.

43. The inner figure becomes the outer one and the outer figure disappears and another figure comes inside in each subsequent figure.

44. The number of circles and the number of triangles increase in every alternate figure.

45. One line in each figure changes to a curve up and down alternately.

46. 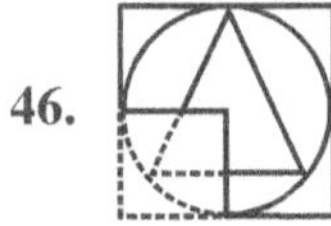

47. 

48. 

49. 

50. 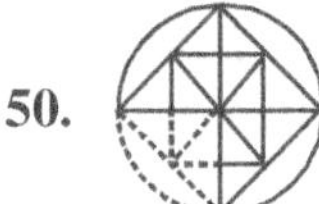

Sainik School Entrance Exam., 2014

(CLASS-VI)

PAPER-I : MATHEMATICS AND LANGUAGE

Time : 2 Hrs.   **Max. Marks : 200**

Part-A : Mathematics

Section-I

(Each questions carries two marks.)

1. Find the lowest common multiple of 2, 4 and 5.

2. What least number should be added to 322516 so that the result is exactly divisible by 543?

3. The weight of book is 1 kg 350 g. Find the weight of 25 boxes if each box contains 38 books.

4. Find the prime factors of 231.

5. Express 20 as percentage of 25.

6. Find the value of $12\frac{1}{5} \div 6\frac{1}{10}$

7. Arrange the following fraction in descending order (Use of > symbol)

   $\dfrac{8}{9}, \dfrac{8}{11}, \dfrac{8}{15}, \dfrac{8}{13}$ and $\dfrac{8}{17}$

8. Find the HCF of 16, 24, 36

9. A shopkeeper sells a cycle for ₹ 575 and incurs a loss of 75. Find his loss percentage.

10. Ram slept at 9:30 PM and got up at 6:00 AM. How much time did he sleep?

Section-II

(Each questions carries three marks.)

11. Simplify: $10 - 2\frac{1}{3} \times 3 + 3\frac{3}{4} \div 2\frac{1}{2}$

12. A train covers a distance of 560 km at a speed of 70 km per hour. Find the time taken by the train to cover this distance.

13. The age of 5 children is 13, 15, 11, 9 and 8 years respectively. Find their average age.

14. A carpet is 6.60 m long and 3.75 m broad. The carpet is surrounded by a lace. Find the length of the lace.

15. Find the measure of the angle ABC in each of the following figures using property of the given figure.

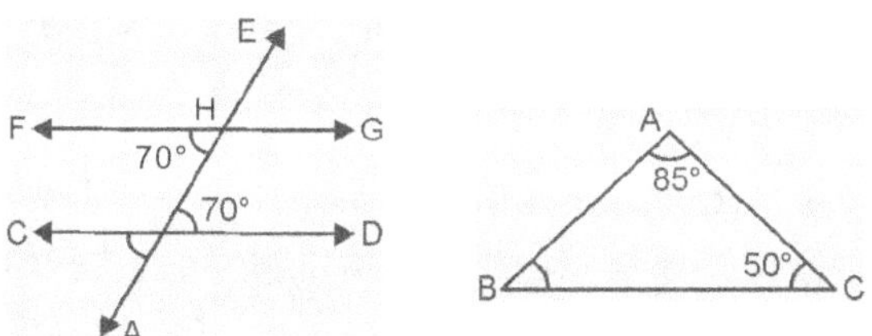

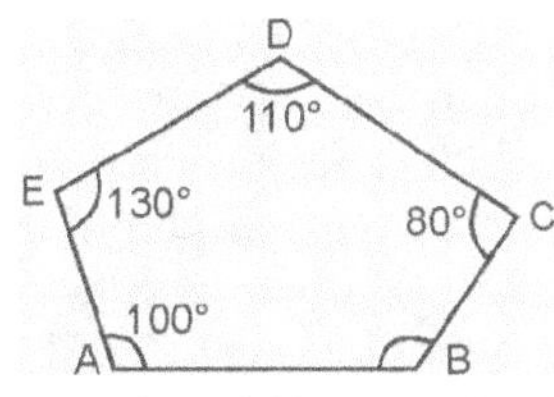

16. A container has 4 liters and 650 ml of curd. In how many glasses each of 25 ml capacity, can it be distributed?

17. A trader paid ₹ 900 as simple interest for 3 years on the sum of ₹ 4500 borrowed by him. Find the rate of interest.

18. Uma can finish a work in 18 days. The same work is finished by Manju in 9 days. In how many days both of them will finish the work while working together.

19. Amit plans to tile his kitchen floor with square tiles. Each side of the tile is 10 cm, his kitchen

is 2.6 m long and 1.7 m wide. How many tiles will Amit need?

20. Find the square root of $2\dfrac{113}{256}$.

Section-III

(Each questions carries five marks.)

21. A library has 1025 books in all. Out of this 205 books are on Science, 164 books are on Philosophy. Find the % of (*i*) Science books, (*ii*) Philosophy books.

22. Akbar gave 1/3rd of his savings to his wife 2/5th to his son. Akbar's total saving was ₹ 24,000. Find the balance amount left with Akbar.

23. A block of wood is in the form of a cube. Its edge is 4 m. How many rectangular pieces of size 20 cm × 10 cm × 5 cm can be cut from the block if there is no wastage of wood?

24. Explain and draw:–
(*a*) Intersecting lines
(*b*) Concurrent lines

25. The total age of three persons is 60 years. The ages are in proportion 1:2:3. What are their ages?

26. A shopkeeper bought 15 tables at the rate of ₹ 50 each, 20 chairs at the rate of ₹ 30 each. He spent ₹ 40 on transportation. He sold all the tables and all the chairs for ₹ 1300. Find his gain or loss.

27. The angles of a triangle are in the ratio of 2:3:5. Find the angles of the triangle. Also write the type of the triangle.

28. The area of a square A is 25 cm^2. The perimeter of square B is 12 cm. What is the area and perimeter of square C?

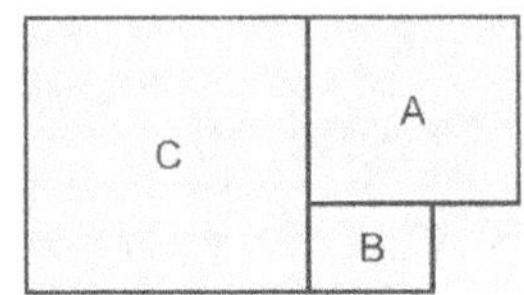

29. Find the amount required to make a circular path around a garden as shown in the picture (shaded portion) if the rate is ₹ 20 per sq metre.

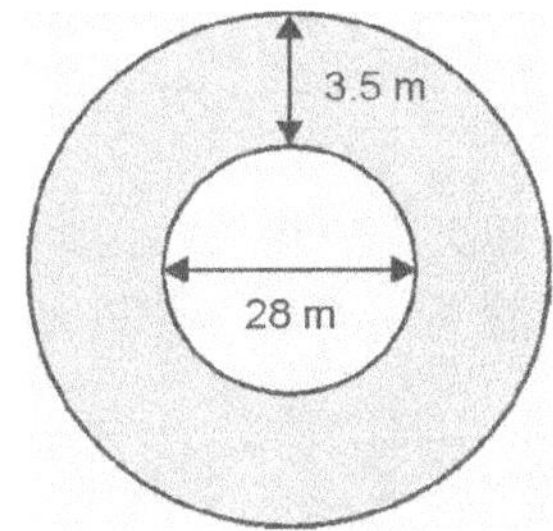

30. The average age of 5 boys is 13 years. One more boy joins them and the average age become 12 years. Find the age of boy who joins last.

EXPLANATORY ANSWERS

1. LCM of 2, 4, 5 = 20

$$\begin{array}{r|l} 2 & 2,4,5 \\ \hline & 1,2,5 \end{array}$$

∴ LCM = 2 × 2 × 5 = 20

2.
$$543\overline{)322516}(594$$
$$\begin{array}{r} 2715 \\ \hline 5101 \\ 4887 \\ \hline 2146 \\ 2172 \\ \hline 26 \end{array}$$

If we add 26 in 322516 then it becomes 322542 which is divisible by 543.
Hence, required number = 26

3. Weight of 1 book = 1350 g
Weight of 38 books = 1350 × 38 = 51300 g
Required weight = 51300 × 25 = 1282500 g
　　　　　　　　　= 1282 kg, 500 g.

4.
$$\begin{array}{r|l} 3 & 231 \\ \hline 7 & 77 \\ \hline 11 & 11 \\ \hline & 1 \end{array}$$

3, 7 and 11 are the prime factors of 231.

5. $$x \% \text{ of } 25 = 20$$

$$\Rightarrow \quad x \times \frac{25}{100} = 20$$

$$\therefore \quad x = \frac{20 \times 100}{25} = 80\%$$

6. $12\frac{1}{5} \div 6\frac{1}{10}$

$$= \frac{61}{5} \div \frac{61}{10} = \frac{61}{5} \times \frac{10}{61} = 2$$

7. $\dfrac{8}{9} > \dfrac{8}{11} > \dfrac{8}{13} > \dfrac{8}{15} > \dfrac{8}{17}$

8. HCF of 16, 24, 36 = 4

```
16 ) 24 ( 1          8 ) 36 ( 4
     16                  32
   8 ) 16 ( 2         4 ) 8 ( 2
        16               8
        ×                ×
```

$\therefore$ HCF = 4

9.
$$\text{SP} = ₹ \ 575$$
$$\text{Loss} = ₹ \ 75$$
$$\therefore \quad \text{CP} = \text{SP} + \text{Loss}$$
$$= 575 + 75 = ₹ \ 650$$

$$\text{Loss}\% = \frac{\text{Loss}}{\text{CP}} \times 100 = \frac{75}{650} \times 100$$

$$= \frac{15 \times 10}{13} = \frac{150}{13} = 11\frac{7}{13}\%$$

10. Required time $= 2\frac{1}{2}$ hrs + 6 hrs $= 8\frac{1}{2}$ hrs

$= 8$ hrs, 30 minutes.

11. $10 - 2\dfrac{1}{3} \times 3 + 3\dfrac{3}{4} \div 2\dfrac{1}{2}$

$$= 10 - \frac{7}{3} \times 3 + \frac{15}{4} \div \frac{5}{2}$$

$$= 10 - 7 + \frac{15}{4} \times \frac{2}{5}$$

$$= 3 + \frac{3}{2} = \frac{9}{2} = 4\frac{1}{2}$$

12. $$\text{Speed} = \frac{\text{distance}}{\text{time}}$$

$$\Rightarrow \quad 70 = \frac{560}{\text{time}}$$

$$\Rightarrow \quad \text{time} = \frac{560}{70} = 8 \text{ hrs.}$$

13. Average age $= \dfrac{13 + 15 + 11 + 9 + 8}{5}$

$$= \frac{56}{5} = 11.2 \text{ years}$$

14. Length of the lace $= 2(l + b)$
$= 2(6.60 + 3.75)$ m
$= 2(10.35)$ m
$= 20.70$ m

15. 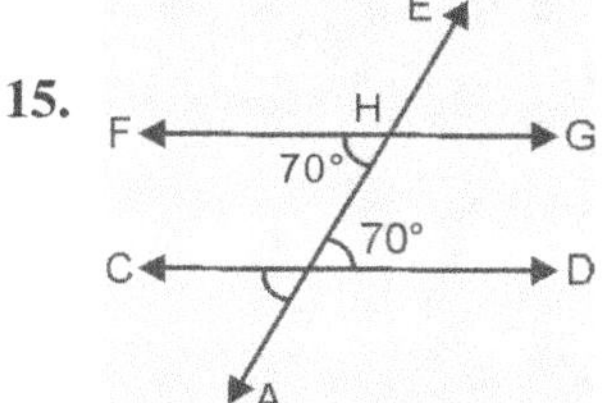

$\angle$ABC = $\angle$HBD = 70°

(vertically opposite angles)

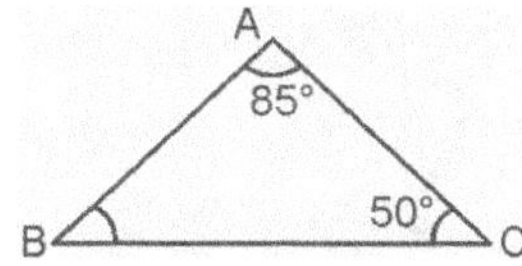

$\angle$ABC = 180° − (85° + 50°)
[Sum of angles of a triangle is 180°]
= 180° − 135° = 45°

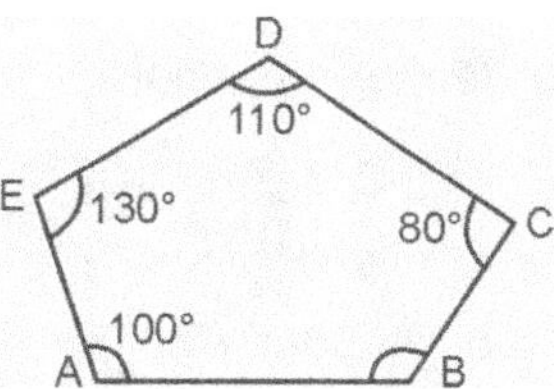

$\angle$ABC = 540° − (100° + 80° + 110° + 130°)
[Sum of angles in a pentagon is 540°]
= 540° − 420°
= 120°

16. Number of glasses $= \dfrac{4650}{25} = 186$

17. Rate of interest $= \dfrac{\text{SI} \times 100}{\text{P} \times t}$

$= \dfrac{900 \times 100}{4500 \times 3} = \dfrac{20}{3} = 6\dfrac{2}{3}\%.$

18. Uma can finish a work in 18 days

Uma's 1 day work $= \dfrac{1}{18}$

Manju can finish the same work in 9 days

Manju's 1 day work $= \dfrac{1}{9}$

(Uma + Manju)'s 1 day work

$= \dfrac{1}{18} + \dfrac{1}{9} = \dfrac{1+2}{18} = \dfrac{3}{18} = \dfrac{1}{6}$

Hence, both can finish the work in 6 days.

19. Number of tiles $= \dfrac{260 \times 170}{10 \times 10}$

$= 26 \times 17 = 442$

20. $2\dfrac{113}{256} = \dfrac{625}{256}$

$\sqrt{\left(\dfrac{625}{256}\right)} = \sqrt{\dfrac{25 \times 25}{16 \times 16}} = \dfrac{25}{16}$

Hence, square root of $2\dfrac{113}{256} = \dfrac{25}{16}.$

21. (*i*) % of Science book

$= \dfrac{205}{1025} \times 100 = 20\%$

(*ii*) % of Philosophy book

$= \dfrac{164}{1025} \times 100 = 4 \times 4 = 16\%$

22. Wife's share $= \dfrac{24000}{3} = ₹\ 8000$

Son's share $= \dfrac{2}{5} \times 24000 = ₹\ 9600$

Required amount $= 24000 - 17600 = ₹\ 6400$

23. Number of pieces $= \dfrac{400 \times 400 \times 400}{20 \times 10 \times 5}$

$= \dfrac{64000000}{1000} = 64000$

24. **Intersecting Lines:** Two lines are intersecting if they have a common point. The common point is called the point of intersection.

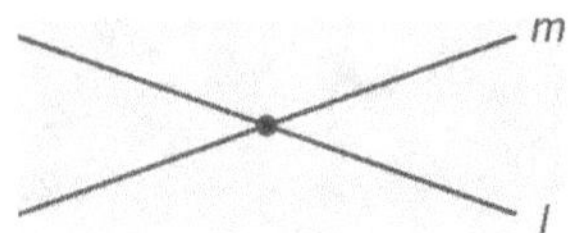

Concurrent Lines: Three or more lines are said to be concurrent if there is a point which lies on all of them.

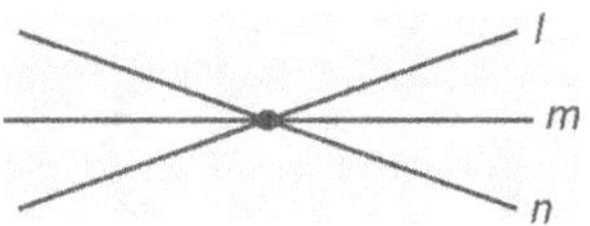

25. Let ages are in x ratios.

According to the question,

$\quad 1x + 2x + 3x = 60$

$\Rightarrow \qquad\qquad 6x = 60 \Rightarrow x = 10$

$1x = 1 \times 10 = 10$ years

$2x = 2 \times 10 = 20$ years

$3x = 3 \times 10 = 30$ years

26. Cost of 15 tables $= 15 \times 50 = ₹\ 750$

Cost of 20 chairs $= 20 \times 30 = ₹\ 600$

Spent on transportation $= ₹\ 40$

$\qquad$ Total CP $= ₹\ 750 + 600 + 40$

$\qquad\qquad\qquad = ₹\ 1390$

$\qquad$ Total SP $= ₹\ 1300$

Clearly $\qquad$ CP $>$ SP

$\therefore \qquad\qquad$ Loss $= 1390 - 1300$

$\qquad\qquad\qquad = ₹\ 90$

27. Let the angles of a triangle are in the x ratios.

According to the question,

$\quad 2x + 3x + 5x = 180°$

$\Rightarrow \qquad\qquad 10x = 180° \Rightarrow x = 18°$

$\qquad\qquad 2x = 2 \times 18 = 36°$

$\qquad\qquad 3x = 3 \times 18 = 54°$

$\qquad\qquad 5x = 5 \times 18 = 90°$

Since one angle is 90°.

Hence, it is right angled triangle.

28.

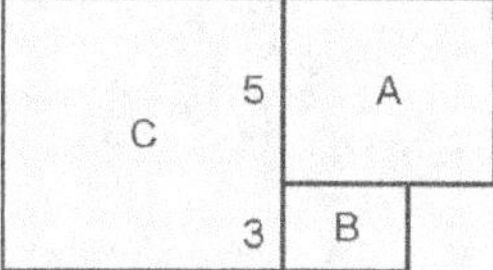

$$\text{Area of square A} = 25 \text{ cm}^2$$
$$\therefore \qquad \text{Side of square} = 5 \text{ cm}$$
$$\text{The perimeter of square B} = 12 \text{ cm}$$
$$\therefore \qquad \text{Side of square B} = \frac{12}{4} = 3 \text{ cm}$$
$$\text{Hence,} \quad \text{side of square C} = 5 + 3 = 8 \text{ cm}$$
$$\text{Area of square C} = 8 \times 8 = 64 \text{ cm}^2$$
$$\text{Perimeter of square C} = 4 \times 8 = 32 \text{ cm}$$

29.

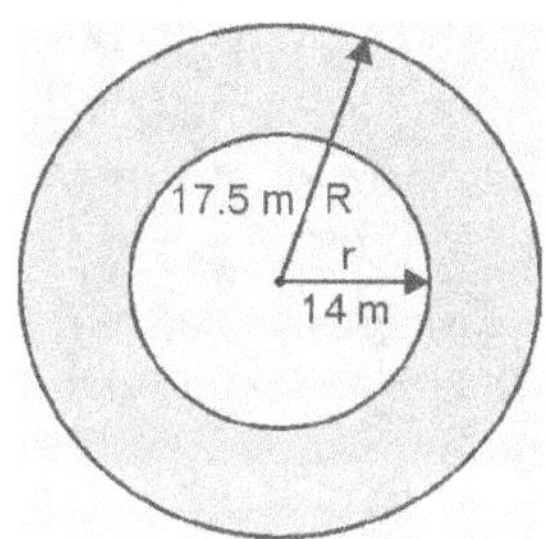

Area of the shaded portion
$$= \pi \,(R^2 - r^2)$$
$$= \pi \,(R + r)\,(R - r)$$
$$= \pi \,(17.5 + 14)\,(17.5 - 14)$$
$$= \frac{22}{7} \times 31.5 \times 3.5$$
$$= 22 \times 31.5 \times .5$$
$$= \frac{22 \times 315 \times 5}{10 \times 10} \text{ m}^2$$

Cost of 1 m^2 = ₹ 20

Cost of $\dfrac{22 \times 315 \times 5}{100}$ m^2

$$= ₹ \,\frac{22 \times 315 \times 5}{100} \times 20$$
$$= ₹ \,22 \times 315 = ₹ \,6930$$

30. Total age of 5 boys = $5 \times 13 = 65$ years
Total age of 6 boys = $6 \times 12 = 72$ years
Hence, age of boy who joins last
$$= 72 - 65 = 7 \text{ years.}$$

PART-B : LANGUAGE ABILITY

1. Write 15 sentences on any one of the following topics— **(15 Marks)**
 (*a*) My Ambition in Life
 (*b*) Importance of Games

2. Read the following passage carefully and answer the questions that follow: **(15 Marks)**

Newspaper, writing paper, printing paper, typing paper, bolting paper, carbon paper, wall paper, stamp paper – who can deny that paper is one of the most useful article in man's daily life? Yet man did not invent paper. The real inventors are the wasps who pile away tiny wood shavings from fence-posts and tree trunks and chew them to a fine pulp from which they make the grey paper walls of their nests. Who were the first paper makers amongst men? Thousands of years ago the people of Egypt made a kind of paper from the pith of the papyrus plant, which grew in marshes near the river Nile. Papyrus paper was made in long rolls, and the books written on it were rolled up, not cut into pages. One ancient book which is to be seen in the British Museum in London is a hundred and twenty feet long.

 (*a*) Name three different types of paper which are used in daily life?
 (*b*) Who invented paper?
 (*c*) Who were the first paper makers amongst men?
 (*d*) How do the wasps make paper walls of their nests?
 (*e*) Where can an ancient book which is one hundred and twenty feet long be seen?

3. Make a sentence of your own for each underlined word given in the following passage. (Do not copy any sentence from the given paragraph.) **(10 Marks)**

<u>Education</u> plays a very <u>important</u> role in the <u>development</u> of mankind. The mental and

<u>intellectual</u> development of a man takes place due to education. Without education man is like an <u>Animal</u>.

(*a*) ....

(*b*) ....

(*c*) ....

(*d*) ....

(*e*) ....

4. Rearrange the jumbled words to form meaningful sentences. **(10 Marks)**

(*a*) of exercise/the oldest form/walking/is/one/of

(*b*) is excellent/an hour's walk/fit and fine/for keeping

(*c*) than/friend/enemy a foolish/a wise/is better

(*d*) to/doctor's advice/should/carefully/your/you/listen

(*e*) vegetables/fresh fruits/sources/and/are vitamins/of minerals/and

5. Give one word for the following: **(5 Marks)**

(*a*) One who makes furniture with wood

....

(*b*) One who designs buildings

....

(*c*) A place where wild animals are kept

....

(*d*) A place where Christians pray

....

(*e*) One who writes poems

....

6. Choose the correct word from the brackets and fill in the blanks: **(5 Marks)**

(*a*) These boys have been .... a great deal of noise. (make, makes, making)

(*b*) Good children are .... by all. (like, liked, liking)

(*c*) The cattle .... grazing in the field. (is, are, was)

(*d*) It .... heavily last month. (rain, raining, rained)

(*e*) My teacher told me to .... a letter. (write, wrote, written)

7. Use each of the word in separate sentences of your own to show the difference in the meaning of the words of the pairs given below:

(10 Marks)

(*a*) male, mail   (*b*) pray, prey

(*c*) break, brake   (*d*) pour, pore

(*e*) buy, by

8. Write the meaning of the following idioms and make meaningful sentences. **(10 Marks)**

(*a*) Hand to hand   (*b*) To and fro

(*c*) Safe and sound   (*d*) Off and on

(*e*) By and by

9. You are Mohan, a resident of Janakpuri, Delhi. Write a letter to your friend requesting him to spend winter vacation with you. **(10 Marks)**

10. Look at the picture and write a story (at least 10 sentences) **(10 Marks)**

EXPLANATORY ANSWERS

1. (*a*)   **My Ambition in Life**

It is rightly said that the chief aim of education is to broaden the horizon of human mind. But we know that in the modern world, we also have to make a living by taking up some profession. I have decided to become a teacher as I grow up. It is rightly said that a teacher is a nation builder. By becoming a teacher, I want to kill two birds with one stone. On the one hand, I want to make a decent living. The teachers are well-paid these day. They also command a high respect in society. On the other hand, my aim is to serve the society at large.

I want to inculcate great moral values of life in the minds of young children. This I'll do while blending matter-of-fact and imaginative elements in my teaching. Fortunately, I'm a brilliant student and I hope I'll achieve my aim in life. Morever, both my father and mother are teachers and they are my good guides and a source of great inspiration to me.

2. (a) Writing paper, printing paper and typing paper.
   (b) Wasps invented paper in real terms.
   (c) The people of Egypt were the first paper makers amongst men.
   (d) Wasps pile away tiny wood shavings from fence-posts and tree trunks and chew them to a fine pulp to make the paper walls of their nests.
   (e) It can be seen in the British museum in London.

3. (a) Education is the key to success in life.
   (b) It is more important to understand books than cramming them.
   (c) We should work for the all-round development of society.
   (d) Intellectual development comes from good education and reading.
   (e) Animals are better than humans in the sense that they do not cheat anyone.

4. (a) One of the oldest form of exercise is walking.
   (b) An hour's walk is excellent for keeping fit and fine.
   (c) A wise enemy is better than a foolish friend.
   (d) You should carefully listen to your doctor's advice.
   (e) Fresh fruits and vegetables are sources of vitamins and minerals.

5. (a) Carpenter   (b) Architect
   (c) Zoo   (d) Church
   (e) Poet

6. (a) making   (b) liked
   (c) are   (d) rained
   (e) write

7. (a) It does not make any difference whether the teacher is male or female. Mail this letter positively today.
   (b) Pray to God for peace of mind. He was an easy prey for the cheats.
   (c) Do not break the glass. Apply brakes to stop the bicycle.
   (d) Pour some water in the bottle. There are many porer in the filter.
   (e) You must buy a book today. He walks by the help of a stick.

8. (a) He gave me my book hand to hand.
   (b) The swing moved to and fro.
   (c) We reached there safe and sound.
   (d) I play football off and on.
   (e) By and by the tortoise reached its destination.

9.
Janakpuri, Delhi
Date ....

Dear Rahul,

It was a moment of joy to receive your letter and learn that you are planning to come to Delhi and stay with us during the Winter vacation. You are most welcome and in fact I shall be waiting for you impatiently. Definitely it will be a nice time for you and me to go around the city and see the beautiful places and historical monuments.

Delhi is a place worth visiting. You will enjoy seeing the Red Fort, then the Mughal dynasty's remains. The beautiful Lotus temple, Kalkaji Mandir, the Mughal Gardens and Kalindi Kunj are other attractions which you would love to see. The Qutab Minar, Ashoka Pillar, Purana Quila and the Jama Masjid are typical examples of architecture and stone work. You will definitely enjoy boating near the zoo and the exciting ride on the metro rail. The Rastrapati Bhavan, Supreme Court, Parliament House will really fill you with pride. You can pay homage to the Samadhis of Mahatma Gandhi at Rajghat, Indira Gandhi at Shaktisthal and various other leaders. For shopping, I shall take you to Chandni Chowk, Connaught Place, Sarojini Nagar and Palika bazaar. Of course, I shall not miss the opportunity to go to malls and movies with you at the various PVRs that have started mushrooming up in the city.

I shall start making all the arrangements and preparation right from today.

Waiting impatiently for your arrival.

Your loving friend,
Mohan

10. Mohinder Singh from his childhood remained absorbed in thoughts. He was always pondering over some or the other problem. In school/ college days, he was always busy with his studies and was on the look out to show his talent and calibre. Here he got a chance. During emergency, he got selected for commission and opted for intelligence corps.

While serving in operational/forward area, he found some torn-out pieces of paper near the bank of a canal, adjacent to enemy borders. He collected and joined these papers, which were thrown away by the enemy (in hurry). These papers contained enemy's plan for attack. Mohinder after careful study of these papers took them to his commander; (who mobilised his trap). Enemy man of attack proved futile, as the Armed troops on our side were fully prepared. Hence our country won the day.

PAPER-II : INTELLIGENCE TEST

Time : 40 Minutes.   **Max. Marks : 100**

Directions (Qs. 1 to 5): *Spot-out odd/extra/wrong number.*

1. 256, 324, 289, 225, 144, 123.
   (*a*) 324   (*b*) 225
   (*c*) 144   (*d*) 123

2. 64, 36, 49, 25, 16, 13, 9.
   (*a*) 49   (*b*) 16
   (*c*) 13   (*d*) 25

3. 35, 28, 42, 49, 14, 53, 63.
   (*a*) 28   (*b*) 49
   (*c*) 53   (*d*) 63

4. 17, 23, 59, 31, 14, 13, 17.
   (*a*) 14   (*b*) 23
   (*c*) 59   (*d*) 31

5. 16, 18, 20, 12, 4, 8.
   (*a*) 16   (*b*) 18
   (*c*) 20   (*d*) 8

Directions (Qs. 6 to 10): *In the following questions you have to find which one of the given five choices will come next in the series:*

6. 31   7   25   13   19   19   13   .....
   (*a*) 14   (*b*) 20
   (*c*) 25   (*d*) 30

7. 3   125   7   25   11   5   15   .....
   (*a*) 19   (*b*) 16
   (*c*) 3   (*d*) 1

8. 4 $5\frac{1}{2}$ 7 $8\frac{1}{2}$ 10 $11\frac{1}{2}$ .....
   (*a*) 12   (*b*) $12\frac{1}{2}$

   (*c*) 13   (*d*) $13\frac{1}{2}$

9. 7   53   21   48   63   43   189   .....
   (*a*) 567   (*b*) 38
   (*c*) 48   (*d*) 42

10. 1   4   9   16   25   36   .....
   (*a*) 37   (*b*) 40
   (*c*) 45   (*d*) 49

Directions (Qs. 11 to 15): *For each of the following questions, four words have been given of which three are alike in someway and one is different. Find the odd word.*

11. (*a*) Blue   (*b*) Red
    (*c*) Yellow   (*d*) Dark

12. (*a*) Hop   (*b*) Dive
    (*c*) Jump   (*d*) Fall

13. (*a*) Mother   (*b*) Sister
    (*c*) Brother   (*d*) Aunt

14. (*a*) Writer   (*b*) Printer
    (*c*) Publisher   (*d*) Reader

15. (*a*) Microphone   (*b*) Microscope
    (*c*) Spectacles   (*d*) Telescope

Directions (Qs. 16 to 20): In each of the questions below, find out the correct answer from the given alternatives.

16. If FRIEND is coded as HUMJTK, how is CANDLE written in that code?
    (*a*) EDRIRL   (*b*) DCQHQK
    (*c*) FROBOC   (*d*) ESJFME

17. If in a certain code YELLOW is written as XFKMNX, how is COUNTRY coded?
(a) DPVOSQX   (b) BNTMSQX
(c) BPTMSSX   (d) AMSLRPW

18. If BATCH is coded as ABSDG, how is FORSAKE coded in that code?
(a) ABDGS   (b) EPQTZLD
(c) EQPZLTD   (d) GDSBA

19. In a certain code, RIPPLE is written as 613382 and LIFE is written as 8192. How is PILLER written in that code?
(a) 318826   (b) 318286
(c) 618826   (d) 328816

20. If PEOPLE is coded as PLPOEE, how is TREND coded?
(a) TREDN   (b) DNERT
(c) NDETR   (d) TNERD

21. 'Data Processing' is related to 'Raw Data' in the same way as 'University' is related to :
(a) Teacher   (b) Building
(c) Students   (d) Principal

22. 'Heart' is related to 'Blood' in the same way as 'Lung' is related to :
(a) Oxygen   (b) Chest
(c) Purification   (d) Air

23. 'Video' is related to 'Cassette' in the same way as 'Computer' is related to :
(a) Reels   (b) Recording
(c) Files   (d) Floppy

24. 'Much' is related to 'Many' in the same way as 'Measure' is related to :
(a) Count   (b) Calculate
(c) Quantity   (d) Weighs

25. 'Liberty' is related to 'Slavery' in the same way as 'Danger' is related to :
(a) Safety   (b) Dangerous
(c) Anger   (d) Stability

26. Some boys are sitting in a row. X is sitting 7th from right and Y is sitting 8th from. If there are 4 boys between X and Y. How many boys are there in the row?
(a) 9   (b) 8
(c) 10   (d) 7

27. Pointing to the lady, Anuj said, "She is the sister of the father of my mother's son". Who is the lady to Anuj.
(a) Niece   (b) Mother
(c) Aunt   (d) Sister

28. Six boys are sitting in a circle facing the centre. Gopal is to the left of Sachin, Sourav is between Ashok and Vikas. Ravi is between Ashok and Gopal. Who is left of Vikas.
(a) Gopal   (b) Ravi
(c) Ashok   (d) Sachin

29. The day before yesterday was saturday so tomorrow will be
(a) Friday   (b) Monday
(c) Wednesday   (d) Tuesday

30. The time on the watch is quarter to three. If the minute hand points to North-East. In which direction does the hour hand points.
(a) South-East   (b) South-West
(c) North-East   (d) North-West

Directions (Qs. 31 to 40): *Each of the following questions consist of problem figures followed by answer figures. Select a figure from amongst the answer figures which will continue the same series or pattern as established by the problem figures.*

31. Problem Figures

Answer Figures

(a)   (b)   (c)   (d)

32. Problem Figures

Answer Figures

(a)   (b)   (c)   (d)

33. Problem Figures

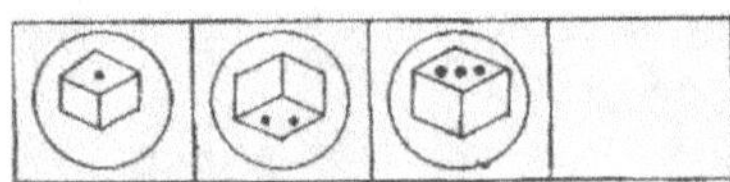

Answer Figures

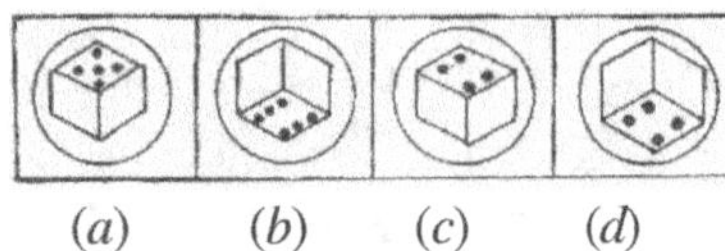

(*a*)　　(*b*)　　(*c*)　　(*d*)

34. Problem Figures

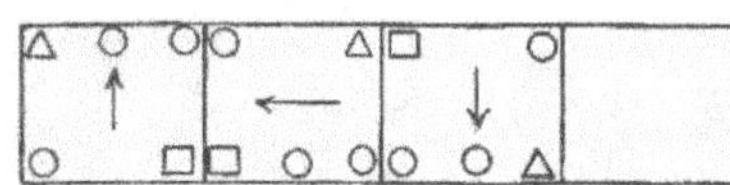

Answer Figures

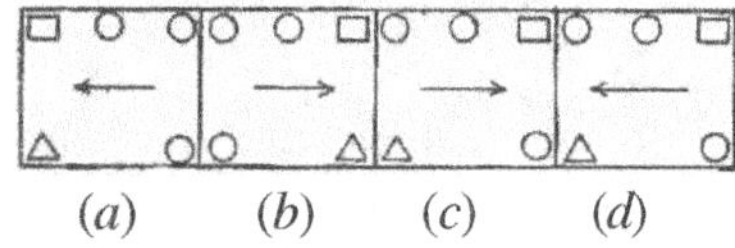

(*a*)　　(*b*)　　(*c*)　　(*d*)

35. Problem Figures

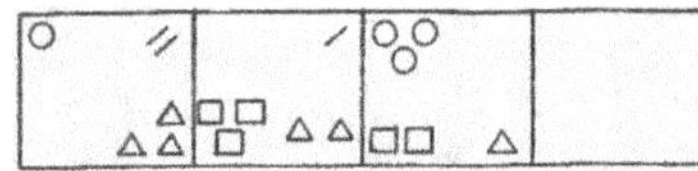

Answer Figures

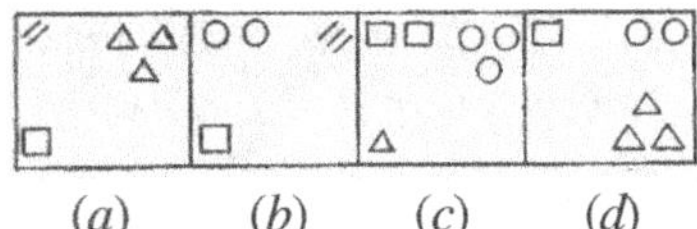

(*a*)　　(*b*)　　(*c*)　　(*d*)

36.

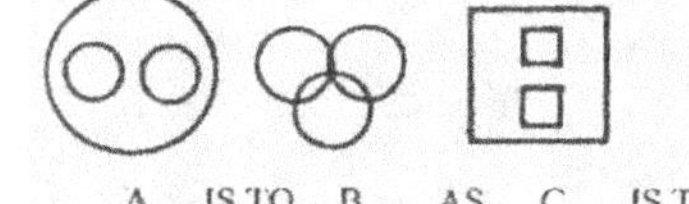

(*a*)　　(*b*)　　(*c*)　　(*d*)

37.

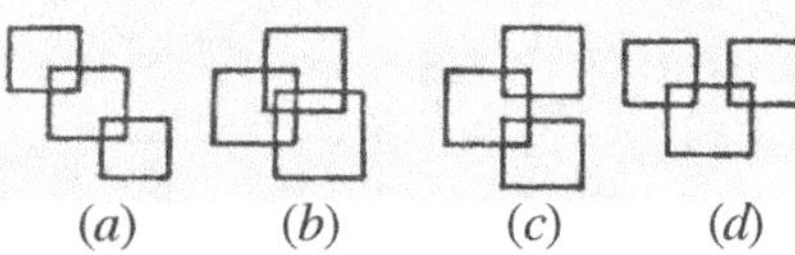

(*a*)　　(*b*)　　(*c*)　　(*d*)

38.

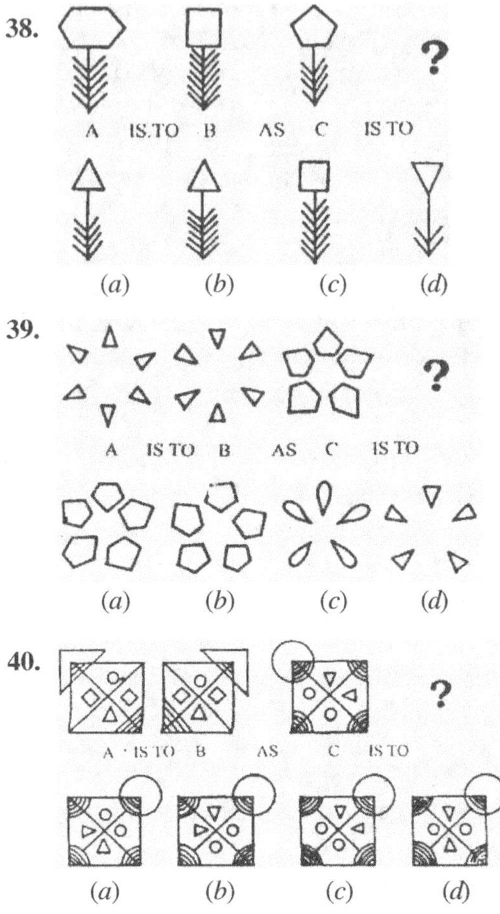

(*a*)　　(*b*)　　(*c*)　　(*d*)

39.

(*a*)　　(*b*)　　(*c*)　　(*d*)

40.

(*a*)　　(*b*)　　(*c*)　　(*d*)

Directions (Qs. 41 to 45): *In each of the following questions one of the figures is different from the rest. Spot the figure.*

41.

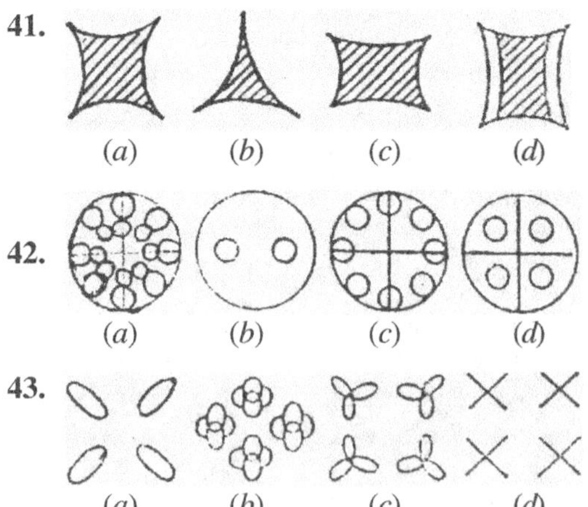

(*a*)　　(*b*)　　(*c*)　　(*d*)

42.

(*a*)　　(*b*)　　(*c*)　　(*d*)

43.

(*a*)　　(*b*)　　(*c*)　　(*d*)

44. 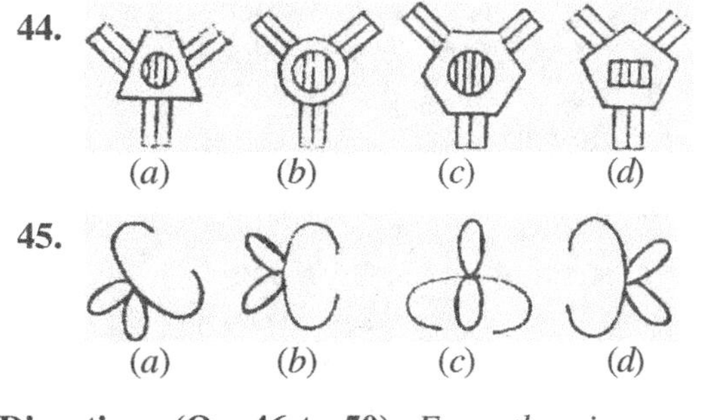

45.

Directions (Qs. 46 to 50): *From the given answer figures, select the one in which the question figure is hidden/embedded?*

46. 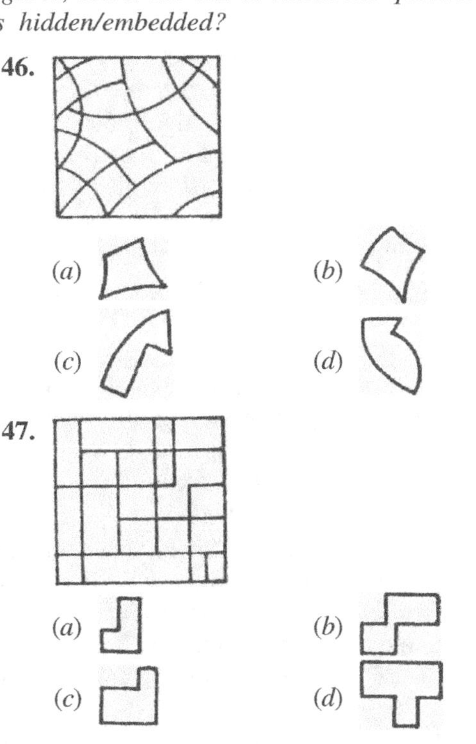

47.

48. 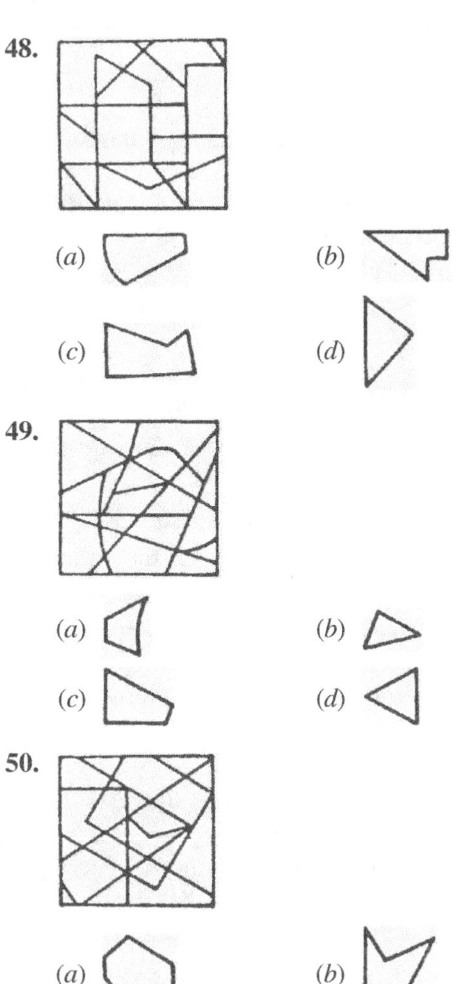

49.

50.

EXPLANATORY ANSWERS

1. (*d*): All other numbers can be expressed as a square of certain number, *i.e.*, $256 = (16)^2$.
2. (*c*): It is the only prime number.
3. (*c*): All other numbers are multiple of 7.
4. (*a*): All other numbers are prime.
5. (*b*): All other numbers are multiple of 4.
6. (*c*): In this alternate series the numbers in the first set starting with 31 have a difference of 6 in decreasing order. In the second set starting with 7 there is a difference of 6 in increasing order. So $19 + 6 = 25$.
7. (*d*): In this alternate series the first set starts with number 3 and increases each time with a difference of 4. In the second set beginning with number 125 the numbers are divided by 5 and so $5 \div 5 = 1$.

8. (*c*): The numbers in this series increase by $1\frac{1}{2}$, *i.e.,* $11\frac{1}{2} + 1\frac{1}{2} = 13$.

9. (*b*): In this alternate series the numbers in the first set 7, 21, 63 are multiplied by 3 and the second set 53, 48 three is a difference of 5 in decreasing order. So, $43 - 5 = 38$.

10. (*d*): In this series the increasing sequence of odd numbers 3, 5, 7, 8, 11 is added to 1, 4, 9, 16, 25. So $36 + 13 = 49$.

11. (*d*): Except (*d*), others are colours, while dark is the attribute of a colour.

12. (*d*): All other terms are related to different exercises.

13. (*c*): All others are female relationship.

14. (*d*): All the persons work for the Readers.

15. (*a*): All the terms except 'Microphone' are related to the vision.

16. (*a*): In the code, the first letter is the second alphabet, the second letter is the third alphabet, the third letter is the fourth alphabet and so on after the corresponding letter in the word.

17. (*c*): In the code, the letters in the odd places are one before and those in the even places are one ahead than the corresponding letter in the word.

18. (*b*): In the code, the letters at odd places are one place before and those at even place are one place after the corresponding letter in the word.

19. (*a*): The alphabets are coded as shown i.e., P as 3, I as 1, L as 8, E as 2 and R as 6. So, PILLER is code as 318826.

20. (*d*): In the code, keeping first and last letters the same, the second and second last, third and third last letters and so on are interchanged.

21. (*c*): 'Data processing' is the process of using 'Raw data' to shape it in the final product. Likewise, 'University' is the place which is used to shape the 'Students' for their career.

22. (*a*): 'Heart' is the organ which deals with the pumping and flow of 'Blood'. In the same way, 'Lungs' deals with the storage and flow of Oxygen.

23. (*d*): 'Cassette' is used as a software in the 'Video'. Similarly, 'Floppy' is used as a software in the 'Computer'.

24. (*a*): 'Much' is synonym of 'Many'. Similarly, 'Measure' is synonym of 'Count'.

25. (*a*): 'Liberty' is opposite to 'Slavery' and 'Danger' is opposite to 'Safety'.

26. (*a*): 27. (*c*): 28. (*a*):

29. (*d*): 30. (*b*):

31. (*c*): PF/2 is obtained from PF/1 by taking out the inner geometrical figure outside and putting a new figure inside. Similarly, AF/'C' is obtained from PF/3. Hence, AF/'C' completes the series.

32. (*a*): PF/2 is obtained from PF/1 by removing one '>' symbol to the right. Similarly, AF/A is obtained from PF/3. Hence, AF/A completes the series.

33. (*d*): PF/2 is obtained from PF/1 by rotating the die clockwise through 180° through 180° and adding one dot. Similarly, AF/'D' is obtained from PF/3. Hence, AF/'D' completes the series.

34. (*c*): PF/2 is obtained from PF/1 by rotating all the four geometrical figures clockwise through 90° and the arrow anti-clockwise through 90°. Similarly, AF/'C' is obtained from PF/3. Hence, AF/'C' completes the series.

35. (*b*): PF/2 is obtained from PF/1 by moving the internal units clockwise through length side of the square and replacing them by equal number of new units. Similarly, AF/'B' is obtained from PF/3. Hence, AF/'B' completes the series.

36. (*d*): 37. (*d*): 38. (*b*):

39. (*b*): 40. (*c*): 41. (*d*):

42. (*b*): 43. (*d*): 44. (*b*):

45. (*c*): 46. (*b*): 47. (*b*):

48. (*d*): 49. (*a*): 50. (*b*):

SAINIK SCHOOL ENTRANCE EXAM, 2013
(CLASS-VI)

PAPER-I : MATHEMATICS AND LANGUAGE

PART-A : MATHEMATICS

Section-I

1. Find the largest and smallest (least) numbers which can be formed by 5, 0, 7, 4.

2. The number 4318 should be divided by which number so that the quotient is 17?

3. The side of a square room is 12 m. Find the cost of carpeting the room at the rate of ₹ 5 per square metre.

4. Find the value: $1\dfrac{1}{2} + 2\dfrac{2}{3} - \dfrac{1}{6}$.

5. The cost of a dozen pens is ₹ 90. Find the cost of 20 such pens.

6. The marks obtained by a student in five examinations are 90, 92, 93, 95 and 90. Find his average marks.

7. What is 15% of ₹ 500?

8. Change 40 m/sec into km/hr.

9. In the given figure, AOB is a straight line.

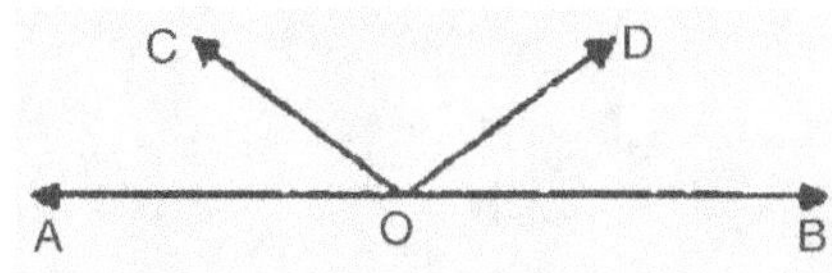

If $\angle AOC + \angle BOD = 85°$, then find the measure of $\angle COD$.

10. The side of a square is 25 m. What is the perimeter of the square.

Section-II

11. Simplify: $1 \div \left\{ \dfrac{1}{2} + \dfrac{1}{3} + \dfrac{1}{6} \div \left(\dfrac{3}{4} - \dfrac{1}{3} \right) \right\}$

12. If 15 men can do a piece of work in 20 days, in how many days can 25 men finish the same work?

13. The radius of a circle is 7 cm. Find its diameter, area and circumference.

14. Find the simple interest on ₹ 5,600/- at the rate of 5% per annum for a period of three years.

15. The LCM of two numbers is 630 and their HCF is 9. If one number is 90, then find out the other number.

16. In a school, 75% of the students are boys. If the number of girls is 420, find the number of boys in that school.

17. The angles of a triangle are in the ratio 1 : 2 : 3. Find the angles. Also write the type of the triangle.

18. Find the average of first ten counting numbers.

19. Find the square root of $5\dfrac{19}{25}$.

20. The radius of a wheel is 35 cm. How much distance will it travel in 100 revolutions?

Section-III

21. A town's population is 2,65,000. In which 40% are males, 30% females and rest are children. Find out the number of males, females and children in the town.

22. The average age of a class of 40 students is 18 years. When a teacher joins them, their average age becomes 19 years. Find the teacher's age.

23. The angles of a triangle are in the ratio of 2 : 3 : 5. Find the angles of the triangle.

24. A man sold two radios at ₹ 924/- each. On one he gains 20% on another he loses 20%. How much does he gain or lose in the whole transaction?

25. Find the area of the figure given below:

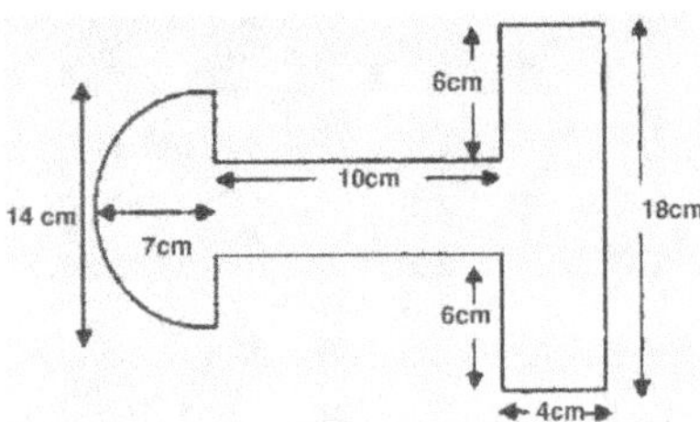

26. How many bricks, each measuring 25 cm × 12.5 cm × 7.5 cm will be needed to construct a wall 15 m long, 1.8 m high and 37.5 cm thick?

27. Calculate the time in which ₹ 1,250/- would become ₹ 1,375/- at 4% rate of interest per annum?

28. A number is divided into two parts such that their sum is 246. One part is twice the other. Find the two parts.

29. How many wooden cubical blocks of edge 20 cm can be cut from a log of wood of size 8 m × 5 m × 80 cm, assuming there is no wastage.

30. The perimeter of a square and circumference of a circle are each equal to 44 cm. Find their areas. Which area is greater and by how much?

EXPLANATORY ANSWERS

1. Given number = 5, 0, 7, 4

Largest number = 7540

Smallest number = 4057.

2. Required number = 4318 ÷ 17 = 254.

3. Side of square = 12 m

Area of square = 12 × 12 = 144 m^2

Cost of 1 m^2 = ₹ 5

Cost of 144 m^2 = ₹ 144 × 5 = ₹ 720.

4. $1\dfrac{1}{2} + 2\dfrac{2}{3} - \dfrac{1}{6} = \dfrac{3}{2} + \dfrac{8}{3} - \dfrac{1}{6}$

$= \dfrac{9 + 16 - 1}{6} = \dfrac{24}{6} = 4.$

5. Cost of 12 pens = ₹ 90

Cost of 20 pens = ₹ $\dfrac{90}{12} \times 20$ = ₹ 150.

6. Average marks $= \dfrac{90 + 92 + 93 + 95 + 90}{5}$

$= \dfrac{460}{5} = 92.$

7. 15% of ₹ 500

$= \dfrac{15}{100} \times ₹\ 500 = ₹\ 75.$

8. 40 m/s $= 40 \times \dfrac{18}{5}$ km/hr

$= 8 \times 18 = 144$ km/hr.

9.

∵ ∠AOC + ∠COD + ∠BOD = 180°

∠COD = 180 − 85 = 95°

[∵ ∠AOC + ∠BOD = 85°].

10. Side of a square = 25 m

Perimeter of square = 4 × 25 = 100 m.

11. Simplify : $1 \div \left\{ \dfrac{1}{2} + \dfrac{1}{3} + \dfrac{1}{6} \div \left(\dfrac{3}{4} - \dfrac{1}{3} \right) \right\}$

$= 1 \div \left\{ \dfrac{1}{2} + \dfrac{1}{3} + \dfrac{1}{6} \div \left(\dfrac{9 - 4}{12} \right) \right\}$

$= 1 \div \left\{ \dfrac{1}{2} + \dfrac{1}{3} + \dfrac{1}{6} \times \dfrac{12}{5} \right\}$

$$= 1 \div \left\{ \frac{1}{2} + \frac{1}{3} + \frac{2}{5} \right\} = 1 \div \left\{ \frac{15 + 10 + 12}{30} \right\}$$

$$= 1 \div \frac{37}{30} = 1 \times \frac{30}{37} = \frac{30}{37}.$$

12. 15 men can do a work in 20 days

25 men can do the same work in

$$\frac{20 \times 15}{25} = 12 \text{ days.}$$

13. The radius of circle = 7 cm

Diameter of circle = 2 × 7 = 14 cm

$$\text{Area of circle} = \pi r^2 = \frac{22}{7} \times 7 \times 7$$

$$= 154 \text{ cm}^2$$

Circumference of circle = $2\pi r$

$$= 2 \times \frac{22}{7} \times 7$$

$$= 44 \text{ cm.}$$

14. Simple Interest $= \dfrac{p \times r \times t}{100}$

$$= \frac{5600 \times 5 \times 3}{100} = ₹\ 840.$$

15. Other number $= \dfrac{\text{LCM} \times \text{HCF}}{\text{One number}}$

$$= \frac{630 \times 9}{90} = 63$$

16. Let total number of students = x

According to question,

25% of x = 420

$$\Rightarrow \quad \frac{25}{100} \times x = 420$$

$$\Rightarrow \quad x = 1680$$

No. of boys = 1680 − 420 = 1260.

17. $x + 2x + 3x = 180°$

$6x = 180° \Rightarrow x = 30°$

∴ Angles of triangle are 30°, 60°, 90°

One angle is 90°. Therefore it is right triangle.

18. Average $= \dfrac{1 + 2 + 3 + 4 + \ldots + 10}{10} = \dfrac{55}{10} = 5.5$

Second Method,

$$\text{Average} = \frac{10 \times 11}{2 \times 10} = \frac{11}{2} = 5.5.$$

19. Square root of $5\dfrac{19}{25} = \sqrt{\dfrac{144}{25}} = \dfrac{12}{5} = 2.4.$

20. $C = 2\pi r = 2 \times \dfrac{22}{7} \times 35 = 220$ cm

1 revolution = 220 cm

100 revolutions = 22000 cm = 220 m.

21. Number of males $= \dfrac{40}{100} \times 265000$

$$= 106000$$

Number of females $= \dfrac{30}{100} \times 265000$

$$= 79500$$

Number of children $= \dfrac{30}{100} \times 265000$

$$= 79500.$$

22. Total age of 40 students = 40 × 18

= 720 years

Total age with teacher = 41 × 19

= 779 years

∴ Age of teacher = 779 − 720

= 59 years.

23. $2x + 3x + 5x = 180°$

$10x = 180°$

$\Rightarrow \quad x = 18°$

Angles of triangle are 36°, 54°, 90°.

24.

First Radio	2nd Radio
SP = ₹ 924	SP = ₹ 924
Profit = 20%	Loss = 20%

$$\text{CP} = \frac{100}{120} \times 924 \qquad \text{CP} = \frac{100}{80} \times 924$$

$$= ₹\ 770 \qquad\qquad = 231 \times 5$$

$$\qquad\qquad\qquad = ₹\ 1155.$$

Total SP = 924 + 924 = ₹ 1848

Total CP = 770 + 1155 = ₹ 1925

Loss = CP − SP = 1925 − 1848 = ₹ 77.

25. Area of the figure = 18 × 4 = 72 cm^2

10 × 6 = 60 cm^2

$$\frac{1}{2} \times \frac{22}{7} \times 7 \times 7 = 77 \text{ cm}^2$$

Total area = 72 + 60 + 77

= 209 cm^2.

26.

$$\text{Volume of wall} = \frac{1500 \times 180 \times 375}{10} \text{ cm}^3$$

$$\text{Volume of each brick} = \frac{25 \times 125 \times 75}{10 \times 10} \text{ cm}^3$$

$$\text{Number of bricks} = \frac{1500 \times 180 \times 375 \times 10 \times 10}{25 \times 125 \times 75 \times 10}$$

$$= 2 \times 180 \times 12 = 4320.$$

27.

$$P = ₹\ 1250$$
$$A = ₹\ 1375$$
$$\text{S.I.} = A - P = 1375 - 1250 = ₹\ 125$$

$$\text{Time} = \frac{\text{S.I.} \times 100}{p \times r}$$

$$= \frac{125 \times 100}{1250 \times 4} = \frac{5}{2} = 2\frac{1}{2} \text{ years.}$$

28. According to question,

$$x + 2x = 246$$
$$\Rightarrow \quad 3x = 246$$
$$\Rightarrow \quad x = \frac{246}{3} = 82$$

So, the first part = x = 82
and, second part = $2x$ = 2 × 82 = 164.

29.

$$\text{Volume of cuboid} = 800 \times 500 \times 80 \text{ cm}^3$$
$$\text{Volume of cube} = 20 \times 20 \times 20 \text{ cm}^3$$

Number of cubical wooden blocks

$$= \frac{800 \times 500 \times 80}{20 \times 20 \times 20}$$

$$= 800 \times 5 = 4000.$$

30.

$$\text{Perimeter of square} = 44 \text{ cm}$$

$$\text{Side of square} = \frac{44}{4} = 11 \text{ cm}$$

$$\text{Area of square} = 11 \times 11 = 121 \text{ cm}^2$$

$$\text{Circumference of circle} = 44 \text{ cm}$$

$$\Rightarrow \quad 2 \times \frac{22}{7} \times r = 44$$

$$r = \frac{7 \times 44}{44} = 7 \text{ cm}$$

$$\text{Area of circle} = \pi r^2 = \frac{22}{7} \times 7 \times 7$$

$$= 154 \text{ cm}^2$$

Clearly area of circle is greater than area of square.

Difference = 154 − 121 = 33 cm^2.

PART-B : LANGUAGE ABILITY

1. Write an essay in 15 sentences on any one of the following topics:

(*a*) My Parents

(*b*) My Favourite Game

2. Read the following passage carefully and answer the questions:

We should eat green vegetables and fresh fruits to remain healthy. The use of carrot, peas, cabbage and spinach protect us from diseases whereas apple, papaya, orange, pomegranate and mango give us energy. Vegetarian food is considered healthier than the non-vegetarian food. We should also avoid fried food stuff. Samosas, Burger, Pizza and Pakodas weaken our digestive system. Chocolates and toffees are the biggest enemies of our teeth. In order to remain healthy, we should inculcate good eating habits.

(*a*) Give a suitable title for the above passage.

(*b*) What should we eat in order to remain healthy?

(*c*) What are the benefits of eating fruits?

(*d*) Name the food items which weaken our digestive system.

(*e*) What are the two main enemies of our dental health?

3. Make a sentence of your own for each underlined word given in the following passage. Do not copy any sentence from the given paragraph.

Do you support a football or hockey team? Perhaps you follow the success of your national cricket team. You know every game has its own importance and follows its own discipline. To become a good player of any game you need to have a <u>regular</u> practice of that game. Learning basic skills of the game is very <u>essential</u>.

(a) ....

(b) ....

(c) ....

(d) ....

(e) ....

4. Form meaningful sentences of the following by rearranging the words/phrases in proper order.

(a) both/likes/Mahesh/and dancing/singing

(b) a lot/cries/baby brother/our

(c) to watch/go out/we/on Saturdays/cinema

(d) of milk/gives/cow/neighbour's/our/a lot

(e) the washing/does/father/on Sundays/my

5. Give one word for the following:

(a) One who paints..

(b) One who treats patients........................

(c) One who sings..

(d) Place where Muslims pray....................

(e) Group of twelve....................................

6. Use each of the word in separate sentences of your own to show the difference in the meaning of the words of the pairs given below:

(a) Pool, Pull..

....

(b) Pen, Pain..

....

(c) Birth, Berth..

....

(d) Their, There..

....

(e) Bare, Bear..

....

7. Write a letter to your uncle informing him why you want to join Sainik School for your further studies.

8. Change each of the following as directed:

(a) Health is wealth.
                    (Change into Interrogative)

(b) This is a lovely view.
                    (Change into Exclamatory)

(c) He likes swimming.
                    (Change into Negative)

(d) Aeroplanes fly in the air.
                    (Change verb to past tense)

(e) I see a dark cloud.
                    (Change into passive voice)

9. Write the opposite words for the following:

(a) Cheap   ....

(b) Safe   ....

(c) Tight   ....

(d) Deep   ....

(e) Smooth   ....

EXPLANATORY ANSWERS

1. (a)   **My Parents**

I belong to a small family. My father's name is Mr. ABC and mother's name is Mrs. XYZ. Both my parents are quite religious. Both of them are working. My father is a bank officer and my mother is a teacher. Both of them work very hard in their respective jobs. They work to run the family and to finance our educational expenses. When they return from their offices they are busy in household chorus like cooking and washing etc. In the evening, they help us in our studies. After the studies, they sit with us and have chats and play with us. We watch television and have dinner together. We go for a walk in the park together. They take care of our every small need. They are very health-conscious and always encourage us to adopt a healthy lifestyle. They love us very much and we also love them immensely.

2. (a) "Good Eating Habits".

(b) We should eat green vegetables and fresh fruits to remain healthy.

(c) We get energy by eating fruits.

(d) Samosas, Burgers, Pizzas and Pakodas weaken our digestive system.

(e) Chocolates and toffees are the two main enemies of our dental health.

3. (*a*) We must support a good cause.
(*b*) Work hard and success will be yours.
(*c*) We must observe discipline in whatever we do.
(*d*) We must do regular exercises.
(*e*) It is essential to wear uniform at school.

4. (*a*) Mahesh likes both singing and dancing.
(*b*) Our baby brother cries a lot.
(*c*) We go out to watch cinema on Saturdays.
(*d*) Our neighbour's cow gives a lot of milk.
(*e*) My father does the washing on Sundays.

5. (*a*) Painter
(*b*) Doctor
(*c*) Singer
(*d*) Mosque
(*e*) Dozen

6. (*a*) We jumped into the pool.
They pulled him out of the ditch.
(*b*) We write with a pen.
I had a little pain in my ear.
(*c*) I took birth in November.
There is no vacant berth in this coach.
(*d*) Their car was stolen.
Go there and send him here.
(*e*) Do not walk with bare foot.
I can not bear this pain any more.

7. ABC
Delhi
16/5 November, 20....
My dear Uncle,

How are you? I have received your letter in which you have asked me why I want to join Sainik School for further studies. There are many reasons behind this wish of mine. As you know, Sainik Schools are very prestigious schools and getting admission there itself is a matter of great pride. Secondly, their educational levels and teaching methods are of highest standards. Moreover, they lay great stress on discipline and all-round development of students. Apart from academic education, ample opportunities are provided for extra-curricular activities, sports and physical training also. Further, I also want to be an army officer like papa and you, so, this will be the right platform for me to start with. I believe you will also agree with me in this. Love & regards,

ABC

8. (*a*) Isn't health wealth?
(*b*) What a lovely view!
(*c*) He doesnot like swimming.
(*d*) Aeroplanes flew in the air.
(*e*) A dark cloud is seen by me.

9. (*a*) Costly
(*b*) Unsafe
(*c*) Loose
(*d*) Shallow
(*e*) Rough

PAPER-II : INTELLIGENCE TEST

Directions (Qs. 1 to 10): *For each of the following questions, four words have been given of which three are alike in someway and one is different. Find the odd word.*

1. (*a*) Frog   (*b*) Tortoise
(*c*) Crab   (*d*) Fish

2. (*a*) IVEF   (*b*) VEENS
(*c*) EINN   (*d*) VEIIDD

3. (*a*) Number   (*b*) Form
(*c*) Weight   (*d*) Size

4. (*a*) Commission   (*b*) Team
(*c*) Agenda   (*d*) Board

5. (*a*) Addition   (*b*) Subtract
(*c*) Multiplication   (*d*) Division

6. (*a*) Prod   (*b*) Sap
(*c*) Jab   (*d*) Thrust

7. (*a*) Flute   (*b*) Violin
(*c*) Guitar   (*d*) Sitar

8. (*a*) Conceal   (*b*) Divulge
(*c*) Cover   (*d*) Hide

9. (*a*) Pistol   (*b*) Sword
(*c*) Gun   (*d*) Rifle

10. (*a*) Aeroplane   (*b*) Bird
(*c*) Tanker   (*d*) Parachute

Directions (Qs. 11 to 15): *Find the odd number pair from the given alternatives.*

11. (*a*) 81   (*b*) 93
   (*c*) 66   (*d*) 72

12. (*a*) 186 - 69   (*b*) 168 - 570
   (*c*) 1001 - 100   (*d*) 5270 - 2936

13. (*a*) 6 3 8 5 2   (*b*) 5 2 6 3 8
   (*c*) 2 8 7 5 1   (*d*) 8 5 3 6 2

14. (*a*) 162   (*b*) 405
   (*c*) 567   (*d*) 644

15. (*a*) 156   (*b*) 201
   (*c*) 273   (*d*) 345

Directions (Qs. 16 to 20): *In each of the questions below, find out the correct answer from the given alternative.*

16. In a certain code, "CERTAIN" is coded as "XVIGZRM", "SEQUENCE" is coded as "HVJFVMXV". How would "REQUIRED" be coded?
   (*a*) VJIFWTRV   (*b*) WVJRIFVI
   (*c*) IVJFRIVW   (*d*) FJIVWVIR

17. If in a certain code HYDROGEN is written as JCJZYSSD, then how can ANTIMONY be written in that code?
   (*a*) CPVKOQPA   (*b*) CRZQWABO
   (*c*) ERXMQSRC   (*d*) GTZOSUTE

18. If DELHI is coded as 73541 and CALCUTTA as 82589662, then how can CALICUT be coded?
   (*a*) 5279431   (*b*) 5978013
   (*c*) 8251896   (*d*) 8543691

19. If HONESTY is written as 5132468 and POVERTY as 7192068, how is HORSE written in a certain code?
   (*a*) 50124   (*b*) 51042
   (*c*) 51024   (*d*) 52014

20. In a certain code SISTER is written as RHRSDQ. How is UNCLE written in that code?
   (*a*) TMBKD   (*b*) TBMKD
   (*c*) TVBOD   (*d*) TMKBD

Directions (Qs. 21 to 25): *Which one set of letters when sequentially placed at the gaps in the given letters series shall complete it?*

21. a_ba_c_aad_aa_ea
   (*a*) babbd   (*b*) babbc
   (*c*) bacde   (*d*) babbb

22. aa_aa bb_b_aa_aa bb_bb.
   (*a*) bbbba   (*b*) aabbb
   (*c*) babba   (*d*) bbbaa

23. _cb_cab_baca_cba_ab
   (*a*) cabcb   (*b*) abccb
   (*c*) bacbc   (*d*) bcaba

24. reoc, pgme, nikg, lkii, ?
   (*a*) acef   (*b*) jmgk
   (*c*) efgh   (*d*) wxyz

25. (?), PSVYB, EHKNQ, TWZCF, ILORU
   (*a*) BEHKN   (*b*) ADGJM
   (*c*) SVYBE   (*d*) ZCFIL

Directions (Qs. 26 to 30): *Complete the following series.*

26. 8, 15, 36, 99, 288, ?
   (*a*) 368   (*b*) 676
   (*c*) 855   (*d*) 908

27. 4, 196, 16, 169, ?, 144, 64
   (*a*) 21   (*b*) 81
   (*c*) 36   (*d*) 32

28. 0, 4, 18, 48, ?, 180
   (*a*) 58   (*b*) 68
   (*c*) 84   (*d*) 100

29. 36, 28, 24, 22, ?
   (*a*) 18   (*b*) 19
   (*c*) 21   (*d*) 22

30. 7, 9, 13, 21, 37, ?
   (*a*) 58   (*b*) 63
   (*c*) 69   (*d*) 72

Directions (Qs. 31 to 35): *Each of the following questions consist of problem figures followed by answer figures. Select a figure from amongst the answer figures which will continue the same series or pattern as established by the problem figures.*

31. Problem Figures

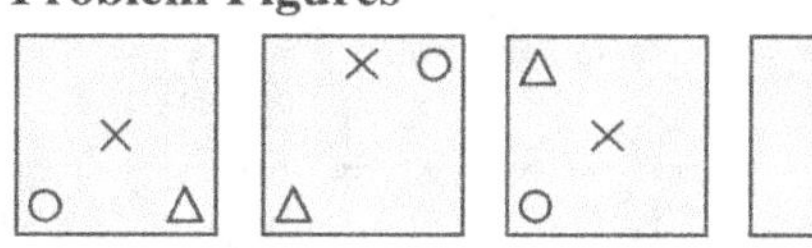

Answer Figures

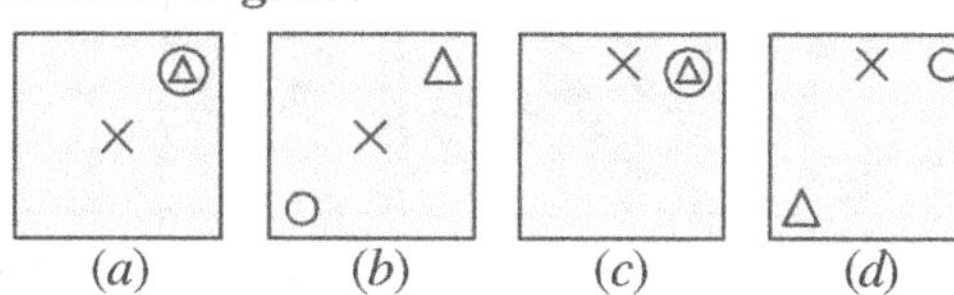

32. Problem Figures

 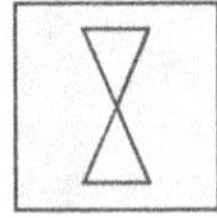 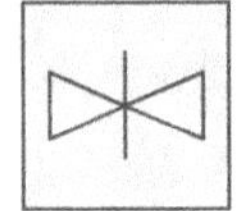 

Answer Figures

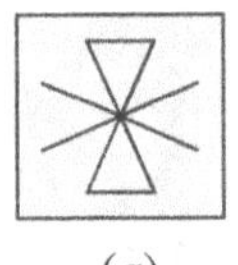 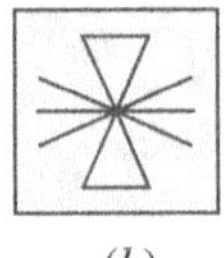 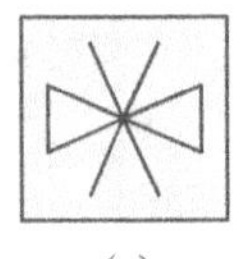 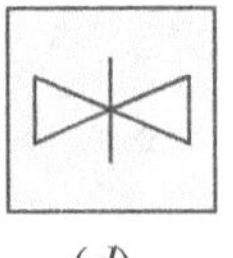

    (a)   (b)   (c)   (d)

33. Problem Figures

 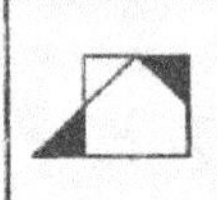  

Answer Figures

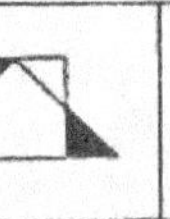   

    (a)   (b)   (c)   (d)

34. Problem Figures

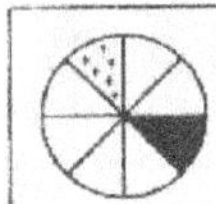  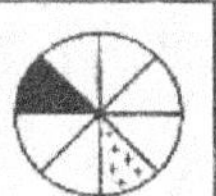 

Answer Figures

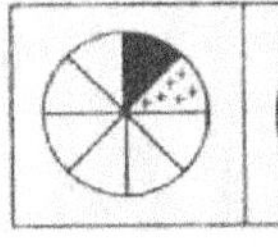  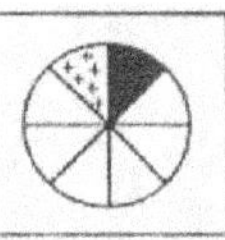 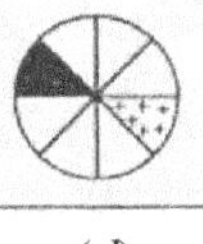

    (a)   (b)   (c)   (d)

35. Problem Figures

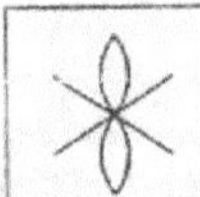   

Answer Figures

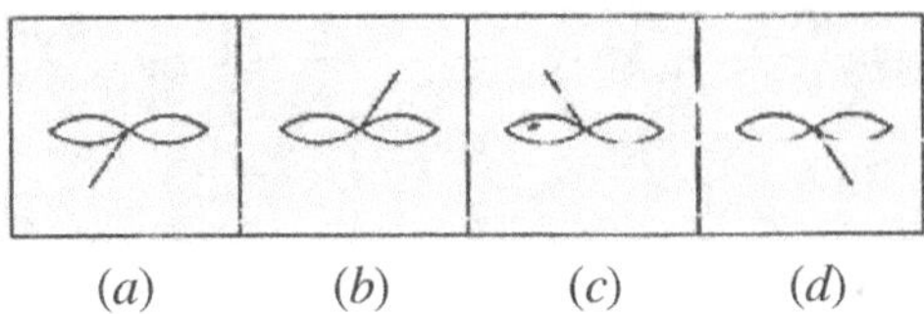

    (a)   (b)   (c)   (d)

Directions (Qs. 36 to 40): *The second figure in the first unit of the Problem Figures bears a certain relationship to the first figure. Similarly, one of the figures in the Answer Figures bears the same relationship to the first figure in the second unit of the Problem Figures. Locate the figure which would fit the question mark.*

36. Problem Figures

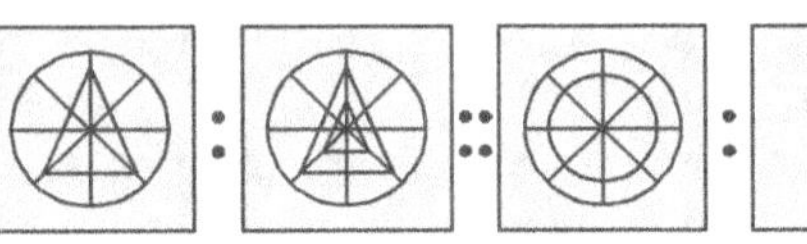

Answers Figures
उत्तर आकृतियाँ

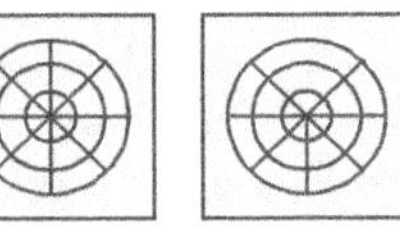 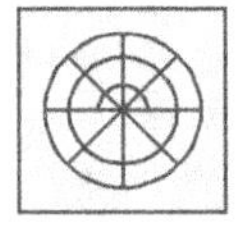 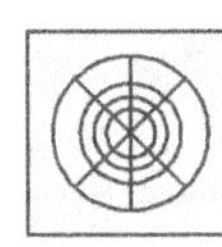

    (a)   (b)   (c)   (d)

37. Problem Figures

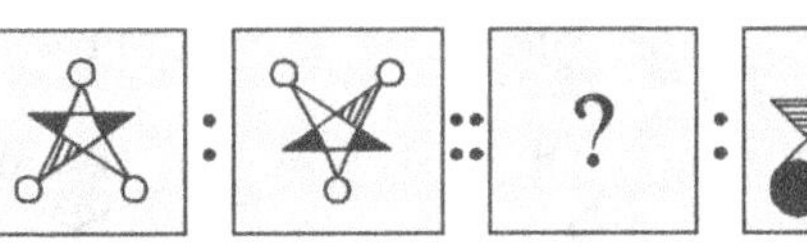

Answer Figures

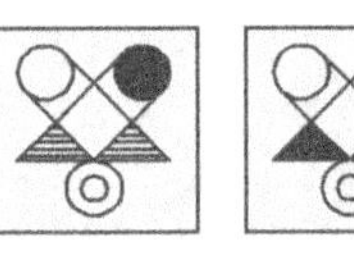   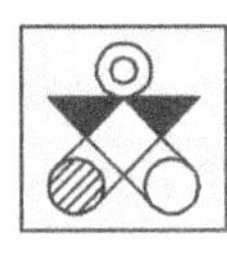

    (a)   (b)   (c)   (d)

38. Problem Figures

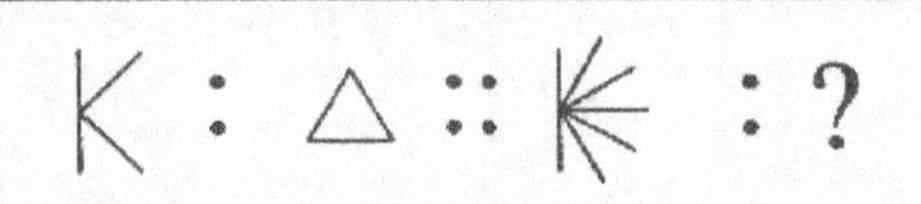

Answer Figures

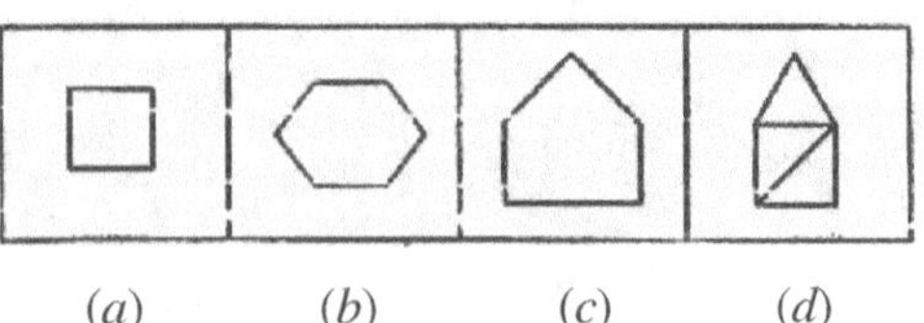

    (a)   (b)   (c)   (d)

39. Problem Figures

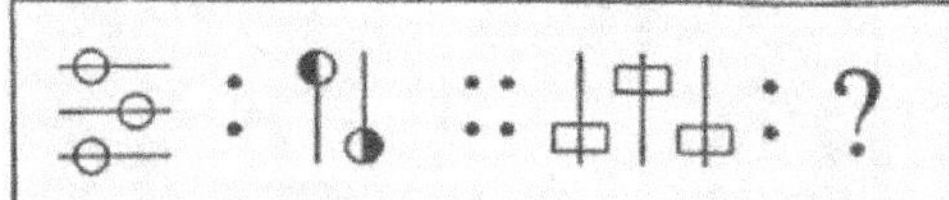

Answer Figures

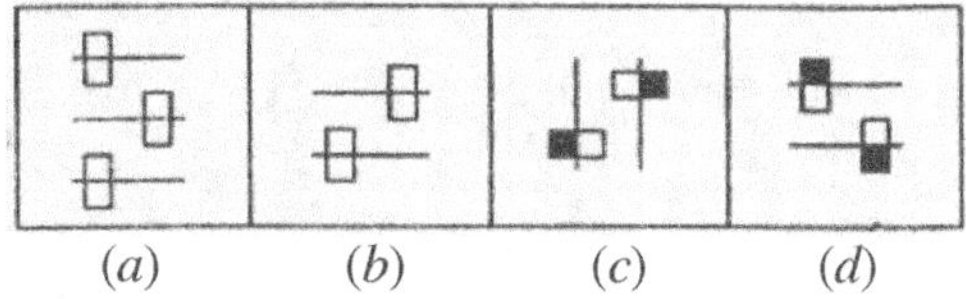

(a)   (b)   (c)   (d)

40. Problem Figures

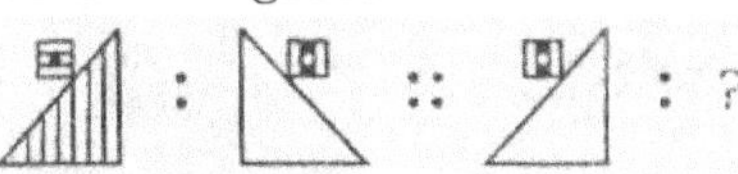

Answer Figures

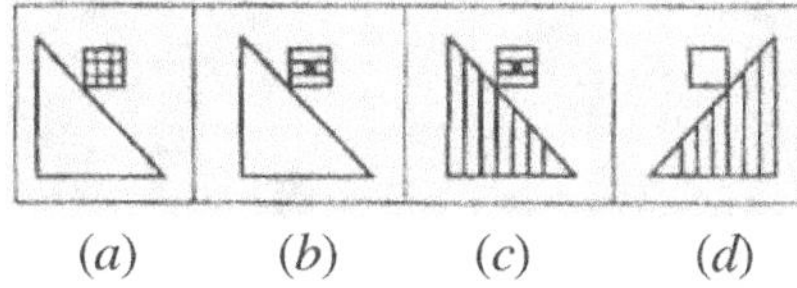

(a)   (b)   (c)   (d)

Directions (Qs. 41 to 45): *In each of the following questions one of the figures is different from the rest. Spot the figure.*

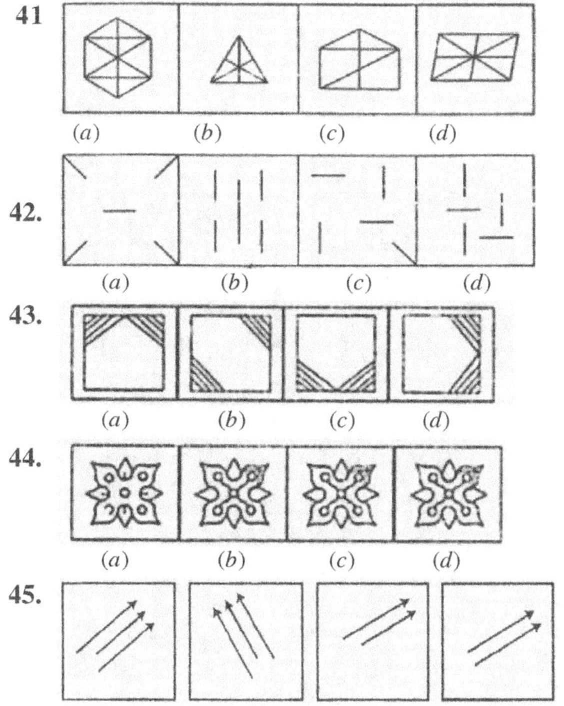

41

(a)   (b)   (c)   (d)

42.

(a)   (b)   (c)   (d)

43.

(a)   (b)   (c)   (d)

44.

(a)   (b)   (c)   (d)

45.

(a)   (b)   (c)   (d)

Directions (Qs. 46 to 50): *From the given answer figures, select the one in which the question figure is hidden/embedded.*

46. Question figure:

Answer figures:

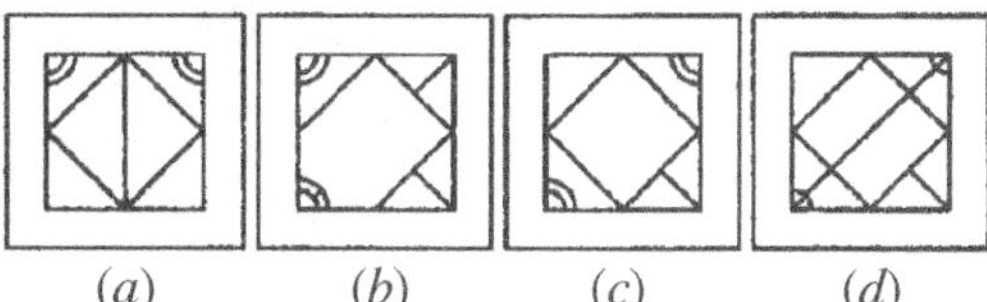

(a)   (b)   (c)   (d)

47. Question Figure:

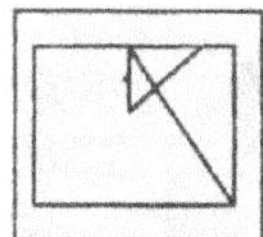

Answer Figures:

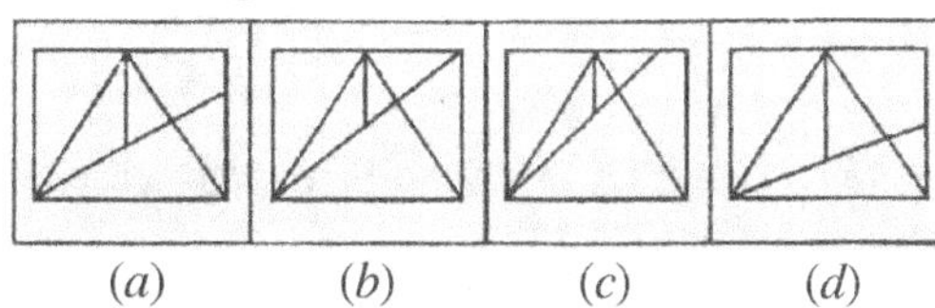

(a)   (b)   (c)   (d)

48. Question Figure:

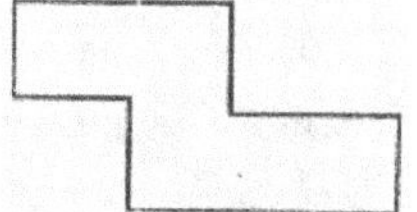

Answer Figure:

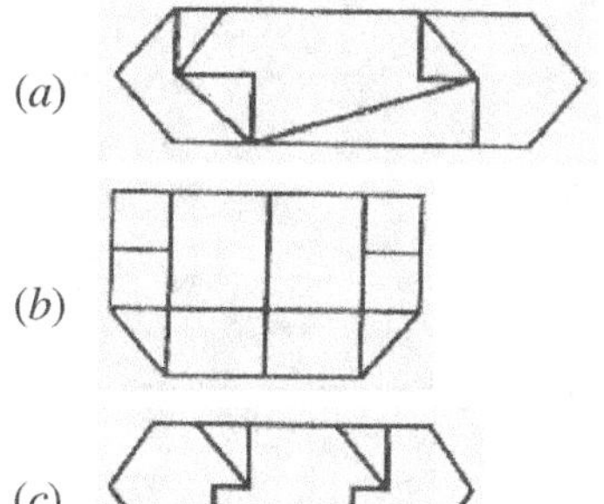

(a)

(b)

(c)

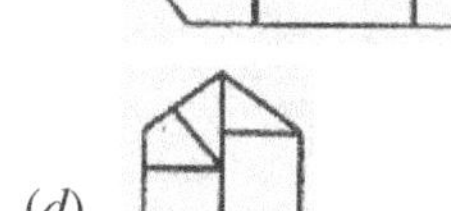

(d)

49. Question Figure

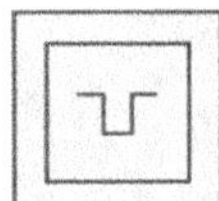

Answer Figures

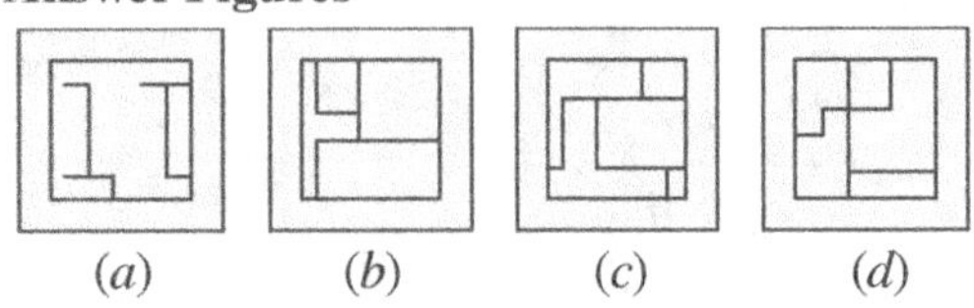

(*a*) (*b*) (*c*) (*d*)

50. Question Figure:

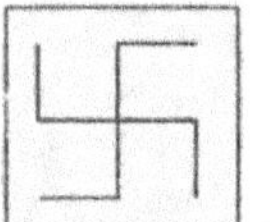

Answer Figures:

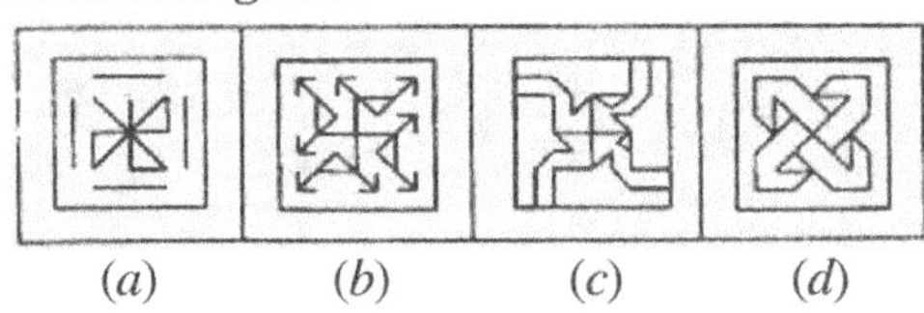

(*a*) (*b*) (*c*) (*d*)

EXPLANATORY ANSWERS

1. (*d*) : Fish swims in water only while rest all are amphibians.

2. (*d*) : Every group of letters have two vowels except 'VEIIDD'.

3. (*b*) : Form can not be calculated but rest all can be calculated.

4. (*c*) : Agenda is not a collective word but rest all are collective.

5. (*b*) : Subtract is a verb while rest all are noun.

6. (*b*)

7. (*a*)

8. (*b*) : Except (*b*), all has similar sense.

9. (*b*)

10. (*c*) : Except (*c*), all are moving in the sky.

11. (*a*) : Only 81 is a perfect square.

12. (*b*) : In every pair of numbers the first number is greater than the second. But in option (*b*) the second number is greater than the first.

13. (*c*) : Only 28751 is odd number, rest all are even numbers.

14. (*d*) : Rest all the numbers are divided by 3.

15. (*b*) : Sum of digits are 12.

16. (*c*) :

C E R T A I N
X V I G Z R M

S E Q U E N C E
H V J F V M X V

Hence, R E Q U I R E D = I V J F R I V W.

17. (*b*)

18. (*c*)

19. (*b*) :

H O N E S T Y
↓ ↓ ↓ ↓ ↓ ↓ ↓
5 1 3 2 4 6 8

P O V E R T Y
↓ ↓ ↓ ↓ ↓ ↓ ↓
7 1 9 2 0 6 8

Therefore,

H O R S E
↓ ↓ ↓ ↓ ↓
5 1 0 4 2

20. (*a*) :

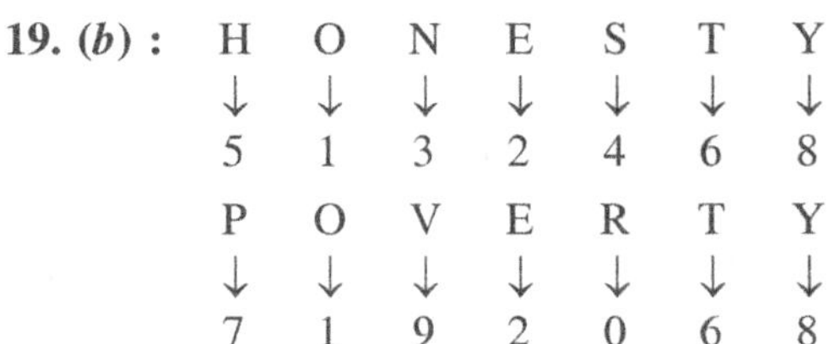

S I S T E R ⟶ R H R S D Q

Similarly,

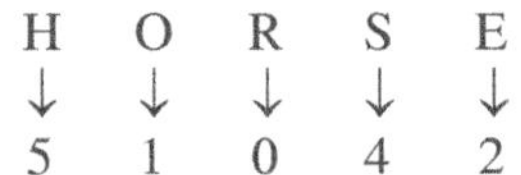

U N C L E ⟶ T M B K D

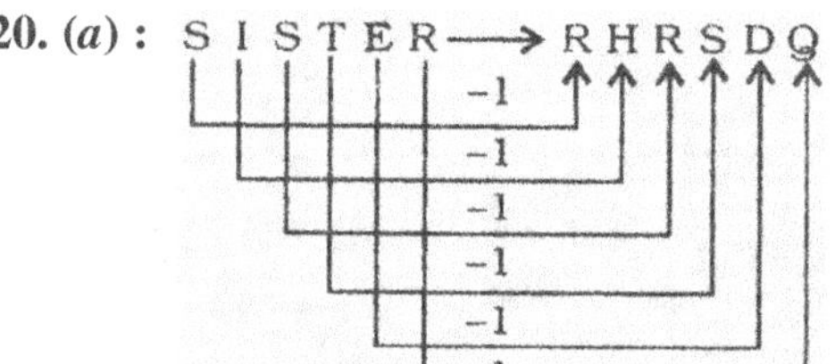

21. (*c*) : The correct sequence of letters is:

a b *ba* a *c* c *aad* d *aa* e *ea*

22. (c) : The correct sequence of letters is:

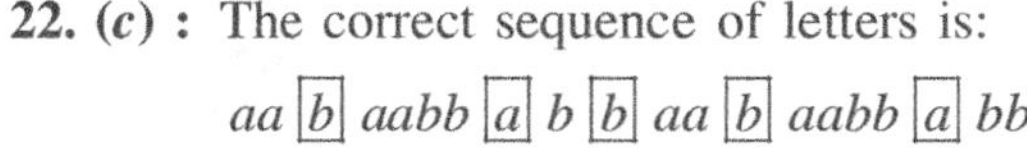

23. (c)

24. (b)

25. (b) : $P \xrightarrow{+3} S \xrightarrow{+3} V \xrightarrow{+3} Y \xrightarrow{+3} B$

$E \xrightarrow{+3} H \xrightarrow{+3} K \xrightarrow{+3} N \xrightarrow{+3} Q$

$T \xrightarrow{+3} W \xrightarrow{+3} Z \xrightarrow{+3} C \xrightarrow{+3} F$

$I \xrightarrow{+3} L \xrightarrow{+3} O \xrightarrow{+3} R \xrightarrow{+3} U$

Now, $P \xrightarrow{+3} T \cdot \bullet E \xrightarrow{+4} I$

Therefore, the first letter of the first term

should be $E \xrightarrow{-4} A$

$A \xrightarrow{+3} D \xrightarrow{+3} G \xrightarrow{+3} J \xrightarrow{+3} M$

26. (c) :
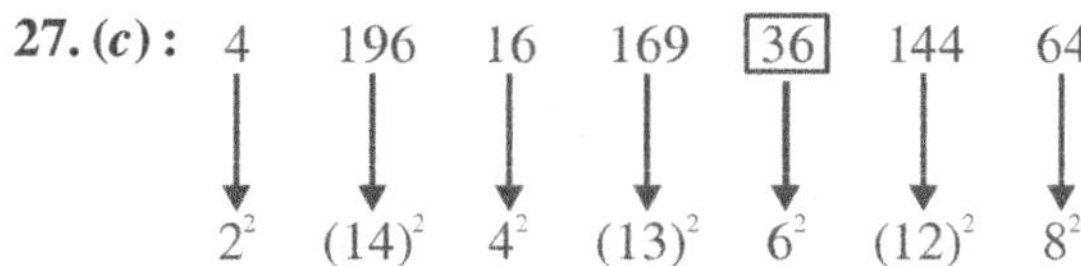

27. (c) :
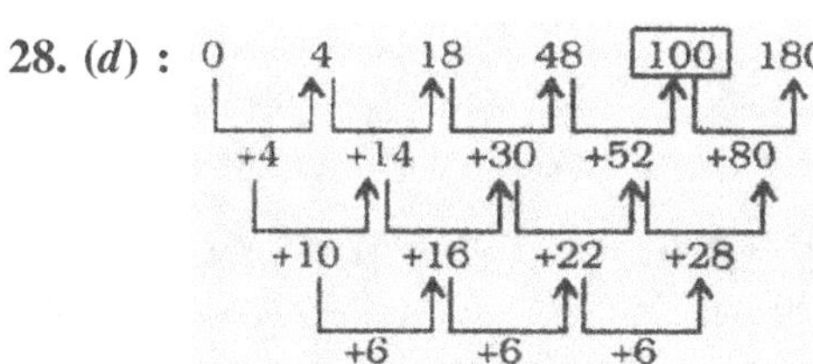

28. (d) :
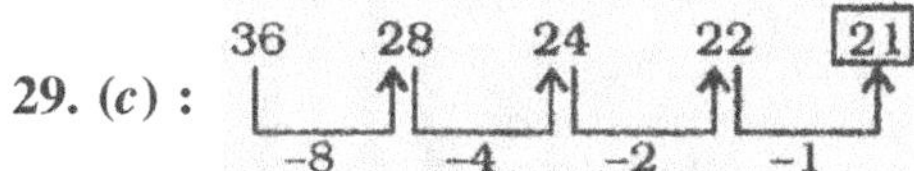

29. (c) :

30. (c) :
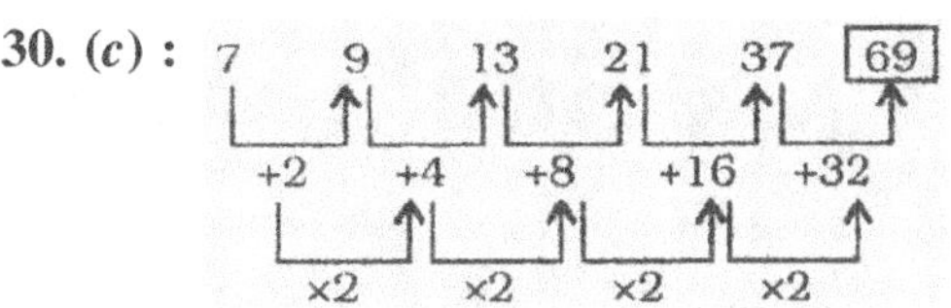

31. (c)

32. (a)

33. (d) : In each next figure, main design moves through 90° in clockwise direction.

34. (a)

35. (d) : In each next figure main design moves through 90° in anticlockwise direction and also having one less line segment.

36. (a)

37. (c)

38. (b) : The first figure is made by three lines, which changes into triangle in IInd figure. Similarly third figure is made by six lines, which changes as rhombus in IVth figure.

39. (d)

40. (c)

41. (c) : Except (c), in all figures, inside lines are making triangles.

42. (b)

43. (b)

44. (a)

45. (d) : In figure (d) both the arrows are same in length while in the rest figures the length of arrows are different.

46. (b)

47. (c)

48. (a)

49. (b)

50. (b)

Sainik School Entrance Exam, 2012
(CLASS-VI)

PAPER-I : MATHEMATICS AND LANGUAGE

PART-A : MATHEMATICS

Section-I

1. Write the smallest and greatest five digit numbers using 5, 0, 3, 7 and 4.

2. Find the product of 7765 and 137.

3. Find lowest common multiple of 2, 4 and 5.

4. Find the value of $3\frac{5}{7}$.

5. Find the sum of $1\frac{3}{5}$ and $2\frac{7}{10}$.

6. A lawn tennis match starts at 9:15 am and finishes at 4:10 pm. Find the duration of the match.

7. Convert 2222 hours into days and hours.

8. Which of the following can be the angles of a triangle?
   (a) 90°, 70°, 20°
   (b) 105°, 35°, 40°

9. Simplify: $\dfrac{11}{12} + \dfrac{15}{16} - \dfrac{13}{24}$.

10. Find the radius of a circle whose circumference is 79.2 cm. Given that $\pi = \dfrac{22}{7}$.

Section-II

11. State True or False:
    (a) The sum of four angles of a quadrilateral is 360°. ( )
    (b) A line segment has one end point. ( )
    (c) Every natural number is whole number. ( )

12. Find the interval between 7.25 AM and 3.10 PM.

13. If the average of 14, 17, 21 , 24, 26 and X is 20, then find the value of X.

14. Jubaida took a loan of Rs. 4000/- on 12% annual interest. After 3 years how much money she will have to return?

15. Add 3 hours 50 minutes 55 seconds to 4 hours 55 minutes 30 seconds.

16. A carpet is 5m.50 cm. long and 3m.25cm. broad. The carpet is surrounded by a lace. Find the length of the lace.

17. John plans to tile his kitchen floor with square tiles. Each side of the tile is 10 cm. His kitchen is 2.2 m long and 1.8 m wide. How many tiles will John need?

18. A pond is 5 m long, 4 m wide and 2.5 m deep. How much water does it contain?

19. A shopkeeper earns a profit of Rs. 80 by selling an article for Rs. 490. Find the cost price of the article.

20. The circumference of a circle is 22 cm. Find the radius of the circle.

Section-III

21. Ashok got 366 marks out of 600 and Brij Mohan got 300 marks out of 500. Whose score is better. Also find their per cent of marks.

22. Solve
    (a) 25.43 × 4.61
    (b) 526.880 ÷ 3.2

23. Arrange the following fractions in descending order:

5/8, 5/6, 2/7, 1/4, 1/2, 1/3.

24. Find out perimeter and area of the given diagram.

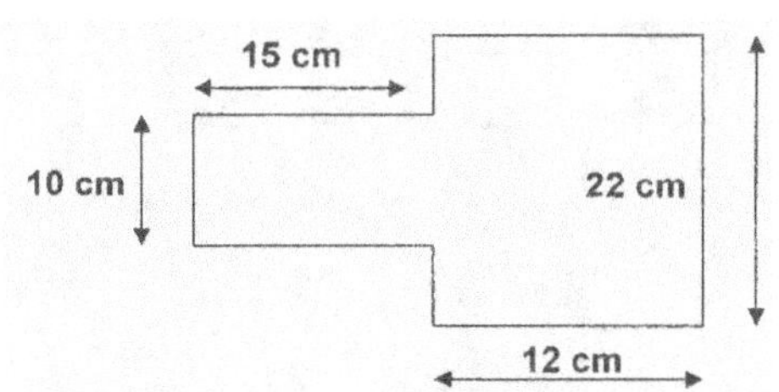

25. A, B and C have a total Rs. 4,600/-. The ratio of the money between B and C is 3:5. If share of A is Rs. 1,400/- then find shares of B and C. Whose share is minimum?

26. In a class the height of 6 students are 162 cm, 170 cm, 158 cm, 160 cm, 170 cm and 165 cm, respectively. Find the average of their height.

How many students are having more than average height?

27. Average of 9 numbers is 24. If the average of first 5 numbers is 23 and that of the last 5 is 26, find the fifth number.

28. Capacity of two types of containers is 6.5 litres and 9.5 litres, respectively. How much oil will be required to fill 6 tins of first type and 8 tins of second type of containers?

29. A swimming pool of 90 m. length and 60 m. breadth is to be laid with tiles of length 30 cm. and breadth 20 cm. Find the number of tiles required. Also find the total cost if cost of 100 tiles is Rs. 525.

30. How many stones of 0.50 m^2 can be fixed in a court yard of length 15 m and width 10 m. If cost of fixing one stone is Rs. 2.50, what will be the expenditure on fixing stones in the courtyard?

EXPLANATORY ANSWERS

1. Smallest number = 30457

Greatest number = 75430.

2.
$$
\begin{array}{r}
7\ 7\ 6\ 5 \\
1\ 3\ 7 \\
\hline
5\ 4\ 3\ 5\ 5 \\
2\ 3\ 2\ 9\ 5 \\
7\ 7\ 6\ 5 \\
\hline
1\ 0\ 6\ 3\ 8\ 0\ 5
\end{array}
$$

3.
$$
\begin{array}{c|ccc}
2 & 2, & 4, & 4 \\
\hline
 & 1, & 2, & 5
\end{array}
$$

L.C.M. = $2 \times 2 \times 5 = 20$

Hence L.C.M. of 2, 4 and 5 = 20.

4. $3\dfrac{5}{7} = \dfrac{26}{7}$.

5. $1\dfrac{3}{5} + 2\dfrac{7}{10} = \dfrac{8}{5} + \dfrac{27}{10}$

$= \dfrac{16+27}{10} = \dfrac{43}{10} = 4\dfrac{3}{10}$.

6. Duration of the match = hours minute

$$
\begin{array}{rr}
16 & 10 \\
-9 & 15 \\
\hline
6 & 55
\end{array}
$$

Hence, required time = 6 hrs 55 minutes.

7. $\dfrac{2222}{24}$ = 92 days and 14 hrs.

$$
\begin{array}{r}
92 \\
24\overline{)2222} \\
216 \\
\hline
62 \\
48 \\
\hline
14
\end{array}
$$

Hence, 2222 hrs. = 92 days and 14 hrs.

8. (*a*) Right angles triangle

(*b*) Obtuse angle triangle.

9. $\dfrac{11}{12} + \dfrac{15}{16} - \dfrac{13}{24} = \dfrac{44+45-26}{48}$

$= \dfrac{89-26}{48} = \dfrac{63}{48} = \dfrac{21}{16} = 1\dfrac{5}{16}$.

10. $C = 2\pi r$

$$79.2 = 2 \times \frac{22}{7} \times r$$

$$r = \frac{79.2 \times 7}{2 \times 22} = \frac{7 \times 3.6}{2} = 7 \times 1.8 = 12.6\,cm$$

$\therefore$ required radius = 12.6 cm.

11. (*a*) T   (*b*) F   (*c*) T.

12. Required time = 15.10 – 7.25

$$= 7.45$$
$$= 7 \text{ hrs } 45 \text{ minutes.}$$

13. Average $= \dfrac{14 + 17 + 21 + 24 + 26 + X}{6}$

$$20 = \frac{X + 102}{6}$$

$$X + 102 = 120$$
$$X = 120 - 102 = 18.$$

14. $SI = \dfrac{P \times r \times t}{100} = \dfrac{4000 \times 12 \times 3}{100}$

$$= 36 \times 40 = 1440$$

Amount = 4000 + 1440 = ₹ 5440.

15.

Hours	Minutes	Seconds
3	50	55
+ 4	55	30
8	46	25

Hence required sum = 8 hrs 46 minutes and 25 seconds.

16. Perimeter of the Carpet = 2(5.50 + 3.25)

$$= 2(8.75) = 17.50 \text{ m}$$

$\therefore$ Length of the lace = 5.50 + 3.25 + 5.50 + 3.25

$$= 17.50 \text{ m}$$
$$= 17 \text{ m and } 50 \text{ cm.}$$

17. Length of the kitchen = 2.2 m = 220 cm

breadth of the kitchen = 1.8 m = 180 cm

Area of the kitchen = 220 × 180 square cm

Area of each square tile = 10 × 10

$$= 100 \text{ square cm}$$

Number of tiles $= \dfrac{220 \times 180}{100} = 396.$

18. Volume of water in pond = $l \times b \times h$

$$= 5 \times 4 \times 2.5$$
$$= 50 \text{ m}^3.$$

19. SP of the article = ₹ 490

Profit = ₹ 80

Hence C.P. of the article = 490 – 80 = ₹ 410.

20. Circumference of a circle = $2\pi r$

$$22 = 2 \times \frac{22}{7} r$$

$$r = \frac{22 \times 7}{2 \times 22} = \frac{7}{2} = 3.5\,cm$$

Hence radius = 3.5 cm.

21. Ashok's marks $= \dfrac{366}{600} = 0.61$

% marks of Ashok $= \dfrac{366}{600} \times 100 = 61$

Brij Mohan's marks $= \dfrac{300}{500} = 0.60$

% marks of Brij Mohan $= \dfrac{300}{500} \times 100 = 60$

Clearly Ashok's score is better.

22. (*a*) $\dfrac{2543}{100} \times \dfrac{461}{100} = \dfrac{1172323}{10000} = 117.2323$

(*b*) $\dfrac{526.880}{3.2} = \dfrac{526880}{1000} \times \dfrac{10}{32}$

$$= \frac{52688}{10 \times 32} = \frac{3293}{20} = 164.65.$$

23. $\dfrac{5}{8}, \dfrac{5}{6}, \dfrac{2}{7}, \dfrac{1}{4}, \dfrac{1}{2}, \dfrac{1}{3}$

LCM of 8, 6, 7, 4, 2, 3 = 168

$$\frac{105, 140, 48, 42, 84, 56}{168}$$

Hence $\dfrac{5}{6}, \dfrac{5}{8}, \dfrac{1}{2}, \dfrac{1}{3}, \dfrac{2}{7}, \dfrac{1}{4}$ are in descending order.

24. Perimeter of the given figure

$$= 12 + 22 + 12 + 6 + 15 + 10 + 15 + 6$$
$$= 98 \text{ cm}$$

Area of the given diagram

$$= 10 \times 15 + 12 \times 22$$
$$= 150 + 264 = 414 \text{ cm}^2.$$

25. Total amount = ₹ 4600

A's share = ₹ 1400

Hence B's and C's share = 4600 − 1400

$$= ₹ \ 3200$$

$3x + 5x = 3200 \Rightarrow 8x = 3200$

$\therefore \quad x = 400$

B's share = 3 × 400 = ₹ 1200

C's share = 5 × 400 = ₹ 2000

Hence B's share is minimum.

26. Average height

$$= \frac{162 + 170 + 158 + 160 + 170 + 165}{6}$$

$$= \frac{985}{6} = 164.16 \text{ cm}$$

Number of students more than average height = 3.

27. According to the question,

$$24 \times 9 = 216$$
$$5 \times 23 = 115$$
$$5 \times 26 = 130$$

Hence fifth number = (115 + 130) − 216

$$= 245 − 216 = 29.$$

28. Required Oil = (6 × 6.5 + 8 × 9.5) litres

$$= (39 + 76) \text{ litres}$$
$$= 115 \text{ litres.}$$

29. Area of Swimming pool = 9000 × 5000 cm^2

Area of each tile = 30 × 20 cm^2

Number of tiles = $\dfrac{9000 \times 5000}{30 \times 20}$ = 75000

Cost of 100 tiles = ₹ 525

Cost of 75000 tiles = ₹ $\dfrac{525 \times 75000}{100}$ = ₹ 393750.

30. Area of court yard = 15 × 10 m^2

Area of 1 stone = 0.50 m^2 = $\dfrac{1}{2}$ m^2

Number of Stones = $\dfrac{15 \times 10}{\dfrac{1}{2}}$

$$= 15 \times 10 \times 2 = 300$$

Cost of 1 stone = ₹ 2.50

Cost of 300 stones = ₹ 300 × 2.50

$$= ₹ \ 750.$$

PART-B : LANGUAGE

1. Write an essay in 15 sentences on any one of the following topics:

(*a*) A Visit to Zoo

(*b*) My Favourite Sport

2. Read the following passage and answer the questions:

My own recollection is that I had not any high regard for my ability. I used to be surprised whenever I won prizes and scholarships. But I very jealously guarded my character. The least little blame drew tears from my eyes. When I merited, or seemed to the teacher to merit, a scolding, it was unbearable for me. I remember having once received physical punishment. I did not so much mind the punishment, as the fact I considered it as my dessert. I wept piteously. That was when I was in the first or second standard.   (M.K. Gandhi)

(*a*) What kind of regard did M.K. Gandhi has for his ability?

(*b*) How did M.K. Gandhi guard his character?

(*c*) What was unbearable for him?

(*d*) What did M.K. Gandhi do when once he received physical punishment?

(*e*) In which class was he studying at that time?

3. Make a sentence of your own for each underlined word given in the following passage. (Do not copy any sentence from the given paragraph):

The next evening, my mother told me that she had <u>spotted</u> another egg. Wonderful news! This meant we had a regular visitor. I have always <u>longed</u> for a pet, now I was lucky to own one! The next evening I <u>noticed</u> another egg and I was sure of our friend's <u>intentions</u>.

She had decided to make our roof her home!
The following day was the most <u>memorable</u> —
there were four eggs.

(a) ....

(b) ....

(c) ....

(d) ....

(e) ....

4. Form meaningful sentences by rearranging the words in proper order—
(a) Go/shall/tomorrow/we/picnic/for
(b) to/your/school?/do/how/go
(c) mistake/for/the/his/teacher/boy/punished
(d) plants/the/is/gardener/watering/the
(e) book?/which/your/is/favourite.

5. Use each of the following words in separate sentences of your own to show the difference in the meaning of the pairs given below:
(a) Write, Right
(b) Steel, Steal
(c) Two, Too
(d) Sheet, Seat
(e) Rain, Reign

6. Change each of the following as directed:
(a) Without effort nothing can be gained.
(Change into Interrogative)
(b) By this time tomorrow I shall have reached home. (Change into Negative)
(c) The moonlight very sweetly sleeps upon this bank. (Change into Exclamatory)
(d) If only I had a good horse!
(Change into Assertive)
(e) Shall I ever forget those happy days?
(Change into Assertive)

7. Fill in the blanks by using the correct form of verb given in bracket:
(a) He .... a letter to his father yesterday. (Write)
(b) The cat .... on the rug. (Sleep)
(c) Cocks .... in the morning. (Crow)
(d) I have already .... my application to the Principal. (Send)
(e) The Moon .... early last night. (Rise)

8. Choose the correct article (a, an or the) and fill in the blanks.
(a) He is .... honourable member of the society.
(b) He looks as stupid as .... owl.
(c) Let us discuss .... matter seriously.
(d) Yesterday .... European came to visit our school.
(e) You are .... fool to say that.

9. Write antonyms of the following words:
(a) Young ....
(b) Warm ....
(c) Comfort ....
(d) Happy ....
(e) Big ....

EXPLANATORY ANSWERS

1. (A)　　　　**A Visit to Zoo**

A visit to a zoo is quite interesting. It has an educative and recreational value too. It gives us practical knowledge of different types of animals and birds. I along with my classmates had a chance to visit a zoo in Delhi.

Our class-teacher bought entrance tickets and we went into zoo. First of all we saw a lion inside a cage. He looked weak but still roared and moved about here and there. In the next cage, there were some monkeys, who were chattering and making nice gestures. They jumped from one bar to another. We threw grains and corns etc. and they readily accepted.

At a short distance, there was a pond of water, where some ducks, swans and cranes were swimming. Crocodiles and rhinoes were also lying in the adjacent ponds. Next we saw different kinds of animals like zebras, kangaroos, ostriches, camels, elephants, wild-horses, neel-gais, cheetahs and tigers etc. Peacocks were seen dancing while sparrows of various colours and beautiful parrots were twittering. Lastly we saw cobras and poisonous snakes; some lying on ground, while others were entering holes nearby.

2. (*a*)   M.K. Gandhi had no high regard for his ability.
   (*b*)   M.K. Gandhi jealously guarded his character.
   (*c*)   A scolding was unbearable for him.
   (*d*)   M.K. Gandhi wept bitterly when he received physical punishment.
   (*e*)   He was studying in first or second class at that time.

3. (*a*)   He easily spotted the lost coin.
   (*b*)   He always longed for this chance.
   (*c*)   She noticed a great change in him.
   (*d*)   His intentions were quite clear.
   (*e*)   The tour to Agra was really memorable.

4. (*a*)   We shall go for picnic tomorrow.
   (*b*)   How do you go to school.
   (*c*)   Teacher punished the boy for his mistake.
   (*d*)   The gardener is watering the plants.
   (*e*)   Which is your favourite book?

5. (*a*)   Write your name clearly.
      Always eat with your right hand.
   (*b*)   The machine was made of steel.
      Never steal anything.
   (*c*)   One and one make two.
      She is too shy to talk.

   (*d*)   Write on a sheet of paper.
      Sit properly on your seat.
   (*e*)   It may rain tonight.
      The king's reign was peaceful.

6. (*a*)   Can anything be gained without effort?
   (*b*)   I shall not have reached home by this time tomorrow.
   (*c*)   How sweetly moonlight sleeps upon this bank!
   (*d*)   I wish, I had a good horse.
   (*e*)   I will never forget those happy days.

7. (*a*)   He had written a letter to his father yesterday.
   (*b*)   The cat has slept on the rug.
   (*c*)   Cocks crow in the morning.
   (*d*)   I have already sent my application to the Principal.
   (*e*)   The moon had risen early last night.

8. (*a*)   an   (*b*)   an
   (*c*)   the   (*d*)   a
   (*e*)   a

9. (*a*)   Old   (*b*)   Cool
   (*c*)   Discomfort   (*d*)   Sad
   (*e*)   Small

PAPER-II : INTELLIGENCE TEST

Directions (Qs. 1 to 10): *For each of the following questions, four words have been given of which three are alike in someway and one is different. Find the odd word.*

1. (*a*)   Blue   (*b*)   Red
   (*c*)   Yellow   (*d*)   Dark

2. (*a*)   Writer   (*b*)   Actor
   (*c*)   Singer   (*d*)   Dancer

3. (*a*)   Cactus   (*b*)   Rose
   (*c*)   Lotus   (*d*)   Sunflower

4. (*a*)   Football   (*b*)   Cricket
   (*c*)   Chess   (*d*)   Hockey

5. (*a*)   Sun   (*b*)   Moon
   (*c*)   Venus   (*d*)   Earth

6. (*a*)   Microphone   (*b*)   Microscope
   (*c*)   Spectacles   (*d*)   Telescope

7. (*a*)   Artery   (*b*)   Ventricle
   (*c*)   Pharynx   (*d*)   Aorta

8. (*a*)   Diamond   (*b*)   Ruby
   (*c*)   Emerald   (*d*)   Turquoise

9. (*a*)   Crimson   (*b*)   Scarlet
   (*c*)   Vermilion   (*d*)   Cardinal

10. (*a*)   Swim   (*b*)   Run
   (*c*)   Anticipate   (*d*)   Dance

Directions (Qs. 11 to 15): *In the following questions, numbers given in four out of the five alternatives have same relationship. You have to choose the one which does not belong to the group.*

11. (*a*)   4   (*b*)   8
   (*c*)   16   (*d*)   9
   (*e*)   25

12. (*a*) 125   (*b*) 216
(*c*) 27   (*d*) 121
(*e*) 1

13. (*a*) 43   (*b*) 53
(*c*) 63   (*d*) 73
(*e*) 83

14. (*a*) 26   (*b*) 124
(*c*) 728   (*d*) 64
(*e*) 215

15. (*a*) 22 : 8   (*b*) 24 : 20
(*c*) 32 : 15   (*d*) 14 : 17
(*e*) 91 : 82

Directions (Qs. 16 to 20): *In each of the questions below, find out the correct answer from the given alternatives.*

16. If in a certain language DISPEL is coded as IDPSLE, how is EFFECT coded in that language?
(*a*) FEEFTC   (*b*) CTFEEF
(*c*) EFFETC   (*d*) ECTEFF

17. If in a certain language HUNTER is coded as UHNTRE, how is MANAGE coded in that code?
(*a*) MAANGE   (*b*) MNAAEG
(*c*) AMNAEG   (*d*) EGNAAM

18. If RAMAYANA is coded as AMARANAY, how is TULSIDAS written?
(*a*) SLUTSADI   (*b*) UTSLIDSA
(*c*) SADISLUT   (*d*) SADITULS

19. If CANOE is coded as IFRRG, how is MUSIC written in that code?
(*a*) NWVNI   (*b*) MWVMH
(*c*) NTULB   (*d*) SZWLE

20. If HOBBY is coded as IOBY and LOBBY is coded as MOBY; then BOBBY is coded as
(*a*) BOBY   (*b*) COBY
(*c*) DOBY   (*d*) OOBY

Directions (Qs. 21 to 25): *Write next four letters to complete the series.*

21. COXTOCOXTO.... .

22. CCOXCOXC.... .

23. CCCOXCCOXCCOX.... .

24. COXTVCOXTVCO.... .

25. COXTCOXXTT.... .

Directions (Qs. 26 to 30): *Complete the following series.*

26. 5, 10, 13, 26, 29, 58, 61, ?

27. 2, 3, 5, 7, 11, ?, 17

28. 5, 11, 17, 25, 33, 43, ?

29. 2, 9, 28, 65, 126, ?

30. 3, 7, 15, 31, 63, ?

Directions (Qs. 31 to 35): *Each of the following questions consist of problem figures followed by answer figures. Select a figure from amongst the answer figures which will continue the same series or pattern as established by the problem figures.*

31. Problem Figures

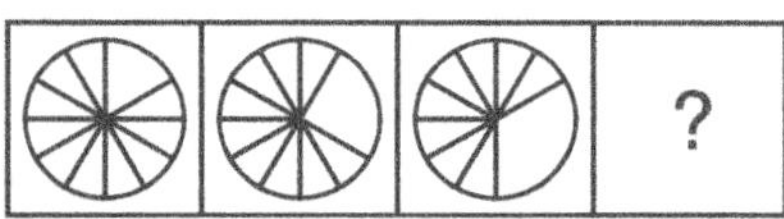

Answer Figures

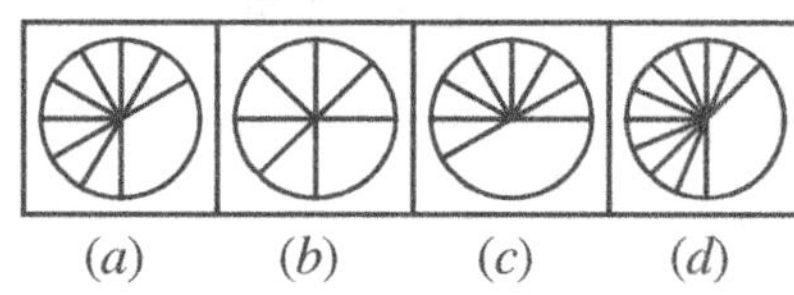

(*a*)   (*b*)   (*c*)   (*d*)

32. Problem Figures

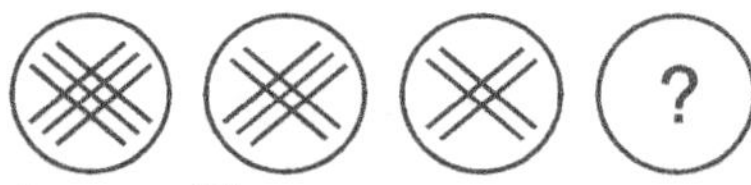

Answer Figures

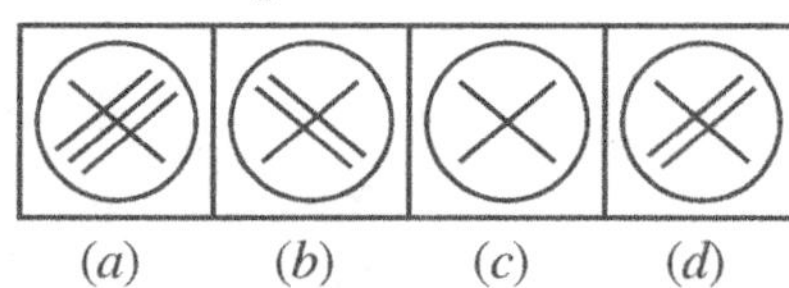

(*a*)   (*b*)   (*c*)   (*d*)

33. Problem Figures

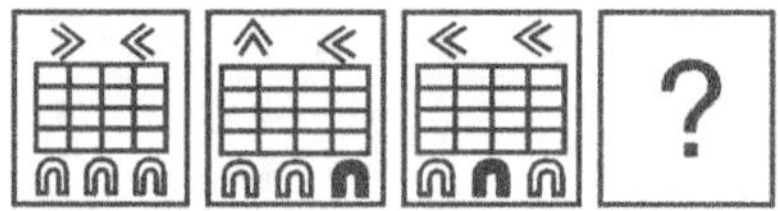

Answer Figures

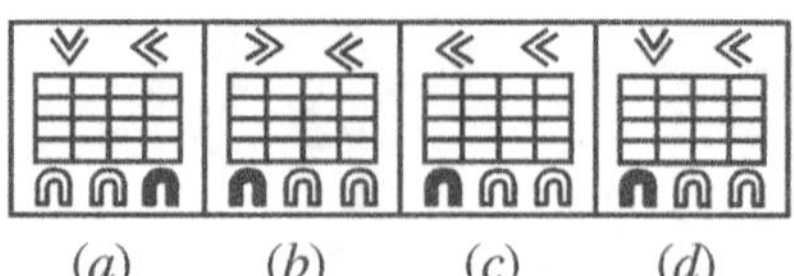

(*a*)   (*b*)   (*c*)   (*d*)

34. Problem Figures

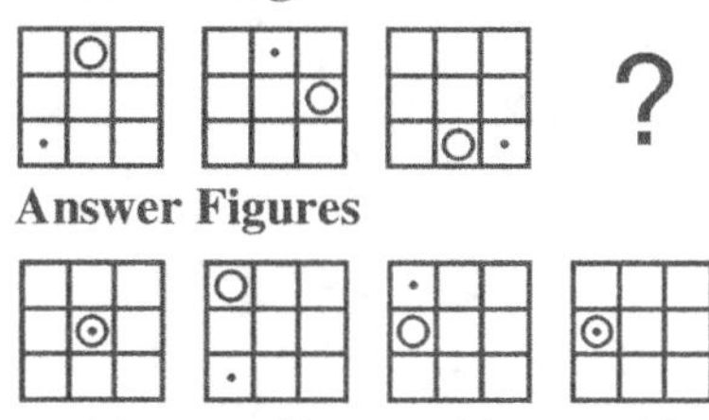

Answer Figures

   (*a*)   (*b*)   (*c*)   (*d*)

35. Problem Figures

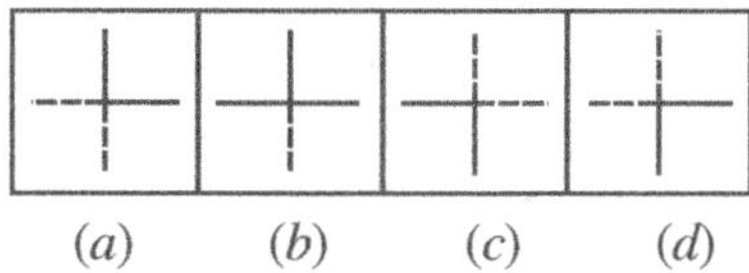

Answer Figures

   (*a*)   (*b*)   (*c*)   (*d*)

Directions (Qs. 36 to 40): *The second figure in the first unit of the Problem Figures bears a certain relationship to the first figure. Similarly, one of the figures in the Answer Figures bears the same relationship to the first figure in the second unit of the Problem Figures. Locate the figure which would fit the question mark.*

36. Problem Figures

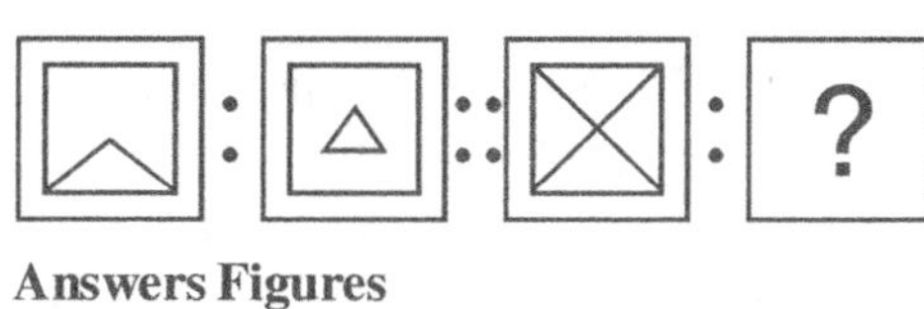

Answers Figures

   (*a*)   (*b*)   (*c*)   (*d*)

37. Problem Figures

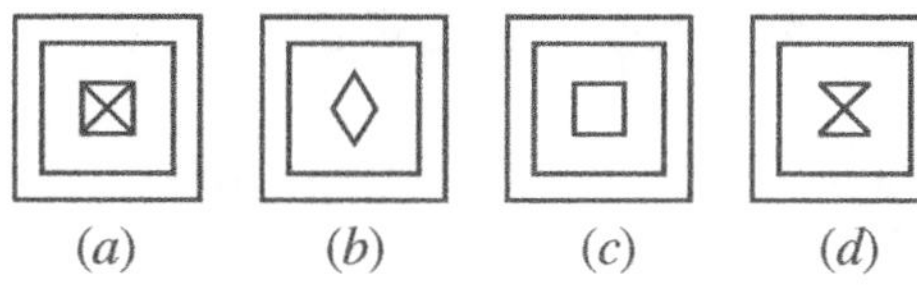

Answer Figures

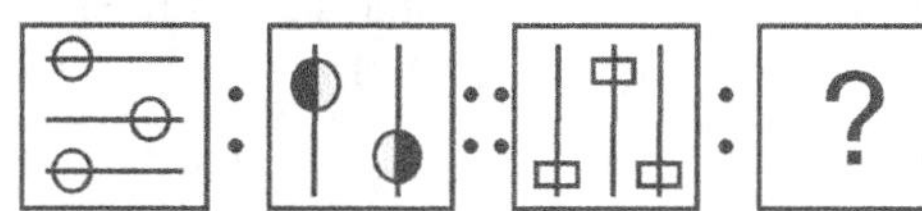

   (*a*)   (*b*)   (*c*)   (*d*)

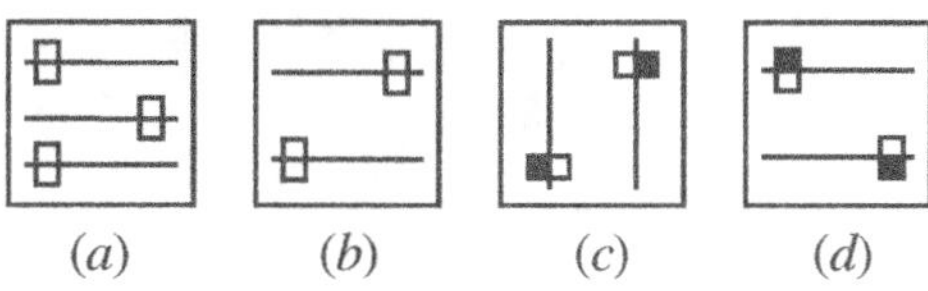

38. Problem Figures

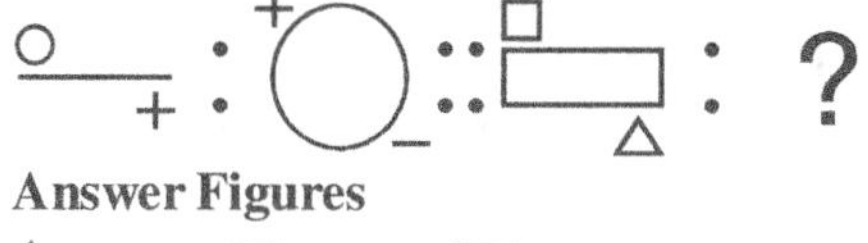

Answer Figures

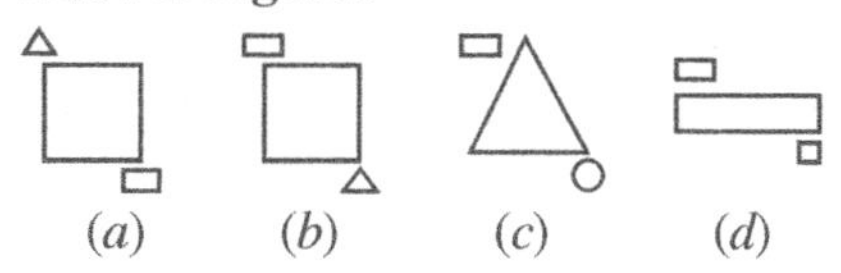

   (*a*)   (*b*)   (*c*)   (*d*)

39. Problem Figures

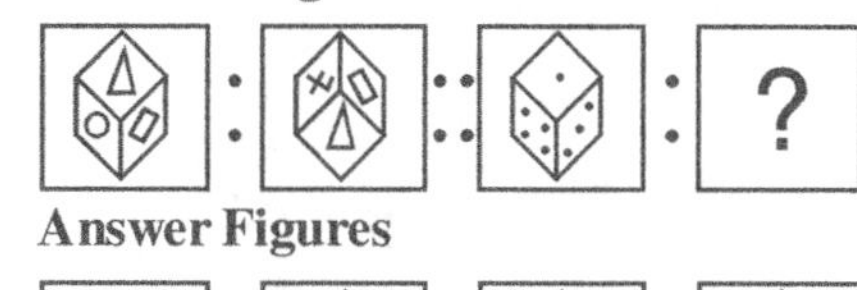

Answer Figures

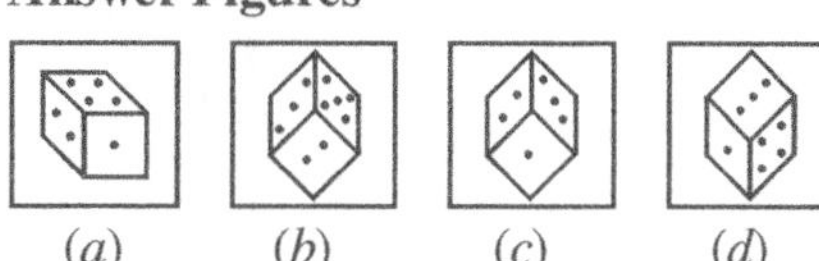

   (*a*)   (*b*)   (*c*)   (*d*)

40. Problem Figures

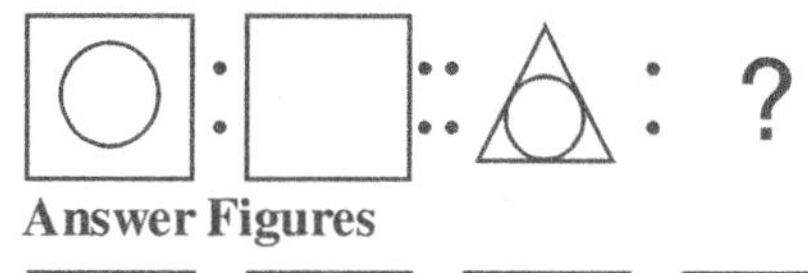

Answer Figures

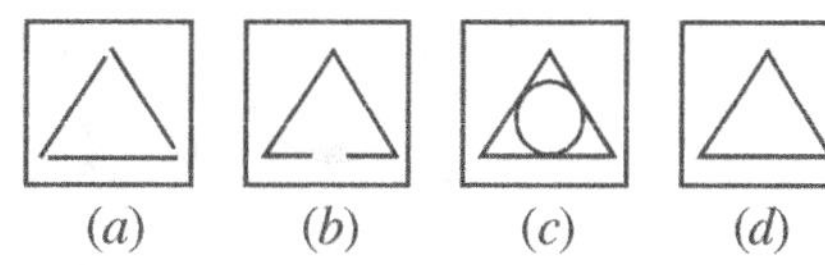

   (*a*)   (*b*)   (*c*)   (*d*)

Directions (Qs. 41 to 45): *In each of the following questions one of the figures is different from the rest. Spot the figure.*

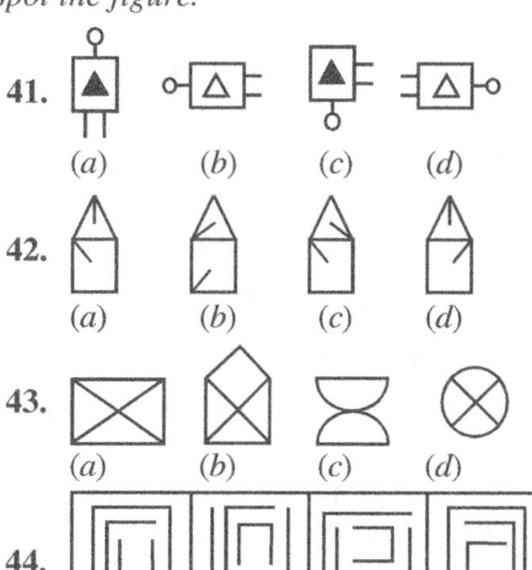

41.

   (*a*)   (*b*)   (*c*)   (*d*)

42.

   (*a*)   (*b*)   (*c*)   (*d*)

43.

   (*a*)   (*b*)   (*c*)   (*d*)

44.

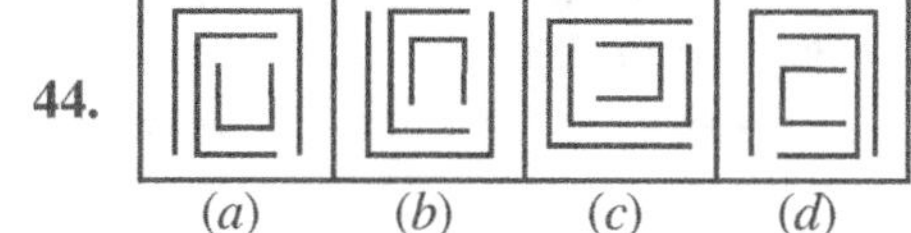

   (*a*)   (*b*)   (*c*)   (*d*)

45. 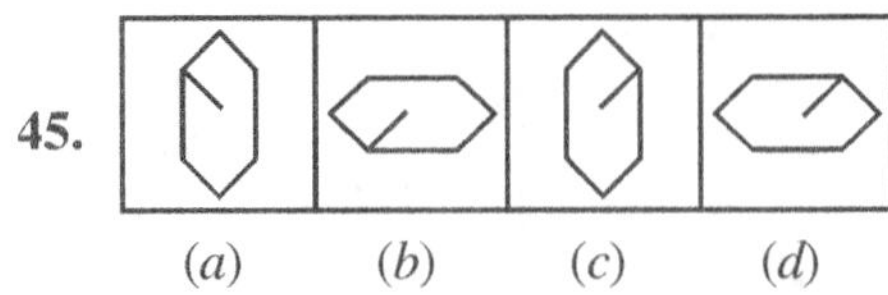

(*a*)   (*b*)   (*c*)   (*d*)

Directions (Qs. 46 to 50): *In each question, which one of the alternative figures will complete the given figure pattern?*

46. Pattern 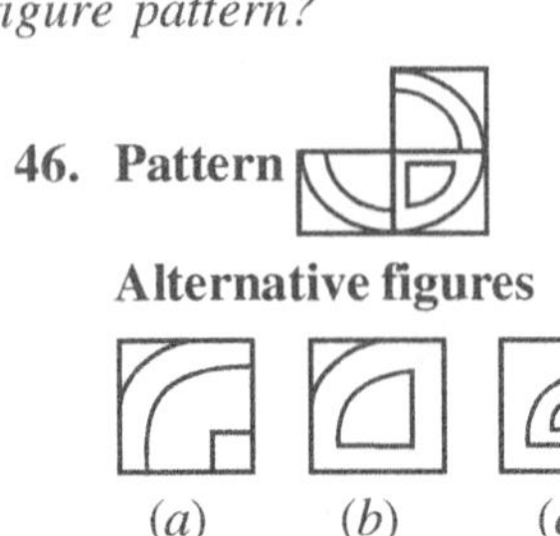

Alternative figures

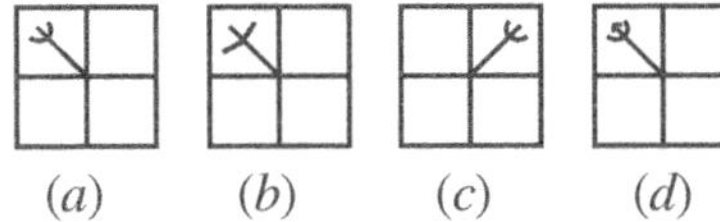

(*a*)   (*b*)   (*c*)   (*d*)

47. Pattern

Alternative figures

(*a*)   (*b*)   (*c*)   (*d*)

48. Pattern 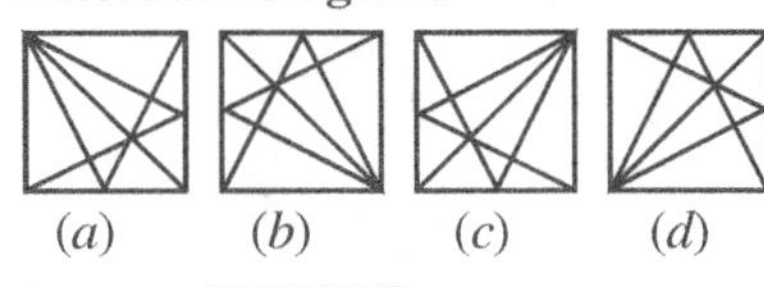

Alternative figures

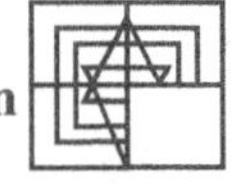

(*a*)   (*b*)   (*c*)   (*d*)

49. Pattern 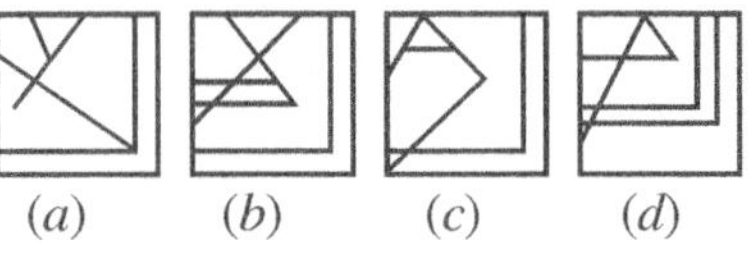

Alternative figures

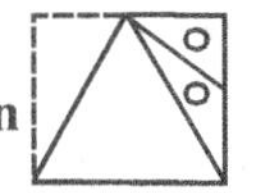

(*a*)   (*b*)   (*c*)   (*d*)

50. Pattern 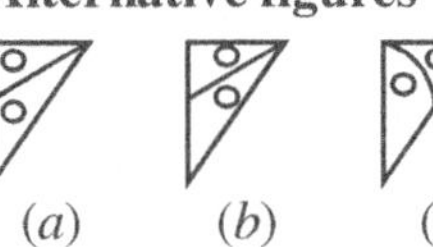

Alternative figures

(*a*)   (*b*)   (*c*)   (*d*)

EXPLANATORY ANSWERS

1. (*d*) : Except (*d*), others are colours, while dark is the attribute of a colour.

2. (*a*) : Except (*a*), others are professional workers, while writer is a creater.

3. (*a*) : Except (*a*), others are flowers, while cactus is a leafless plant.

4. (*a*) : Except (*a*), others are played by hands, while football is played by feet.

5. (*b*) : All the term except 'Moon' are related to the Solar system.

6. (*a*) : All the terms except 'Microphone' are related to the vision.

7. (*c*) : Except 'Pharynx' all other terms are related to heart.

8. (*a*) : Except 'Diamond' all the jewels contain some colour in it.

9. (*d*) : Except 'Cardinal' all the terms are related to colours.

10. (*c*) : Except 'Anticipate' all the terms are related to body movement or exercise.

11. (*b*) : All other numbers are square of natural numbers.

12. (*d*) : All other numbers are cubes of natural numbers.

13. (*c*) : All other numbers are prime number.

14. (*d*) : All other numbers are one less than the cube of natural numbers.

15. (*c*) : Second number is the sum of the square of the digits of first number.

16. (*a*) : Since

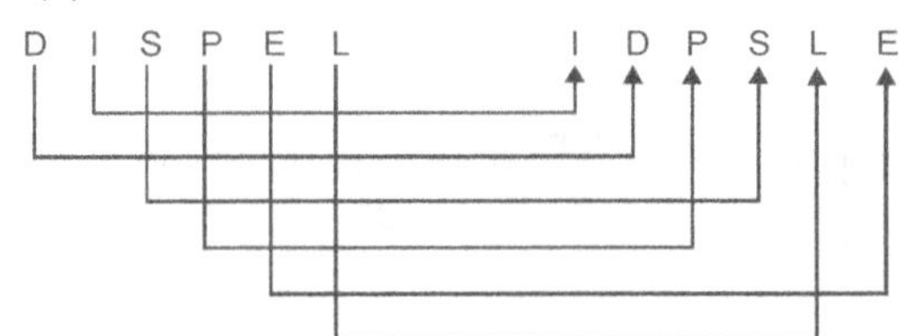

Therefore

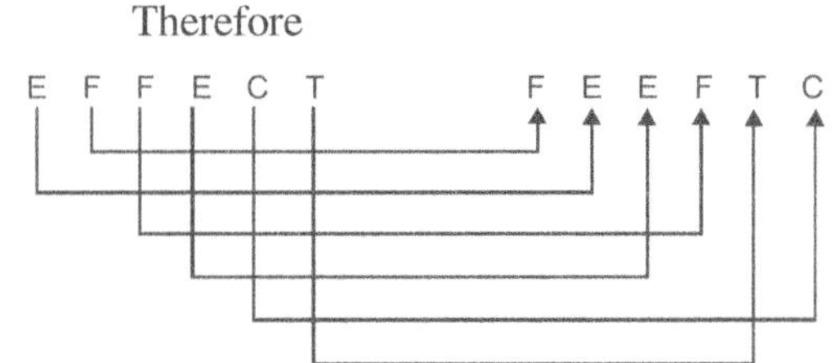

17. (*c*) : Since

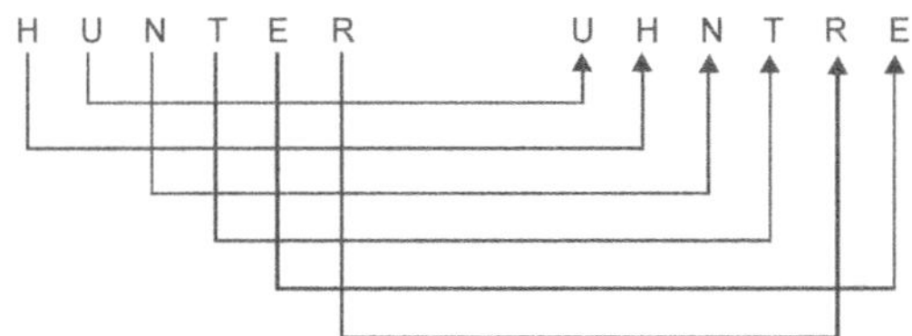

Therefore

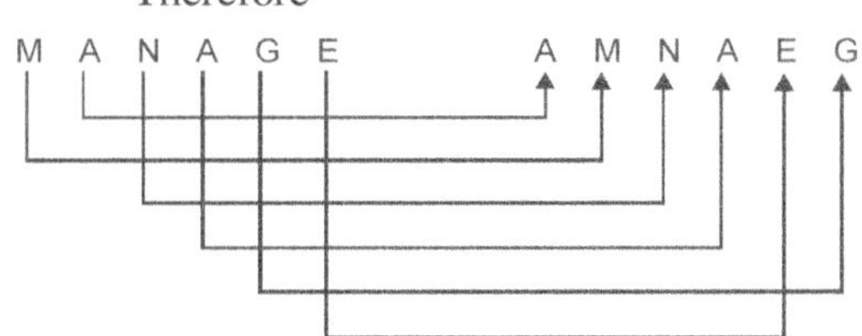

18. (*a*) : Since

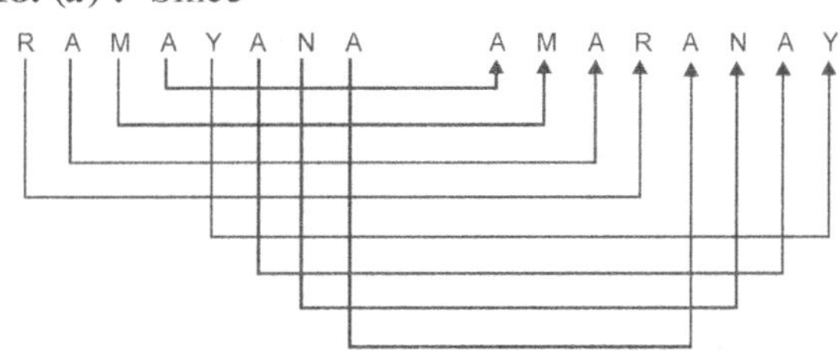

Therefore

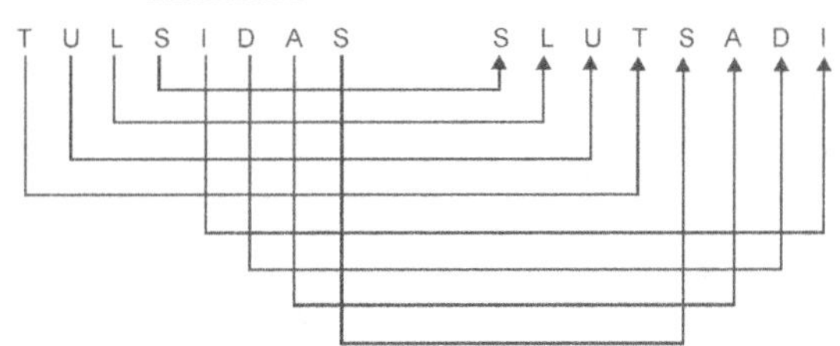

19. (*d*) : Since

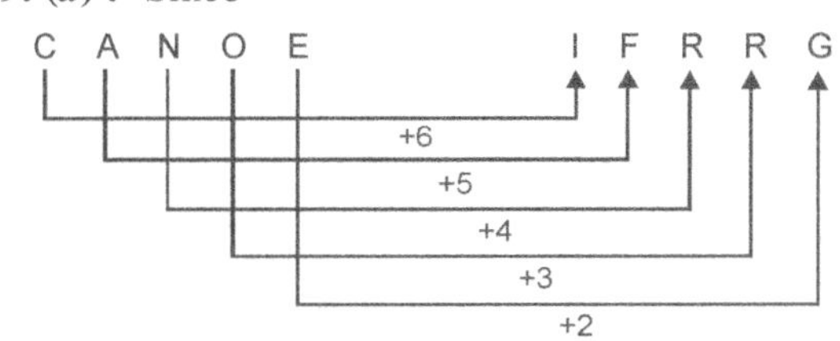

Therefore

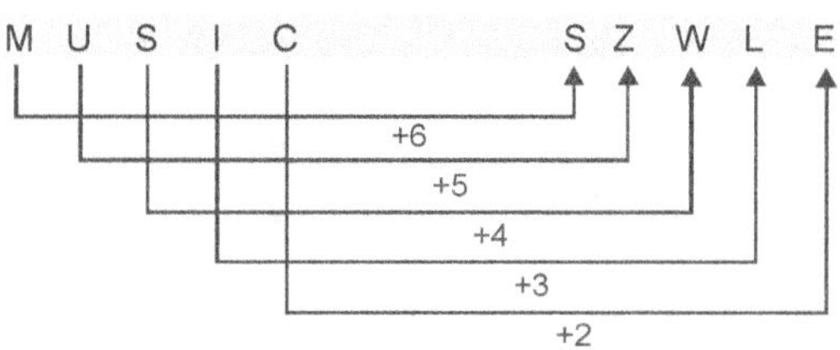

20. (*b*) : Since

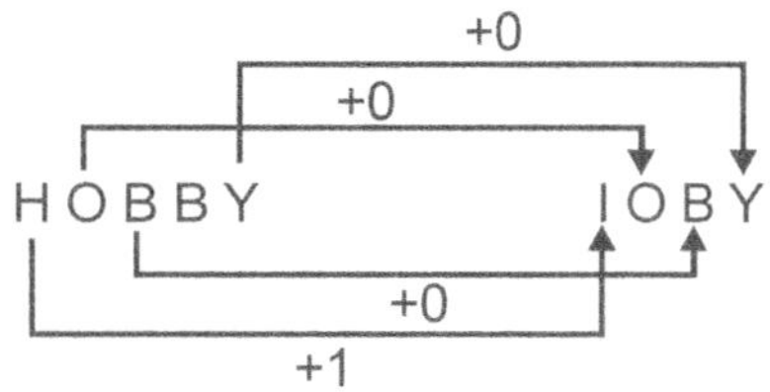

And

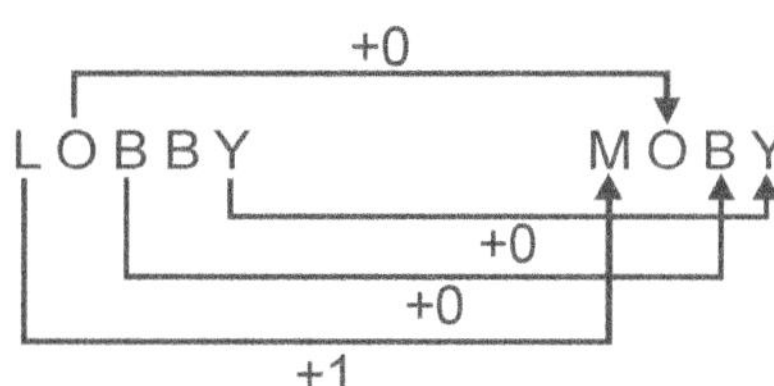

Therefore

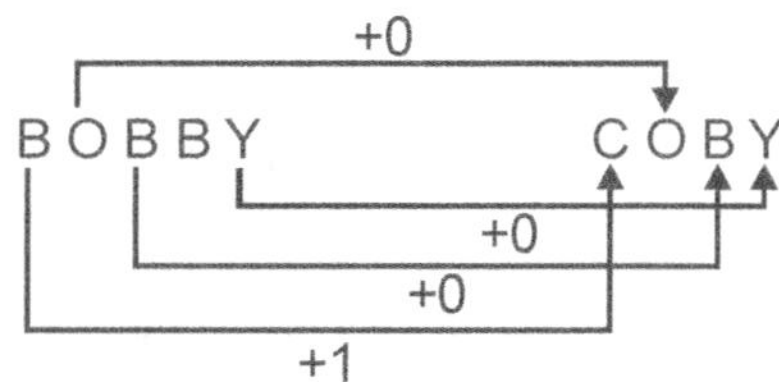

21. (COXT) : On writing COXT in the blank spaces, the sequence COXTOCOXTOCOXT is formed, in which COXTO is repeated partially three times.

22. (OXCC) : On writing OXCC in the blank spaces, the sequence CCOXCOXCOXCC is formed.

23. (CCCO) : On writing CCCO in the blank spaces, the sequence CCCOXCCOXCCOXCCCO is formed, in which C is decreasing by 1, then remaining constant, and then increasing by 1.

24. (XTVC) : On writing XTVC in the blank spaces, the sequence COXTVCOXTVCO-XTVC is formed, in which COXTV is repeated partially 4 times.

25. (COXX) : On writing COXX in the blank spaces, the sequence COXTCOXXTTCOXX is formed, in which X and T are increasing by 1 only once.

26. The numbers are alternately multiplied by 2 and increased by 3.
Thus, $5 \times 2 = 10$, $10 + 3 = 13$, $13 \times 2 = 26$, $26 + 3 = 29$ and so on.
$\therefore$ answer is $61 \times 2 = 122$.

27. Clearly the given series consists of prime numbers starting from 2. The prime number after 11 is 13. So, 13 is our answer.

28. The sequence is $+ 6, + 6, + 8, + 8, + 10, \ldots$
So, answer is $43 + 10 = 53$.

29. The sequence is $1^3 + 1, 2^3 + 1, 3^3 + 1, 4^3 + 1, 5^3 + 1$.
$\therefore$ Missing number $= 6^3 + 1 = 216 + 1 = 217$.

30. Each number in the series is the preceding number multiplied by 2 and then increased by 1.
Thus, $(3 \times 2) + 1 = 7$, $(7 \times 2) + 1 = 15$, $(15 \times 2) + 1 = 31$ and so on.
$\therefore$ Missing number
$= (63 \times 2) + 1 = 126 + 1 = 127$.

31. (c) : Clockwise, the circle is turned by 30° and also one radial line segment is removed.

32. (d) : The diagonal line segments are removed one by one in a set order.

33. (d) : The 'V' shape on the top left is rotated 90° anticlockwise. The three figures at the bottom are shaded one at a time beginning from the right figure and moving to the left.

34. (d) : The circle and the dot are moved two and three sections clockwise respectively.

35. (a) : The cross is turned 90° clockwise at each step.

36. (d) : The triangle in the first figure is moved to the centre of the second figure. Similarly, the two triangles joined at the apex are moved to the centre in answer figure.

37. (d) : The first figure is turned by 90° one of the bars is removed and opposite sides of the element attached to the bar are shaded to get the second figure.

38. (a) : The element at the bottom is moved to the diagonal corner, the element in the top is enlarged and moved to the centre and element in the middle is reduced and moved to the bottom right corner.

39. (c) : The view of the cube is changed from top to bottom. The design on the right side remains unchanged while the design on the left side is changed.

40. (d) : The inner shape in the first figure is removed to get the second figure.

41. (c) : In all other figures the line with a circle and the two line segments are on opposite sides of the square.

42. (c) : In all other figures the two line segments are drawn on same side from the corners of same line. In this figure they are drawn on opposite sides.

43. (c) : All other figures are divided into four parts.

44. (d) : Only in this figure the middle and the centre shapes are opposite to each other.

45. (c) : All other figures can be rotated into each other. In this figure the line segment is on the wrong side.

46. (b) : 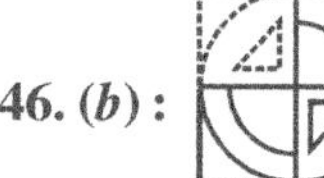

47. (a) : 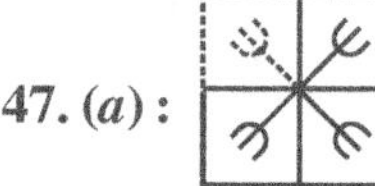

48. (d) : 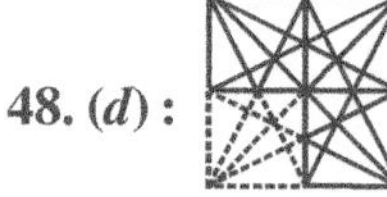

49. (d) : 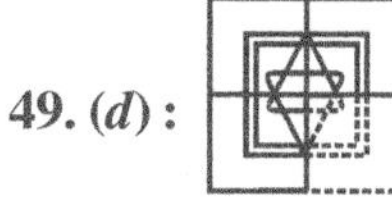

50. (a) : 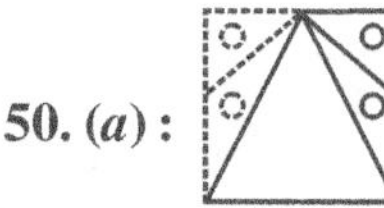

Sainik School Entrance Exam, 2011
(CLASS-VI)

PAPER-I : MATHEMATICS AND LANGUAGE

PART-A : MATHEMATICS

Section-I

1. Find the sum of two numbers if one number is 41628 and the other number is 1235 greater than the first number.

2. Arrange the numbers in ascending order—631997, 514245, 51437, 631460.

3. The side of a square is 8m. The same square is divided into four equal squares. Find the area of the square.

4. Find prime factors of 216 and 90.

5. Find the value of $11\dfrac{1}{5} \div 6\dfrac{1}{10}$.

6. Find 10% of 95.

7. A train starts from Delhi at 9.15 p.m and reaches Jammu Tawi next day at 11.30 am. Find the total time taken by the train.

8. The weight of 25 bags of sugar is 625 kg. Find the weight of 35 bags of the sugar.

9. Find out LCM of 75, 90 and 125.

10. Find the perimeter of rectangle of length 60 cm and breadth 30 cm.

Section-II

11. Simplify: $16 - \left[4 \div 2\left\{ 6 - \left(8 \text{ of } \dfrac{1}{2} \right) \right\} \right]$.

12. A rectangular lawn is 40m by 30m. It has two roads of 2m wide running in the middle one parallel to the length and the other parallel to the breadth. Find the area of the roads.

13. A pit of 50 meter long, 40 meter wide and 1 meter deep is dug. Find the volume of earth dug out from the pit.

14. Find the Area and circumference of a circle with diameter 14 cm.

15. An angle is twice of its complement. Find the measures of the angle and its complement.

16. The LCM of two numbers is 1080 and their HCF is 18. One of the numbers is 216, find the other number.

17. Asha can finish a work in 15 days . The same work is finished by Nirmala in 12 days . In how many days both of them will finish the work while working together?

18. A carpenter bought 6 chairs for Rs 90 each. He spent Rs 10 on each chair for painting. He then sold all the six chairs for Rs. 795. Find his profit or loss.

19. Write true or false for the following statements.
    (*a*) A cylinder has two curved surfaces and one flat base.
    (*b*) A cone has two curved surfaces and one flat base.
    (*c*) A sphere has no flat faces.

20. In the following pictograph the number of students liking various sports have been represented:

    Scale = 5 students

    Cricket

    Football

    Kabbadi

    Kho-kho

With the help of this answer the following questions

(*a*) Which is the most favourite game of the students?

(*b*) How many students like Cricket?

(*c*) What is the difference between the number of students liking Kho-kho and Kabbadi.

Section-III

21. Sahil scored 95 marks out of 150 and Ankit scored 180 marks out of 250. Whose score is higher?

22. Jatin borrowed Rs 4500 at 12 paise for every rupee per annum. After 3 years he returned Rs 4000 and a wrist watch. Find the cost of the wrist watch.

23. Draw a circle with radius 3 cm and mark.
(*a*) Its centre O
(*b*) Diameter AB
(*c*) An Arc CD
(*d*) a chord PQ.

24. A, B and C have a total of Rs 1500. The ratio of the money between A and B is 4:5. If C has Rs. 600, calculate the shares of A and B.

25. What is the greatest 6 digit number which is exactly divisible by 24, 15 and 36?

26. By selling a bed sheet for Rs. 75, a man suffers 4% loss. What amount should he sell it so as to gain 20% profit?

27. If $a = 2$, $b = 3$, and c = 4, find value of
(*a*) $ab + bc$

(*b*) $\dfrac{a(b + c)}{b(a + c)}$

28. A chalk box measures 7 cm in length, 5 cm in breadth and 3 cm in height. How many chalk boxes can be placed in a box whose length, breadth and height are respectively 49 cm, 25 cm and 15 cm?

29. Find average of 12 numbers if the average of the first 8 numbers is 21 and the average of the last four numbers is 18.

30. Find the perimeter and area of the given figure?

EXPLANATORY ANSWERS

1. One number = 41628
Other number = 41628 + 1235 = 42863
Sum of the numbers = 41628 + 42863
$\qquad\qquad = 84491.$

2. 51437, 51425, 631460, 631997.

3. Side of a square = 8 m.

Area of square = 8 × 8 = 64 m^2
It is divided into 4 equal parts.

4	4
4	4

area of each square = 16 m^2.

4.

2	216
2	108
2	54
3	27
3	9
3	3
	1

Prime factors of 216 = $2^3 \times 3^3$

2	90
3	45
3	15
5	5
	1

Prime factors of 90 = 3 × 3 × 2 × 5.

5. $11\dfrac{1}{5} \div 6\dfrac{1}{10} = \dfrac{56}{5} \div \dfrac{61}{10}$

$\qquad = \dfrac{56}{5} \times \dfrac{10}{61} = \dfrac{112}{61} = 1\dfrac{51}{61}.$

6. 10% of $95 = \dfrac{10}{100} \times 95 = \dfrac{19}{2} = 9.5.$

7. Total time taken by the train
$= 12$ hrs $+ 2$hrs 15 min. $= 14$ hrs 15 min.

8. Weight of 25 bags of sugar $= 625$ kg

Weight of 1 bags of sugar $= \dfrac{625}{25}$ kg

Weight of 35 bags of sugar $= \dfrac{625}{25} \times 35$

$\qquad\qquad\qquad = 25 \times 35 = 875$ kg.

9.

5	75, 90, 125
5	15, 18,　25
3	3, 18,　5
	1,　6,　5

LCM $= 5 \times 5 \times 3 \times 6 \times 5 = 2250.$

10. Perimeter of rectangle $= 2\,(l + b)$
$\qquad\qquad = 2\,(60 + 30) = 2 \times 90 = 180$ cm.

11. $\left[16 - 4 \div 2\left\{6 - \left(8 \text{ of } \dfrac{1}{2}\right)\right\}\right]$

$= [16 - 4 \div 2\,\{6 - 4\}]$

$= [16 - 4 \div 2 \times 2]$

$= 16 - 4 = 12.$

12.

Area of the road $= 40 \times 2 + 30 \times 2$
$\qquad = 80 + 60 = 140$ m^2 $= 140 - 4 = 136$ m^2.

13. Volume of earth dug out from the pit
$= l \times b \times h = 50 \times 40 \times 1 = 2000$ m^3.

14. Diameter of circle $= 14$ cm
$\therefore$ radius of circle $= 7$ cm

Circumference $= 2\pi r = 2 \times \dfrac{22}{7} \times 7 = 44$ cm.

Area of circle $= \pi r^2 = \dfrac{22}{7} \times 7 \times 7 = 154$ cm^2.

15. $x + 2x = 90°$
$3x = 90°$
$x = 30°$
its complement $= 2 \times 30 = 60°.$

16. Other number $= \dfrac{\text{LCM} \times \text{HCF}}{\text{One number}} = \dfrac{1080 \times 18}{216} = 90.$

17. Asha can finish a work in 15 days.

Asha's one day work $= \dfrac{1}{15}$

Nirmala can finish the same work in 12 days.

Nirmala's one day work $= \dfrac{1}{12}$

(Asha's + Nirmala's) one day work

$\qquad = \dfrac{1}{15} + \dfrac{1}{12} = \dfrac{4+5}{60} = \dfrac{9}{60}$

$\therefore$ They can do the work in $\dfrac{60}{9}$ days

$\qquad\qquad = 6\dfrac{2}{3}$ days.

18. CP of 6 chairs $= 100 \times 6 = ₹\,600$
SP of 6 chairs $= ₹\,795$
Profit $=$ SP $-$ CP $= 795 - 600 = ₹\,195.$

19. (a) False
(b) False
(c) True

20. Scale $= 5$ students

Cricket

Football

Kabbadi

Kho-kho

(a) Kho-kho
(b) 40
(c) 15.

21. % marks of Sahil $= \dfrac{95}{150} \times 100 = \dfrac{190}{3} = 63.33\%$

% marks of Ankit $= \dfrac{180}{250} \times 100 = 72\%$

$\therefore$ Ankit score is higher.

22. SI $= \dfrac{P \times r \times t}{100} = \dfrac{4500 \times 12 \times 3}{100} = ₹\ 1620$

Amount $= P + SI = 4500 + 1620 = ₹\ 6120.$

$\therefore$ Cost of the wrist watch

$$= 6120 - 4000 = ₹\ 2120.$$

23.

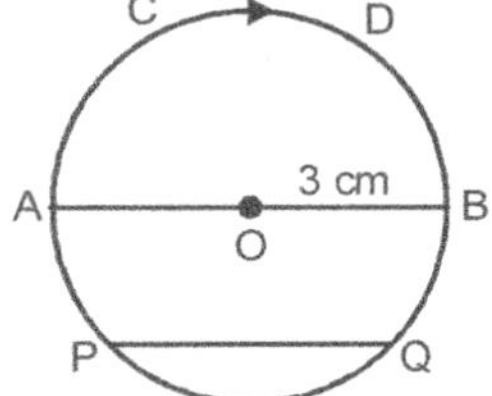

24. $1500 - 600 = ₹\ 900$

Let A has $₹\ 4x$ and B has $₹\ 5x$

$4x + 5x = 900$

$9x = 900$

$x = 100$

$\therefore$ A has $4 \times 100 = ₹\ 400$

B has $5 \times 100 = ₹\ 500.$

25. The greatest number of 6 digits $= 999999$

LCM of 24, 15 and 36 $= 360$

$999999 \div 360$ then we get remainder $= 279$

$999999 - 279 = 999720$

$\therefore$ Required number $= 999720.$

26. SP $= ₹\ 75$

Loss $= 4\%$

Let CP $= ₹\ 100$

SP $= ₹\ 100 - 4 = ₹\ 96$

When SP ₹ 96 then CP $= ₹$ 100

When SP ₹ 75 then CP

$$= ₹\ \dfrac{100}{96} \times 75 = ₹\ \dfrac{625}{8} = ₹\ 78.125$$

Again $100 + 20 = 120$

When CP ₹ 100 then SP $= ₹$ 120

When CP ₹ $\dfrac{625}{8}$ then

$$SP = ₹\ \dfrac{120}{100} \times \dfrac{625}{8} = ₹\ \dfrac{375}{4} = ₹\ 93.75.$$

27. Given that $a = 2$, $b = 3$ and $c = 4$

(a) Then value of $ab + bc$

$$= 2(3) + 3(4) = 6 + 12 = 18$$

(b) $\dfrac{a(b+c)}{b(a+c)} = \dfrac{2(3+4)}{3(2+4)} = \dfrac{14}{18} = \dfrac{7}{9}.$

28. Number of chalk boxes

$$= \dfrac{49 \times 25 \times 15}{7 \times 5 \times 3} = 7 \times 5 \times 5 = 175.$$

29. Total of number of first 8 numbers

$= 21 \times 8 = 168$

Total number of last 4 numbers $= 18 \times 4 = 72$

Total number of 12 numbers $= 168 + 72 = 240$

Average of 12 numbers $= \dfrac{240}{12} = 20.$

30.

Perimeter $= 2(30 + 20) = 100$ m

Area $= 30 \times 20 = 600$ m^2.

PART-B : LANGUAGE ABILITY

1. Write a paragraph of 15 sentences on the topic:

(a) An Important Day in My Life *OR*

(b) My Aim in Life

2. Read the following passage carefully and answer the questions:

Kalidas is known as the Shakespeare of India. His name has been immortalised in the history of Sanskrit literature. He was at the head of the celebrated nine gems which adorned the court of King Vikramaditya. The poems and dramas of Kalidas have elicited unreserved praise not only from Indian Scholars but also from European critics like Maxmuller, a German. The age in which Kalidas flourished and the place where he was born are matters of dispute. But true genius is independent of time and place although the century of Kalidas is far more remote, his fame in shining with undiminished grandeur even in our own days.

(*a*) Who is the Shakespeare of India?

(*b*) Who was Maxmuller?

(*c*) What is the language used by Kalidas for his literary works?

(*d*) Where was Kalidas born?

(*e*) What was the position of Kalidas in the court of King Vikramaditya?

3. Make a sentence of your own for each underlined word given in the following passage. (Do not copy any sentence from the given paragraph).

Once a smart looking young man visited the office of a businessman to look for a job. The manager though <u>pleased</u> with his <u>behaviour</u> said, "There is no <u>vacancy</u> for a clerk." The young man was very unhappy and turned to go. As he was passing out of the door way, he found waste papers scattered all around the entrance. He at once picked them up and dropped in the dust bin. The manager saw this and was greatly <u>impressed</u>. He thought that the <u>applicant </u>was good enough to be employed in the office. So he called him back and appointed him a clerk in his office.

4. Form meaningful sentences by rearranging the words/phrases in the proper order.

(*a*) animal/man/a/is/social

(*b*) Shimla/winter/went/we/during/to/holidays.

(*c*) neighbour/is/photographer/a/our/good/very.

(*d*) sentences/meaningful/the/make/following/ to/words/phrases/and/rearrange.

(*e*) will/next/my/be/parents/meet/coming/to/me/ week.

5. Write a Leave application addressed to your Headmaster seeking two days leave to appear in Sainik Schools entrance examination.

6. Use each of the word in separate sentences of your own to show the difference in the meaning of the words of the pairs given below:

(*a*) Sale, sail

(*b*) Throne, thorn

(*c*) whether, weather

(*d*) earn, yearn

(*e*) cattle, kettle

7. Choose correct form of pronouns from the brackets and fill in the blanks.

(*a*) We scored as many goals as ....
(they, them, their)

(*b*) The horse fell down and broke .... leg.
(it, its, his)

(*c*) The presents are for .... and me.
(you, yours, yourself)

(*d*) Wait for Hari and .... (I, me, mine)

(*e*) Nobody but .... was present,
(he, his, him)

8. Change each of the following as directed.

(*a*) He had been sleeping till now since morning.
(Change into Interrogative)

(*b*) The garden will be looking its best next month. (Change into Negative)

(*c*) He leads a most unhappy life.
(Change into Exclamatory)

(*d*) How beautiful is night!
(Change into Assertive)

(*e*) Who does not know the owl?
(Change into Assertive

9. (*a*) Don't sit .... the grass. It is wet.
(in/at/on)

(*b*) There is a pair of shoes .... the bed.
(above/around/under)

(*c*) The dog swam .... the river.
(by/beside/across)

(*d*) I am sorry .... what I have done.
(by/for/with)

(*e*) I felt nervous .... the exam.
(since/before/while)

EXPLANATORY ANSWERS

1. (*a*) An Important Day in My Life

I was studying in 5th class in D.A.V. Public School. I took up scholarship examination. I was expecting good result, since I was good at studies. On 11th March Raman, my classmate, came running to my house early in the morning. He disclosed that the scholarship result was out and I was lucky to be one of the successful candidates. He congratulated me and embraced me. I also thanked him and wished him 'best of luck'.

On hearing the good news of my scholarship, most of my relatives and friends visited my house. In the evening, my parents and uncles brought for me good gifts a wristwatch, a bicycle and some good books. They all prayed for my further success in life.

Thus, 11th March was an important day of my life.

(*b*) My Aim in Life

My aim in life is to become a doctor. I want to serve sick people, give them proper medical treatment. I am very much impressed with Dr. P.K. Arora. Dr. Arora's clinic is very near to our house. I keep on watching Dr. Arora working with the patients. He works more than 15-16 hours a day. I have seen him going out at night to visit the sick people. He is a very good doctor. He has a smiling face. He never becomes angry. He does not take fee from poor sick people.

After becoming a doctor I will open my clinic in a remote village. Medical facilities are not available in remote villages. Sick people of the village are taken from the village to the town or city for medical treatment. My ambition is to live in a far distant village, open a good clinic and serve the poor sick people.

2. (*a*) Kalidas is the Shakespeare of India.

(*b*) Maxmuller was a German scholar and critic.

(*c*) Kalidas used Sanskrit language for his literary works.

(*d*) Kalidas was born in ancient India but the exact place of birth is disputed.

(*e*) Kalidas was at the head of the celebrated nine gems in the court of king Vikramaditya.

3. (*a*) The teacher was <u>pleased</u> with his answer.

(*b*) His <u>behaviour</u> was really good.

(*c*) He was looking for a <u>vacancy</u> in the newspaper.

(*d*) She was <u>impressed</u> with his personality.

(*e*) The <u>applicant</u> was selected for the post.

4. (*a*) Man is a social animal.

(*b*) We went to Shimla during winter holidays.

(*c*) Our neighbour is a very good photographer.

(*d*) Rearrange the following words to make the meaningful phrases and sentences.

(*e*) My parents will be coming next week to meet me.

5. The Headmaster, Dated : ....
ABC Primary School,
Daryaganj,
New Delhi-110002.

Respected Sir,

With due respect I beg to state that I have to appear in my Sainik Schools entrance examination on 04-05 August. Please grant me leave for two days to enable me to appear in it and raise the name of our school higher with pride.

Thanking you.

Your sincerely,

XYZ

Class V-A

Roll No. 1

6. (a) (i) There was a grand sale of garments going on.

    (ii) The ship set sail for Rome.

  (b) (i) He sat on the throne like a king.

    (ii) He never cared for thorns on the way.

  (c) (i) No one can surely say whether it will rain tonight or not.

    (ii) The weather in Shimla is pleasant.

  (d) (i) No one knows how much money he earns.

    (ii) He was yearning to have the new game.

  (e) (i) The cattle were grazing in the field.

    (ii) There is a little tea in the kettle.

7. (a) We scored as many goals as they.

  (b) The horse fell down and broke its leg.

  (c) The presents are for you and me.

  (d) Wait for Hari and me.

  (e) Nobody but he was present.

8. (a) Had he been sleeping till now since morning?

  (b) The garden will not be looking its best next month.

  (c) What an unhappy life he leads?

  (d) The night is beautiful.

  (e) Everyone knows the owl.

9. (a) Don't sit on the grass. It is wet.

  (b) The is a pair of shoes under the bed.

  (c) The dog swam across the river.

  (d) I am sorry for what I have done.

  (e) I felt nervous before the exam.

PAPER-II : INTELLIGENCE TEST

Directions (Qs. 1 to 10): *For each of the following questions, four words have been given of which three are alike in someway and one is different. Find the odd word.*

1. (a) Shorthand   (b) Morse
   (c) Semaphore   (d) Record

2. (a) Green   (b) Violet
   (c) Brown   (d) Yellow

3. (a) City   (b) Town
   (c) Village   (d) Home

4. (a) Writer   (b) Printer
   (c) Publisher   (d) Reader

5. (a) Under   (b) Near
   (c) Above   (d) Where

6. (a) Fragrance   (b) Smell
   (c) Aroma   (d) A foul smell

7. (a) Motorcar   (b) Tractor
   (c) Bus   (d) Train

8. (a) Stammer   (b) Whisper
   (c) Drawl   (d) Taunt (Speech)

9. (a) Portrait   (b) Snapshot
   (c) Diagram   (d) Painting

10. (a) Silk   (b) Fur
    (c) Milk   (d) Rubber

Directions (Qs. 11 to 15): *In the following questions, numbers given in four out of the five alternatives have same relationship. You have to choose the one which does not belong to the group.*

11. (a) 1 : 4   (b) 10 : 24
    (c) 8 : 18   (d) 22 : 46
    (e) 50 : 102

12. (a) 22 : 42   (b) 4 : 6
    (c) 11 : 20   (d) 5 : 14
    (e) 9 : 16

13 (a) 3 : 8   (b) 6 : 35
    (c) 7 : 50   (d) 1 : 0
    (e) 9 : 80

14. (a) 385   (b) 572
    (c) 671   (d) 264
    (e) 427

15. (a) 9 : 80   (b) 1 : 0
    (c) 6 : 35   (d) 12 : 143
    (e) 10 : 91

Directions (Qs. 16 to 20): *In each of the questions below, find out the correct answer from the given alternatives.*

16. If FRIEND is coded as HUMJTK, how is CANDLE written in that code?
    (a) EDRIRL   (b) DCQHQK
    (c) FROBOC   (d) ESJFME

17. If ADVENTURE is coded as ERUTNEVDA, how is GREEN coded in that code?
    (a) NEERG   (b) ENEGR
    (c) GEREN   (d) NEEGR

18. If CAB is coded as WUV, how is DEAF coded in that language?
    (a) XYUZ   (b) UWYV
    (c) XWUY   (d) UYXZ

19. If in a certain code YELLOW is written as XFKMNX, how is COUNTRY coded?
    (a) DPVOSQX   (b) BNTMSQX
    (c) BPTMSSX   (d) AMSLRPW

20. If QUICK is coded as PSFYF, how is NEST coded?
    (a) MCPP   (b) MDQS
    (c) OGUV   (d) TESN

Directions (Qs. 21 to 25): *Write next four letters to complete the series.*

21. COXTCCCOXTC.... .

22. COCXOCXCCXCO.... .

23. COXVTCOOXXVVTT.... .

24. COXTOXTCXTC.... .

25. COXTCOXTCOX.... .

Directions (Qs. 26 to 30): *Complete the following series.*

26. 4, 9, 13, 22, 35, ?

27. 18, 36, 54, 72, 90, ?

28. 2, 4, 7, 11, 16, ?

29. 0, 2, 6, ?, 20, 30, 42

30. 1, 8, 27, 64, 125, 216, ?

Direction (Qs. 31 to 35): *Each of the following questions consist of problem figures followed by answer figures. Select a figure from amongst the answer figures which will continue the same series or pattern as established by the problem figures.*

31. **Problem Figures**

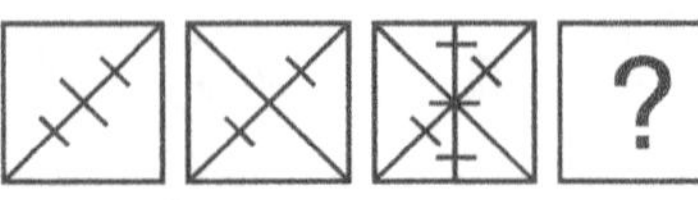

Answer Figures

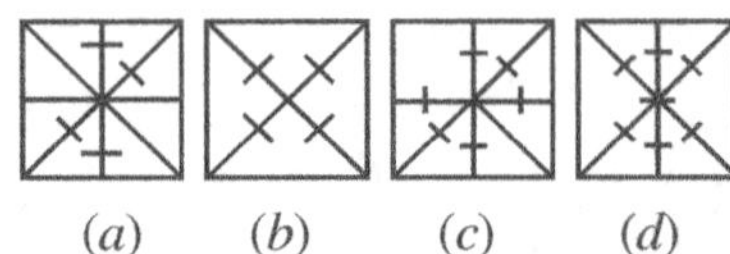

   (a)   (b)   (c)   (d)

32. **Problem Figures**

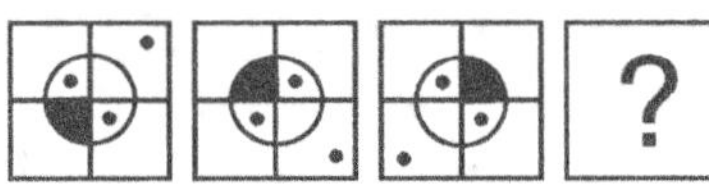

Answer Figures

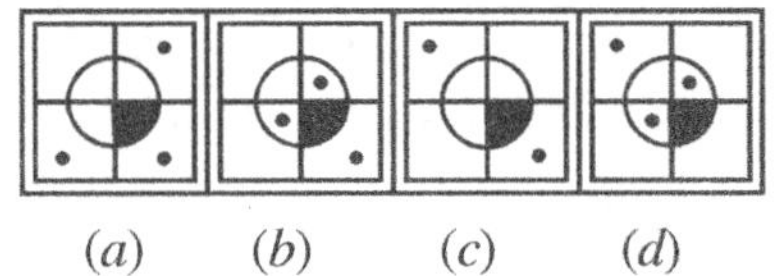

   (a)   (b)   (c)   (d)

33. **Problem Figures**

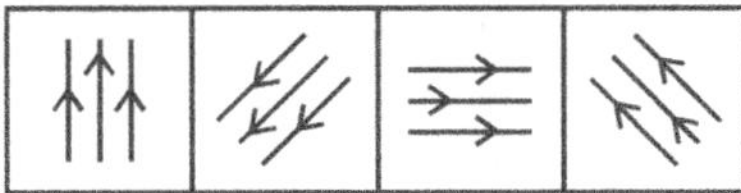

Answer Figures

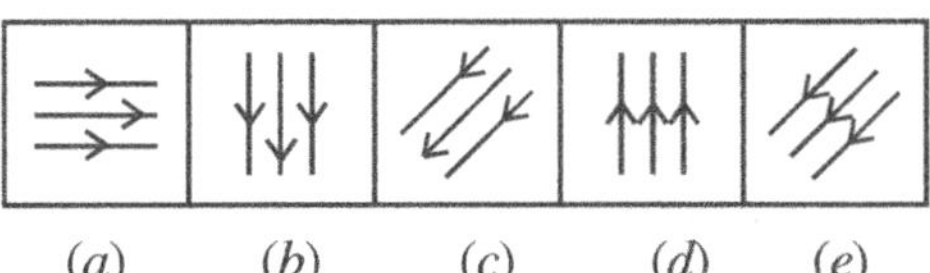

   (a)   (b)   (c)   (d)   (e)

34. **Problem Figures**

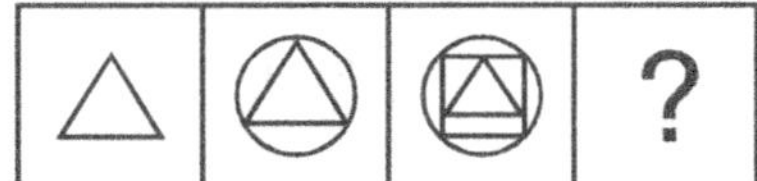

Answer Figures

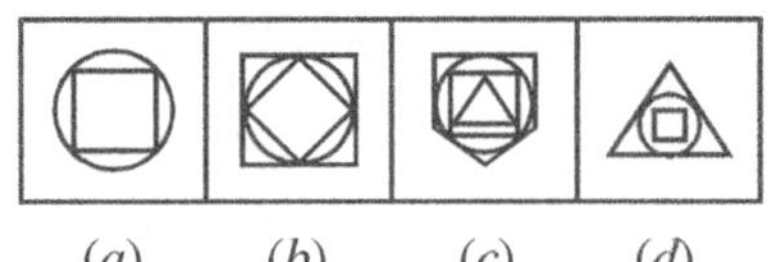

   (a)   (b)   (c)   (d)

35. **Problem Figures**

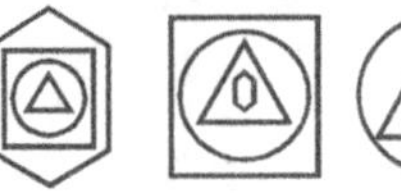

Answer Figures

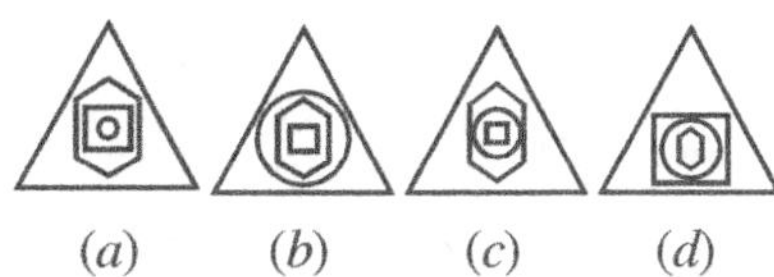

(a)   (b)   (c)   (d)

Directions (Qs. 36 to 40): *The second figure in the first unit of the Problem Figures bears a certain relationship to the first figure. Similarly, one of the figures in the Answer Figures bears the same relationship to the first figure in the second unit of the Problem Figures. Locate the figure which would fit the question mark.*

36. Problem Figures

Answer Figures

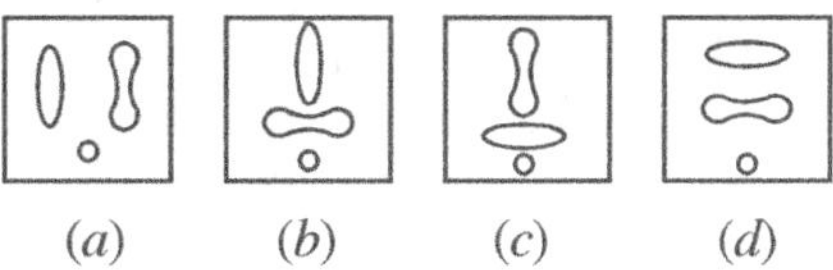

(a)   (b)   (c)   (d)

37. Problem Figures

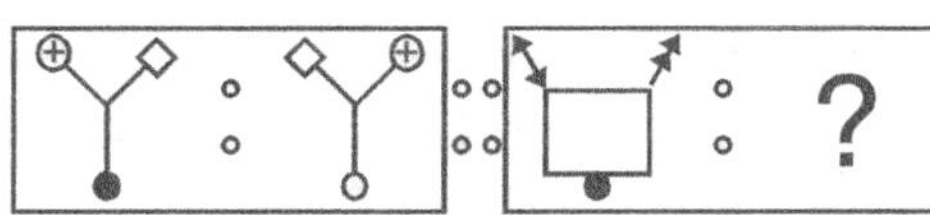

Answer Figures

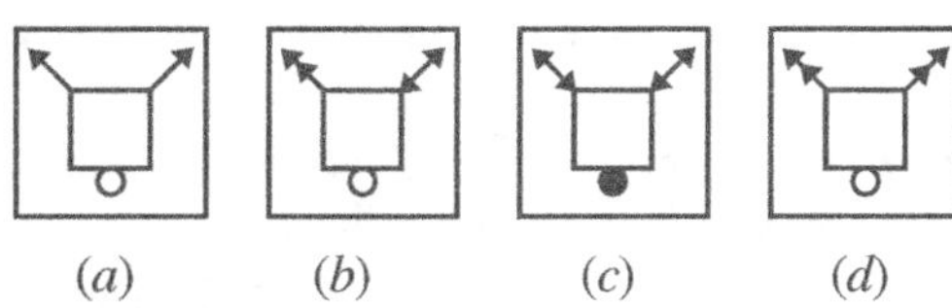

(a)   (b)   (c)   (d)

38. Problem Figures

Answer Figures

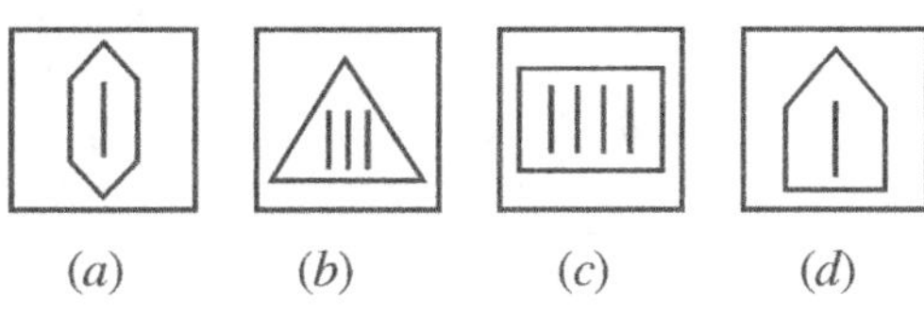

(a)   (b)   (c)   (d)

39. Problem Figures

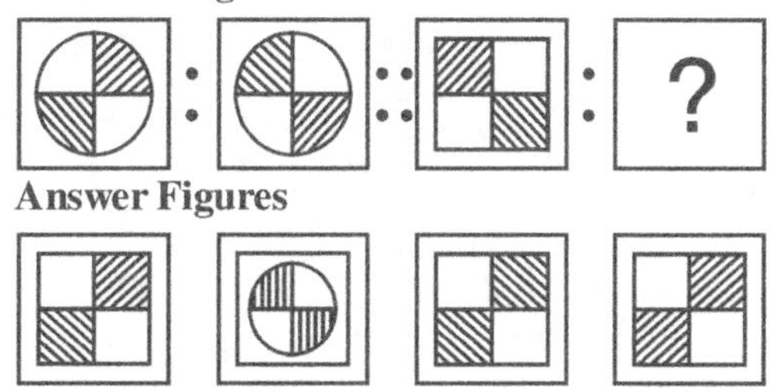

Answer Figures

(a)   (b)   (c)   (d)

40. Problem Figures

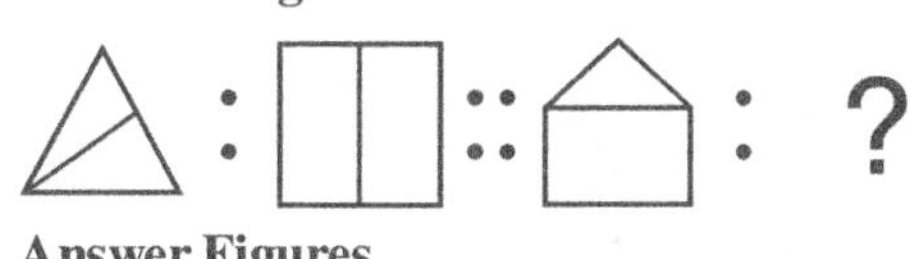

Answer Figures

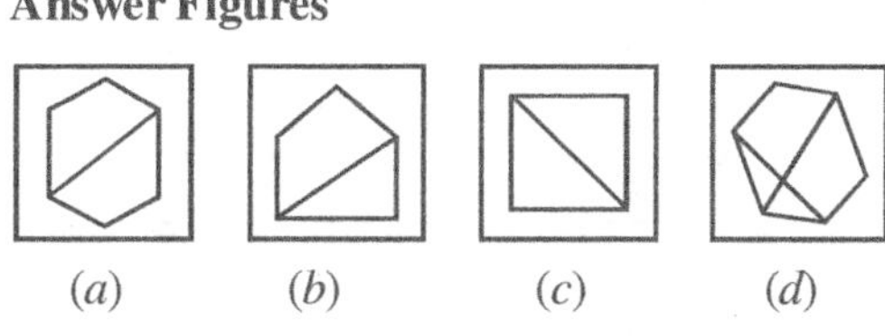

(a)   (b)   (c)   (d)

Directions (Qs. 41 to 45): *In each of the following questions one of the figures is different from the rest. Spot the figure.*

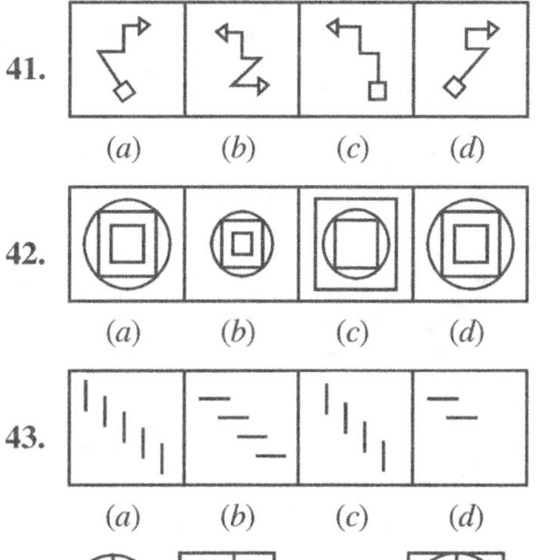

41.   (a)   (b)   (c)   (d)

42.   (a)   (b)   (c)   (d)

43.   (a)   (b)   (c)   (d)

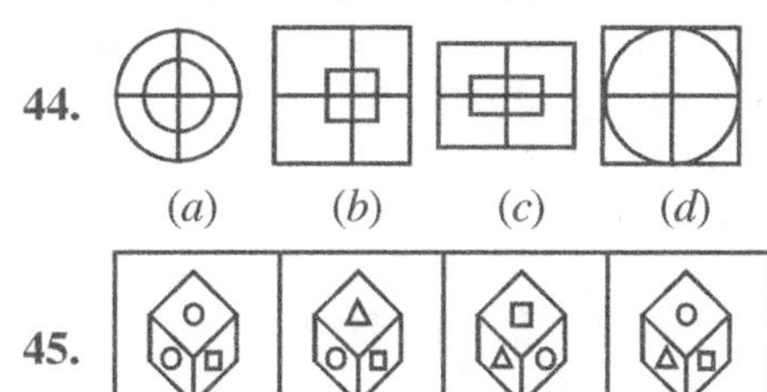

44.   (a)   (b)   (c)   (d)

45.   (a)   (b)   (c)   (d)

Directions (Qs. 46 to 50): *In each question, which one of the alternative figures will complete the given figure pattern?*

46. Pattern 

Alternative figures

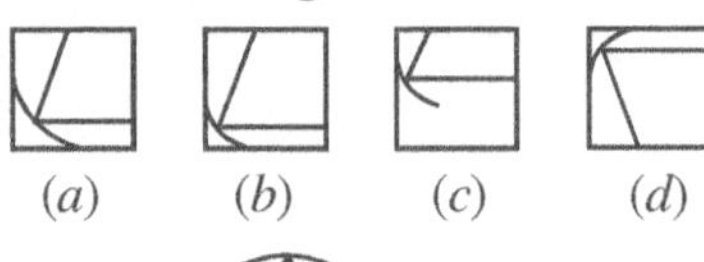

   (*a*)   (*b*)   (*c*)   (*d*)

47. Pattern

Alternative figures

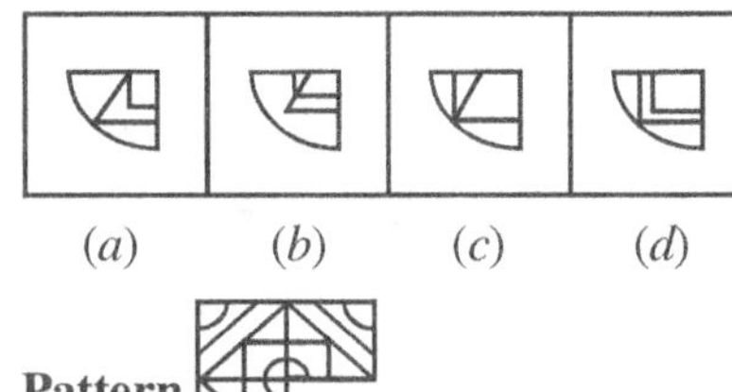

   (*a*)   (*b*)   (*c*)   (*d*)

48. Pattern

Alternative figures

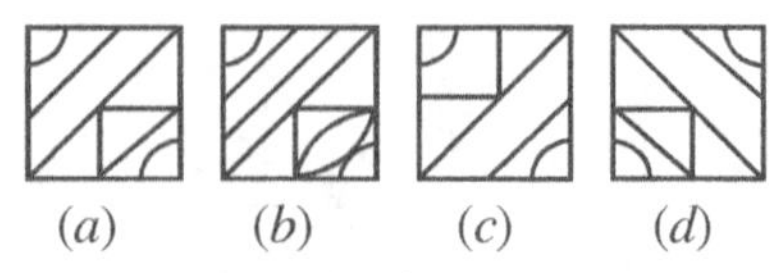

   (*a*)   (*b*)   (*c*)   (*d*)

49. Pattern

Alternative figures

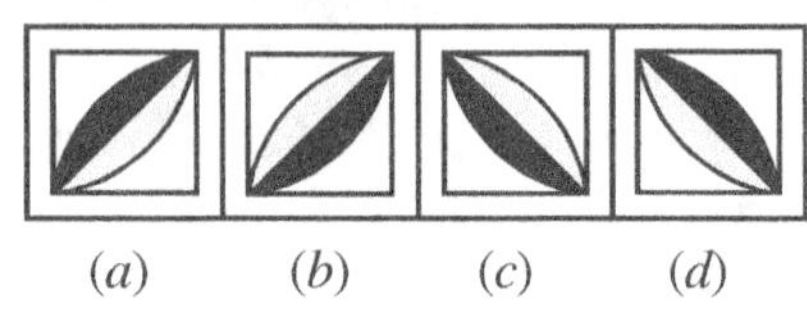

   (*a*)   (*b*)   (*c*)   (*d*)

50. Pattern

Alternative figures

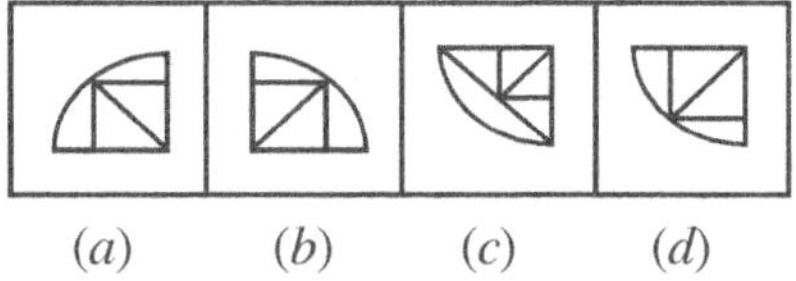

   (*a*)   (*b*)   (*c*)   (*d*)

EXPLANATORY ANSWERS

1. (*d*) : Except 'Record' all the terms are related to secret systems of sending messages.

2. (*c*) : Except 'Brown' all the colours are present in the rainbow.

3. (*d*) : Except 'Home' all the terms represent different sections of area present on the earth. Home can be located in any of these sections of area.

4. (*d*) : All the persons work for the Readers.

5. (*d*) : All the terms represent the different position except Where.

6. (*d*) : All others terms are generally used for pleasant Smell.

7. (*b*) : All other vehicles are used to carry goods and passengers. Tractor is meant for farming.

8. (*d*) : All other terms are related to the Speech.

9. (*b*) : All other arts are hand works on the paper drawn by artist.

10. (*d*) : Only 'Rubber' is a tree product.

11. (*b*) : Second number is double the one more than first number.

12. (*d*) : First number is one more than the half of second number.

13. (*c*) : In other numbers second number is one less than the square of first number.
$(3)^2 - 1 = 8$, $(6)^2 - 1 = 35$ . . . and so on.

14. (*e*) : Digit in the middle is the sum of the other two digits.

15. (*e*) : Second number is one less than the square of first number.

16. (*a*) : Since,

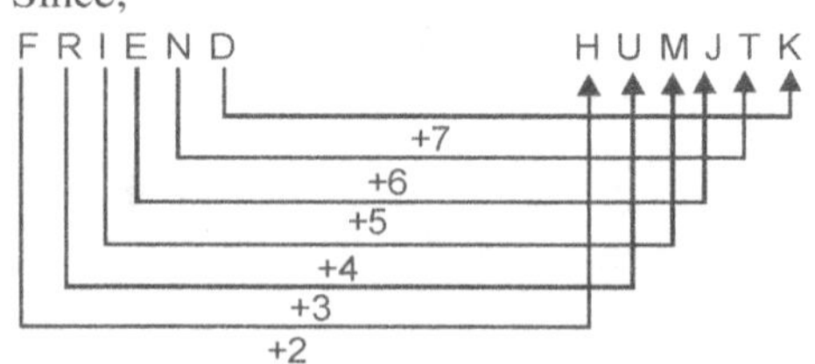

Therefore,

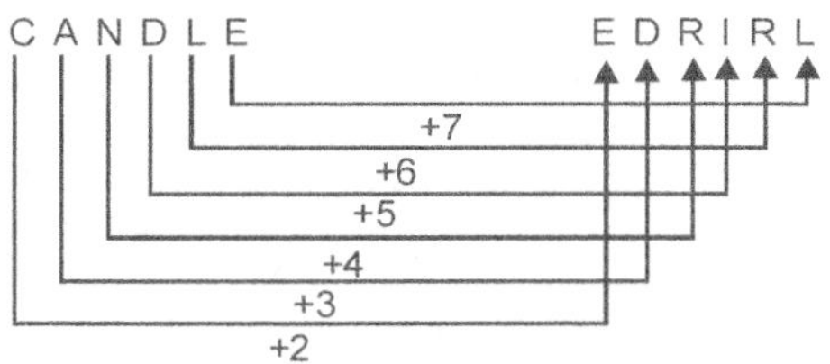

17. (*a*) : Since,

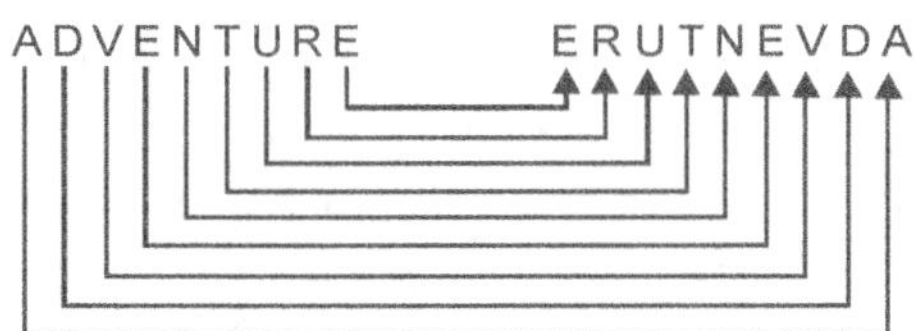

Therefore,

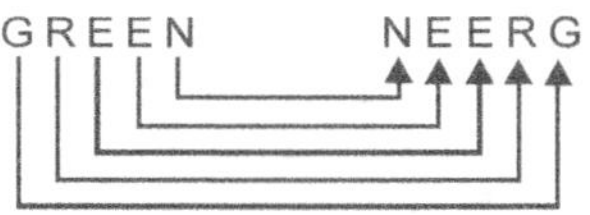

18. (*a*) : Since,

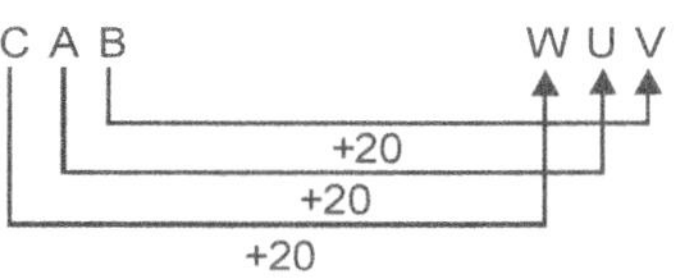

Therefore,

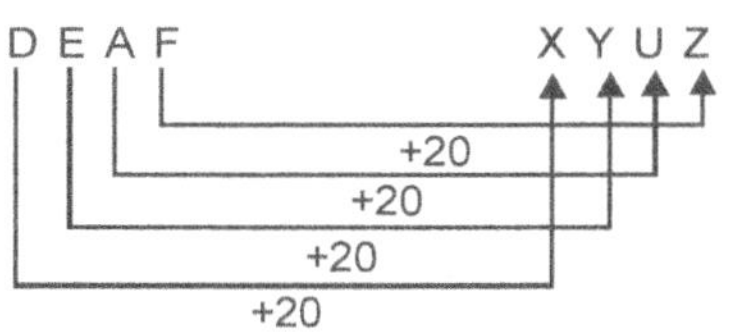

19. (*c*) : Since,

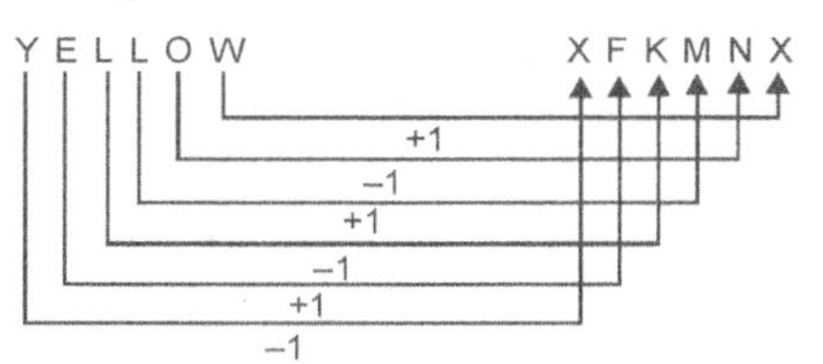

Therefore,

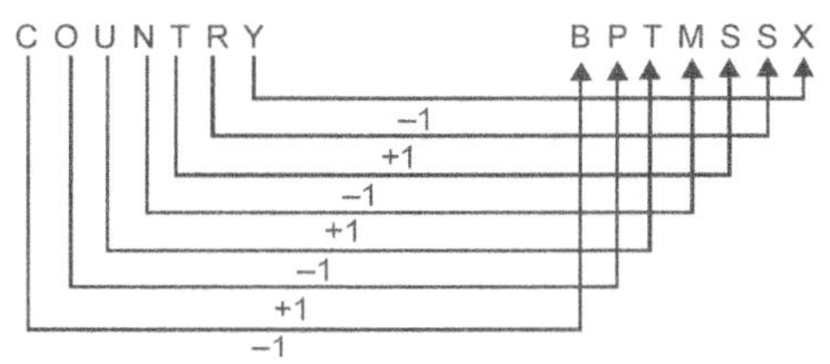

20. (*a*) : Since,

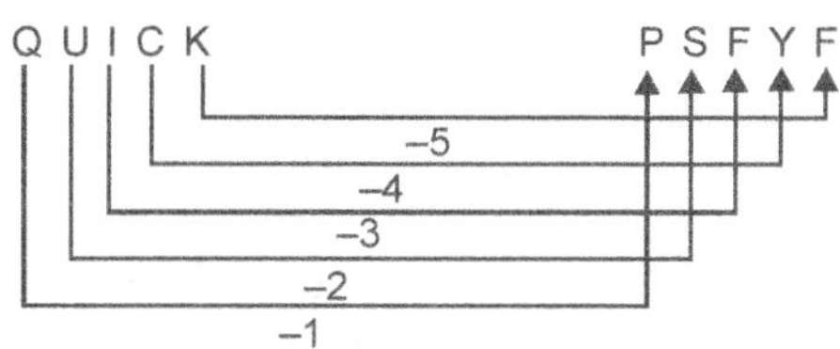

Therefore,

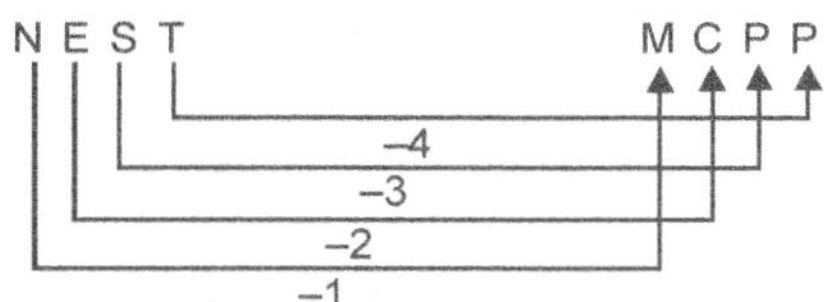

21. (CCOX) : On writing CCOX in the blank spaces, the sequence COXTCCCOXTCCCOX is formed, in which C is increasing by 2 only once.

22. (XCOC) : On writing XCOC in the blank spaces, the sequence COCXOCXCCXCOX-COC is formed.

23. (COOO) : On writing COOO in the blank spaces, the sequence COXVTCOOXXVVTT-COOO is formed, in which O, X, V, T are increasing by 1.

24. (OTCO) : On writing OTCO in the blank spaces, the sequence COXTOXTCXTCOTCO is formed.

25. (TCOX) : On writing TCOX in the blank spaces, the sequence COXTCOXTCOXTCOX is formed, in which COXT is repeated partially four times.

26. The sum of two consecutive numbers of the series gives the next number.

Thus, $4 + 9 = 13$, $9 + 13 = 22$, $13 + 22 = 35$ and so on.

$\therefore$ Missing number $= 22 + 35 = 57$.

27. The sequences is 18×1, 18×2, 18×3, 18×4, $18 \times 5, \ldots$

$\therefore$ Our answer is $18 \times 6 = 108$.

28. The difference between consecutive numbers increases by 1.

Thus, the sequence is $+ 2, + 3, + 4, + 5, \ldots$

$\therefore$ Missing number $= 16 + 6 = 22$.

29. The sequence is $+ 2, + 4, \ldots, \ldots, + 10, + 12$.

Clearly, missing number $= 6 + 6 = 12$.

30. The numbers are $1^3, 2^3, 3^3, 4^3, 5^3, 6^3$.

∴ Our answer is $7^3 = 343$.

31. (*a*) : The middle line segment on the diagonal is extended to touch the corners of the square. In the next figure a new line with three line segments is added. To continue the series the middle line segment should be extended to touch the sides of the square.

32. (*d*) : The complete figure is turned 90° clockwise at each step.

33. (*b*) : In alternate figures the arrows are turned 90° clockwise and the positioning of arrow heads is shifted from front to back and vice versa.

34. (*c*) : A new figure is added to the previous set of figures at each step.

35. (*a*) : The outermost shape is made the innermost shape in the next figure.

36. (*b*) : The two half shapes placed vertically are turned upside down and joined, and this new shape is moved to the top. The two curved shapes placed horizontally are joined and this new shape is moved to the centre. One of the two remaining corner shapes is moved to the bottom.

37. (*b*) : The places of elements on the top are interchanged and the shade inside the circle is removed.

38. (*a*) : One of the vertical lines is removed and the number of lines making the second figure is increased by one.

39. (*a*) : First figure is rotated 90° anticlockwise to get the second figure.

40. (*a*) : The number of lines making the second figure is one more than the number of lines making the first figure.

41. (*b*) : Only this figure has identical design on the corners of the bent line.

42. (*c*) : In all other figures the middle and the centre designs are identical.

43. (*a*) : Only this figure has odd number of line segments.

44. (*d*) : Only this figure has two different shapes divided into equal parts.

45. (*a*) : Only this figure has two identical shapes (circles).

46. (*a*) : 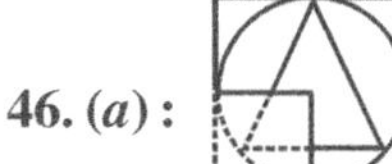

47. (*b*) : 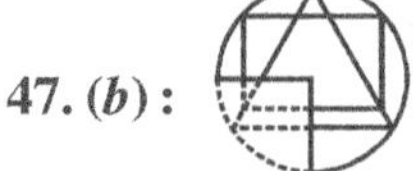

48. (*c*) : 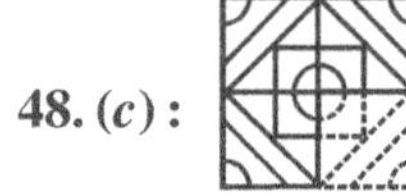

49. (*b*) : 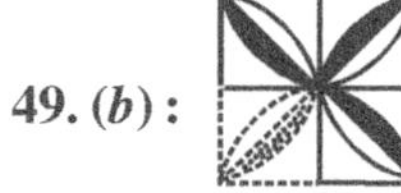

50. (*c*) : 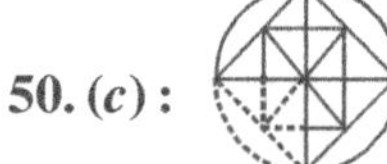

SAINIK SCHOOL ENTRANCE EXAM, 2010
(CLASS-VI)

PAPER-I : MATHEMATICS AND LANGUAGE

PART-A : MATHEMATICS

Section-I

1. Write the smallest and greatest 5-digit number using 8, 0, 3, 2 and 6.

2. Arrange the numbers in descending order—

   53003, 99530, 53050, 53330

3. Write the following Roman numerals in Hindu Arabic numerals—

   (*a*) MMCCCXIV

   (*b*) DCCLXXVII

4. Four traffic signals glow at intervals of 5, 10, 15 and 20 minutes. When will they glow together?

5. Find the value of—

   $8\dfrac{9}{13} + \dfrac{8}{9}$

6. Find the quotient of the following –

   (*a*) $87 \div 4.1$

   (*b*) $1330 \div 0.22$

7. A swimming pool opens at 7:45 a.m. and closes from 1:30 p.m. to 3:30 p.m. Thereafter it remains open till 5:30 p.m. Find the duration for which the swimming pool remains open?

8. The cost of 103 chairs is Rs. 29335, Find the cost 1031 chairs.

9. Which of the following can be the angles of a quadrilateral?

   (*a*) 120°, 60°, 45°, 135°

   (*b*) 105°, 55°, 40°, 45°

10. The length of a rectangular field is twice of its breadth and its breadth is 105/2 m. Find the area of the field.

Section-II

11. Simplify—

    $\dfrac{2}{5}$ of $[2 + \{3 + (12 + 4 + 3)\}]$

12. Find the volume of a Geometry Box whose length is 11.05 cm, breadth is 5.05 cm and height is 1.03 cm.

13. A park of 15 m. 30 cm. length and 12 m. 20 cm. in breadth, is to be surrounded by a barbed wire of four layers. Find the length of barbed wire required.

14. Find the circumference of the circles whose diameters are 16 cm and 20 cm.

15. Name the triangles with following dimensions—

    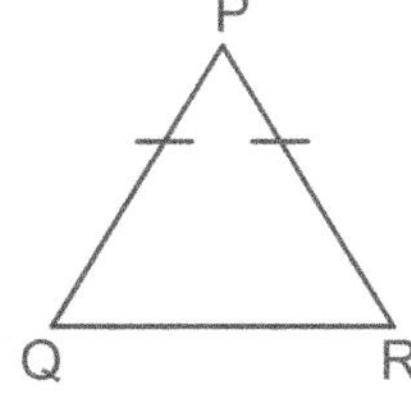

    (*a*) Opposite sides and base angles are equal ....

    (*b*) Three angles $\angle P = 50°$, $\angle Q = 60°$ and $\angle R = 70°$ ....

    (*c*) Three angles $\angle P = 110°$, $\angle Q = 35°$ and $\angle R = 35°$..........

16. Classify each of the following as acute, obtuse or right angle—

    (*a*) 120°   (*b*) 35°

    (*c*) 45° + 45°   (*d*) 85°

    (*e*) 160°   (*f*) 45°

17. On a deposit of ₹ 6000, Sham received at the end of 1 year ₹ 6900. What was his interest and rate of interest?

18. Write True or False.

(a) $\dfrac{4}{6} < \dfrac{7}{8}$

(b) $13 \times \left(\dfrac{15}{9}\right) = \left(\dfrac{13 \times 15}{13 \times 7}\right)$

(c) $88 : 8 = 121 : 11$

19. A School employed a daily-wager for 59 days. He joined the School on 12 Feb., 2000. On which date his term would be completed.
[**Note:** 2000 was a leap year]

20. Add 42 hours 35 minutes 30 seconds and 14 hours 20 minutes and 35 seconds.

Section-III

21. (a) Mohan got 76 marks out of 150, Ravi got 344 marks out of 500, whose score is better?

(b) A bus travelled a distance of 360 km in 10 hrs. Calculate its speed in m/sec. How far will it travel in 18 hrs.?

22. (a) Convert the following into decimal.
   (i) 11%   (ii) 33%
   (iii) $\dfrac{2}{5}$ (iv) 2%
   (v) $\dfrac{8}{9}$

(b) Convert the following decimals into a fraction—
   (i) 3.03   (ii) 0.04
   (iii) 6.7   (iv) 0.300

23. Arrange the following fractions in descending order—
$$\dfrac{3}{4}, \dfrac{6}{8}, \dfrac{3}{5}, \dfrac{4}{6}, \dfrac{5}{3}, \dfrac{7}{3}$$

24. How many spoons will be required to make complete sets of 30, 34 and 40?

25. Sh. Mani went to Jain Stores on 15 Lal Chowk, J & K on the 4 Dec., 2008. He bought the following items— $8\dfrac{1}{2}$ kg flour at ₹ 9.40 per kg. $9\dfrac{1}{4}$ kg Oil at ₹ 64.70 per kg, $6\dfrac{3}{4}$ kg. rice at ₹ 27.30 per kg. Make a bill for what he received. His bill number was 555.

26. Draw a circle whose length of diameter is 14 cm with the help of compass. Calculate the length of the circumference.

27. A man bought 800 orange for ₹ 560.00. Seventy oranges got crushed. He sold the remaining for 80 p each. Find the gain or loss %.

28. A, B and C have a total of ₹ 8855. The ratio of the money between A and B is 9 : 11. If C has ₹ 2855. Calculate A's and B's Share.

29. Fill in the blanks—
   (a) 5.35 : .... = 0.00535
   (b) SP = Rs. 2175, CP = ₹ 1740, Profit/Loss% = ...
   (c) Sum of the angles of a quadrilateral is ....
   (d) Volume of a cube = ...
   (e) Perimeter of Square of side = A/3 is ....

30. Match the following—
   (a) If two angles have a common vertex they are   (i) 60°
   (b) Measurement of two right angles   (ii) Complementary
   (c) Equilateral triangle has each angle   (iii) 130°
   (d) If the sum of the two angles is 90° then they are   (iv) Adjacent
   (e) Supplementary angle of 50°   (v) 180°

EXPLANATORY ANSWERS

1. From the given digits 8, 0, 3, 2 and 6.
Smallest number of five digits = 20368.
Greatest number = 86320.

2. Given numbers are—
53003, 99530, 53050 and 53330
In descending order it will be written as
99530, 53330, 53050, 53003.

3. In Roman Numerals
M = 1000, D = 500, C = 100, L = 50, X = 10,
V = 5, I = 1, II = 2, III = 3 and IV = 4.
 (*a*) MMCCCXIV
  $= 2 \times 1000 + 3 \times 100 + 10 + 4 = 2314.$
 (*b*) DCCLXXVII
  $= 500 + 2 \times 100 + 50 + 2 \times 10 + 7 = 777.$

4. L.C.M. of 5, 10, 15 and 20 = 60
They will glow together after 60 minutes.

5. $$8\frac{9}{13} + \frac{8}{9} = \frac{113}{13} + \frac{8}{9}$$
$$= \frac{1017 + 104}{117}$$
$$= \frac{1121}{117} = 9\frac{68}{117}.$$

6. (*a*) $$87 \div 4.1 = \frac{87}{4.1}$$
$$= \frac{870}{41}$$
$$= 21\frac{9}{41}$$
∴ Quotient = 21.

 (*b*) $$1330 \div 0.22 = \frac{1330}{.22}$$
$$= \frac{133000}{22} = \frac{66500}{11}$$
$$= 6045\frac{5}{11}$$
∴ Quotient = 6045.

7. Duration between 7.45 am to 1.30 pm
  = 5.45 hrs.
  = 5 hrs. 45 minutes.
Duration again between 3.30 pm to 5.30 pm
  = 2 hours
Total duration = 5 hrs. 45 minutes + 2 hrs.
  = 7 hrs. 45 minutes.

8. ∵ Cost of 103 chairs = ₹ 29335
 ∴ Cost of 1 chair $= \dfrac{29335}{103}$
  = 284.31
  = ₹ 285 (approximately)
Also cost of 1030 chairs = 293350
 ∴ Cost of 1031 chairs
  = ₹ 285 + ₹ 293350
  = ₹ 293635.

9. We have, sum of angles of a quadrilateral = 360°
 (*a*) Sum of the angles = 120° + 60° + 45° + 135°
  = 360°
   ∴ A is the angles of a quadrilateral.
 (*b*) Sum of the angles = 105° + 55° + 40° + 45°
  = 245°
   ∴ B is not the angles of a quadrilateral.

10. ∵ Breadth $= \dfrac{105}{2}$ m
 ∴ Length $= 2 \times \dfrac{105}{2}$ m = 105 m
Area of the rectangular field = $l \times b$
$$= \frac{105 \times 105}{2}$$
$$= \frac{11025}{2} \text{ m}^2$$
$$= 5512.50 \text{ m}^2.$$

11. $$\frac{2}{5} \times [2 + \{3 + (12 + 4 + 3)\}]$$
$$= \frac{2}{3} \times [2 + \{3 + 19\}]$$
$$= \frac{2}{5} \times [2 + 22]$$

$= \dfrac{2}{5} \times 24$

$= \dfrac{48}{5} = 9\dfrac{3}{5}.$

12. Volume $= l \times b \times h$

Volume $= 11.05 \times 5.05 \times 1.03$

$\qquad = 57.476$ cm^3

$\qquad = 57.48$ cm^3 (approximately).

13. Perimeter of the rectangular park

$\qquad = 2\,(L + B)$

$\qquad = 2\,(15 \text{ m } 30 \text{ cm} + 12 \text{ m } 20 \text{ cm})$

$\qquad = 2 \times (27 \text{ m } 50 \text{ cm})$

$\qquad = 55$ m.

$\because$ Length of one layer $= 55$m

Length of the barbed wire of four layers

$= 55 \times 4 = 220$ m.

14. $D_1 = 16$ cm

$\quad C_1 = \pi \times$ Diameter

$\qquad = \pi \times 16$

$\qquad = 16\pi$ cm

$\quad D_2 = 20$ cm

$\quad C_2 = \pi \times 20$

$\qquad = 20\pi$ cm.

15. (*a*) Isosceles triangle.

(*b*) Scalene triangle.

(*c*) Obtuse isosceles triangle.

16. (*a*) = Obtuse angle

(*b*) = Acute angle

(*c*) = Right angle

(*d*) = Acute angle

(*e*) = Obtuse angle

(F) = Acute angle.

17. P $= ₹\ 6000$

A $= ₹\ 6900$

(S.I.) $= ₹\ 6900 - 6000$

$\qquad = ₹\ 900$

T $= 1$ year

$r = \dfrac{100 \times \text{S.I.}}{\text{T} \times \text{P}}$

$\quad = \dfrac{100 \times 900}{1 \times 6000}$

$\quad = 15\%$ per annum.

18. (*a*) $\because \qquad \dfrac{4}{6} < \dfrac{7}{8}$

$\Rightarrow \qquad 4 \times 8 < 7 \times 6$

$\therefore \qquad 32 < 42.$ **True**

(*b*) $\because \quad 13 \times \left(\dfrac{15}{9}\right) = \dfrac{13 \times 15}{13 \times 7}$

$\Rightarrow \qquad \dfrac{65}{3} = \dfrac{15}{7}$

$\therefore \qquad 455 = 45$ **False**

(*c*) $\because \qquad 88 : 8 = 121 : 11$

$\Rightarrow \qquad \dfrac{88}{8} = \dfrac{121}{11}$

$\therefore \qquad 11 = 11.$ **True**

19. In a leap year February $= 29$ days.

Number of working days in February

$\qquad = 29 - 11$

$\qquad = 18$ days

March $= 31$ days

April $= 10$ days

Total $= 18 + 31 + 10 = 59$ days.

$\therefore$ Last date of the term $= $ 10th April, 2000.

20.

$$
\begin{array}{r}
42 \text{ hrs} \quad 35' \quad 30'' \\
+\ 14 \text{ hrs} \quad 20' \quad 35'' \\
\hline
56 \text{ hrs} \quad 56' \quad 5'' \\
\end{array}
$$

$= 56$ hrs $56'$ $5''.$

21. (*a*) Mohan's % $= \dfrac{76}{150} \times 100$

$\qquad\qquad\qquad = \dfrac{152}{3}\%$

$\qquad\qquad\qquad = 50.667\%$

Ravi's % $= \dfrac{344}{500} \times 100$

$\qquad\qquad = \dfrac{344}{5}\% = 68.8\%$

Ravi is better than Mohan.

(*b*) Speed of the bus

$\qquad\qquad = \dfrac{360}{10}$ km/hr

$\qquad\qquad = 36$ km/hr

$$= \frac{36 \times 5}{18} \text{ m/s}$$
$$= 10 \text{ m/s}$$
$$\text{D} = \text{S} \times t$$
$$\therefore \quad \text{Distance} = 18 \times 36 \text{ kms}$$
$$= 648 \text{ kms.}$$

22. (*a*) (*i*) $\quad 11\% = \dfrac{11}{100} = 0.11$

(*ii*) $\quad 33\% = \dfrac{33}{100} = 0.33$

(*iii*) $\quad \dfrac{2}{5} = 0.4$

(*iv*) $\quad 2\% = \dfrac{2}{100} = 0.02$

(*v*) $\quad \dfrac{8}{9} = 0.88$

(*b*) (*i*) $\quad 3.03 = \dfrac{303}{100} = 3\dfrac{3}{100}$

(*ii*) $\quad 0.04 = \dfrac{4}{100} = \dfrac{1}{25}$

(*iii*) $\quad 6.7 = \dfrac{67}{10} = 6\dfrac{7}{10}$

(*iv*) $\quad 0.300 = \dfrac{3}{10}$

23. It can be written as
$$\frac{3}{4}, \frac{6}{8}, \frac{3}{5}, \frac{4}{6}, \frac{5}{3}, \frac{7}{3}$$
$$\Rightarrow \quad \frac{3}{4}, \frac{3}{4}, \frac{3}{5}, \frac{2}{3}, \frac{5}{3}, \frac{7}{3}$$
$$\Rightarrow \quad \frac{3}{4}, \frac{3}{5}, \frac{2}{3}, \frac{5}{3}, \frac{7}{3}$$
L.C.M. of $4, 5, 3 = 4 \times 5 \times 3 = 60$
$$\text{Given fractions} = \frac{3}{4}, \frac{3}{5}, \frac{2}{3}, \frac{5}{3}, \frac{7}{3}$$
$$= \frac{45, 36, 40, 100, 140}{60}$$
$$\therefore \quad \frac{7}{3}, \frac{5}{3}, \frac{3}{4}, \frac{2}{3} \text{ and } \frac{3}{5} \text{ are in descending order.}$$

24. Number of Spoons = L.C.M. of 30, 34, 40
$$= 2040$$

25. Jain Stores

15 Lal Chowk, J & K $\hspace{2cm}$ Bill No. 555

Date..........

| 0 | 4 | 1 | 2 | 2 | 0 | 0 | 8 |

Customers Name.......... Shri Mani

S. No.	Name of the Article	Weight	Rate per kg		Amount	
			₹	P.	₹	P.
1.	Flour	$8\frac{1}{2}$ kg	9	40	79	90
2.	Oil	$9\frac{1}{4}$ kg	64	70	598	48
3.	Rice	$6\frac{3}{4}$ kg	27	30	184	28
			Total		862	66

Thank you $\hspace{3cm}$ Signature

....

26.

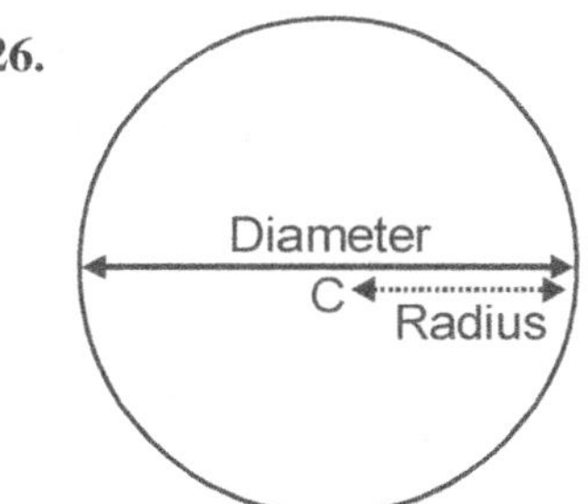

$$\text{C} = \pi \times \text{diameter}$$
$$= \frac{22}{7} \times 14$$
$$= 44 \text{ cm.}$$

27. $\hspace{3cm}$ C.P. = ₹ 560.

Number of crushed oranges = 70

Number of good oranges = 800 − 70
$$= 730$$
$$\text{S.P.} = ₹ 584$$
$$\text{Profit} = \text{S.P.} - \text{C.P.}$$
$$= ₹ 584 - ₹ 560$$
$$= ₹ 24$$

88

$$\text{Profit \%} = \frac{\text{Profit}}{\text{CP}} \times 100$$

$$= \frac{24 \times 100}{560}\%$$

$$= \frac{30}{7}\% = 4\frac{2}{7}\%.$$

28. Total amount of A, B and C = ₹ 8855

C's share = ₹ 2855

∴ Amount (A and B have)

$$= ₹ 8855 - ₹ 2855$$

$$= ₹ 6000$$

According to the question,

$$A : B = 9 : 11$$

∴   A's share $= \dfrac{9}{20} \times 6000$

$$= ₹ 2700$$

∴   B's share $= \dfrac{11}{20} \times 6000$

$$= ₹ 3300.$$

29. (*a*) $5.35 \div 1000 = 0.00535$

(*b*)   Profit $=$ SP $-$ CP

$$= 2175 - 1740$$

$$= ₹ 435$$

Profit \% $= \dfrac{\text{Profit}}{\text{CP}} \times 100$

$$= \frac{435 \times 100}{1740}\% = 25\%.$$

(*c*) Sum of the angles of a quadrilateral is $360°$

(*d*) Volume of a cube $= (\text{side})^3$

(*e*) Perimeter of a square $= 4 \times$ side

$$= \frac{4 \times A}{3}$$

$$= \frac{4A}{3}.$$

30. (*a*)   (*iv*)   Adjacent

(*b*)   (*v*) $180°$

(*c*)   (*i*) $60°$

(*d*)   (*ii*)   Complementary

(*e*)   (*iii*) $180° - 50° = 130°.$

PART-B : LANGUAGE

1. Write an essay in 15 sentences on any one of the following topics—

(*a*) My Dream

(*b*) A Visit to Fair

2. Read the following passage carefully and answer the questions—

City children suffer from great disability. They have little contact with Nature. They do not know the joy of living in the open air. In cities there is no space to live. So one storey is piled upon another. Their lives have become so artificial that they can not see the stars at night. They get flower pots and put paper flowers in them. They hang pictures of Sunrise and Sunset on the walls. Wherever one turns, one finds artificial lights during the day as well as night. They have lost even the darkness of the night which was given to man for peace, rest and quiet thought. The task before education is to change the whole system of values that is current in our cities. Distance in large cities are long. All the people don't have their own means of transport. They have to depend upon the State or private buses. The number of bus users is very large. Every bus stop is, therefore, crowded. The number of buses is inadequate. Thus people suffer the torture of long wait at the bus stop. Some bus stops are quite orderly.

(*a*) Which disability do the city children suffer from?

(*b*) How have their lives become artificial?

(*c*) What is the importance of darkness of night for man?

(*d*) Where do they hang pictures of Sunrise?

(*e*) What does the world 'adequate' means in the passage? Tick the correct answer.

  (i) much

  (ii) proper

  (*iii*) sufficient

  (*iv*) just

3. Make a sentences of your own for each underlined word given in the following passage. (Do not copy any sentence from the given paragraph)—

   Milk is a <u>complete</u> food full of vitamins and proteins. Children should <u>drink</u> it regularly otherwise they might <u>suffer</u> from under-nourishment. Elders must take it but those who can not <u>afford</u> it should take pulses, fruits and vegetables as an alternative. We should <u>purchase</u> milk of good quality from milk booths opened by the Government.

4. Form meaningful sentences by rearranging the words in proper order—
   (*a*) Decided/down/go/to/I/shore/to the/again.
   (*b*) Book/his/a/wanted/birthday/for/he.
   (*c*) Under/a/standing/the/boy/tree/is.
   (*d*) Poem/to/below/listen/given/the.
   (*e*) New/bought/My/a/car/Father.

5. Give one word for the following—
   (*a*) One who makes iron goods.
   (*b*) One hundred years.
   (*c*) One who mends shoes.
   (*d*) One who believes in God.
   (*e*) A place where science practicals are performed.

6. Use each of the word in separate sentences of your own to show the difference in the meaning of the words of the pairs given below—
   (*a*) Story, Storey
   (*b*) Floor, Flour
   (*c*) Prey, Pray
   (*d*) Tail, Tale
   (*e*) Lone, Loan

7. Choose the correct article/conjunction/prepositions (a, an, and, else, to still, but and fill) in the blanks—
   (*a*) I prefer coffee .... Milk.
   (*b*) He tried often .... he could not pass.
   (*c*) Work hard .... you will fail in the examination.
   (*d*) He is .... able man.
   (*e*) Man proposes .... God disposes.

8. Change each of the following as directed—
   (*a*) Sohan is a Goldsmith.
                    (Change into Interrogative)
   (*b*) Mohan says, ''Kailash was lazy''.
                    (Change into Indirect Speech)
   (*c*) Neha said that she was busy then.
                    (Change into Direct Speech)
   (*d*) Who broke this plate?
                    (Change into Passive Voice)
   (*e*) He is dead.   (Change into Exclamatory)

9. Fill in the blanks with words that are opposite in meaning to those given in the brackets—
   (*a*) This news is ....   (false)
   (*b*) This shirt is .....   (dirty)
   (*c*) Chinese Language is .... to learn. (easy)
   (*d*) He is a .... boy.   (rude)
   (*e*) She is a .... girl.   (bold)

EXPLANATORY ANSWERS

1. (A)   **My Dream**

I live in a village near Gwalior city. The distance between Gwalior aerodrome and my village is about 6 km. Aircrafts and helicopters keep on hovering my house day and night. I also want to become a pilot. I want to join Indian Air Force. I want to fly high in the sky. One day, I saw the live telecast of the Air Force. About a dozen aircrafts and six helicopters took part in the air show. Many types of aerobatics were performed by the aircrafts and helicopters. I saw a dream in the night. I saw that I was a pilot in Indian Air Force posted at Gwalior aerodrome. In the dream, I saw that I was sitting in the cockpit. After getting orders from the

senior officer I started the plane. Within few minutes my plane was flying in the sky. After half an hour my plane landed at Indira Gandhi National Airport. New Delhi. I switched off the engine and stepped out of the plane. Suddenly, I fell down from the bed with a big sound. My mother came running and lifted me from the floor. I told her about my dream. She hugged me and said, ''My son, you will be a pilot.'' I am sure that my mother's blessing will come true in the coming years.

2. (*a*) City children suffer from the disability of living away from the open air and nature.

(*b*) Their lives have become artificial because they can not see Sunrise and Sunset.

(*c*) Darkness of night gives a man mental peace, rest and a quiet thought.

(*d*) They hang the pictures of rising sun on the walls.

(*e*) Sufficient.

3. (*a*) **Complete**—The doctor advised patient to take complete bed rest.

(*b*) **Drink**—I drink coco-cola only once or twice in a month.

(*c*) **Suffer**—Many people suffer from Malaria during rainy season.

(*d*) **Afford**—Many poor people can not afford to send their children in costly schools.

(*e*) **Purchase**—I always purchase good magazines.

4. (*a*) I decided to go to the shore again.

(*b*) He wanted a book for his birthday.

(*c*) A boy is standing under the tree.

(*d*) Listen to the poem given below.

(*e*) My father bought a new car.

5. (*a*) Blacksmith (*b*) Century

(*c*) Cobbler (*d*) Theist

(*e*) Laboratory

6. (*a*) **Story**—My grandmother told me a story yesterday.

Storey—My house is a double storey house.

(*b*) **Floor**—My mother cleans the floor daily.

Flour—Wheat flour is liked by all.

(*c*) **Prey**—Eagles are birds of prey.

Pray—Christians pray in a church.

(*d*) **Tail**—A dog wags his tail when it's happy.

Tale—My mother told us a tale yesterday.

(*e*) **Lone**—A lone tree stood out on the bare ridge.

Loan—My father took loan from a bank.

7. (*a*) to (*b*) but

(*c*) else (*d*) an

(*e*) but

8. (*a*) Is Sohan a goldsmith?

(*b*) Mohan says that Kailash was lazy.

(*c*) Neha said, ''She is busy now.''

(*d*) By whom this plate was broken?

(*e*) Alas! He is dead.

9. (*a*) true (*b*) clean

(*c*) difficult (*d*) polite

(*e*) timid

PAPER-II : INTELLIGENCE TEST

Directions (Qs. 1 to 10): *In each of the following questions find the odd one—*

1. (*a*) Mango (*b*) Guava

(*c*) Papaya (*d*) Neem

2. (*a*) Ginger (*b*) Cauliflower

(*c*) Potato (*d*) Arum

3. (*a*) Dog (*b*) Cat

(*c*) Cow (*d*) Tiger

4. (*a*) Clock (*b*) Ring

(*c*) Chain (*d*) Tie

5. (*a*) Paper (*b*) Pen

(*c*) Ink (*d*) Student

6. (*a*) Lucknow (*b*) Patna

(*c*) Jaipur (*d*) Delhi

7. (*a*) Hair (*b*) Nail

(*c*) Teeth (*d*) Clean

8. (*a*) Crow (*b*) Owl

(*c*) Eagle (*d*) Pigeon

9. (*a*) Flower (*b*) Leaf

(*c*) Fruit (*d*) Garden

10. (*a*) Ear (*b*) Eye

(*c*) Heart (*d*) Lung

Directions (Qs. 11 to 20): *Each of the following questions complete the series—*

11. 1, 7, 14, 22, ...

(*a*) 30 (*b*) 29

(*c*) 31 (*d*) 32

12. 35, 33, 30, 26, ...

(*a*) 19 (*b*) 21

(*c*) 22 (*d*) 26

13. 2, 6, 14, 30, ...
   (*a*) 52   (*b*) 48
   (*c*) 42   (*d*) 62

14. 5, 9, 18, 34, ...
   (*a*) 59   (*b*) 49
   (*c*) 45   (*d*) 54

15. 4, 6, 9, 13.5, ...
   (*a*) 20.25   (*b*) 17.25
   (*c*) 19.25   (*d*) 18.25

16. 6, 19, 58, ...
   (*a*) 170   (*b*) 175
   (*c*) 165   (*d*) 145

17. A, E, I, O, ...
   (*a*) W   (*b*) U
   (*c*) A   (*d*) Y

18. C, E, H, L, ...
   (*a*) P   (*b*) O
   (*c*) Q   (*d*) R

19. 5, 15, 55, 235, ...
   (*a*) 855   (*b*) 665
   (*c*) 725   (*d*) 1195

20. 1, 8, 27, 64, ...
   (*a*) 128   (*b*) 216
   (*c*) 256   (*d*) 125

Directions (Qs. 21 to 30): *In a certain code language PRODUCER is coded as 56437286 and KINDER is coded as 190386. How are the following words coded in that code language—*

21. RENDER
   (*a*) 680386   (*b*) 680836
   (*c*) 683086   (*d*) 670538

22. POURD
   (*a*) 54673   (*b*) 57636
   (*c*) 54763   (*d*) 75432

23. DRINK
   (*a*) 90136   (*b*) 36901
   (*c*) 36109   (*d*) 36190

24. DONER
   (*a*) 34086   (*b*) 30486
   (*c*) 35086   (*d*) 34096

25. REDOP
   (*a*) 68347   (*b*) 68340
   (*c*) 68343   (*d*) 68345

26. DROPPED
   (*a*) 3645583   (*b*) 3645582
   (*c*) 3645853   (*d*) 3645830

27. REPRODUCE
   (*a*) 685643728   (*b*) 685643722
   (*c*) 685647328   (*d*) 685634722

28. DIPPER
   (*a*) 395568   (*b*) 395486
   (*c*) 395586   (*d*) 395587

29. UNDER
   (*a*) 70385   (*b*) 70386
   (*c*) 70383   (*d*) 70387

30. NIKDORE
   (*a*) 0913478   (*b*) 0913498
   (*c*) 3913468   (*d*) 3914398

Directions (Qs. 31 to 40): *In each of the following questions four words have been given, out of which three are alike in some manner and the fourth one is different. Choose out the odd one—*

31. (*a*) Patna   (*b*) Lucknow
   (*c*) Bhopal   (*d*) Delhi

32. (*a*) Tendulkar   (*b*) Sangkara
   (*c*) Jadeja   (*d*) Saniya

33. (*a*) River   (*b*) Drain
   (*c*) Canal   (*d*) Pond

34. (*a*) Crow   (*b*) Eagle
   (*c*) Kite   (*d*) Pigeon

35. (*a*) Boat   (*b*) Train
   (*c*) Truck   (*d*) Car

36. (*a*) Crocodile   (*b*) Whale
   (*c*) Tortoise   (*d*) Frog

37. (*a*) Rajeev Gandhi

   (*b*) Morarjee Desai
   (*c*) Chandra Shekhar Azad
   (*d*) Atal Bihari Vajpayee

38. (*a*) Length   (*b*) Breadth
   (*c*) Height   (*d*) Volume

39. (*a*) Table   (*b*) Chair
   (*c*) Stool   (*d*) Furniture

40. (*a*) Car   (*b*) Scooter
   (*c*) Jeep   (*d*) Van

Directions (Qs. 41 to 45): *In each of the following sets of figures, select the one that is different from the rest—*

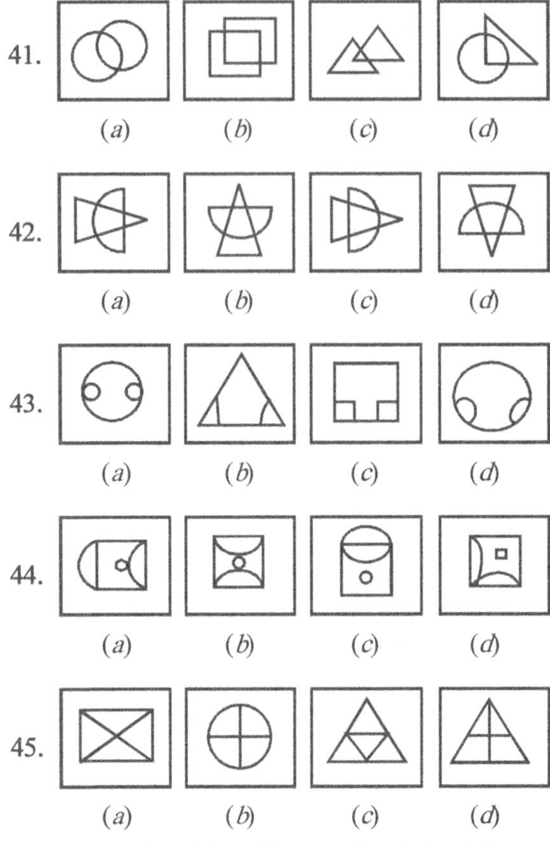

41.
(a) (b) (c) (d)

42.
(a) (b) (c) (d)

43.
(a) (b) (c) (d)

44.
(a) (b) (c) (d)

45.
(a) (b) (c) (d)

Directions (Qs. 46 to 50): *Each of the following questions consists of four unmarked figures followed by four figures marked (a), (b), (c) and (d). Select a figure from the marked figures which will continue the series established by the unmarked figures—*

46. Problem Set

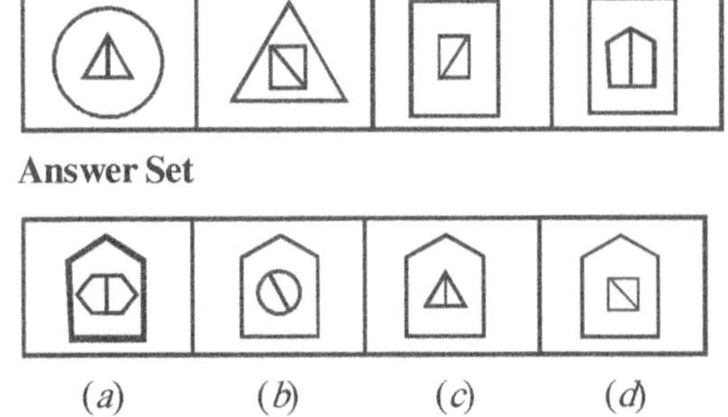

Answer Set

(a) (b) (c) (d)

47. Problem Set

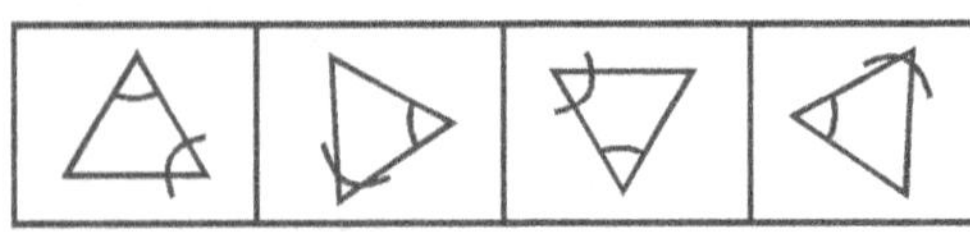

Answer Set

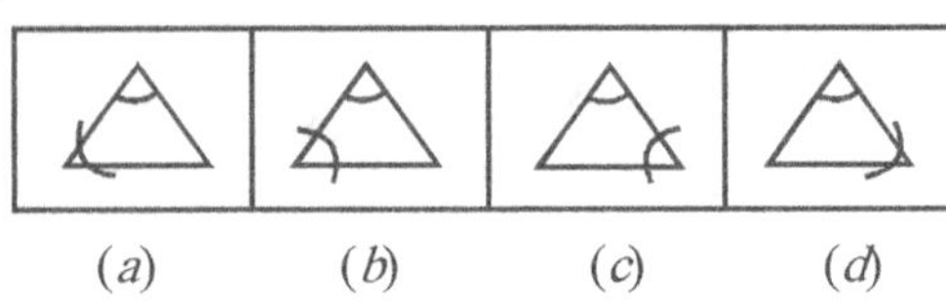

(a) (b) (c) (d)

48. Problem Set

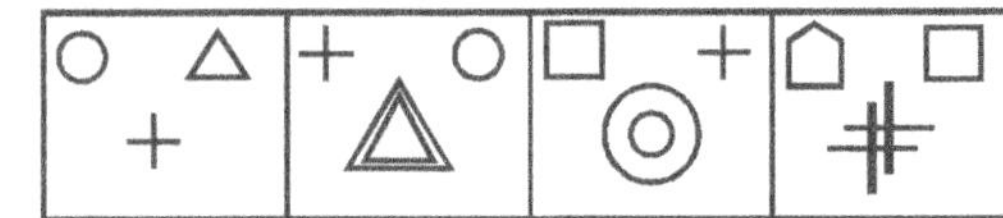

Answer Set

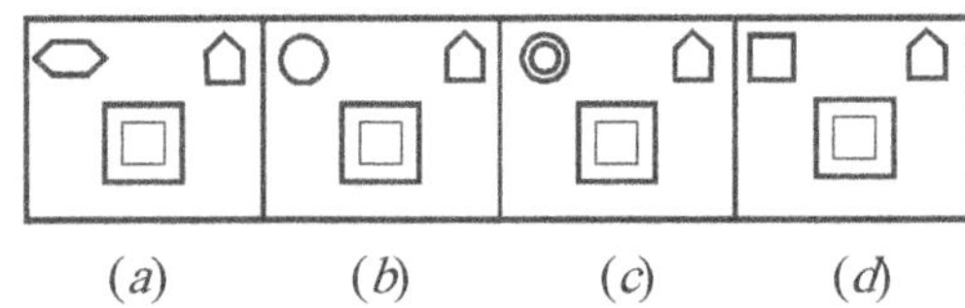

(a) (b) (c) (d)

49. Problem Set

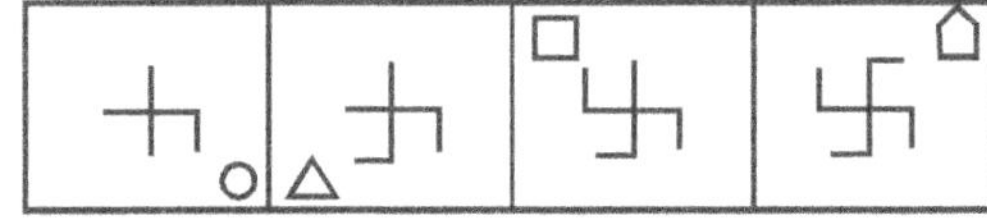

Answer Set

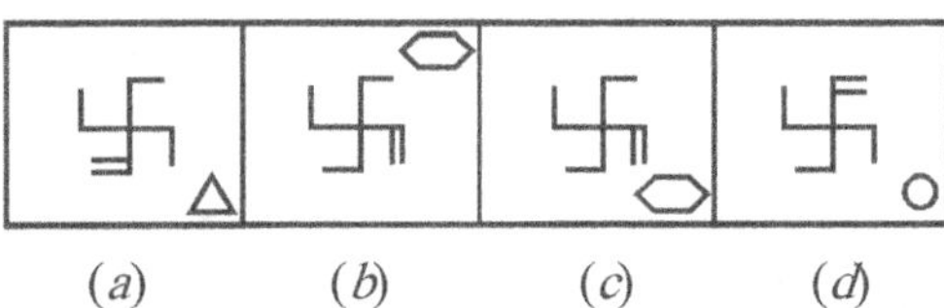

(a) (b) (c) (d)

50. Problem Set

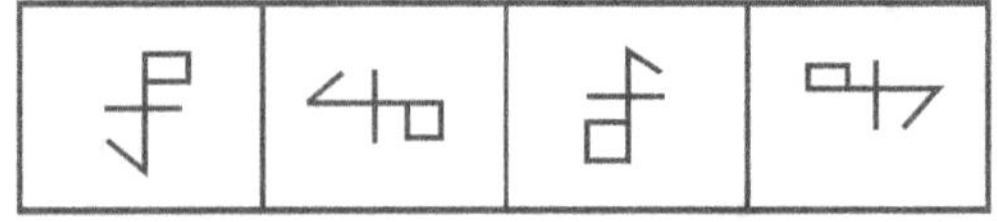

Answer Set

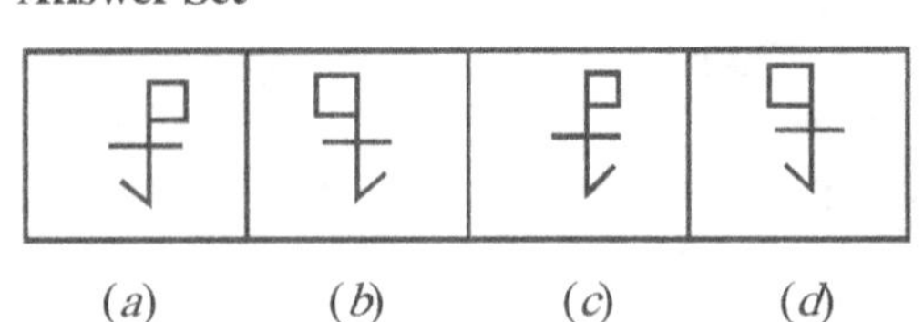

(a) (b) (c) (d)

EXPLANATORY ANSWERS

1. (*d*) : All the rest are fruit tree.

2. (*b*) : All the rest are found inside the soil.

3. (*c*) : All the rest are non-vegetarian.

4. (*d*) : All the rest are made of metals.

5. (*d*) : All the rest are things.

6. (*d*) : All the rest are capitals of states.

7. (*d*) : All the rest are parts of body.

8. (*d*) : All the rest are hunters.

9. (*d*) : All the rest are part of tree.

10. (*c*) : All the rest are in pairs.

11. (*c*) : 1   7   14   22 $\boxed{31}$
$+6$ $+7$ $+8$ $+9$

12. (*b*) : 35   33   30   26 $\boxed{21}$
-2 -3 -4 -5

13. (*d*) : 2   6   14   30 $\boxed{62}$
$\times2+2$ $\times2+2$ $\times2+2$ $\times2+2$

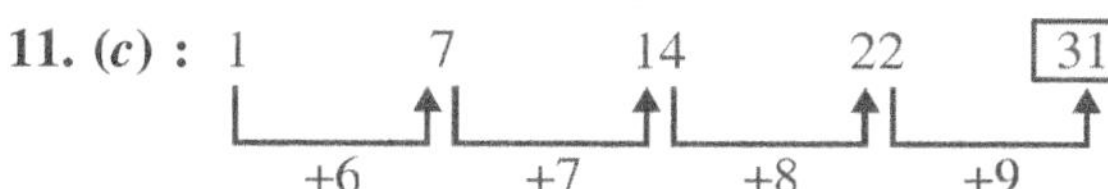

14. (*a*) : 5   9   18   34 $\boxed{59}$
$+(2)^2$ $+(3)^2$ $+(4)^2$ $+(5)^2$

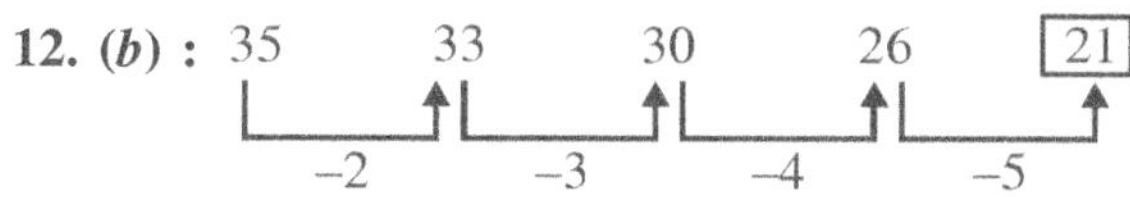

15. (*a*) : 4   6   9   13.5 $\boxed{20.25}$
$\times3/2$ $\times3/2$ $\times3/2$ $\times3/2$

16. (*b*) : 6   19   58 $\boxed{175}$
$\times3+1$ $\times3+1$ $\times3+1$

17. (*b*) : A, E, I, O, $\boxed{U}$ continues vowels.

18. (*c*) : C   E   H   L $\boxed{Q}$
$+2$ $+3$ $+4$ $+5$

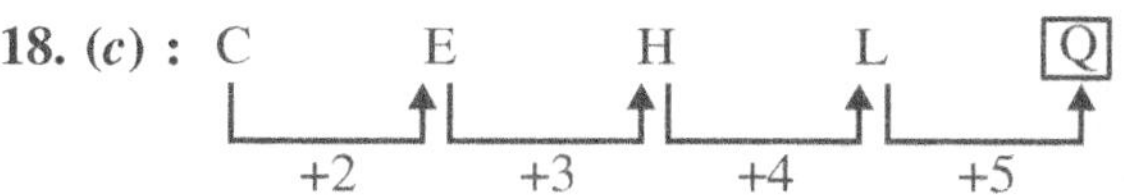

19. (*d*) : 5   15   55   235 $\boxed{1195}$
$\times2+5$ $\times3+10$ $\times4+15$ $\times5+20$

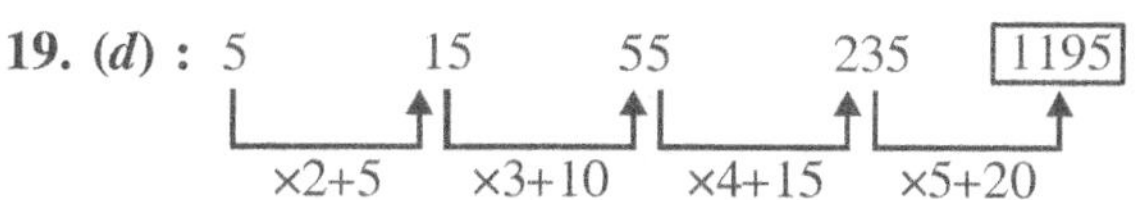

20. (*d*) : 1   8   27   64 $\boxed{125}$
$(1)^3$ $(2)^3$ $(3)^3$ $(4)^3$ $(5)^3$

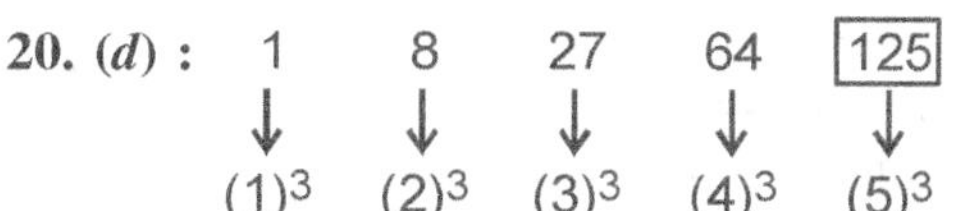

21. (*a*)

22. (*c*)

23. (*b*)

24. (*a*)

25. (*d*)

26. (*a*)

27. (*a*)

28. (*c*)

29. (*b*)

30. (*c*)

31. (*d*) : All the rest are capitals of states.

32. (*d*) : All the rest are male gender and are related to cricket.

33. (*d*) : In all the rest water flows.

34. (*a*) : All the rest are non-vegetarian.

35. (*a*) : All the rest have wheels.

36. (*b*) : All the rest lay eggs.

37. (*c*) : All the rest were Prime Minister of our country.

38. (*d*) : All the rest are measured in a length.

39. (*d*) : All the rest belong to furniture.

40. (*b*) : All the rest have four wheels.

41. (*d*) : All the rest have same figures.

42. (*c*) : Rotating all the rest figures, the same figure is obtained.

43. (*d*) : In all the rest outer and inner designs are same.

44. (*d*) : In all the rest a semicircle is situated on the opposite side.

45. (*c*) : In all the rest two lines across.

46. (*a*) : In each successive problem figure, inner design comes out and inside of that design a new figure occurs. Thus the answer figure (*a*) is obtained.

47. (*c*) : In each successive problem figure, design rotates through 90° clockwise, and the curve at the corner reverse each time. Thus the answer figure (*c*) is obtained.

48. (*a*) : In each successive problem figure, right corner design reaching at centre becomes double and the design at centre reaches to the left upper corner and left upper corner design reaches at right upper corner. Thus, the answer figure (*a*) is obtained.

49. (*c*) : In each successive problem figure, a small line increase in the main design anticlockwise. The small design moves an arm ahead anticlockwise and takes a new shape.

Thus, the answer figure (*c*) is obtained.

50. (*a*) : In each successive problem figure, whole design rotates through 90° clockwise. Thus, the answer figure (*a*) is obtained.

SAINIK SCHOOL ENTRANCE EXAM, 2009
(CLASS-VI)

PAPER-I : MATHEMATICS AND LANGUAGE

PART-A : MATHEMATICS

Section-I

1. Find $\dfrac{5}{7}$ of $2\dfrac{1}{3}$ kg.

2. What should be added to 21.707 to get 29.053?

3. Find the square root of 0.0625

4. Divide 1.36 by 0.4.

5. The cost of 103 chairs is ₹ 29335, find the cost of 1031 chairs.

6. Find the value of $3\dfrac{1}{2} \div 2\dfrac{1}{14} \times \dfrac{1}{2} \times \dfrac{4}{5}$

7. Arrange the following in ascending order:
   7.275, 7.305, 7.265, 7.432, 7.135

8. Find the suface area of a cube of side 6 cm.

9. Madhubala purchased 15 books for ₹ 180. If she purchases 20 more books then how much total amount she has to pay?

10. Find $\dfrac{4}{9}$ of $5\dfrac{2}{3}$.

Section-II

11. Simplify:

$$\left\{\left(2-\dfrac{1}{3}\right)+\left(\dfrac{2}{3}\times 1\dfrac{1}{4}\right)\right\}+\dfrac{3}{7}\ \text{ of }\ 2\dfrac{5}{8}$$

12. Find simple interest on ₹ 975.60 for 9 months at 10% p.a.

13. Find the cube of the following:

$$\dfrac{3}{5}+\dfrac{1}{5}+\dfrac{2}{5}\div\dfrac{1}{5}-\dfrac{1}{5}$$

14. A park of 15 m 30 cm length and 12 m 20 cm breadth is to be surrounded by 4 layers of barbed wire. Find the length of barbed wire required.

15. A number is multiplied by $\dfrac{7}{5}$. What is the percentage increase in it?

16. Divide ₹ 345.45 in the ratio $1\dfrac{1}{2}:1\dfrac{1}{3}:1\dfrac{1}{4}$

17. A litre of petrol costs ₹ 46.75 and a litre of diesel costs ₹ 34.16. Find the total cost of 600 litres of diesel and 100 litres of petrol.

18. A car travels 58 km in the first hour, 62 km in the second hour, 75 km in the third hour. Find the average speed of the car.

19. Subtract the difference of 8.362 and 7.942 from the sum of 5.675 and 1.327.

20. A man can finish a piece of work in 12 days when he works 8 hours a day. In how many days will be finish the piece of work if he works 6 hours a day?

Section-III

21. The average age of 25 students of a class is 13 years. Out of them the average age of 15 students is 18 years. Find the average age of remaining students.

22. Find the length of tunnel which a man travelling

by train can cross in $5\dfrac{1}{2}$ minutes. The speed of the train is 40 km/h.

23. An ore contains 16% zinc. How many kg of ore will be required to get 36 kg of zinc?

24. Simplify:

$$1+\dfrac{3}{7}\text{ of }\left(6+8\times\overline{3-2}\right)+\left\{\left(\dfrac{1}{5}\div\dfrac{7}{25}\right)-\left(\dfrac{3}{7}+\dfrac{8}{14}\right)\right\}$$

25. Find the least number which when divided by 30, 36, 56 and 63 leaves 8 as a remainder in each case.

26. Find the value of x

(*a*) $\dfrac{1}{9}:x::\dfrac{1}{3}:\dfrac{1}{4}$

(*b*) $x:1.6::2.1:8.4$

27. A sum of ₹ 480 is distributed to two persons A and B in the ratio of 3 : 5. Find the share of A and B.

28. A man went to the market for shopping. He bought 2.300 kg of spices, 3.580 kg of fish, 800 gms of tamarind, 950 gms of carrot and 0.250 kg of green chilly. Find the total weight of the items purchased. Express the result in grams only.

29. A man spends 10% of his monthly income on house rent and 30% of it on food. Find how much is left for other expenses if his monthly income is ₹ 10000.

30. Draw a circle with radius 4 cm with the help of compass. Also draw the following—

(*a*) Its diameter AB

(*b*) Minor segment of the circle

(*c*) An angle of 30° at the center

(*d*) A chord CD

EXPLANATORY ANSWERS

1.
$$\dfrac{5}{7}\text{ of }2\dfrac{1}{3}\text{ kg }=\dfrac{5}{7}\text{ of }\dfrac{7}{3}\text{ kg}$$
$$=\dfrac{5}{7}\times\dfrac{7}{3}\text{ kg}=\dfrac{5}{3}\text{ kg}$$
$$=1\dfrac{2}{3}\text{ kg.}$$

2.
Total of the two numbers $= 29.053$
One number $= 21.707$

$\therefore$ We should add $(29.053 - 21.707)$ to get the sum of the two numbers

$\therefore$ We should add 7.346.

3.

```
     | 0.25
   2 | 0.0625
     |   04
  45 |   225
     |   225
     |    ×
```

$\sqrt{0.0625} = 0.25$

4.
$$1.36 \div 0.4 = \dfrac{136}{40} = \dfrac{34}{10} = 3.4$$

5. $\because$ Cost of 103 chairs $=$ ₹ 29335

$\therefore$ Cost of 1 chair $=\dfrac{29335}{103}$

$\therefore$ Cost of 1031 chairs $=\dfrac{29335\times1031}{103}$
$$= 29335 \times 10.009$$
$$= 29335 \times (10.01)$$
$$\text{(Approxi.)}$$
$$= 29335\,(10 + 0.01)$$
$$= 293350 + 293.35$$
$$= 293643.35$$
$$= ₹\ 293643.$$

6. We have Exp. $=$

$$3\dfrac{1}{2}\div2\dfrac{1}{14}\times\dfrac{1}{2}+\dfrac{4}{5}=\dfrac{7}{2}\div\dfrac{29}{14}\times\dfrac{1}{2}+\dfrac{4}{5}$$

$$=\dfrac{7}{2}\times\dfrac{14}{29}\times\dfrac{1}{2}+\dfrac{4}{5}$$

$$=\dfrac{49}{29\times2}+\dfrac{4}{5}$$

$$=\dfrac{49}{58}+\dfrac{4}{5}$$

$$= \frac{245+232}{58\times5} = \frac{477}{290}$$

$$= 1\frac{187}{290}.$$

7. Ascending order of the given fractions 7.275, 7.305, 7.265, 7.432 and 7.135 is = 7.135, 7.265, 7.275, 7.305 and 7.432.

8. $\because$ One side of a cube = 6 cm

$\therefore$ Surface area of a cube = 6 (side)^2

$$= 6 \times (6)^2$$
$$= 216 \text{ cm}^2.$$

9. $\because$ C.P. for 15 books = ₹ 180

$\Rightarrow$ C.P. for 1 book = 180 ÷ 15

$$= ₹ 12$$

$\Rightarrow$ C.P. for 20 books = 12 × 20

$$= ₹ 240$$

Total no. of books = 15 + 20

$$= 35$$

$\therefore$ C.P. for 35 books = 180 + 240

$$= ₹ 420.$$

10. We have Exp. =

$$\frac{4}{9} \text{ of } 5\frac{2}{3} = \frac{4}{9} \text{ of } \frac{17}{3}$$
$$= \frac{4}{9} \times \frac{17}{3}$$
$$= \frac{68}{27} = 2\frac{14}{27}.$$

11. We have Exp. =

$$\left\{\left(2-\frac{1}{3}\right)+\left(\frac{2}{3}\times1\frac{1}{4}\right)\right\}+\frac{3}{7} \text{ of } 2\frac{5}{8}$$

$$= \left\{\left(\frac{6-1}{3}\right)+\left(\frac{2}{3}\times\frac{5}{4}\right)\right\}+\frac{3}{7} \text{ of } \frac{21}{8}$$

$$= \left\{\frac{5}{3}+\frac{5}{6}\right\}+\frac{9}{8}$$

$$= \left\{\frac{10+5}{6}\right\}+\frac{9}{8}$$

$$= \frac{15}{6}+\frac{9}{8} = \frac{5}{2}+\frac{9}{8} = \frac{20+9}{8} = \frac{29}{8} = 3\frac{5}{8}.$$

12. Principal = ₹ 975.60

Rate = 10%

Time = 9 months

$$= \frac{9}{12} \text{ years}$$

$$= \frac{3}{4} \text{ years}$$

$$\text{Simple Interest} = \frac{P \times R \times T}{100}$$

$$= \frac{975.60 \times 10 \times 3}{4 \times 100}$$

$$= \frac{9756 \times 3}{4 \times 100}$$

$$= \frac{2439 \times 3}{100} = \frac{7317}{100}$$

$$= ₹ 73.17.$$

13. We have Exp. $= \frac{3}{5}+\frac{1}{5}+\frac{2}{5}\div\frac{1}{5}-\frac{1}{5}$

$$= \frac{3}{5}+\frac{1}{5}+\frac{2}{5}\times\frac{5}{1}-\frac{1}{5}$$

$$= \frac{3}{5}+\frac{1}{5}+2-\frac{1}{5}$$

$$= \frac{3+1+10-1}{5} = \frac{13}{5}$$

$$\text{Required Cube} = \left(\frac{13}{5}\right)^3 = \frac{2197}{125}.$$

14. Length of the park = 15.30 m

Breadth of the park = 12.20 m

Perimeter = 2 (15.30 + 12.20)

$$= 2 \times 27.50$$
$$= 55 \text{ m.}$$

Length of the barbed wire to go round 4 times the park

$$= 55 \times 4 = 220 \text{ m.}$$

15. Suppose that the number be 100

$$\because \qquad 100 \times \frac{7}{5} = 20 \times 7 = 140$$

$$\therefore \quad \text{Per cent increase} = 140 - 100 = 40\%.$$

16. $1\frac{1}{2} : 1\frac{1}{3} : 1\frac{1}{4} = \frac{3}{2} : \frac{4}{3} : \frac{5}{4}$

$$(\because \text{L.C.M. of } 2, 3, 4 = 12)$$

$$= \frac{3 \times 6}{2 \times 6} : \frac{4 \times 4}{3 \times 4} : \frac{5 \times 3}{4 \times 3}$$

$$= \frac{18}{12} : \frac{16}{12} : \frac{15}{12} = 18 : 16 : 15$$

$$\text{Total of ratio} = 18 + 16 + 15 = 49$$

$$\because \quad \text{Total money} = ₹ \, 345.45$$

$$\therefore \quad \text{First part} = \frac{18}{49} \times 345.45$$

$$= 18 \times 7.05 = ₹ \, 126.90$$

$$\text{Second part} = \frac{16}{49} \times 345.45 = 16 \times 7.05$$

$$= ₹ \, 112.80$$

$$\text{Third part} = \frac{15}{49} \times 345.45 = 15 \times 7.05$$

$$= ₹ \, 105.75.$$

17. $\because \quad$ Cost of 1 litre petrol $= ₹ \, 46.75$

$\therefore$ Cost of 100 litres petrol $= 46.75 \times 100$

$$= ₹ \, 4675$$

$\because \quad$ Cost of 1 litre diesel $= ₹ \, 34.16$

$\therefore$ Cost of 600 litres diesel $= 34.16 \times 600$

$$= ₹ \, 20496$$

Total cost of 100 litres petrol and 600 litres diesel

$$= 4675 + 20496$$

$$= ₹ \, 25171$$

18. Distance covered by the car in three hours

$$= (58 + 62 + 75) \text{ km}$$

$$= 195 \text{ km}$$

$$\text{Average Speed} = \frac{\text{Distance}}{\text{Time}} = \frac{195}{3}$$

$$= 65 \text{ km/h.}$$

19. Difference between 8.362 and 7.942

$$= 8.362 - 7.942$$

$$= 0.420$$

$$\text{Total of 5.675 and 1.327} = 5.675 + 1.327$$

$$= 7.002$$

$$\text{Required difference} = 7.002 - 0.420$$

$$= 6.582.$$

20. Suppose that the man completes the work in x days working 6 hours a day.

Hours	Days
8 ↓	12 ↑
6 ↓	x

This is a question of reverse proportion.
When number of working hours per day decreases, then the number of days for completion of the work will increase.

$$\because \qquad x : 12 = 8 : 6$$

$$\Rightarrow \qquad 6x = 12 \times 8$$

$$\Rightarrow \qquad x = \frac{12 \times 8}{6}$$

$$\therefore \qquad x = 16 \text{ days}$$

Hence, the man will complete the work in 16 days if he works 6 hours per day.

21.

$$\text{Average age of the 25 students} = 13 \text{ years}$$

$$\therefore \text{Total of the ages of 25 students} = 13 \times 25$$

$$= 325 \text{ years}$$

$$\text{Average age of 15 students} = 18 \text{ years}$$

$$\therefore \quad \text{Total ages of 15 students} = 18 \times 15$$

$$= 270 \text{ years}$$

$$\because \qquad 25 - 15 = 10$$

Total Age of remaining 10 students

$$= 325 - 270$$

$$= 55 \text{ years}$$

$$\text{Reqd. Average age} = \frac{55}{10}$$

$$= 5.5 \text{ years.}$$

22.

$$\text{Time} = 5\frac{1}{2} \text{ minutes}$$

$$= \frac{11}{2} \text{ minutes}$$

$$= \frac{11}{2 \times 60} \text{ hours}$$

$$= \frac{11}{120} \text{ hours}$$

Speed of the train $= 40$ km/h.

$\therefore \qquad$ Distance $=$ Speed $\times$ Time

$$= \frac{40 \times 11}{120} = \frac{11}{3} \text{ km}$$

$$= 3\frac{2}{3} \text{ km}$$

Hence, the tunnel is $3\frac{2}{3}$ km long.

23. Amount of Zinc in an ore $= 16\%$

$\because$ For getting 16 kg Zinc we require $= 100$ kg ore

$\therefore$ For getting 36 kg. Zinc we will require

$$= \frac{100 \times 36}{16} \text{ kg ore.}$$

$$= 25 \times 9 \text{ kg ore}$$

$$= 225 \text{ kg ore.}$$

24. We have Exp. $= 1 + \dfrac{3}{7}$ of $\left[6 + 8 \times \overline{3 - 2} \right]$

$$+ \left\{ \left(\frac{1}{5} \div \frac{7}{25} \right) - \left(\frac{3}{7} + \frac{8}{14} \right) \right\}$$

$$= 1 + \frac{3}{7} \text{ of } [6 + 8 \times 1]$$

$$+ \left\{ \left(\frac{1}{5} \times \frac{25}{7} \right) - \left(\frac{6 + 8}{14} \right) \right\}$$

$$= 1 + \frac{3}{7} \times 14 + \frac{5}{7} - 1$$

$$= 1 + 6 + \frac{5}{7} - 1 = 6 + \frac{5}{7} = 6\frac{5}{7}.$$

25. L.C.M. of 30, 36, 56 and 63

2	30,	36,	56,	63
2	15,	18,	28,	63
3	15,	9,	14,	63
3	5,	3,	14,	21
7	5,	1,	14,	7
	5,	1,	2,	1

L.C.M. $= 2 \times 2 \times 3 \times 3 \times 7 \times 5 \times 2$

$$= 4 \times 9 \times 35 \times 2$$

$$= 36 \times 70$$

$$= 2520$$

$\therefore$ Required number

$$= 2520 + 8 = 2528.$$

26. $(a) \because \dfrac{1}{9} : x :: \dfrac{1}{3} : \dfrac{1}{4}$

$$\Rightarrow \qquad \frac{1}{3} x = \frac{1}{9} \times \frac{1}{4}$$

$$\Rightarrow \qquad \frac{1}{3} x = \frac{1}{36}$$

$$\Rightarrow \qquad x = \frac{1}{36} \div \frac{1}{3}$$

$$\Rightarrow \qquad x = \frac{3}{36}$$

$$\therefore \qquad x = \frac{1}{12}.$$

$(b) \because x : 1.6 :: 2.1 : 8.4$

$$\Rightarrow \qquad 8.4x = 1.6 \times 2.1$$

$$\Rightarrow \qquad x = \frac{1.6 \times 2.1}{8.4}$$

$$\Rightarrow \qquad x = \frac{1.6}{4}$$

$$\therefore \qquad x = 0.4.$$

27. $\qquad$ Total of ratio $3 + 5 = 8$

$\qquad$ Total money $= ₹\,480$

$\therefore$ A will get $= \dfrac{3}{8}$ of $480 = \dfrac{3}{8} \times 480$

$$= 3 \times 60$$

$$= ₹\,180$$

$\therefore$ B will get $= \dfrac{5}{8} \times 480 = 5 \times 60$

$$= ₹\,300.$$

28. Total weight $= 2.300$ kg $+ 3.580$ kg $+ 0.800$ kg $+$ 0.950 kg $+ 0.250$ kg $= 7.880$ kg $= 7880$ gm

29.

$$\text{Monthly income} = ₹\ 10000$$

$$\text{Expenditure on rent} = \frac{10}{100} \times 10000$$

$$= ₹\ 1000$$

$$\text{Expenditure on food} = \frac{30 \times 10000}{100}$$

$$= ₹\ 3000$$

$$\text{Total expenditure} = 1000 + 3000$$

$$= ₹\ 4000$$

Money left for other expenses

$$= 10000 - 4000$$

$$= ₹\ 6000.$$

30.

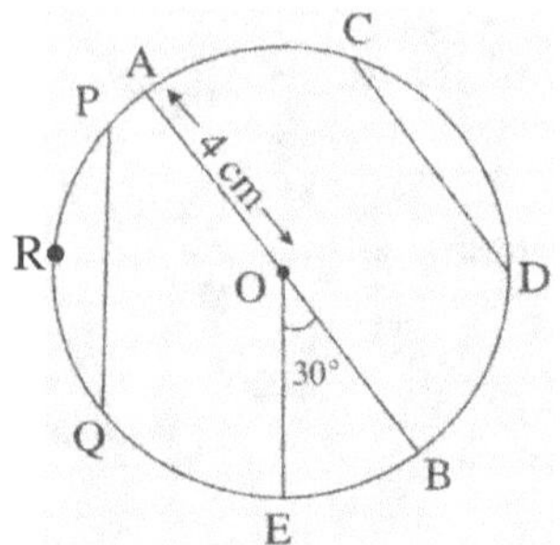

(a)   Diameter – AB

(b)   Minor segment = PQR

(c) $\angle$ BOE = 30°

(d)   Chord = CD.

PART-B : LANGUAGE

1. Write 15 sentences on any one of the following topics—
    (a) Republic Day
    (b) Our National Flag

2. Read the following passage carefully and answer the questions that follow—

    Few animals are as useful or as unpopular as the goat. From ancient times, it has supplied people with milk and meat. Its skin has been made into leather and the wool of some breeds woven into soft, warm cloth. Goats are hardy creatures and can live on the green remains of a thorny bush or a poor grassland. Nevertheless, they have always had a bad reputation. Perhaps this is because the billy goats (Males) often have a bad temper and a strong, unpleasant smell. Goats also do serious damage to young trees and other plants and can quickly reduce a grazing land to barren wasteland. For its size, the goat provides man with more useful things than almost any other animal, yet it often does not receive the food and care given to other animals. The goat will try to eat anything and will put up with the most uncomfortable surroundings. But if it is well fed and carefully housed, the goat will produce much better milk, flesh and wool.

    (a) How is goat a useful animal?
    (b) Why do the goats have a bad reputation?
    (c) What damage is caused by the goats to grazing lands?
    (d) How can the goats produce better milk, flesh and wool?
    (e) Give meanings of the following words:
        (i) Ancient
        (ii) Barren

3. Fill in the blanks by using correct form of verb given in the bracket—
    (a) My brother often ..... to see English films.
        (go)
    (b) Our school ..... with prayer everyday.
        (begin)
    (c) We ..... coffee for breakfast yesterday.
        (drink)
    (d) Radha ..... a new saree last month.   (buy)
    (e) Ashoka ..... to give up war and became a Buddhist.   (decide)

4. Fill in the gaps in the following sentences by using appropriate article:
    (a) The Mount Everest is ..... highest peak in the world.
    (b) You know ..... man by the company he keeps.
    (c) ..... Ganges has overflowed its banks.
    (d) Honesty is ..... best policy.
    (e) ..... apple a day keeps doctor away.

5. Give one word substitute for the following—
  (*a*) Place where books/magazines/newspapers are kept for readers .....
  (*b*) Place where wild animals/birds are protected and kept for public to see .....
  (*c*) Place where vehicles are repaired/serviced .....
  (*d*) Place where fishes are kept in glass containers for public to see.....
  (*e*) Place where objects of artistic, cultural and historical interest are kept for public display .....

6. Do as directed—
  (*a*) I am loved by her.
        (Change into Active Voice)
  (*b*) I am reading a book.
        (Change into Passive Voice)
  (*c*) Sita said, "I am unwell".
        (Change into Indirect Speech)
  (*d*) They are flying kites.
        (Change into Interrogative sentence)
  (*e*) The students were sleeping in the class.
        (Change into Negative sentence)

7. Re-arrange the following words and phrases to form meaningful sentences—
  (*a*) Important/it/is/to observe/rules/traffic.
  (*b*) drive/children/below/of/the age/must not/eighteen years.
  (*c*) protection/our/we/must/helmets/own/wear/for
  (*d*) phones/must/used/not/mobile/be/driving/while
  (*e*) traffic police/making/efforts/is/to increase/on the roads/safety

8. Re-write the following sentences by changing the gender—
  (*a*) My father is writing a letter.
  (*b*) Cow is grazing in the field.
  (*c*) King is loved by all.
  (*d*) He is a poor worker.
  (*e*) I saw a horse on the road.

9. Fill in the blanks with words that are opposite in meaning to those given in the brackets—
  (*a*) A basket is kept ..... the table (under)
  (*b*) This tree is very ..... (short)
  (*c*) Iron is a ..... metal (soft)
  (*d*) Child is ..... in the lap of mother (crying)
  (*e*) It's not a ..... question. (difficult)

EXPLANATORY ANSWERS

1. (*a*)   **Republic Day**

India became free on Aug. 15, 1947, but it became a sovereign republic on 26th of January 1950. This day our constitution was inacted. That's why this day is celebrated as republic day every year. It is a national festival. Tri-colour is hoisted in schools and colleges and in government and private offices/work place. On this day we remember our great leaders who fought for the independence of our country. Today, we are free because of their long struggle against the British rule. They made us free and it is our duty to save our freedom and independence.

It is a day for every Indian to take firm determination to save our nation and national property. Although, we are free and we have some rights but we have some duties too. Our first duty is to our nation. This day makes us proud, feel independence and enthusiasm and makes us full of patriotism.

2. (*a*) A goat gives us milk, meat and leather.
  (*b*) The goats have a bad reputation because billy goats (males) have a bad temper and unpleasant smell.
  (*c*) Goats convert grazing lands into barren wasteland.
  (*d*) Goats can produce better milk, flesh and wool if they are well fed and carefully housed.
  (*e*) (*i*) Ancient — old
       (*ii*) Barren—unfertile

3. (*a*) goes   (*b*) begins
  (*c*) drank   (*d*) bought
  (*e*) decided

4. (*a*) the   (*b*) a
   (*c*) The   (*d*) the
   (*e*) An

5. (*a*) Library   (*b*) Zoo
   (*c*) Workshop   (*d*) Aquarium
   (*e*) Museum

6. (*a*) She loves me.
   (*b*) A book is being read by me.
   (*c*) Sita said that she was unwell.
   (*d*) Are they flying kites?
   (*e*) The students were not sleeping in the class.

7. (*a*) It is important to observe traffic rules.
   (*b*) Children below the age of eighteen years must not drive.
   (*c*) We must wear helmets for our own protection.
   (*d*) Mobile phones must not be used while driving.
   (*e*) Traffic police is making efforts to increase safety on roads.

8. (*a*) My mother is writing a letter.
   (*b*) Bull is grazing in the field.
   (*c*) Queen is loved by all.
   (*d*) She is a poor worker.
   (*e*) I saw a mare on the road.

9. (*a*) on   (*b*) long
   (*c*) hard   (*d*) laughing
   (*e*) simple

PAPER-II : INTELLIGENCE TEST

A. Choose the word, which will come Third in the dictionary and write the choice of the answer.
   (*a*) **Dream**   (*b*) **Direct**
   (*c*) **Discover**   (*d*) **Devotion**
   (*e*) **Drama**

Ans. The word which will come 3rd in the dictionary is Discover. Therefore, the choice (*c*) is the correct answer.

B. Write the second letter of the rearranged word:
   TAEHR is a vital organ of the human body.

Ans. The arrangement of letters in the above given word is not correct. If you rearrange the letters in your mind correctly you will get the correct word as HEART. The second letter of the word HEART is (*e*) Therefore, (*e*) is the correct answer.

C. Write the second word of the rearranged sentence.

(*a*)	(*b*)	(*c*)	(*d*)	(*e*)	(*f*)
the	is	walking	garden	Sohan	in

Ans. If you rearrange the words in your mind, you will get the correct sentence as Sohan is walking in the garden. The second word in the rearranged sentence is 'is'. Therefore letter (*b*) is the correct answer.

D. If 4 + 1 = 4, 2 + 3 = 6, 2 + 7 = 14 then 2 + 6 = ?
   Write the correct choice.
   (*a*) 11   (*b*) 12
   (*c*) 13   (*d*) 15
   (*e*) 16

Ans. If 4 + 1 = 4 then it means that plus sign is treated as multiplication sign. After applying the same reasoning, 2 + 6 will be 12. Therefore, choice letter (*b*) is the correct answer.

E. Write the choice of the word, which does not belong to the same class as the others.
   (*a*) **Forehead**   (*b*) **Heart**
   (*c*) **Liver**   (*d*) **Kidney**
   (*e*) **Lungs**

Ans. Now, Heart, Liver, Kidney and Lungs are found inside the body and a class by themselves, the word. Forehead does not belong to this class. Therefore, (*a*) is the correct answer.

F. Write the number of the group of letters which does not belong to the same class as others—
   (*a*) **ABCD**   (*b*) **GHIJ**
   (*c*) **MNOP**   (*d*) **WXYZ**
   (*e*) **STVU**

Ans. Now, ABCD, GHIJ, MNOP and WXYZ are all in the alphabetical order. The group of letters STUV are not in the alphabetical order and so it does not belong to this class. Therefore, (*e*) is the correct answer.

103

G.. **Which of the given options will complete the series?**

      O Q S U W ....?

(*a*) Z   (*b*) Y

(*c*) X   (*d*) V

Ans. In the above series, every alternate letter of the alphabet has been mentioned. To continue the series the next letter would be Y. Therefore choice (*b*) is the correct answer.

H. **Carpenter is to wood as Tailor is to .....**

(*a*) **Shirt**   (*b*) **Coat**

(*c*) **Cloth**   (*d*) **Wear**

Ans. Carpenter is associated with Wood in the same way as Tailor is associated with Cloth. Therefore, Cloth is the correct answer and option (*c*) is the correct Choice.

I. **Which figure does not belong to the same class as the others?**

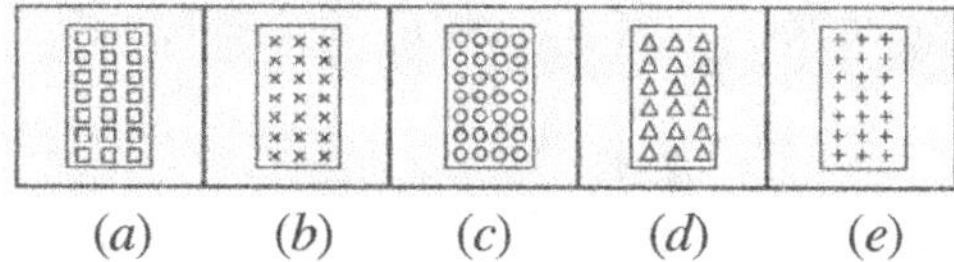

   (*a*)   (*b*)   (*c*)   (*d*)   (*e*)

Ans. Out of the above figures *i.e.* (*a*), (*b*), (*c*), (*d*) and (*e*) except C the rest are similar because they are of same size. Figure (*c*) is dissimilar as it is Broader and one line of design is extra and does not belong to the class of the rest. So, the right answer is (*c*).

J. **Write the number of the figure which will come next in the series.**

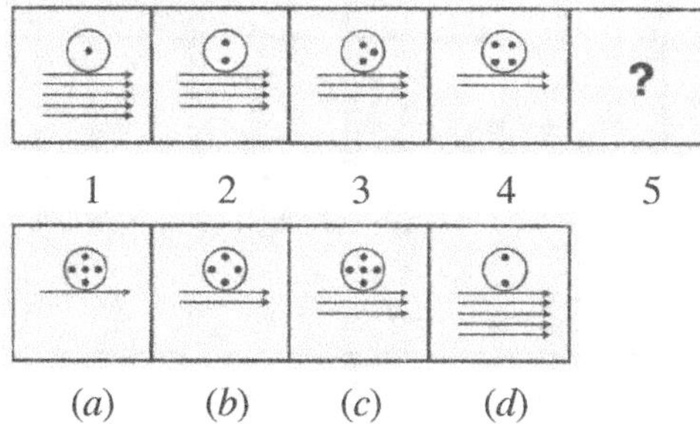

Ans. The series consists of pairs of figures in which dots in the circle keep on increasing and the lines below the circle goes on decreasing. By applying the same rule, you will find that the next figure to come in the series is figure (*a*). Therefore, (*a*) is the correct answer.

K. **In this example, figujre X has some relationship to figure Y. Figure Z has the same relationship with one of the four figures lettered (*a*), (*b*), (*c*) and (*d*). You are required to find out the correct answer.**

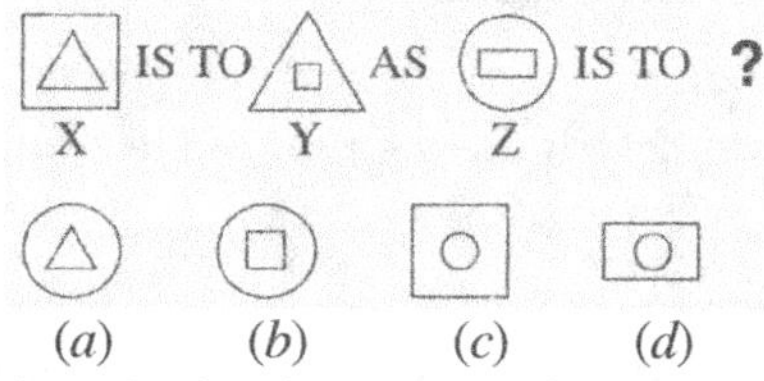

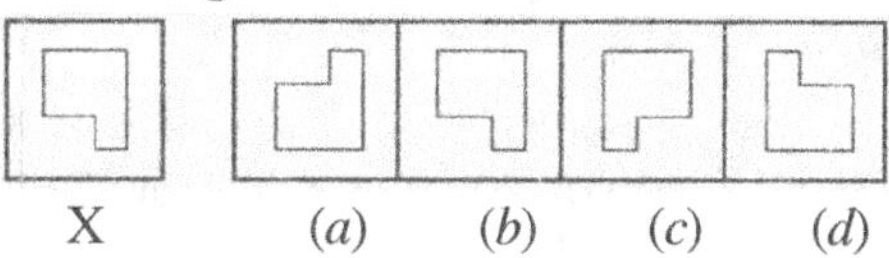

   (*a*)   (*b*)   (*c*)   (*d*)

Ans. In the above example, you will see that in figure X the triangle is inside the square whereas in figure Y, the square comes inside the triangle *i.e.* the position reverses. By applying the same rule we shall find that the figure Z has the same relation with letter D as X has with Y. Therefore (*d*) is the correct answer.

L. **There is one figure X given on the left side followed by four choice figures (*a*), (*b*), (*c*) and (*d*). If you see the figure X in the Mirror, which figure out of the four figures will be like the mirror figure and write the correct answer.**

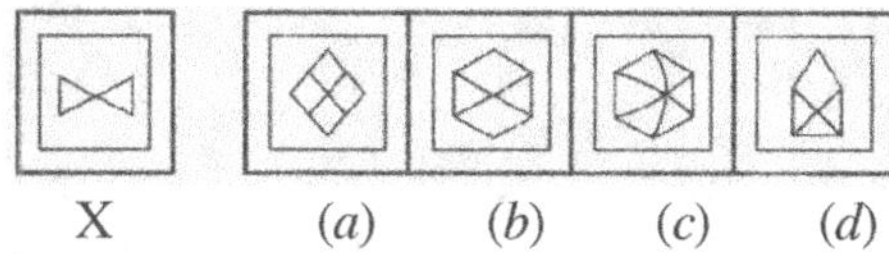

  X   (*a*)   (*b*)   (*c*)   (*d*)

Ans. When you see something in the mirror the left appears right and right appears left. This way figure (*c*) is the right answer.

M. **There is one figure X given on the left side followed by four choice figures (*a*), (*b*), (*c*), (*d*). Find out in which of the choice figures the figure X is hidden and write the correct answer.**

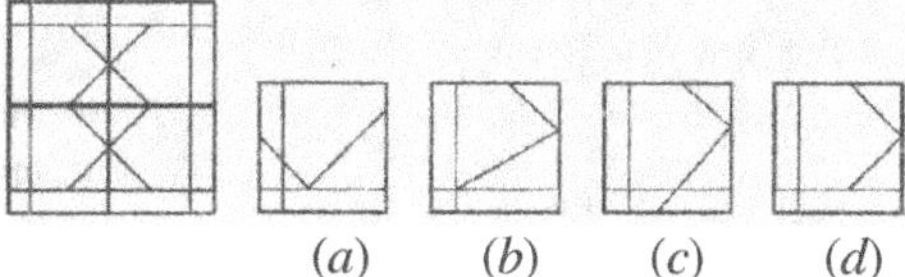

  X   (*a*)   (*b*)   (*c*)   (*d*)

Ans. Now when you see the design clearly you see that figure X is hidden in the choice (*b*). So choice (*b*) is the correct answer.

N. **Four figures marked (*a*), (*b*), (*c*) and (*d*) are given. Below these figures is given pattern X. Out of the four figures one is hidden in the pattern X find the correct option.**

          (*a*)   (*b*)   (*c*)   (*d*)

Ans. Out of the four example figures (*a*), (*b*) and (*c*) does not match with figure X whereas figure (*d*) matches the left box at the lower bottom of the figure X. (*d*) is the write answer.

O. Write the choice of the correct figure, which will complete the design on the left side and write the correct answer.

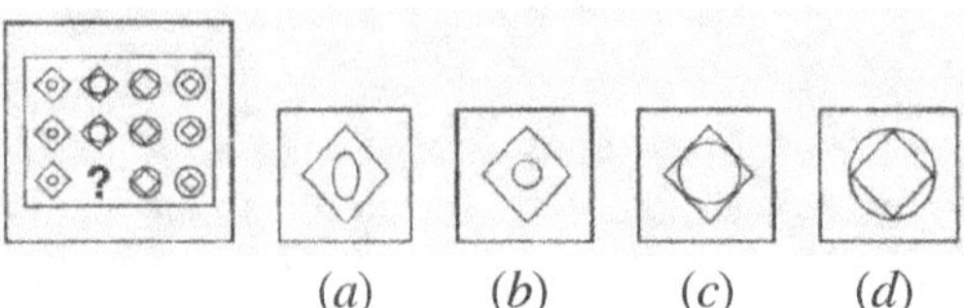

(a)   (b)   (c)   (d)

Ans. If you see the design clearly and put (*c*) figure on the place of the question-mark (?) the design gets completed. So choice (*c*) is the correct answer.

Directions (Qs. 1 to 8): *Out of the five given choices (a), (b), (c), (d) and (e) in each problem, four are similar in one way. However, one choice is not like the other four. Choose the choice, which is different from the rest and write the answer.*

1. (*a*) Sun : Summer   (*b*) Happy : Sad
   (*c*) Good : Bad   (*d*) Hot : Cold
   (*e*) Laugh : Cry

2. 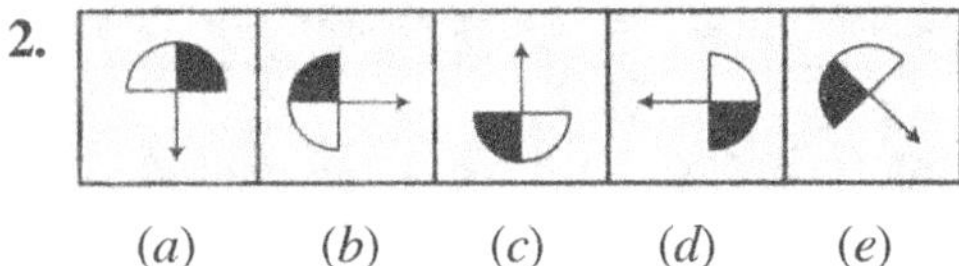

(a)   (b)   (c)   (d)   (e)

3. (*a*) Shillong   (*b*) Bangalore
   (*c*) Hardwar   (*d*) Lucknow
   (*e*) Bhopal

4. 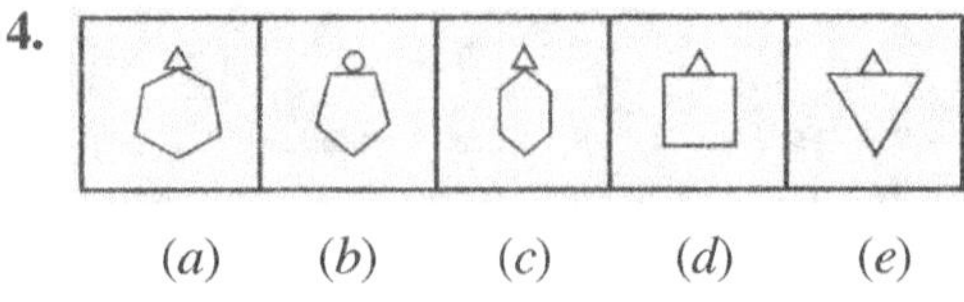

(a)   (b)   (c)   (d)   (e)

5. (*a*) School : Student
   (*b*) Pen : Ink
   (*c*) Son : Daughter
   (*d*) Cup : Tea
   (*e*) Library : Books

6. 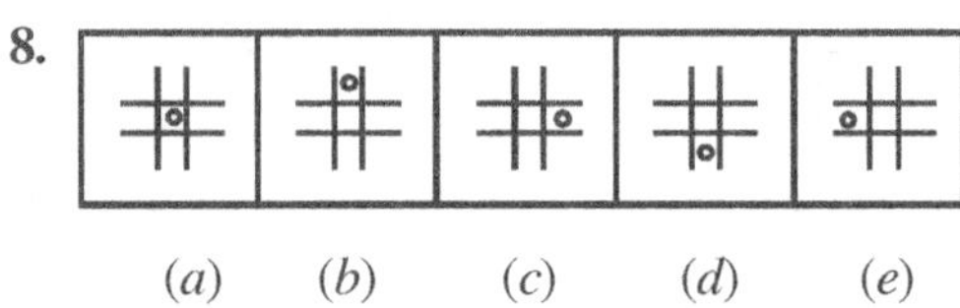

(a)   (b)   (c)   (d)   (e)

7. (*a*) Branch
   (*b*) Stem
   (*c*) Mango
   (*d*) Plant
   (*e*) Tree

8. 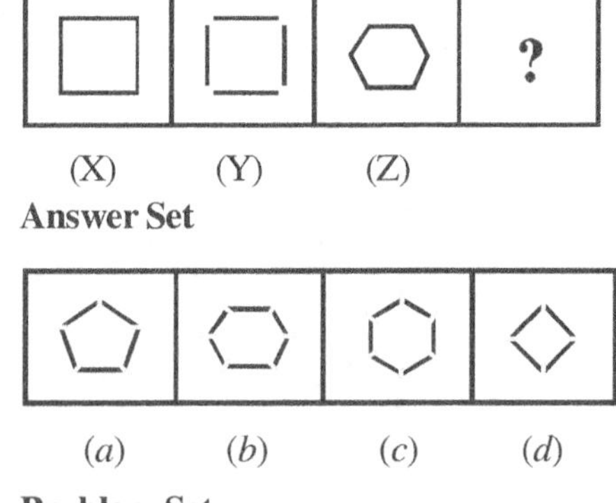

(a)   (b)   (c)   (d)   (e)

Directions (Qs. 9 to 12): *Each of the following questions (X), (Y), (Z) constitute the problem set, while choices (a), (b), (c), (d) constitute the answer set. There is a definite relationship between choice (X) and (Y). Our task is to establish a similar relationship between the choice (Z) and one of the answer choices given in the answer set (a), (b), (c), (d) and write the answer.*

9. Problem Set

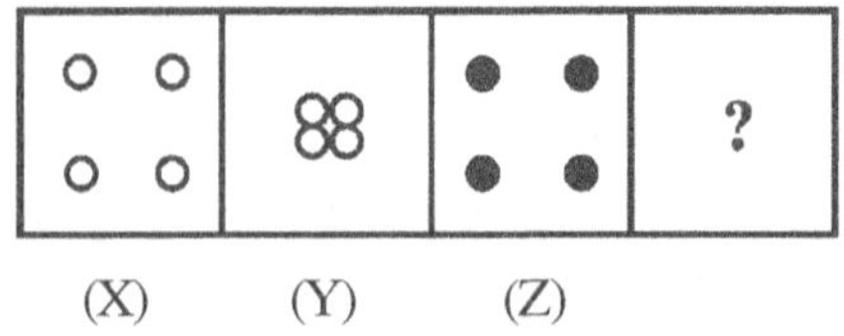

(X)   (Y)   (Z)

Answer Set

(a)   (b)   (c)   (d)

10. Problem Set

(X)   (Y)   (Z)

Answer Set

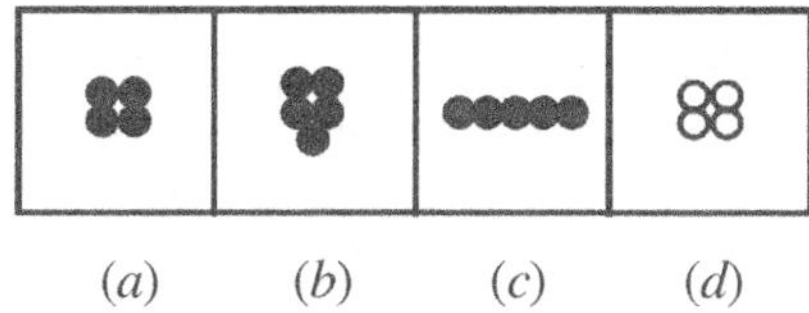

   (a)   (b)   (c)   (d)

11. Problem Set

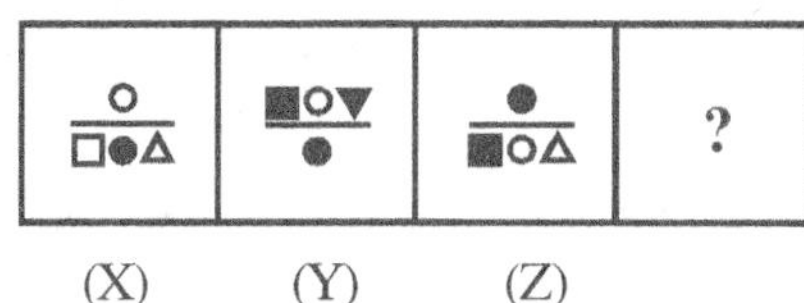

   (X)   (Y)   (Z)

Answer Set

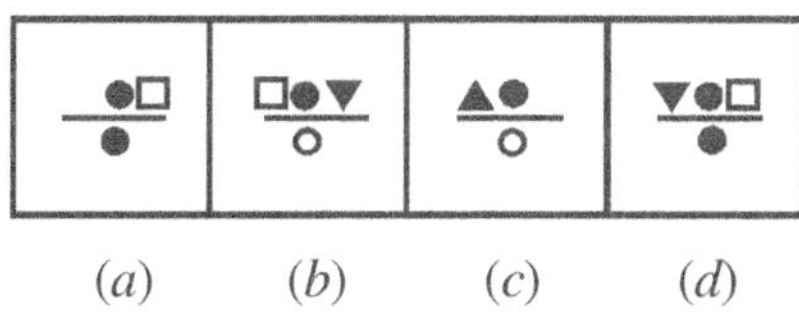

   (a)   (b)   (c)   (d)

12. Problem Set

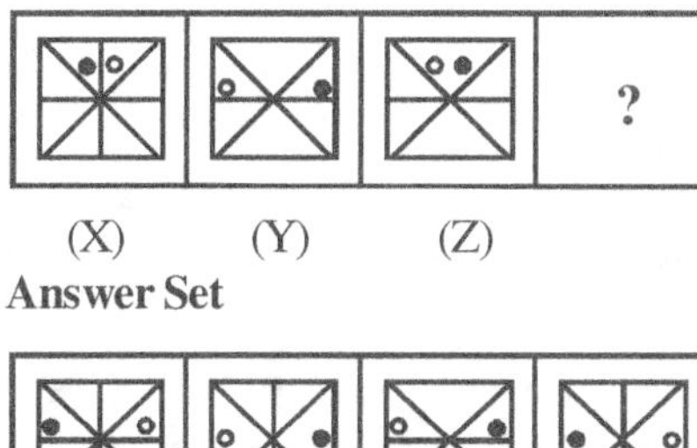

   (X)   (Y)   (Z)

Answer Set

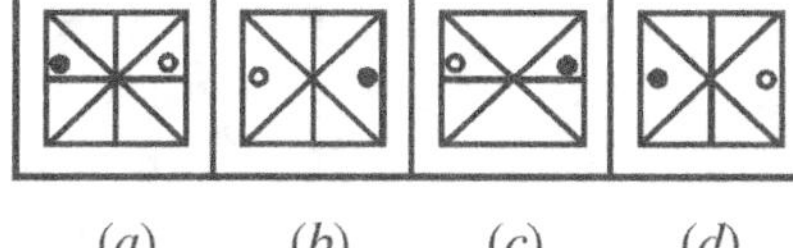

   (a)   (b)   (c)   (d)

Directions (Qs. 13 to 16): *Choose the right answer.*

13. Day is to **week** as **week** is to .....

  (a) Year   (b) Season

  (c) Month   (d) Hour

14. Finger is to **Arm** as **Toe** is to .....

  (a) Knee   (b) Leg

  (c) Foot   (d) Head

15. Snake is to **Reptiles** as **Man** is to .....

  (a) Mammals   (b) Animal

  (c) House   (d) Human

16. Save is to **Rescue** as **Seldom** is to .....

  (a) Often   (b) Frequent

  (c) Rare   (d) Mostly

Directions (Qs. 17 to 24): *Below are given numbers/ alphabets/figures followed by 4 answer choices marked as (a), (b), (c) and (d). Choose a correct answer option, which will continue the series.*

17. 7, 8, 6, 9, 5, ...

  (a) 8   (b) 10

  (c) 4   (d) 3

18.

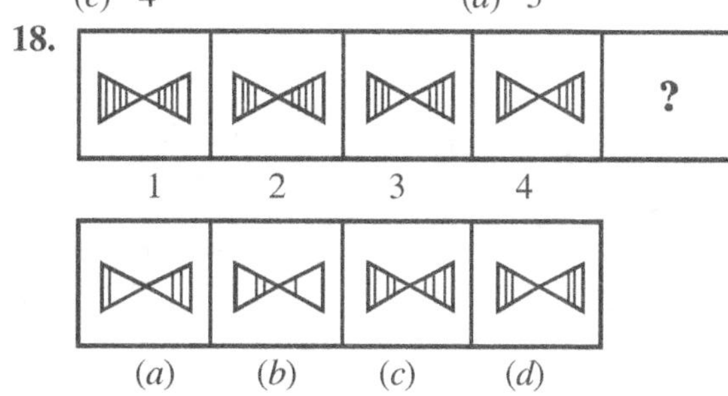

    1   2   3   4

   (a)   (b)   (c)   (d)

19. $\dfrac{P}{M}, \dfrac{R}{O}, \dfrac{T}{Q}, \dfrac{V}{S}$, ...

  (a) $\dfrac{X}{U}$ (b) $\dfrac{V}{S}$

  (c) $\dfrac{W}{U}$ (d) $\dfrac{P}{N}$

20.

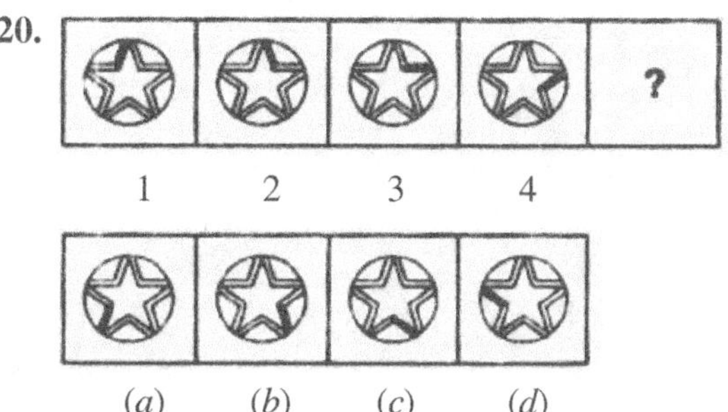

    1   2   3   4

   (a)   (b)   (c)   (d)

21. A, Z, D, Y, G, ...

  (a) W   (b) D

  (c) E   (d) X

22.

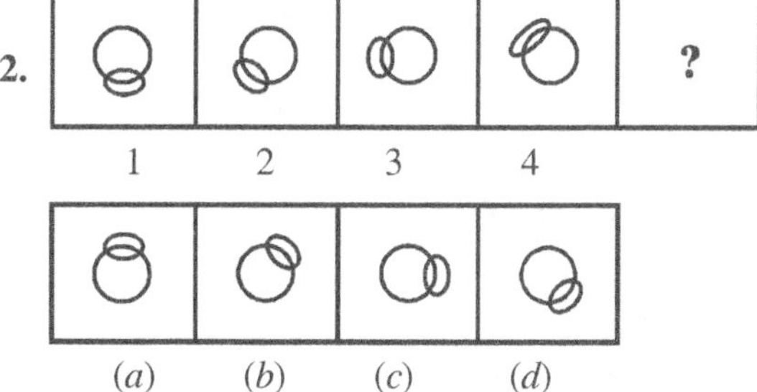

    1   2   3   4

   (a)   (b)   (c)   (d)

23. 54, 52, 49, 45, 40 ....
(a) 30   (b) 29
(c) 35   (d) 34

24.

△	◁	▷	◁	**?**
1	2	3	4	

△	▽	▼	◁
(a)	(b)	(c)	(d)

Directions (Qs. 25 to 26): *Choose the word, which will come THIRD in the dictionary.*

25. (a) Inform   (b) Infinity
(c) Influential   (d) Imbalance
(e) Important

26. (a) Century   (b) Central
(c) Cereal   (d) Certain
(e) Container

Directions (Qs. 27 to 30): *Rearrange the word given in capital letters. Choose the **fourth** letter of the rearranged word.*

27. DNALGNE (Country) .....

28. GORATE (Name of the Poet) .....

29. TEKCAJ (Dress) .....

30. YHCOEK (A Game) .....

Directions (Qs. 31 and 32): *Choose the right answer.*

31. If $1 \times 2 \times 3 = 312$, $2 \times 3 \times 4 = 423$ what will be $2 \times 4 \times 3 = $ .....
(a) 324   (b) 243
(c) 342   (d) 423

32. If $6 \times 2 = 31$, $8 \times 4 = 42$, $2 \times 2 = 11$ then 8×6 will be = ...
(a) 42   (b) 31
(c) 43   (d) 48

Directions (Qs. 33 and 34): *Choose the **third** word of the rearranged sentence.*

33. (a)   (b)   (c)   (d)   (e)
are   june   in   summers   hot

34. (a)   (b)   (c)   (d)   (e)
breakfast   I   my   taken   have

Directions (Qs. 35 to 38): *In these questions try to understand how codes are given to the words. Choose the right code for the asked word from the given choices (a), (b), (c) and (d).*

35. If **BAD** is coded as **896**, then **EGG** will be coded as .....
(a) 534   (b) 533
(c) 431   (d) 422

36. If **HIDE** stands for **2165** then **HIGH** will stand for .....
(a) 2132   (b) 1232
(c) 2131   (d) 2562

37. If **ANX** is coded as **BOY**, then **RNM** will be coded as .....
(a) RAT   (b) DOG
(c) PEN   (d) SON

38. If **RSNO** is coded as **STOP**, then **CNMD** will be coded as .....
(a) DARE   (b) DONE
(c) DUTY   (d) DONT

Directions (Qs. 39 to 42): *Choose the correct mirror image of the figure (X) from the four alternatives given along with it.*

39.

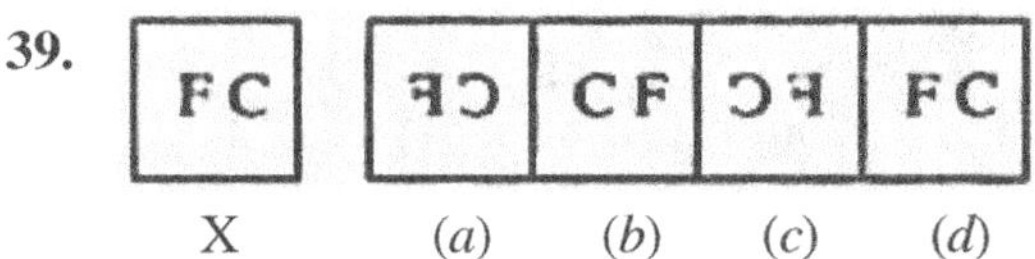

X   (a)   (b)   (c)   (d)

40.

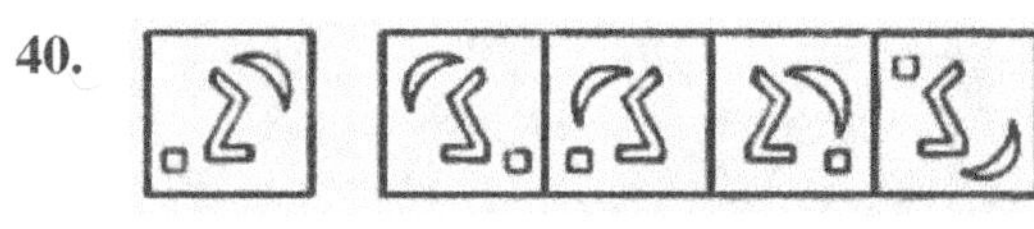

X   (a)   (b)   (c)   (d)

41.

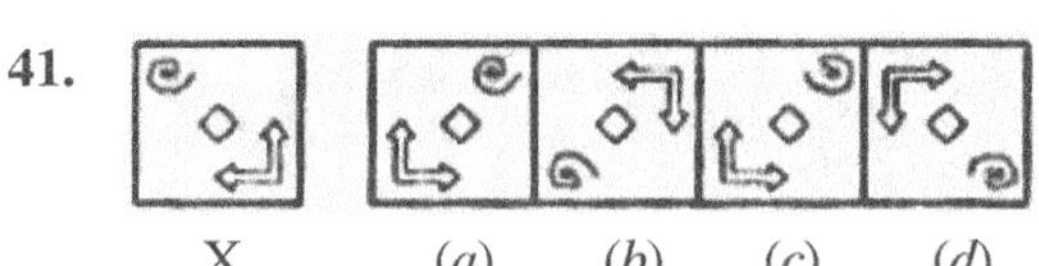

X   (a)   (b)   (c)   (d)

42.

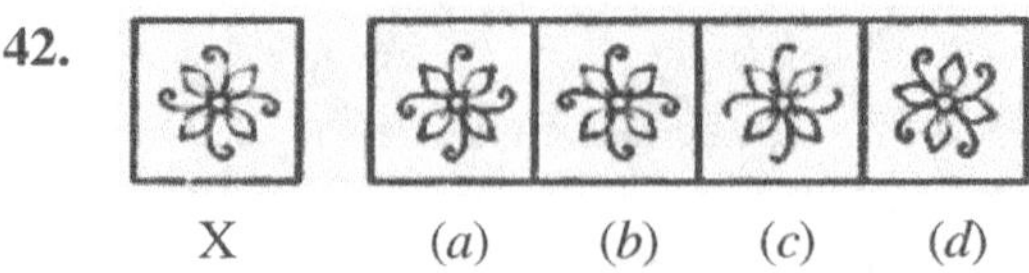

X   (a)   (b)   (c)   (d)

107

Directions (Qs. 43 to 46): *Write the choice of the correct figure, which will complete the given design on the left side.*

43.

44.

45.

46.

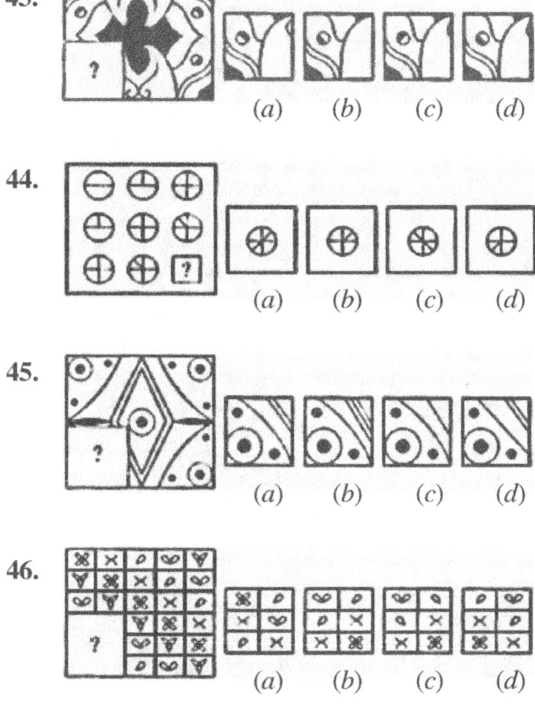

Directions (Qs. 47 to 48): *Four simple figures are marked (a), (b), (c) and (d). Find out one of the figures, which is hidden in the **pattern X**.*

47.

48.

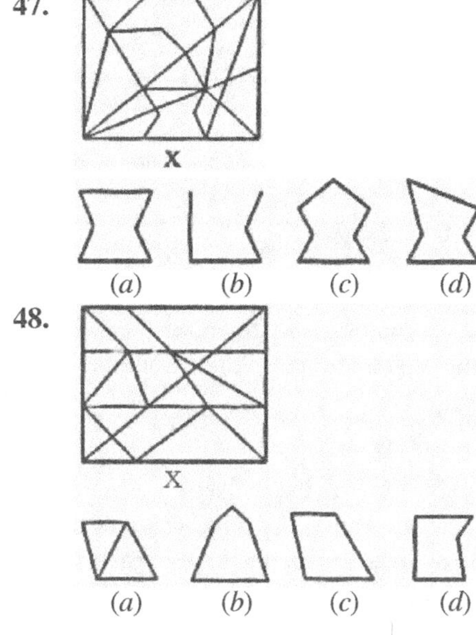

Directions (Qs. 49 to 50): *There is one figure X given on the left side followed by four choice figures (a), (b), (c), (d). Find out in which of the choice figures the figures X is hidden.*

49.

50.

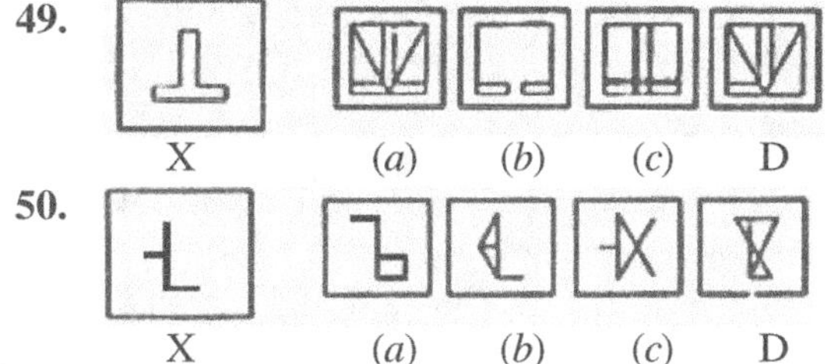

X   (a)   (b)   (c)   D

EXPLANATORY ANSWERS

1. (a) Except choice (a) all the choices are the pairs of words and their (opposite word) antonyms.

2. (e) All figures are either horizontal or vertical, but straight while fig. (e) is not straight. It is slanting.

3. (c) Except option (c) all the choices are capitals of some Indian states.

4. (b) All figures have a triangle on the design top. while fig. (b) has a circle on the top.

5. (c) In the remaining of others the things of second words become inside of first words. As :

Student inside of school, tea inside of the cup and the books inside of library.

6. (d) Except in fig. (d) arcs of the circles are going out of the circle.

7. (c) Except option (c) all choices are the different parts of a tree including tree itself.

8. (a) All the figures have circles outside the closed square. Except in fig. (a).

9. (b) If we open all the corners of the figure X's design we will get Y. By the same way if we open all the corners of fig. Z's design we will get answer figure (b).

10. (*a*) If we put together all the four small circles of the fig. X we will get fig. Y. By the same way if we put all the blackened circles of fig. Z we will get fig. (*a*).

11. (*b*)

12. (*d*)

13. (*c*) Day is to week as week is to month.

14. (*b*) Finger is to arm as toe is to Leg.

15. (*a*) Snake belongs to the group of reptiles as Man belongs to the group of Mammals.

16. (*c*) Synonym of Save is Rescue. Synonym of Seldom is Rare.

17. (*b*) Numbers on the even places are increasing by 1 but numbers on the odd places are decreasing by 1. Hence the blank space will be occupied by the number $9 + 1 = 10$.

18. (*d*) In each subsequent figure one by one lines are decreasing in the main design from left and right respectively.

19. (*a*) In the given fractions Denominators and Numerators are the alphabets coming on the second places respectively. P → R : R → T.

T → V, M → O; O → Q etc. Hence $\dfrac{X}{U}$ will occupy the blank space.

20. (*b*) Considering the movement of blackened small line fig. (*b*) will occupy the blank space.

21. (*d*)

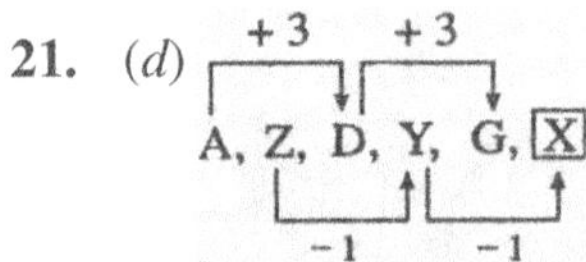

22. (*a*) In each subsequent figure the small circle on the circumference of main circle is revolving 45° clockwise.

23. (*d*) Numbers are decreasing by 2, 3, 4, 5. Hence $40 - 6 = 34$ will occupy the blank space.

24. (*c*) Considering the clockwise movement of the figures alongwith the change of place of the darkened portion, fig. (*c*) will occupy the blank space.

25. (*b*) Imbalance → Important → Infinity → Influence → Inform will be arranged according to dictionary. Hence the word Infinity will occupy the third place.

26. (*c*) Central → Century → Cereal → Certain → Container will be arranged according to dictionary. Hence the word cereal will be the third.

27. (L) ENGLAND. The fourth letter is L.

28. (O) TAGORE. The fourth letter is O.

29. (K) JACKET. The fourth letter is K.

30. (K) HOCKEY. The fourth letter is K.

31. (*a*) Given that $1 \times 2 \times 3 = 312$; $2 \times 3 \times 4 = 423$. It is clear from the above two examples that the number on third place will occupy the first place followed by the numbers of first place and second place.
Hence, $2 \times 4 \times 3 = 324$

32. (*c*) $6 \times 2 = 31$

This means that $\dfrac{6}{2} \times \dfrac{2}{2} = 3 \times 1 = 31$

$8 \times 4 = 42$

This means that $\dfrac{8}{2} \times \dfrac{4}{2} = 4 \times 2 = 42$

$2 \times 2 = 11$

This means that $\dfrac{2}{2} \times \dfrac{2}{2} = 1 \times 1 = 11$

Hence, $8 \times 6 = \dfrac{8}{2} \times \dfrac{6}{2}$

$= 4 \times 3 = 43.$

33. (*e*) Summers are hot in June. Hence the word 'hot' will occupy the third place.

34. (*d*) I have taken my breakfast. Hence the word 'taken' will occupy the third place.

35. (*b*) BAD is coded as 896. This means that A = 9, B = 8, C = 7, D = 6, E = 5, F = 4, G = 3. Hence the word 'EGG' will be coded as 533.

36. (*a*) HIDE stands for 2165. This means that D = 6, E = 5, F = 4, G = 3, H = 2, I = 1. Hence the word HIGH will stand for 2132.

37. (*d*) ANX is coded as BOY. Therefore 'A' is coded with B' 'N' is coded with O and 'X' is coded with Y. So the word RNM will be coded with SON.

38. (*b*) RSNO is coded with STOP. Hence, R is coded with S; S is coded with T; N is coded with O and O is coded with P. So the word CNMD will be coded with DONE.

39. (*c*)		**40.** (*a*)	
41. (*c*)		**42.** (*a*)	
43. (*d*)		**44.** (*c*)	
45. (*a*)		**46.** (*d*)	
47. (*a*)		**48.** (*c*)	
49. (*c*)		**50.** (*b*)	

SAINIK SCHOOL ENTRANCE EXAM, 2008
(CLASS-VI)

PAPER-I : MATHEMATICS AND LANGUAGE

PART-A : MATHEMATICS

Section-I

1. Find the quotient of the following—
   (*i*) $93 \div 3.1$ (*ii*) $144 \div 0.12$

2. A school starts at 8.20 am and closes at 1.50 pm. Find the duration for which the school remains open?

3. The cost of 13 school bags is ₹ 1950, find the cost of 4 such bags.

4. Which of the following can be the angles of a triangle?
   (*i*) $90°, 55°, 35°$ (*ii*) $105°, 55°, 40°$

5. The length of a rectangular field is 45 m. and breadth is 35 m. Find the area of the field.

6. Write the smallest and greatest 5-digit number using 9, 0, 4, 2 and 7.

7. Arrange the numbers in descending order—
   42059, 40259, 40529, 40592, 42952

8. Write the following Hindu-Arabic numerals in Roman numerals—
   (*i*) 44   (*ii*) 95

9. Find first four common multiples of 5, 2 and 3.

10. Find the value of —

$$6\frac{2}{5} \div \frac{8}{11}$$

Section-II

11. Classify each of the following as acute, obtuse or right angle—
    (*i*) $138°$ (*ii*) $76°$
    (*iii*) $90°$ (*iv*) $32°$
    (*v*) $92°$ (*vi*) $89°$

12. A shopkeeper earns a profit of ₹ 75 on a sewing machine. If the cost price of the machine is ₹ 2018.50, what is its SP?

13. Write True or False—
    (*i*) $\dfrac{3}{4} < \dfrac{5}{6}$

    (*ii*) $12 \times \left(\dfrac{14}{7}\right) = (12 \times 14)/12 \times 7$

    (*iii*) $66 : 6 = 55 : 11$

14. A Bank employed a daily-wager for 89 days. He joined the Bank on Feb. 10, 2004. On which date his term would be completed?

15. Add 2 hours 40 minutes 40 seconds and 4 hours 30 minutes 50 seconds.

16. Simplify—

$$5\frac{7}{8} \div 3\frac{1}{4} \times 7\frac{5}{16} + \frac{7}{8} \text{ of } 16$$

17. Find the volume of a brick whose length is 22.5 cm, breadth is 10.5 cm and height is 9 cm.

18. A carpet 5 m. 20 cm. long and 3 m. 20 cm. broad, is to be surrounded by a lace. Find the length of lace required.

19. Find the circumference of the circles whose diameters are 8 cm and 14 cm.

20. In the adjoining figure, PQR is a triangle and PQ = PR and ∠Q = 50°. Find the values of other two angles of the triangle.

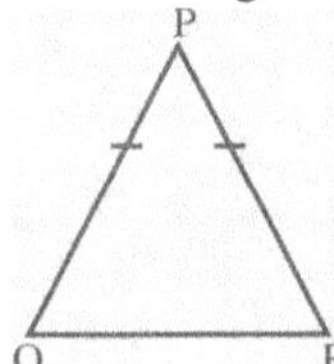

Section-III

21. Draw a circle whose length of circumference is 44 cm with the help of compass and write the length of the diameter by measuring.

22. The depth of a swimming pool at six different places is 344 cm., 275 cm., 192 cm., 147 cm., 233 cm. and 300 cm.
    (i) Find the average depth of the swimming pool.
    (ii) At how many places the depth is more than the average depth?

23. A, B and C have a total of ₹ 1771. The ratio of the money between A and B is 5 : 7. If C has ₹ 571, calculate A's and B's share.

24. Fill in the blanks—
    (i) $4.3 \div \text{........} = 0.043$
    (ii) SP = ₹ 820, Loss = ₹ 40, CP = ...
    (iii) Sum of the three angles of a triangle is ....
    (iv) Circumference = ... × diameter
    (v) Perimeter of square = ...

25. Match the following—
    (i) The complementary angle of 45° (a) 90°
    (ii) Measurement of right angle (b) Supplementary
    (iii) The quadrilateral has the sides (c) 45°
    (iv) If the sum of the two angles is 180°, then they are (d) 110°
    (v) Supplementary angle of 70° (e) Four

26. Anil got 60 marks out of 125, Ankit got 140 marks out of 280, whose score is better?

27. (i) Convert the following into decimal—
    (a) 9% (b) 25%
    (c) $\dfrac{3}{4}$ (d) 1%
    (e) $\dfrac{4}{5}$
    (ii) Convert the following decimals into a fraction—
    (a) 2.02 (b) 0.01
    (c) 5.9 (d) 0.100

28. Arrange the following fractions in descending order—
    $$\frac{5}{8}, \quad \frac{5}{6}, \quad \frac{2}{4}, \quad \frac{1}{5}, \quad \frac{1}{3}, \quad \frac{3}{2}$$

29. Which is the least 6-digit number exactly divisible by 83.

30. A boy spends $\dfrac{1}{3}$ of his money in a shop, then he goes to another shop and spends $\dfrac{1}{2}$ of that was left. He is left with ₹ 15. Find out how much total money did he has?

EXPLANATORY ANSWERS

1. (i) $93 \div 3.1 = \dfrac{930}{31}$
   $$= 30.$$
   (ii) $144 \div 0.12 = \dfrac{14400}{12}$
   $$= 1200.$$

2. 1.50 pm = 13 : 50
   Required duration = 13 : 50 − 8.20
   $$= 5 \text{ hrs. } 30 \text{ min.}$$

3. Cost of 4 such bags = $\dfrac{1950}{13} \times 4$ = ₹ 600.

4. (i) ∵ $90° + 55° + 35° = 180°$
   ∴ These angles are the angle of a triangle.
   (ii) ∵ $105° + 55° + 40° = 200°$
   ∴ These angles are not the angles of a triangle.

5. Area of the rectangular field
   = Length × Breadth
   = 45m × 35m
   = 1575 m²

6. The smallest and greatest numbers of 5 digit number using 9, 0, 4, 2 and 7 are 20479 and 97420 respectively.

7. In descending order—
   42952; 42059; 40592; 40529; 40259.

8. (*i*) $44 \rightarrow$ XLIV

(*ii*) $95 \rightarrow$ XCV

9. First four common multiples of 5, 2 and 3 are 30, 60, 90 and 120.

10.
$$6\frac{2}{5} \div \frac{8}{11} \;=\; \frac{32}{5} \div \frac{8}{11}$$
$$=\; \frac{32}{5} \times \frac{11}{8} = \frac{44}{5}$$
$$=\; 8\frac{4}{5}.$$

11. (*i*) $138°$ — obtuse angle

(*ii*) $76°$ — acute angle

(*iii*) $90°$ — right angle

(*iv*) $32°$ — acute angle

(*v*) $92°$ — obtuse angle

(*vi*) $89°$ — acute angle

12. S.P. $=$ C.P. $+$ Profit $= 2018.50 + 75$

$\qquad = ₹\ 2093.50.$

13. (*i*) $\dfrac{3}{4} < \dfrac{5}{6} \Rightarrow 0.75 < 0.83$ (True)

(*ii*) $12 \times \dfrac{14}{7} = \dfrac{12 \times 14}{12} \times 7$ (False)

(*iii*) $66 : 6 = 55 : 11 \Rightarrow 11 : 1 = 5 : 1$ (False).

14. (Here Feb. 10, 2004 including)

$$\begin{aligned}
\text{Feb.} &= 20 \\
\text{March} &= 31 \\
\text{April} &= 30 \\
\text{May} &= \underline{08} \\
& \;\;89 \text{ days}
\end{aligned}$$

Hence, on 8th May 89 days will be completed.

15.

	Hr.	Min.	Sec.
	2	40	40
+	4	30	50
	7	11	30

Hence, required total $= 7$ hrs 11 min. 30 sec.

16. $5\dfrac{7}{8} \div 3\dfrac{1}{4} \times 7\dfrac{5}{16} + \dfrac{7}{8}$ of 16

$$=\; \frac{47}{8} \div \frac{13}{4} \times \frac{117}{16} + \frac{7}{8} \times 16$$

$$=\; \frac{47}{8} \div \frac{13}{4} \times \frac{117}{16} + 14$$

$$=\; \frac{47}{8} \times \frac{4}{13} \times \frac{117}{16} + 14 = \frac{423}{32} + \frac{14}{1}$$

$$=\; \frac{423 + 448}{32} = \frac{871}{32}$$

$$=\; 27\frac{7}{32}.$$

17. Volume of the brick $= l \times b \times h$

$$= 22.5 \times 10.5 \times 9$$
$$= 2126.25 \text{ cm}^3.$$

18.
$$\begin{aligned}
\text{Length} &= 5 \text{ m } 20 \text{ cm} \\
&= 5.2 \text{ m.} \\
\text{Breadth} &= 3 \text{ m } 20 \text{ cm} \\
&= 3.2 \text{ m}
\end{aligned}$$

Hence, length of the lace required

$$\begin{aligned}
&= 2(l + b) \\
&= 2(5.2 + 3.2) \\
&= 2 \times 8.4 \\
&= 16.8 \text{ m} \\
&= 16 \text{ m. } 80 \text{ cm.}
\end{aligned}$$

19. Circumference of the first circle

$$= \pi \times d = \frac{22}{7} \times 8$$
$$= \frac{176}{7} = 25\frac{1}{7} \text{ cm}$$

Circumference of the second circle

$$= \pi \times d = \frac{22}{7} \times 14 = 44 \text{ cm.}$$

20.

In $\triangle$PQR, PQ $=$ PR

$$\angle \text{Q} = \angle \text{R} = 50°$$

and $\angle \text{P} = 180° - (\angle \text{Q} + \angle \text{R})$

$$= 180° - (50° + 50°)$$
$$= 180° - 100° = 80°.$$

21. Here, $2\pi r = 44$ $\therefore\ r = \dfrac{44 \times 7}{2 \times 22} = 7$ cm

[**Note** : Draw yourself a circle of radius 7 cm with the help of compass and measure the length of diameter.]

22. (*i*)
$$= \frac{344 + 275 + 192 + 147 + 233 + 300}{6}$$

$$= \frac{1491}{6}$$

$$= 248.5 \text{ cm.}$$

    (*ii*) At 344 cm, 275 cm and 300 cm (3 places) the depth is more than the average depth.

23. Total money with A and B
$$= 1771 - 571 = ₹ \ 1200$$
Ratio of A and B = 5 : 7

$$\text{Share of A} = \frac{5}{5+7} \times 1200$$

$$= \frac{5}{12} \times 1200 = ₹ \ 500$$

$$\text{and share of B} = \frac{7}{5+7} \times 1200 = \frac{7}{12} \times 1200$$

$$= ₹ \ 700.$$

24. (*i*) $4.3 \div x = 0.043 \therefore x = \dfrac{4.3}{0.043} = \dfrac{4300}{43} = 100$

    (*ii*) **C.P = S.P. + Loss** = 820 + 40 = **₹ 860.**

    (*iii*) Sum of the three angles of a triangle is **180°**

    (*iv*) Circumference   = **π** × diameter

    (*v*) Perimeter of square = **4** × side of the square.

25. (*i*) ⟶ (*c*)

    (*ii*) ⟶ (*a*)

   (*iii*) ⟶ (*e*)

   (*iv*) ⟶ (*b*)

    (*v*) ⟶ (*d*)

26. Percentage of marks of Anil

$$= \frac{60}{125} \times 100\%$$

$$= 48\%$$

and percentage of marks of Ankit

$$= \frac{140}{280} \times 100\%$$

$$= 50\%$$

Hence, score of Ankit is better.

27. (*i*) (*a*) $9\% = \dfrac{9}{100} = 0.09$

      (*b*) $25\% = \dfrac{25}{100} = 0.25$

      (*c*) $\dfrac{3}{4} = \dfrac{75}{100} = 0.75$

      (*d*) $1\% = \dfrac{1}{100} = 0.01$

      (*e*) $\dfrac{4}{5} = 0.8$

  (*ii*) (*a*) $2.02 = \dfrac{202}{100} = \dfrac{101}{50}$

      (*b*) $0.01 = \dfrac{1}{100}$

      (*c*) $5.9 = \dfrac{59}{10}$

      (*d*) $0.100 = \dfrac{1}{10}$

28. $\because \quad \dfrac{5}{8}, \dfrac{5}{6}, \dfrac{2}{4}, \dfrac{1}{5}, \dfrac{1}{3}, \dfrac{3}{2}$

$\Rightarrow 0.625, 0.833, 0.5, 0.2, 0.33, 1.5$

Hence, in descending order—

$$\frac{3}{2} > \frac{5}{6} > \frac{5}{8} > \frac{2}{4} > \frac{1}{3} > \frac{1}{5}$$

29.

```
83)100000(1205
   83
   170
   166
    400
    415
    -15
```

Hence, required number = 100000 + 15
$$= 100015.$$

30. Let the total money with the boy be ₹ x

Money spent on first shop $= \dfrac{1}{3}$ of $x = ₹ \dfrac{x}{3}$

Remaining money $= x - \dfrac{x}{3} = ₹ \dfrac{2x}{3}$

Money spent on second shop $= \dfrac{1}{2}$ of $\dfrac{2x}{3} = ₹ \ \dfrac{x}{3}$

Remaining money $= \dfrac{2x}{3} - \dfrac{x}{3} = ₹ \dfrac{x}{3}$

Now, $\dfrac{x}{3} = ₹ 15$

$\therefore$ $x = 3 \times 15 = ₹ \ 45.$

PART–B : LANGUAGE

1. Read the following passage carefully and answer the questions—

Narmada is one of the great rivers of India. She is the longest river in Penninsular India. She is believed to be older than Himalayan rivers. Scholars say that the rocks she flows over are so old that they were there when dinosaurs roamed the earth. Today this river is known all over the world for the large number of massive dams that are to be built across her.

Narmada springs from the top of Amar Kantak the highest peak of the Maikal mountain in eastern Madhya Pradesh, to begin her course of 1,245 kilometres between the Vindhya and Satpura ranges. She flows west-south-west towards the Arabian sea, until she pours out her water into the Gulf of Khambat in Gujarat.

(*a*) Which is the longest river in Penninsular India?

(*b*) Where does river Narmada spring from?

(*c*) What is the total course of river Narmada?

(*d*) Into which Gulf, river Narmada finally pours her water in Gujarat state.

(*e*) Which of the following statements is true?

    (*i*) Narmada springs from Amarnath peak.
                            (True/False)

    (*ii*) Narmada pours her waters into the Bay of Bengal.   (True/False)

    (*iii*) Narmada is believed to be even older than Himalayan rivers.   (True/False)

Ans.

(*a*) Narmada is the longest river in Penninsular India.

(*b*) Narmada springs from the top of Amar Kantak the highest peak.

(*c*) The total course of River Narmada is 1,245 kilometres.

(*d*) Narmada river pours her water into the Gulf of Khambat in Gujarat.

(*e*) (*i*) False.

    (*ii*) False.

    (*iii*) True.

2. Write an essay in 15 sentences on any one of the following topics—

(*a*) My School

(*b*) A Visit to Market.

(a) My School

I read in A.K. Model School. It is situated on the Pusa Road. It is one of the best schools in Delhi.

It is a very big school. It is spread on a vast stretch of land. The land for the school was donated by some renowned philanthropists.

It has a huge building. It has about one hundred rooms. All the rooms are spacious, airy and well-ventilated.

About four thousand students study in my school. There are over one hundred teachers who teach them. All the teachers are great scholars. They have mastery over their subjects. They are also very hardworking.

There is a big auditorium hall in my school. There is also a stadium where matches and other sports events are held.

In my school there are so many other things such as a big library, a beautiful canteen, a swimming pool, a cycle and scooter shed, a car parking shed, a badminton court, a boxing court, a gymnasium, etc.

The administrative block is situated near the gate of the school. The gate is guarded by a security man. In my school there is also a garden-cum-nursery. It is supervised by two gardeners. There are also a number of officials, peons and sweepers in the school.

The name of my school Principal is Mrs. Kusum Lata. She is a highly learned middle-aged lady. She is very kind-hearted. But she is a strict disciplinarian.

Our school excels in studies as well as sports and extra curricular activities. It shows very good results every year. Its various teams often win trophies. So many students of our school have often won prizes at local, district, state and even national levels.

I am proud of my school. At present, it is progressing by leaps and bounds. I hope it will continue progressing rapidly for ever.

3. Form meaningful sentences by rearranging the words in proper order.

(*a*) The / belongs / to / book / Ramesh.

(*b*) is / good / a / player / Dhoni / cricket.

(*c*) will / today / come / they / us / see / to.

(*d*) Fond of / she / music / is.

Ans. (*a*) The book belongs to Ramesh.

(*b*) Dhoni is a good cricket player.

(*c*) They will come today to see us.

(*d*) She is fond of music.

4. **Make a sentence of your own for each *Bold* word given in the following passage.**

(Do not copy any sentence from the given paragraph)

At morning time I have the **desire** to read the Newspaper. Newspaper reading gives us the detailed **knowledge** of world events. It also gives us a chance to read stories, poems and jokes and all this **entertain** us. I find the Newspaper reading as most interesting **activity** of the day. We all should develop **habit** of Newspaper reading.

Ans. 1. I have no **desire** to become a millionaire.

2. I have no deep **knowledge** of computer.

3. Samir **entertained** us much with his humorous remarks.

4. A man is known by his **activity**.

5. Students should cultivate good **habits**.

5. **Use each word in separate sentences of your own to show the difference in the meaning of the words of the pairs given below—**

(*a*) Sad, Said   (*b*) Wet, Weight

(*c*) Suit, Shoot   (*d*) Rich, Reach

(*e*) Here, Hear

Ans. (*a*) **Sad**—The bad activity of his son made him **sad.**

Said—Sanjay **said** that he was my friend.

(*b*) **Wet**—His clothes got **wet** when he went out in the rains.

Weight—His **weight** is 65 kg.

(*c*) **Suit**—My father bought me a **suit.**

Shoot—The hunter is **shooting** at the wolf.

(*d*) **Rich**—Saurabh is a **rich** man.

Reach—You should **reach** the office in time.

(*e*) **Here**—Please come **here.**

Hear—He did not **hear** what I said.

6. **Choose the correct article (a, an or the) and fill in the blanks—**

(*a*) .... Bible is a pious book.

(*b*) Raja is .... honest boy.

(*c*) Iron is .... useful metal.

(*d*) The train is late by .... hour.

(*e*) The sun rises in .... East.

Ans. (*a*) The   (*b*) an   (*c*) a

(*d*) an   (*e*) the

7. **Give one word for the following—**

(*a*) One who treats patients?

(*b*) One who dances?

(*c*) One who takes photographs?

(*d*) One who plays Guitar?

(*e*) One who makes furniture?

Ans. (*a*) Doctor   (*b*) Dancer

(*c*) Photographer   (*d*) Guitarist

(*e*) Carpenter

8. **Fill in the blanks with the words that are opposite in meaning to those given in the brackets—**

(*a*) These are .... mangoes.   (raw)

(*b*) That is very .... building.   (small)

(*c*) These are .... paintings.   (new)

(*d*) She is a .... girl.   (ugly)

(*e*) These are .... grapes.   (sour)

Ans. (*a*) ripe   (*b*) big   (*c*) old

(*d*) beautiful   (*e*) sweet.

9. **Change each of the following as directed—**

(*c*) Sachin is a good player.

           (Change into Interrogative)

(*b*) This is a lovely flower.

           (Change into Exclamatory)

(*c*) He is going to school.

           (Change into Negative)

(*d*) There are 500 cadets in my school.

           (Change into Interrogative)

(*e*) We have won the match.

           (Change into Exclamatory)

Ans. (*a*) Is Sachin a good player?

(*b*) What a lovely flower this is!

(*c*) He is not going to school.

(*d*) Are there 500 cadets in my school?

(*e*) Hurrah! We have won the match.

PAPER–II : INTELLIGENCE TEST

Directions : *In each of the following questions find the odd one.*

1. (*a*) Jesus   (*b*) Buddha
   (*c*) Gandhi   (*d*) Mohammad

2. (*a*) Raincoat   (*b*) Umbrella
   (*c*) Gun boats   (*d*) Sari

3. (*a*) Fox   (*b*) Wolf
   (*c*) Deer   (*d*) Panther

4. (*a*) Barber   (*b*) Carpenter
   (*c*) Blacksmith   (*d*) Tailor

5. (*a*) Gangtok   (*b*) Singhbhum
   (*c*) Hyderabad   (*d*) Chennai

6. (*a*) Carrot   (*b*) Potato
   (*c*) Spinach   (*d*) Turnip

7. (*a*) Coat   (*b*) Socks
   (*c*) Shirts   (*d*) Jacket

8. (*a*) January   (*b*) March
   (*c*) July   (*d*) September

9. (*a*) Bulb   (*b*) Fan
   (*c*) Candle   (*d*) Sun

10. (*a*) Lungs   (*b*) Liver
    (*c*) Ear   (*d*) Eyes

Directions : *In each of the following questions complete the series.*

11. U, O, I, E, ...
    (*a*) B   (*b*) C
    (*c*) A   (*d*) Z

12. A, C, F, H, ...
    (*a*) I   (*b*) J
    (*c*) K   (*d*) L

13. 3, 6, 18, 72, ...
    (*a*) 144   (*b*) 288
    (*c*) 350   (*d*) 360

14. 1, 2, 6, 24, ...
    (*a*) 72   (*b*) 120
    (*c*) 48   (*d*) 96

15. 5, 16, 49, 104, ...
    (*a*) 133   (*b*) 144
    (*c*) 180   (*d*) 181

16. 1, 4, 9, 16, 25, ...
    (*a*) 35   (*b*) 36
    (*c*) 49   (*d*) 64

17. 20, 19, 17, ...
    (*a*) 12   (*b*) 13
    (*c*) 14   (*d*) 15

18. 2, 3, 5, 7, 11, ...
    (*a*) 12   (*b*) 13
    (*c*) 14   (*d*) 15

19. 3, 9, 27, 81, ...
    (*a*) 243   (*b*) 343
    (*c*) 210   (*d*) 324

20. A, B, D, G, ...
    (*a*) M   (*b*) L
    (*c*) K   (*d*) H

Directions : *In a certain language **CHARCOAL** is coded as 45164913 and MORALE is coded as 296137, how are the following words coded in that language?*

21. ARCHER
    (*a*) 164576   (*b*) 185476
    (*c*) 197457   (*d*) 184576

22. MECHRALE
    (*a*) 26756137   (*b*) 27456137
    (*c*) 47956137   (*d*) 29456137

23. ROCHEL
    (*a*) 695478   (*b*) 691387
    (*c*) 994537   (*d*) 694573

24. LARCH
    (*a*) 36145   (*b*) 31645
    (*c*) 31546   (*d*) 31456

25. MARCH
    (*a*) 24615   (*b*) 25416
    (*c*) 21645   (*d*) 23456

26. COLLER
    (*a*) 397758   (*b*) 497782
    (*c*) 483359   (*d*) 493376

27. REAL
    (*a*) 8519   (*b*) 6713
    (*c*) 6513   (*d*) 6719

28. COACH
    (*a*) 38137   (*b*) 49145
    (*c*) 49451   (*d*) 85145

29. ALLOCHRE
   (*a*) 17693935   (*b*) 15933653
   (*c*) 13394567   (*d*) 13368957

30. HEARL
   (*a*) 57361   (*b*) 57163
   (*c*) 75613   (*d*) 57931

Directions : *In each of the following questions, four words have been given, out of which three are alike in some manner and the fourth one is different. Choose out the odd one.*

31 (*a*) Jasmine   (*b*) Coriander
    (*c*) Lotus   (*d*) Rose

32. (*a*) Diving   (*b*) Driving
    (*c*) Swimming   (*d*) Sailing

33. (*a*) Cochin   (*b*) Vishakhapatanam
    (*c*) Mysore   (*d*) Mumbai

34. (*a*) Charan Singh   (*b*) S. Radhakrishnan
    (*c*) Morarji Desai   (*d*) Chandrashekhar

35. (*a*) Potato   (*b*) Ginger
    (*c*) Carrot   (*d*) Cabbage

36. (*a*) Birbal   (*b*) Faiz Ahmed
    (*c*) Abul Fazal   (*d*) Tansen

37. (*a*) Lakshadweep   (*b*) Sikkim
    (*c*) Maharashtra   (*d*) Manipur

38. (*a*) Father   (*b*) Sister
    (*c*) Mother   (*d*) Friend

39. (*a*) Thin   (*b*) Tall
    (*c*) Sharp   (*d*) Small

40. (*a*) Man   (*b*) Lion
    (*c*) Elephant   (*d*) Deer

Directions : *Each of the following questions consists of unmarked figures followed by four figures mark (a), (b), (c) and (d). Select a figure from the marked figures which will continue the series established by the unmarked figures.*

41. Problem Figures

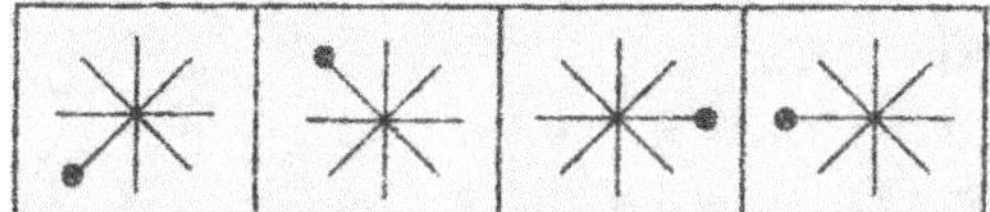

Answer Figures

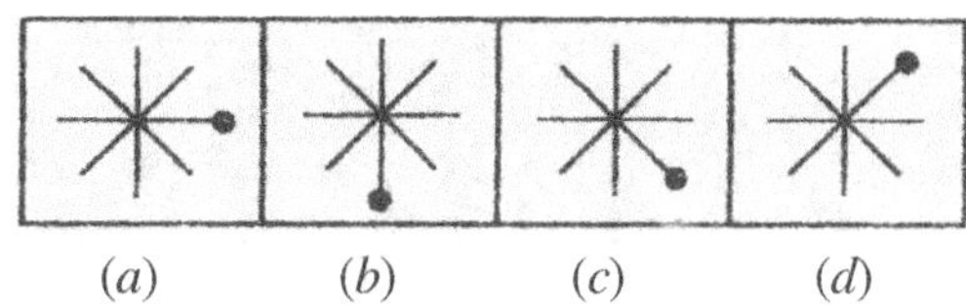

   (*a*)   (*b*)   (*c*)   (*d*)

42. Problem Figures

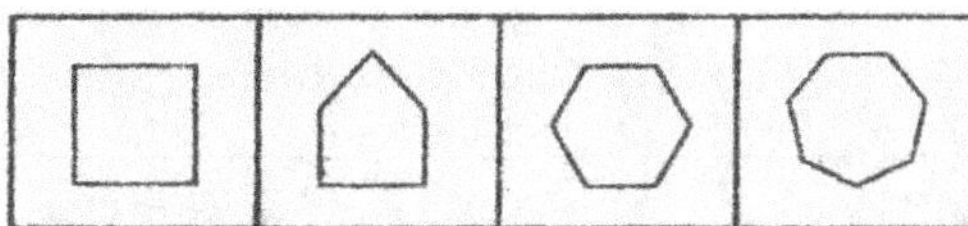

Answer Figures

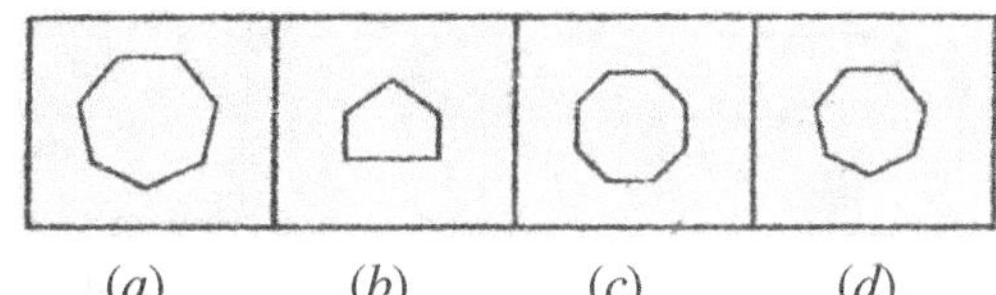

   (*a*)   (*b*)   (*c*)   (*d*)

43. Problem Figures

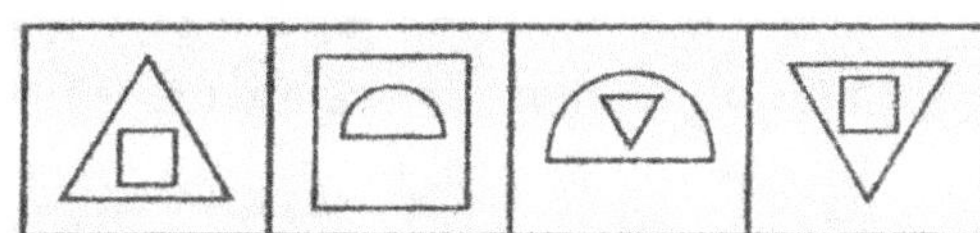

Answer Figures

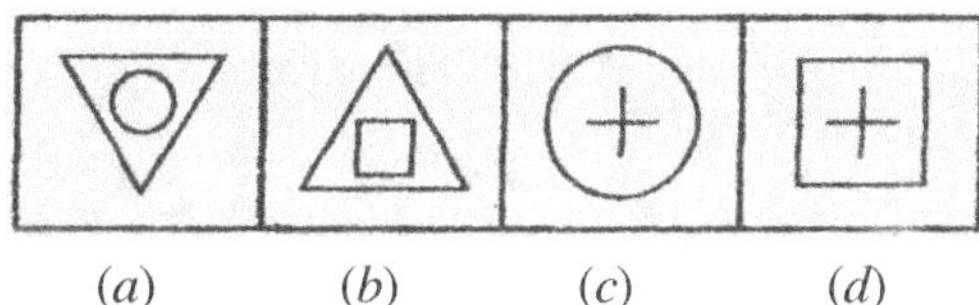

   (*a*)   (*b*)   (*c*)   (*d*)

44. Problem Figures

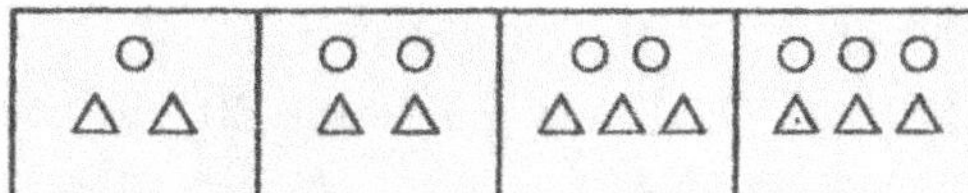

Answer Figures

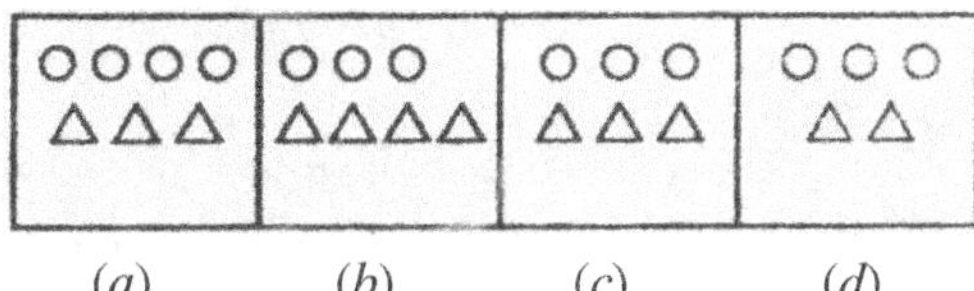

   (*a*)   (*b*)   (*c*)   (*d*)

45. Problem Figures

Answer Figures

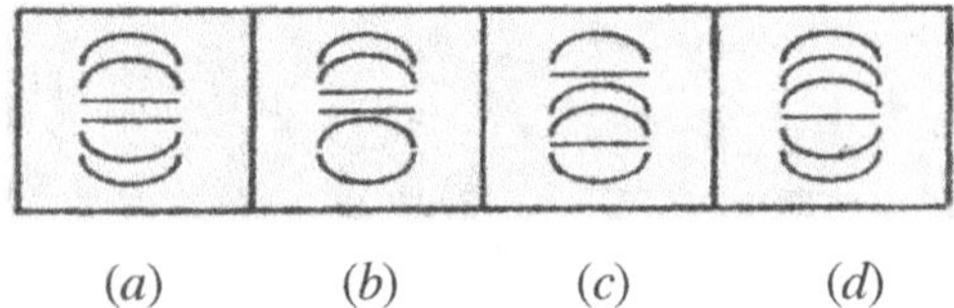

(a)   (b)   (c)   (d)

Directions: *In each of the following sets of figures, select the one that is different from the rest.*

46.

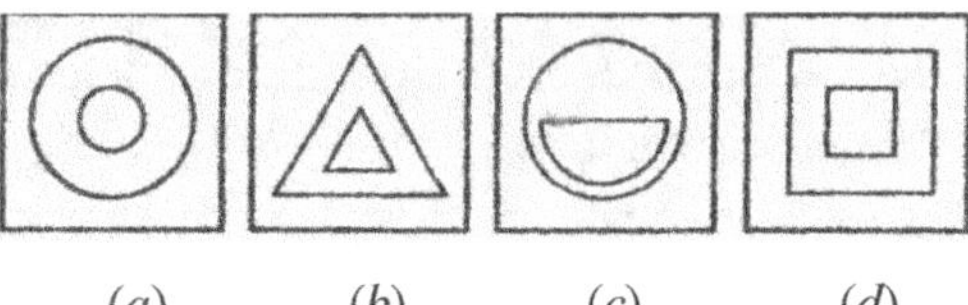

(a)   (b)   (c)   (d)

47. 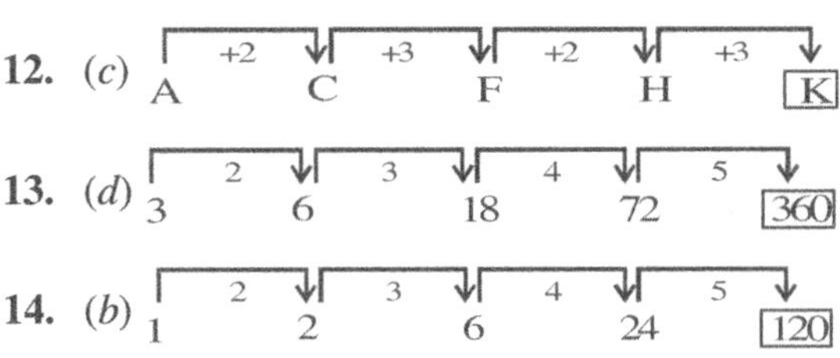

   (a)   (b)   (c)   (d)

48.

   (a)   (b)   (c)   (d)

49.

   (a)   (b)   (c)   (d)

50.

   (a)   (b)   (c)   (d)

EXPLANATORY ANSWERS

1. Except (c), all others are founders of religions.

2. Except (d), all others are used for protection from rain.

3. (c), Except Deer, all are flesh eating animals.

4. (a), Except Barber, all work with raw material.

5. (b), Except Singhbhum all are capitals of states of India.

6. Except (c), all other vegetables grow under the ground.

7. Except (b), all other garments are put on the upper part of the body.

8. (d). Only September have 30 days while all other months have 31 days.

9. Except (b), all others are sources of light.

10. Except (b), all others are organs while liver is a gland.

11. (c) The series consists of vowels in reverse order.

12. (c) A $\xrightarrow{+2}$ C $\xrightarrow{+3}$ F $\xrightarrow{+2}$ H $\xrightarrow{+3}$ $\boxed{K}$

13. (d) 3 $\xrightarrow{2}$ 6 $\xrightarrow{3}$ 18 $\xrightarrow{4}$ 72 $\xrightarrow{5}$ $\boxed{360}$

14. (b) 1 $\xrightarrow{2}$ 2 $\xrightarrow{3}$ 6 $\xrightarrow{4}$ 24 $\xrightarrow{5}$ $\boxed{120}$

15. (d) 5 $\xrightarrow{+11}$ 16 $\xrightarrow{+33}$ 49 $\xrightarrow{+55}$ 104 $\xrightarrow{+77}$ $\boxed{181}$

16. (b) The series is $1^2, 2^2, 3^2, 4^2, 5^2$

    Hence, next number $= 6^2 = 36$.

17. (c) The series is based on the pattern $-1, -2, \dots$

    Hence, next number $= 17 - 3 = 14$.

18. (b) The given series consists of prime numbers, hence next prime number is 13.

19. (a) 3, $\xrightarrow{3}$ 9, $\xrightarrow{3}$ 27, $\xrightarrow{3}$ 81 $\xrightarrow{3}$ $\boxed{243}$

20. (c) A $\xrightarrow{+1}$ B $\xrightarrow{+2}$ D $\xrightarrow{+3}$ G $\xrightarrow{+4}$ $\boxed{K}$

For Q. No. 21 to 30:

CHARCOAL $\rightarrow$ 45164913; MORALE $\rightarrow$ 296137

Hence, A $\rightarrow$ 1, C $\rightarrow$ 4, E $\rightarrow$ 7, H $\rightarrow$ 5, L $\rightarrow$ 3, M $\rightarrow$ 2, O $\rightarrow$ 9, R $\rightarrow$ 6

21. ARCHER $\rightarrow$ 164576

22. MECHRALE $\rightarrow$ 27456137

23. ROCHEL $\rightarrow$ 694573

24. LARCH $\rightarrow$ 31645

25. MARCH $\rightarrow$ 21645

26. COLLER $\rightarrow$ 493376

27. REAL $\rightarrow$ 6713

28. COACH → 49145

29. ALLOCHRE → 13357163164576

30. HEARL → 57163

31. (*b*) Except coriander, all are flowers.

32. (*b*) Except driving, all are activities preformed in water.

33. (*c*) Except Mysore, all are harbours.

34. (*b*) Except S. Radhakrishnan, all were the Prime Ministers of India.

35. (*d*) Except cabbage, all grow under the ground.

36. (*b*) Except Faiz Ahmed, all were among the nine gems in Akbar's court.

37. (*a*) Except Lakshadweep, all are states of India.

38. (*d*) Except friend, all represent blood relations.

39. (*c*) Except sharp, all are related to dimensions.

40. (*b*) Except man, all are animals.

41. (*c*) The dots move, two, three, four, five steps respectively in a clockwise direction.

42. (*c*) The number of sides in each figure increases by one in each next figure.

43. (*d*) The inner figure becomes the outer one and the outer figure disappears and another figure comes inside in each subsequent figure.

44. (*b*) The number of circles and the number of triangles increase in every alternate figure.

45. (*d*) One line in each figure changes to a curve up and down alternately.

46. Except (*c*), all others have similar figures inside as well as outside.

47. Except (*c*), in all others the outer and inner figures are the same.

48. Except (*a*), in all others the outer and inner figures are the same.

49. Except (*a*), in all others the outer and mid figures are same.

50. Except (*d*), all others have parallel lines inside.

Sainik School Entrance Exam, 2007
(CLASS VI)

PAPER–I : MATHEMATICS AND LANGUAGE

PART–A : MATHEMATICS

1. How much per cent is 15 of 75?

2. How much is subtracted from 21.049, so that it will remain 9.2603?

3. Sunita earns ₹ 1500 in 10 days, then how much she will earn in 30 days?

4. What will be the next two-digit numbers for the blanks to continue the series?

   (*i*) 3, 5, 8, 12, ... , ...

   (*ii*) 1, 2, 4, 8, ... , ...

5. Sonia pays rent ₹ 7500 for 3 months. If the rate of rent remains the same, then how much rent she will pay for one complete year?

6. What will be $\dfrac{3}{8}$ of $1\dfrac{2}{3}$?

7. Write the following in descending order :
   4.012, 40.12, .4012, 4.210

8. What is the value of – $4\dfrac{1}{2} \div 2\dfrac{1}{2} + \dfrac{1}{2}$

9. Find the volume of a cube in cubic metres, whose one side is 75 cms.

10. In triangle ABC, AB = AC and $\angle$B = 40°, then find the values of other two angles.

11. Divide ₹ 345.45 in the given ratio

    $1\dfrac{1}{2} : 1\dfrac{1}{3} : 1\dfrac{1}{4}$.

12. Transform the speed $22\dfrac{1}{2}$ metres per second into kilometres per hour.

13. The area of a plot is 6000 sq. metres. If the ratio of its length and breadth is 12 : 5, then find the length of its diagonal.

14. The ratio of two acute angles of a right-angled triangle is 4 : 5, then find the value of both acute angles.

15. A number is multiplied by $\dfrac{3}{2}$. How much per cent the obtained number is increased?

16. Find square of : $1\dfrac{1}{14} - 2\dfrac{1}{7} + 3\dfrac{1}{2} - 1\dfrac{6}{7}$

17. The weight of 25 bags of rice is 876.5 kg, then find the weight of one bag of rice.

18. Vimla scored 70% marks in an examination. If she obtained 280 marks in the examination, then find the maximum marks of the examination.

19. Fill up the blanks :

    (*i*) $0 \div 10 = $ . . . .

    (*ii*) If $\dfrac{1}{25} = 0.04$, then $\dfrac{17}{25} = $ . . . .

20. Find Highest Common Factor of 320, 48, 1500.

21. There is a ration of 65 days for 84 men. How many men should go out so that the ration may last for 78 days?

22. The average age of a class of 30 students is 13 years. The average age of 18 students out of them is 15 years. Find the average age of the remaining students.

23. Find the smallest number which, when divided by 3, 5, 12, 15 has in each case 2 as a remainder.

24. Write true or false :
  (*i*) Two sides of an equilateral triangle are equal.
  (*ii*) 21.07 is less than 50.06.
  (*iii*) The volume of one litre milk is equal to 100 cubic centimetres.
  (*iv*) The radii of concentric circles are equal.
  (*v*) All the sides of a regular hexagon are equal.

25. Roshni can row a boat at the rate 3 kms/hour in still water. If the speed of the stream is 2 kms/hour, then in how much time she will complete the distance of 5 kms against the stream?

26. What will be the simple interest on ₹ 462.50 for $3\frac{1}{2}$ years at the rate of 4% per annum?
Also find the total amount.

27. Draw a circle of diameter 8 cms. with the help of a compass and express :

  (*i*) Its radius OP, where O is the centre of the circle and P is any point on its circumference.
  (*ii*) Construct an angle of 60° at its centre.
  (*iii*) Construct the minor segment of the circle.

28. On selling an article for ₹ 75, Alka loses $6\frac{1}{4}\%$, then find the cost price of the article.

29. A person travelling by a train, crosses a tunnel in $4\frac{1}{2}$ minutes. If the speed of the train is 36 kms per hour, then find the length of the tunnel.

30. A rectangular field is 38 m 5 dm long and 21 m 5 dm wide. How much would be the cost of fencing around the field at the rate of ₹ 15.50 per metre?

$$\boxed{\textbf{EXPLANATORY ANSWERS}}$$

1. Let the per cent be x
Now, $x\%$ of $75 = 15$

$\Rightarrow \quad \dfrac{x}{100} \times 75 = 15$

$\Rightarrow \qquad x = 15 \times \dfrac{100}{75}$

$\qquad\qquad = 20$

Thus, the required per cent is 20.

2. Let the value be x so that
$21.049 - x = 9.2603$
$\therefore \qquad x = 21.049 - 9.2603$
$\qquad\qquad = 11.7887.$

3. One day's earning of Sunita $= \dfrac{1500}{10}$

$\qquad\qquad\qquad = ₹ 150$

$\therefore$ 30 days' earning of Sunita $= 150 \times 30$

$\qquad\qquad\qquad\qquad = ₹ 4500.$

4. (*i*) $3 + 2 = 5$
$\qquad 5 + 3 = 8$
$\qquad 8 + 4 = 12$
$\qquad 12 + 5 = 17$
$\qquad 17 + 6 = 23$
(*ii*) $1 \times 2 = 2$
$\qquad 2 \times 2 = 4$
$\qquad 4 \times 2 = 8$
$\qquad 8 \times 2 = 16$
$\qquad 16 \times 2 = 32.$

5. Rate of rent $= \dfrac{7500}{3}$

$\qquad\qquad\quad = ₹ 2500$

Thus, the amount paid by her for one complete year
$= 12 \times 2500$
$= ₹ 30,000$

6. The value of $\dfrac{3}{8}$ of $1\dfrac{2}{3} = \dfrac{3}{8} \times \dfrac{5}{3}$

$\qquad\qquad\qquad\qquad = \dfrac{5}{8}.$

7. On arranging all the numbers 4.012, 40.12, .4012, 4.210 in descending order, we get 40.12, 4.210, 4.012, .4012.

8. The value of $4\dfrac{1}{2} \div 2\dfrac{1}{2} + \dfrac{1}{2}$ $= \dfrac{9}{2} \div \dfrac{5}{2} + \dfrac{1}{2}$

$$= \dfrac{9}{2} \times \dfrac{2}{5} + \dfrac{1}{2}$$

$$= \dfrac{9}{5} + \dfrac{1}{2}$$

$$= \dfrac{18+5}{10}$$

$$= \dfrac{23}{10}$$

$$= 2\dfrac{3}{10}.$$

9. Side = 75 cm

$\therefore$ The volume of the cube $= (\text{side})^3$

$$= (75)^3$$
$$= 75 \times 75 \times 75$$
$$= 421875 \text{ cu cm.}$$

10. In Δ ABC

AB = AC

$\therefore \angle ABC = \angle ACB = 40°$

(Angles opposite to equal sides are also equal)

$\because \angle A + \angle ABC + \angle ACB = 180°$

(Sum of angles of a triangle is equal to 180°)

$\Rightarrow \angle A + 40° + 40° = 180°$

$\Rightarrow \angle A + 80° = 180°$

$\therefore \angle A = 180° - 80° = 100°.$

11. $1\dfrac{1}{2} : 1\dfrac{1}{3} : 1\dfrac{1}{4} = \dfrac{3}{2} : \dfrac{4}{3} : \dfrac{5}{4}$

$$= \dfrac{18}{12} : \dfrac{16}{12} : \dfrac{15}{12}$$

Suppose, $\dfrac{18x}{12} + \dfrac{16x}{12} + \dfrac{15x}{12} = 345.45$

$\Rightarrow \dfrac{18x + 16x + 15x}{12} = 345.45$

$\Rightarrow \dfrac{49x}{12} = 345.45$

$\therefore \quad x = \dfrac{345.45 \times 12}{49} = 84.60$

First part $= \dfrac{18}{12} \times 84.60 = 18 \times 7.05$
$$= ₹\ 126.90$$

Second part $= \dfrac{16}{12} \times 84.60 = 112.80$

Third part $= \dfrac{15}{12} \times 84.60 = 105.75.$

12. Speed $= 22\dfrac{1}{2}$ m/s

$$= \dfrac{45}{2} \text{ m/s}$$

$$= \dfrac{\dfrac{45}{2 \times 1000} \text{ km}}{\dfrac{1}{60} \times \dfrac{1}{60} \text{ hour}}$$

$$= \dfrac{45}{2 \times 1000} \times 60 \times 60$$

$$= 81 \text{ km/ hour.}$$

13. Suppose the length, $l = 12x$

and the breadth, $b = 5x$

$\because 12x \times 5x = 6000$

$\Rightarrow 60x^2 = 6000$

$\Rightarrow x^2 = \dfrac{6000}{60} = 100$

$\therefore \quad x = 10$

So, $l = 12 \times 10 = 120$ m

and $b = 5 \times 10 = 50$ m

Diagonal $= \sqrt{(120)^2 + (50)^2}$

$$= \sqrt{14400 + 2500}$$

$$= \sqrt{16900}$$

$$= 130 \text{ m.}$$

14. Let the angles be $4x$ and $5x$, so

$\because 4x + 5x + 90 = 180$

$\Rightarrow 4x + 5x = 90$

$\Rightarrow 9x = 90$

$\therefore \quad x = 10$

Thus, first acute angle $= 4 \times 10 = 40°$

and, second acute angle $= 5 \times 10 = 50°.$

15. Let original number be x

The new number $= \dfrac{3}{2}x$

$$\text{Increase} = \dfrac{3}{2}x - x$$

$$= \dfrac{3x - 2x}{2}$$

$$= \dfrac{1}{2}x$$

Thus, percent increase $= \dfrac{\frac{1}{2}x}{x} \times 100$

$$= \dfrac{1}{2} \times 100$$

$$= 50\%.$$

16. $1\dfrac{1}{14} - 2\dfrac{1}{7} + 3\dfrac{1}{2} - 1\dfrac{6}{7} = \dfrac{15}{14} - \dfrac{15}{7} + \dfrac{7}{2} - \dfrac{13}{7}$

$$= \dfrac{15 - 30 + 49 - 26}{14}$$

$$= \dfrac{64 - 56}{14}$$

$$= \dfrac{8}{14}$$

$$= \dfrac{4}{7}$$

Thus, the square of $\dfrac{4}{7} = \left(\dfrac{4}{7}\right)^2$

$$= \dfrac{16}{49}.$$

17. $\because$ 25 bags of rice weighs $= 876.5$ kg

$\therefore$ 1 beg of rice weighs $= \dfrac{876.5}{25}$

$$= 35.06 \text{ kg}$$

18. Suppose the maximum marks $= x$

So, 70% of $x = 280$

$$\Rightarrow \quad \dfrac{70}{100} \times x = 280$$

$$\therefore \quad x = 280 \times \dfrac{100}{70} = 400.$$

19. (*i*) $0 \div 10 = 0$

(*ii*) $\dfrac{1}{25} = 0.04$

$\therefore \dfrac{17}{25} = \dfrac{17 \times 4}{25 \times 4} = \dfrac{68}{100} = .68.$

20.

2	320		2	48		2	1500
2	160		2	24		2	750
2	80		2	12		3	375
2	40		2	6		5	125
2	20			3		5	25
2	10						5
	5						

$\therefore$ 320 $= 2 \times 2 \times 2 \times 2 \times 2 \times 2 \times 5$

 48 $= 2 \times 2 \times 2 \times 2 \times 3$

 1500 $= 2 \times 2 \times 3 \times 5 \times 5 \times 5$

Thus, the highest common factor $= 2 \times 2 = 4$.

21. $\because$ Ration of 65 days is available for 84 men

$\therefore$ Ration of 1 day is available for 65×84 men

$\therefore$ Ration of 78 days is available for $= \dfrac{65 \times 84}{78}$

$$= 70 \text{ men}$$

So, the required number of men $= 84 - 70$

$$= 14 \text{ men}$$

22. The average age of 30 students $= 13$ years

$\therefore$ Total age of 30 students $= 30 \times 13$

$$= 390 \text{ years.}$$

Again, the average age of 18 students

$$= 15 \text{ years}$$

$\therefore$ Total age of 18 students $= 18 \times 15$

$$= 270 \text{ years}$$

So, total age of 12 students $= 390 - 270$

$$= 120 \text{ years}$$

Thus, the average age of remaining students

$$= \dfrac{120}{12} = 10 \text{ years}$$

23. LCM of 3, 5, 12 and 15 $= 3 \times 5 \times 4$

$$= 60$$

3	3, 5, 12, 15
5	1, 5, 4, 5
	1, 1, 4, 1

Thus, the smaller number $= 60 + 2$

$$= 62.$$

24. (*i*) False (An equilateral triangle has all sides equal)

(*ii*) True

(*iii*) False

(*iv*) False

(*v*) True

25. Speed of boat in still water = 3 kms/ hour
Speed of stream = 2 kms/ hour
Speed of boat against the stream = 3 − 2
$$= 1 \text{ km/hr}$$
Time taken by boat against the stream

$$= \frac{5 \text{ km}}{1 \text{ km}} \times \text{hour} = 5 \text{ hours}.$$

26. $p = ₹ 462.50$

$t = 3\frac{1}{2} = \frac{7}{2}$ years

$r = 4\%$ p.a.
Amount = ?

$$\text{S.I} = \frac{p \times r \times t}{100}$$

$$= \frac{462.50 \times 7 \times 4}{100 \times 2}$$

$$= 64.7500$$

$\therefore$ Amount $= ₹\ 462.50 + ₹\ 64.75$
$$= ₹\ 527.25.$$

27. (*i*) Draw PR = 8 cm
Draw perpendicular bisector of PR which meets PR at O .

Thus OP $= \frac{1}{2} \times 8 = 4$ cm

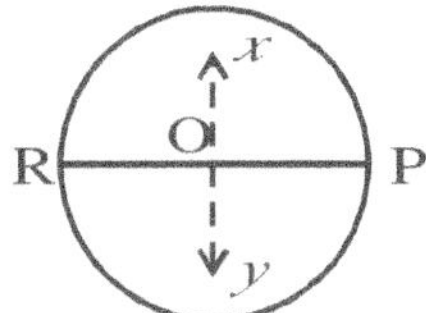

(*ii*) $\angle$POR = 60°

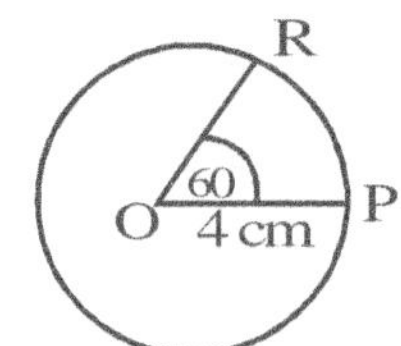

(*iii*)

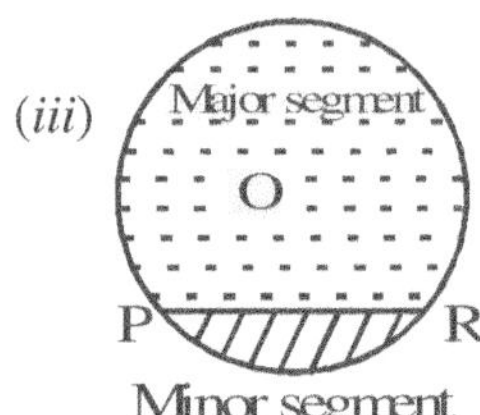

28. Suppose CP = x

Now, $x - 6\frac{1}{4}\%$ of $x = 75$

$$\Rightarrow \quad x - \frac{25x}{4 \times 100} = 75$$

$$\Rightarrow \quad x - \frac{x}{16} = 75$$

$$\Rightarrow \quad \frac{16x - x}{16} = 75$$

$$\Rightarrow \quad \frac{15x}{16} = 75$$

$$\therefore \quad x = \frac{75 \times 16}{15} = ₹\ 80$$

Thus, CP = ₹ 80.

29. Time $= 4\frac{1}{2}$ minutes

$$= \frac{9}{2} \text{ minutes}$$

$$= \frac{9}{2 \times 60} \text{ hours}$$

Speed = 36 km/ hour

$\therefore$ The length of the tunnel $= \dfrac{36 \times 9}{2 \times 60}$

$$= \frac{27}{10} \text{ km}$$

$$= 2.7 \text{ km}.$$

30. Length = 38 m 5 dm
$$= 38.5 \text{ m}$$
Width = 21 m 5 dm
$$= 21.5 \text{ m}$$
Perimeter of rectangular field = $2(l + b)$
$$= 2(38.5 + 21.5)$$
$$= 2 \times 60.0$$
$$= 120 \text{ m}$$
Thus, the cost of fencing $= 120 \times 15.50$
$$= 1860$$
$$= ₹\ 1860.$$

PART–B : LANGUAGE

1. Write an essay on any one of the following :
(*a*) The Problem of Nutrition in India
(*b*) The Problem of Unemployment
(*c*) Population Explosion in India.

2. Read the following passage and answer the questions that follow:

Newton was born in 1642 at Woolsthorpe in England. His father, a farmer, had died before Newton was born. Newton's mother was an intelligent lady. Newton had great affection and regard for his mother. As a boy, he was greatly interested in scientific experiments. He loved to play with mechanical toys and loved to make and fly kites. He invented a small windmill in his childhood. He often watched the stars and made a number of sundials. Immediately after joining college, Newton began to work on the problems that made him so famous. He made many discoveries and inventions. He was a great scholar and genius. Many scientists were inspired by him.

(*a*) What did Newton invent as a young child?
(*b*) In what kind of things was Newton interested as a boy?
(*c*) What are sundials?
(*d*) How did Newton influence other scientists?
(*e*) Give the meaning of each of the following words as used in the passage– (1) Regard (2) Scholar (3) Genius.

3. Fill in the blanks by selecting the correct word:
(*a*) He is .... glad to see you in such a good health.

(very, most)

(*b*) It is necessary to have trust .... God.

(in, on)

(*c*) .... I could sing, I would have sung.

(until, if)

(*d*) I sent him a letter but he had .... left the place.

(already, before)

(*e*) I met him last year and have not seen him ever ....

(thereafter, since)

(*f*) He was .... tired to walk.

(so, too)

(*g*) I was .... troubled by the news.

(much, very)

(*h*) I am .... glad to see you.

(very, too)

(*i*) The work is .... finished.

(near, nearly)

(*j*) We have .... food for a weak.

(much, enough)

4. Make meaningful sentences from words written below :
(*a*) correct, of, neither, is, them
(*b*) studious, I, more, he, than, is
(*c*) go, home, we, immediately, shall
(*d*) us, running, they, away, saw
(*e*) paintings, are, these, whose ?

5. Make a sentence each with the given words.
(*a*) Quarrel   (*b*) Cheat
(*c*) Praise   (*d*) Blame
(*e*) Deserve

6. Correct the following sentences :
(*a*) The cattles were going to the fields.
(*b*) One of my sister is a Ph.D.
(*c*) They enjoyed during the picnic.
(*d*) Whom do you think has torn this book?
(*e*) It was me who addressed the gathering in the playground.

7. Fill in the blanks with appropriate prepositions.
(*a*) He is very good .... drawing.

(at, in)

(*b*) She wanted to sit .... me.

(besides, beside)

(*c*) The two brothers shared the cake .... themselves.

(between, among)

(*d*) Gandhiji had great love .... his country. (for, to)

(*e*) She wants to withdraw .... the contest. (of, from)

8. Do as directed—

(*a*) He failed in the examination.

(change into negative)

(*b*) He informed me that his friends had arrived.

(change into simple sentence)

(*c*) Smoking is not harmless for health.

(change into affirmative)

(*d*) No one in his family is as tall as he is.

(change into superlative degree)

(*e*) Although she is thin, she is healthy.

(change into compound)

9. Make sentences in order to bring out the difference between each pair of words in the following:

(*a*) Ancient, Old

(*b*) Artiste, Artisan

(*c*) Cheat, Deceive

(*d*) Doubt, Suspect

(*e*) Hear, Listen

EXPLANATORY ANSWERS

1. The Problem of Unemployment

In a country like India unemployment is a sheer wastage of manpower resources. Since Independence, various new job opportunities have been created but these have not kept pace with the increasing number of employment-seekers. Problem of unemployment is becoming all the more serious each year. So far the problem remains unsolved. It leads to frustration and crimes which hamper the progress of the country.

There are various causes of unemployment. The galloping birth rate results in a larger and larger proportion of job seekers everywhere. To add to it our system of education is not employment-oriented. The industries, establishments and other institutions seek suitable professionals. Science has replaced man by machinery, thus reducing the number of persons otherwise engaged for the job. Rapid industrialisation and neglect of small-scale industries have thrown many people out of job. Those who have the will and the knowledge to begin a venture on their own meet the drawback of lack of funds and finance. The faulty manpower planning by the planners and administrators is also aggrevating the problem.

The steps taken to solve the problem of unemployment through the years have not been satisfactory. As such India faces an acute problem of finding ways to provide employment to all those who are able and capable of working. A complete reorientation is required to deal with this problem.

The greatest need is the proper utilisation of human resources by proper manpower planning. The education system must stress on job-oriented or vocational training. Along with rapid industrialisation proper encouragement must be given to small-scale or cottage industries. The schemes of employment need due attention for successful outcome. Government aid and encouragement is required for the dynamic youth to start their own ventures. Apart from these, there is a necessity to check the rapid growth of population in the country.

Suitable and proper employment opportunities ensure the happiness of the citizens of a prospering country. If the problem of unemployment is not dealt with seriously, it will become a threat some day. A solution to this critical problem must be arrived at before it is too late. Only then can every man have a decent living and keep away from indulging in wrong activities.

2. (*a*) Newton invented a windmill, when he was a young child.

(*b*) Newton was keenly interested in scientific experiments. He used to play with mechanical toys and would love to make and fly kites.

(*c*) Sundial is an instrument which shows time by the shadow of a pointer in the sunlight.

(*d*) Newton influenced other scientists by making many discoveries and inventions.

(*e*) 1. Regard – Respect
2. Scholar – Learned man
3. Genius – An extra-ordinary intelligent person.

3. (*a*) very   (*b*) in

(*c*) if   (*d*) already

(*e*) since   (*f*) too

(*g*) much   (*h*) very

(*i*) nearly   (*j*) enough

4. (*a*) Neither of them is correct.

(*b*) He is more studious than I.

(*c*) We shall go home immediately.

(*d*) They saw us running away.

(*e*) Whose paintings are these?

5. (*a*) All of the students quarrelled over a trifle thing.

(*b*) The boys were cheated badly.

(*c*) She praised those boys who had done fairly well in the examination.

(*d*) One must blame oneself for his failure in life.

(e) The brave deserves a good deal.

6. (*a*) The **cattle** were going to the fields.

(*b*) One of my **sisters** is a Ph.D.

(*c*) They enjoyed **themselves** during the picnic.

(*d*) **Who** do you think has torn this book?

(*e*) It was **I** who addressed the gathering in the playground.

7. (*a*) at   (*b*) beside

(*c*) between   (*d*) for

(*e*) from

8. (*a*) He did not pass in the examination.

(*b*) He informed me of his friends' arrival.

(*c*) Smoking is harmful for health.

(*d*) He is the tallest of all in his family.

(*e*) She is thin, but she is healthy.

9. (*a*) **Ancient**—(belonging to times long past)
In the *ancient* times, the king dictated the states.
Old—(refers to age)
He is so *old*, that he cannot walk properly.

(*b*) **Artiste**—(professional entertainer *e.g.*, singer, dancer etc.)
Muhammad Rafi was a great *artiste*.
Artisan—(skilled workman)
The time gone when many *artisans* were required in the factory to complete a piece of work.

(*c*) **Cheat**—(act dishonestly in order to get something)
The shopkeeper used to *cheat* his customers by using weights less than the standard ones.
Deceive—(make somebody believe something that is not true)
They were *deceived* by his words and gave him a big loan which he couldn't return.

(*d*) **Doubt**—(feel uncertain about something)
I *doubt* your integrity and can not trust you.
Suspect—(have a feeling that somebody may be guilty)
The police arrested him due to his *suspected* nature.

(*e*) **Hear**—(perceive sounds with the ears)
Have you ever *heard* the roar of a tiger?
Listen—(pay attention)
Listen me first what I am telling you now.

PAPER–II : INTELLIGENCE TEST

Directions (Q. 1 to 8): *In each of these questions, four of the five options (a), (b), (c), (d) and (e) are alike in a certain way, but one of the rest is different from others. Find the different one.*

1. (*a*) R5A1T6   (*b*) B2A1D4
   (*c*) C3E5A1   (*d*) H8B2D4
   (*e*) E5G7G7

2. 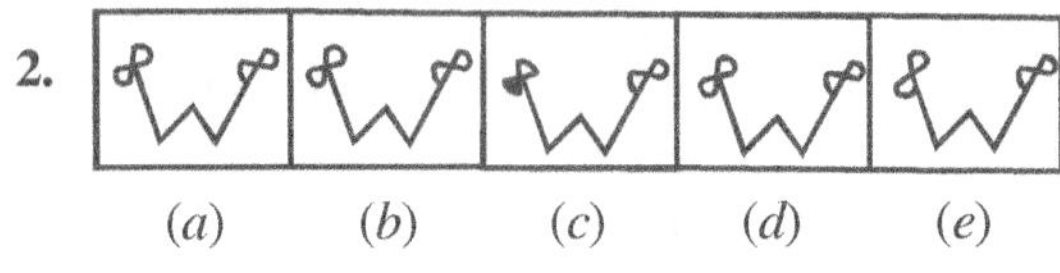
    (*a*)   (*b*)   (*c*)   (*d*)   (*e*)

3. (*a*) 7   (*b*) 21
   (*c*) 29   (*d*) 490
   (*e*) 105

4. 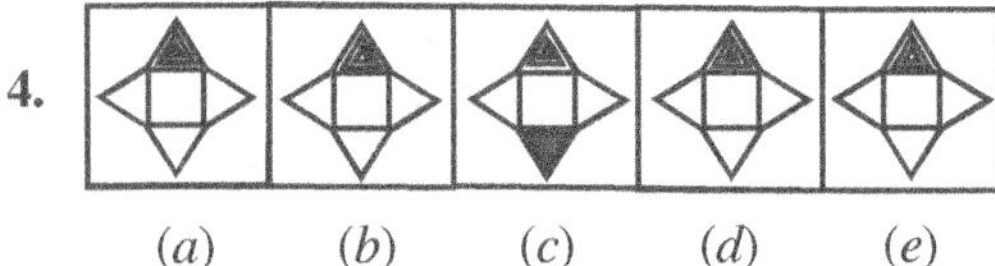
    (*a*)   (*b*)   (*c*)   (*d*)   (*e*)

5. (*a*) Open and Close   (*b*) Hate and Dislike
   (*c*) Rise and Sleep   (*d*) Go and Come
   (*e*) Friend and Enemy

6. 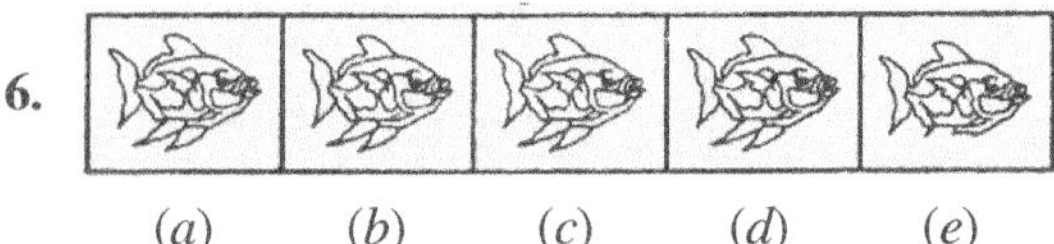
    (*a*)   (*b*)   (*c*)   (*d*)   (*e*)

7. (*a*) 1   (*b*) 8
   (*c*) 26   (*d*) 64
   (*e*) 125

8. 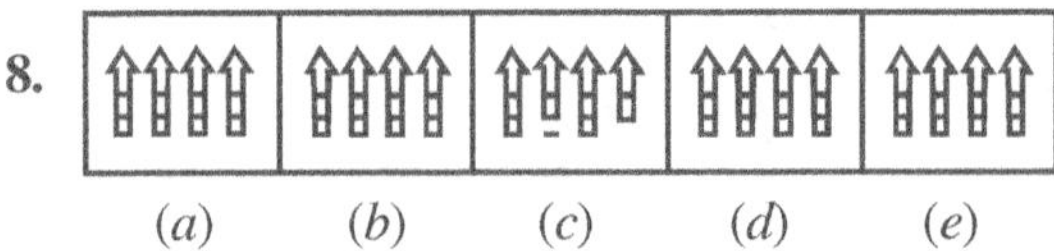
    (*a*)   (*b*)   (*c*)   (*d*)   (*e*)

Directions (Q. 9 to 12): *In each of these questions, problem figures are given in two units. (X), (Y) and (Z) and problem figures while (a), (b), (c), (d) are answer figures. There is some relation between (X) and (Y). The same relation exists between (Z) and one of the answer figures. Find correct answer figure.*

9. **Problem figure**

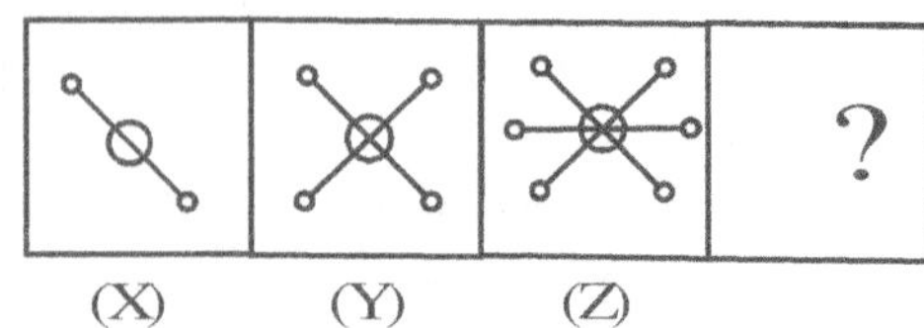

(X)   (Y)   (Z)

Answer figure

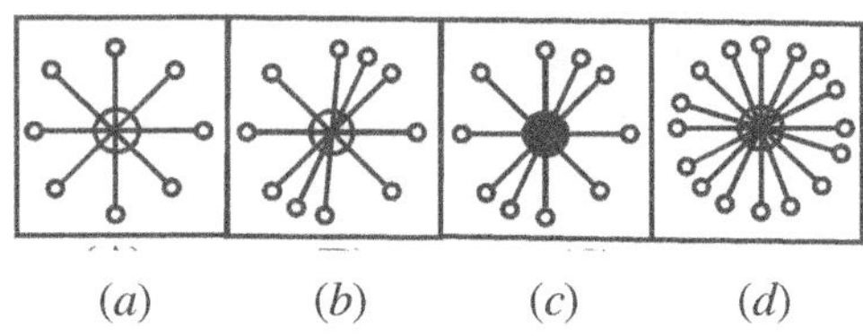

(*a*)   (*b*)   (*c*)   (*d*)

10. **Problem figure**

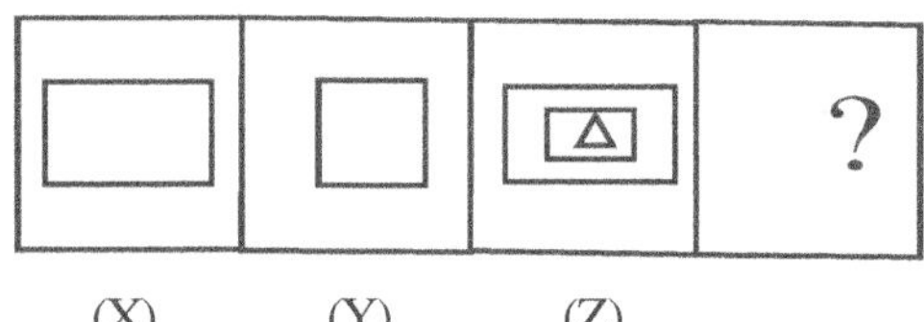

(X)   (Y)   (Z)

Answer figure

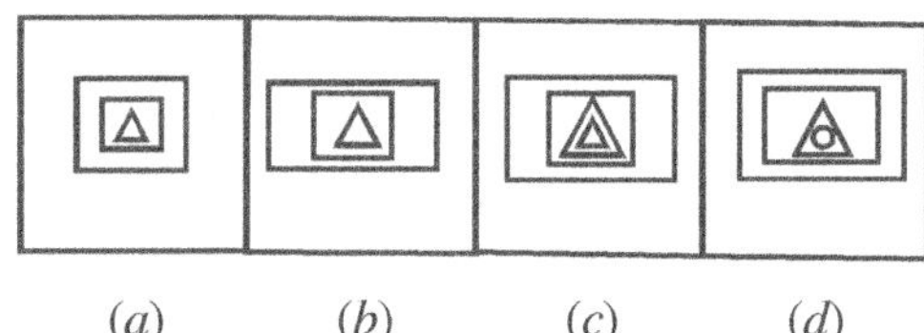

(*a*)   (*b*)   (*c*)   (*d*)

11. **Problem figure**

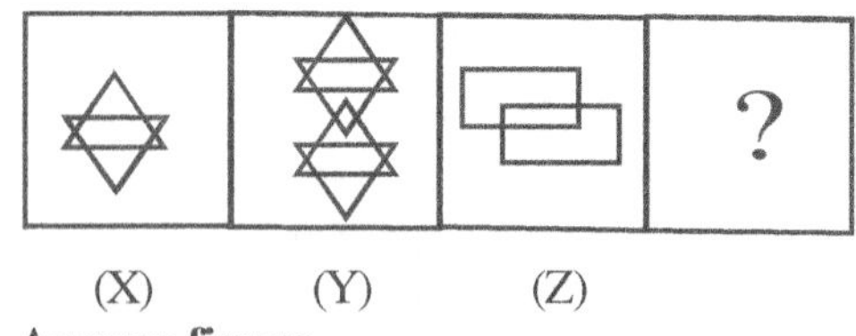

(X)   (Y)   (Z)

Answer figure

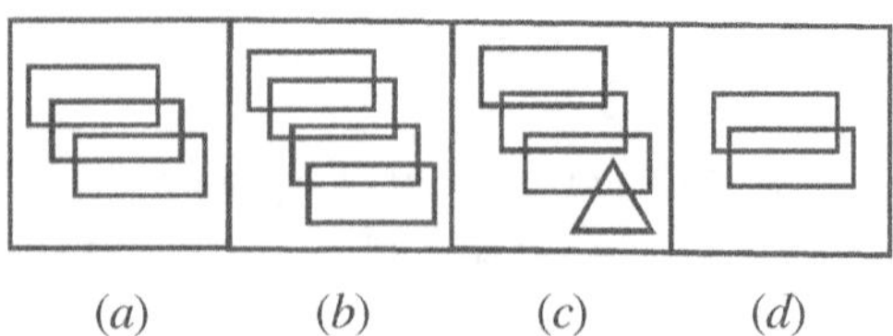

(*a*)   (*b*)   (*c*)   (*d*)

12. Problem figure

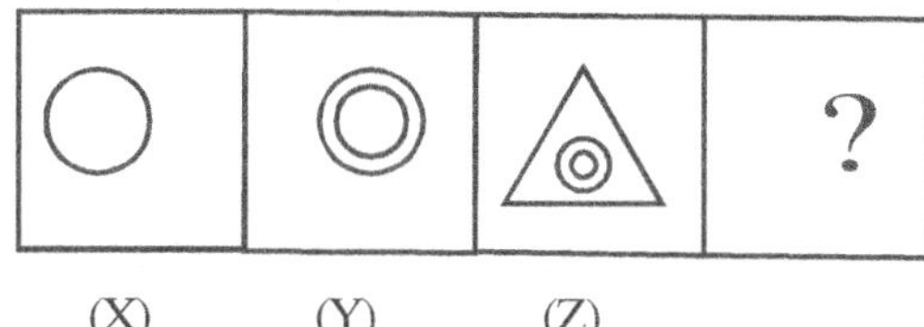

(X)   (Y)   (Z)

Answer figure

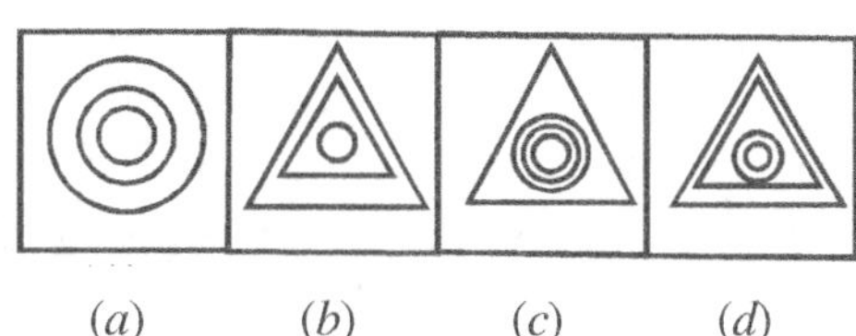

(a)   (b)   (c)   (d)

Directions (Q. 13 to 16): *Find the correct answer.*

13. 'Wood' is related to 'Table' in the same way .... is related to 'Coat' :
(a) Shirt   (b) Wear
(c) Pantaloons   (d) Cloth

14. 'Boy' is related to 'Girl' in the same way 'Nephew' is related to :
(a) Uncle   (b) Niece
(c) Brother-in-law   (d) Aunt

15. 'Fish' is related to 'Bird' in the same way 'Submarine' is related to :
(a) Ship   (b) Train
(c) Aeroplane   (d) Car

16. 'Uncle' is related to 'Aunt' in the same way 'Cock' is related to :
(a) Bird   (b) Hen
(c) Chicken   (d) Duck

Direction (Q. 17 to 24): *In each of the following questions complete the series.*

17. B, D, G, K, ...
(a) P   (b) A
(c) O   (d) N

18. Problem figures

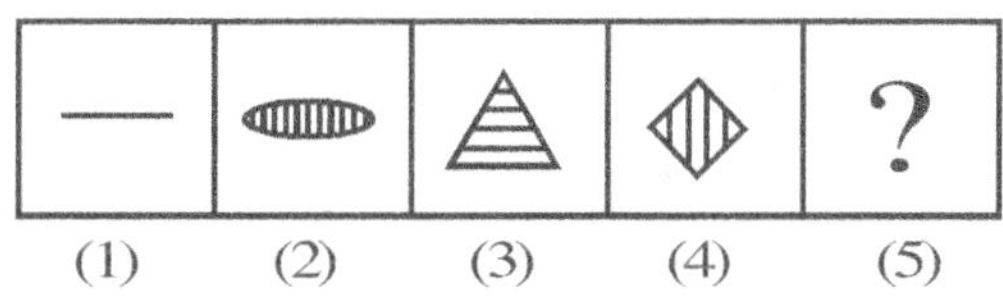

(1)   (2)   (3)   (4)   (5)

Answer figures

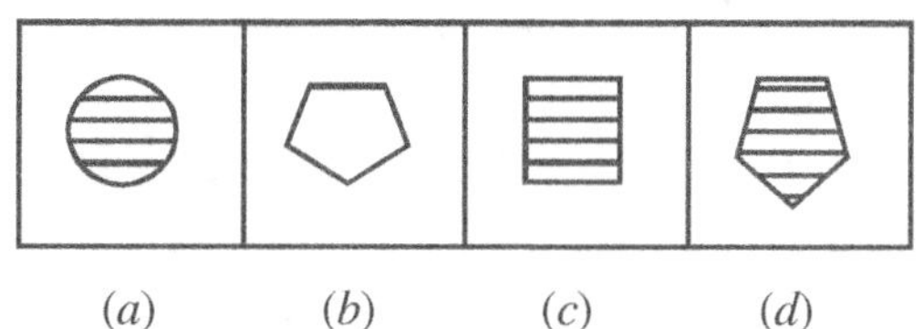

(a)   (b)   (c)   (d)

19. 1243, 2354, 3465 . . . .
(a) 4576   (b) 4675
(c) 4796   (d) 4367

20. Problem figures

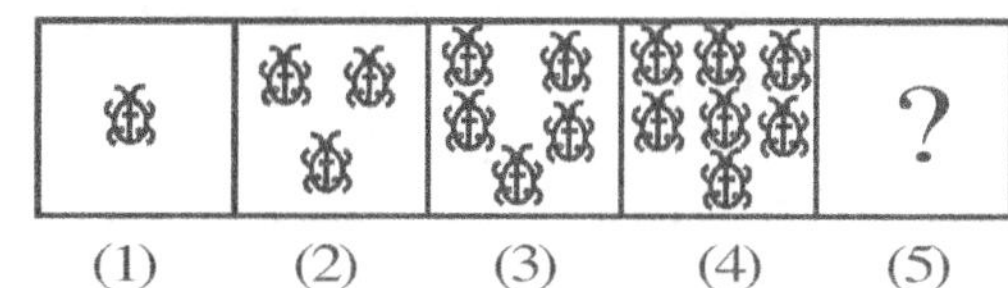

(1)   (2)   (3)   (4)   (5)

Answer figures

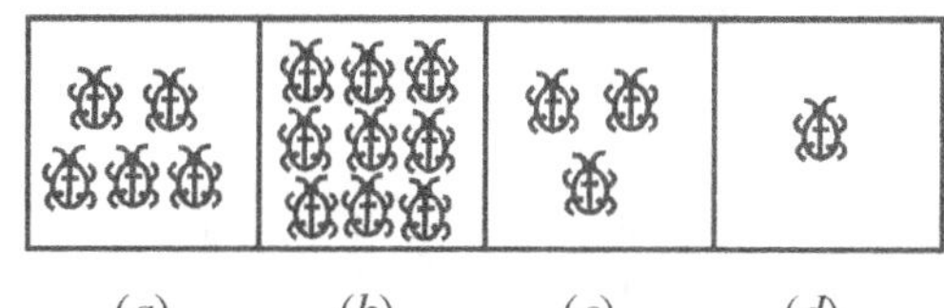

(a)   (b)   (c)   (d)

21. 246, 357, 468, 579, ...
(a) 579   (b) 680
(c) 678   (d) 459

22. Problem figures

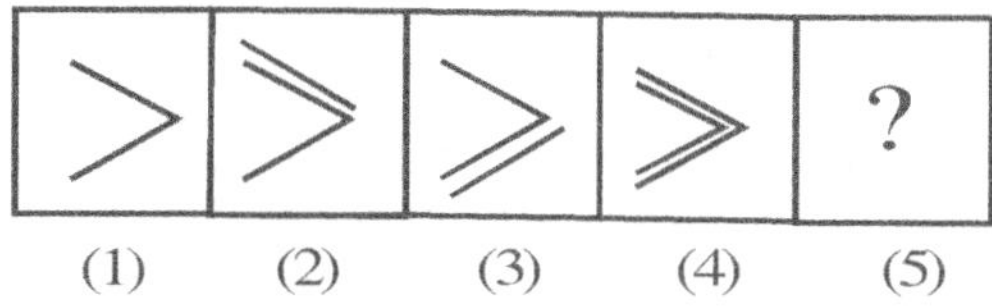

(1)   (2)   (3)   (4)   (5)

Answer figures

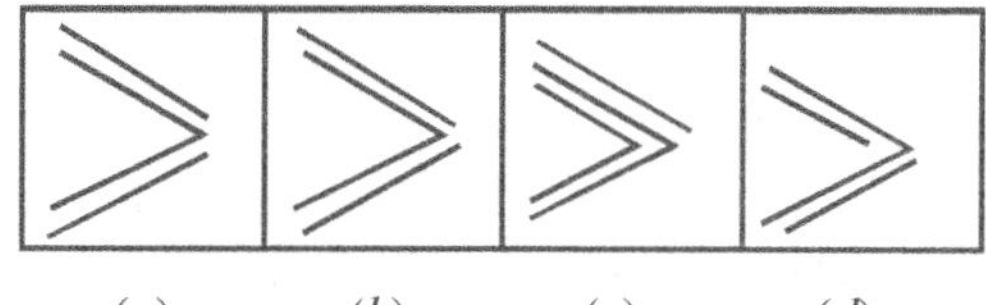

(a)   (b)   (c)   (d)

23. A/2, 4/C, E/6 . . . .
(a) 8/G   (b) 8/K
(c) 7/G   (d) G/8

24. Problem figures

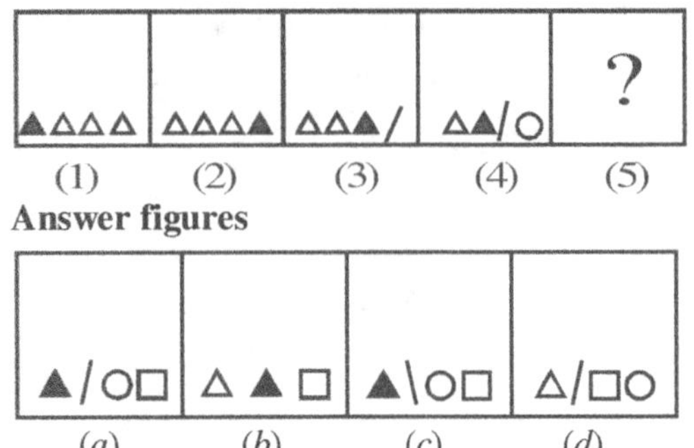

(1)   (2)   (3)   (4)   (5)

Answer figures

(a)   (b)   (c)   (d)

Directions (Q. 25 to 26): *In each of the following questions if words are arranged according to dictionary, which will appear in the third place?*

25. (a) Battalian   (b) Barrister
(c) Banana   (d) Balance
(e) Bachelor

26. (a) Dear   (b) Decide
(c) Diagram   (d) Departure
(e) Dawn

Directions (Q. 27 to 30): *In each of the following questions, arrange the letters of each word then find fourth letter.*

27. ENKAL (A BODY PART)   ....

28. HCDNGRHAIA (A UNION TERRETORY)

       ....

29. HEPES (AN ANIMAL)   ....

30. NEGOAR (A FRUIT)   ....

31. If $2 \times 8 = 4$ and $4 \times 9 = 6$, then what will be 5×5?
(a) 10   (b) 6
(c) 5   (d) 25

32. If $A + E = 6$, then what will be $A \times E$?
(a) 3   (b) 6
(c) 8   (d) 5

Directions (Q. 33 to 34): *In each question arrange the word to make a meaningful sentence, then write its second word.*

33. (a) the   (b) in
(c) is   (d) room
(e) he

34. (a) mango   (b) this
(c) a   (d) is
(e) sweet

35. If the code of ANKLE is CRANKLE, what is the code of OWN?
(a) PERSONAL   (b) HAVING
(c) OWNER   (d) CROWN

36. If the code of ARE is STARE, what will be the code of ARCH?
(a) SYMBOL   (b) PAINT
(c) MART   (d) STARCH

37. If the code of QBSJT is PARIS what will be the code of MPOEPO?
(a) KANPUR
(b) LONDON
(c) MYSOREYORK
(d) MOSCOW

38. If the code of STAND is TSBME, what will be the code of SLEEP?
(a) MKOOS   (b) TKFDQ
(c) FKKQS   (d) RGMMB

Directions (Q. 39 to 42): *In each of these questions which one of the answer figure is the mirror image of the given figure 'X'?*

39. Problem figure

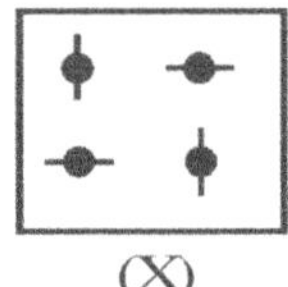

(X)

Answer figures

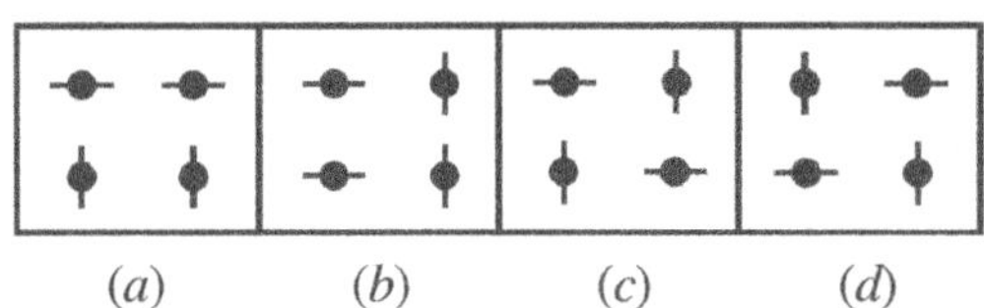

(a)   (b)   (c)   (d)

40. Problem figure

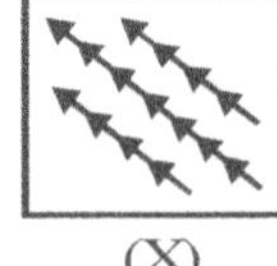

(X)

Answer figures

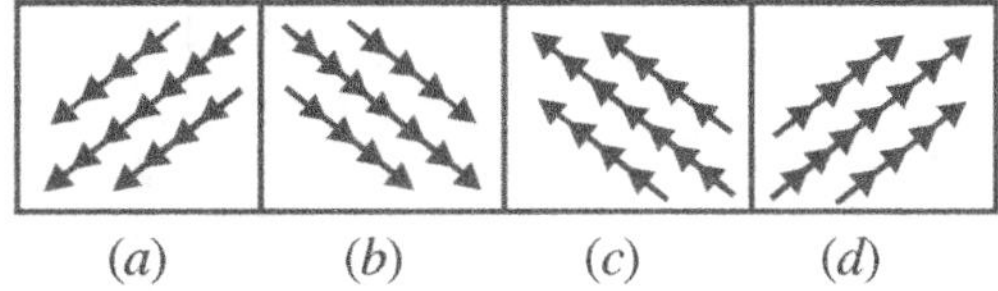

(*a*) (*b*) (*c*) (*d*)

41. Problem figure

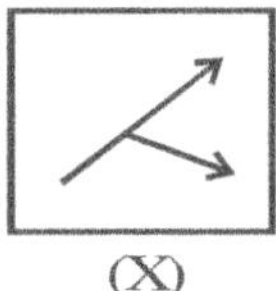

(X)

Answer figures

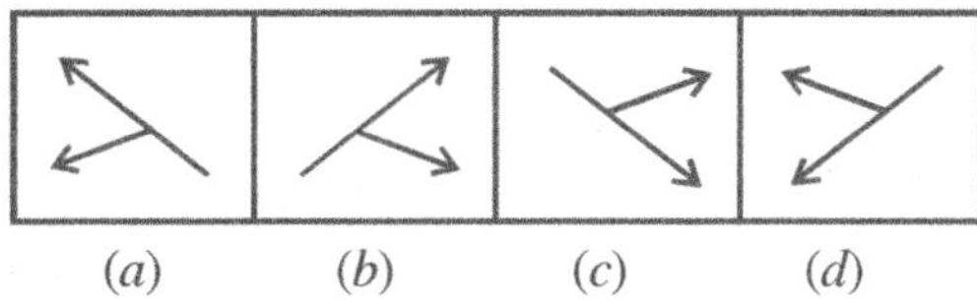

(*a*) (*b*) (*c*) (*d*)

42. Problem figure

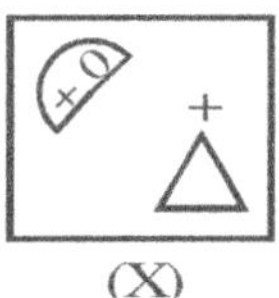

(X)

Answer figures

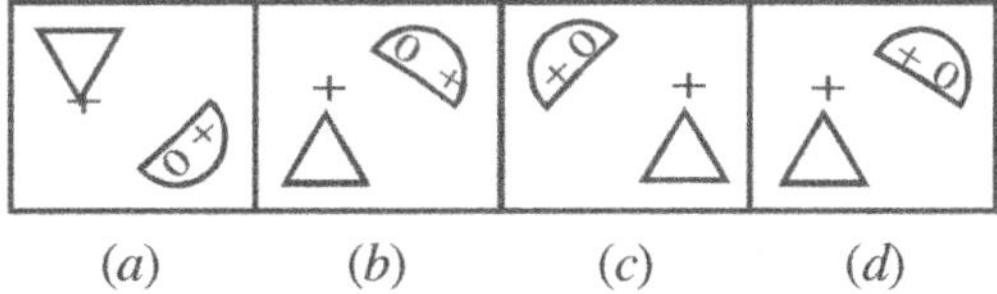

(*a*) (*b*) (*c*) (*d*)

Directions (Q. 43 to 46): *In each of these questions which of the answers figures will complete the given design?*

43. Problem figure

Answer figures

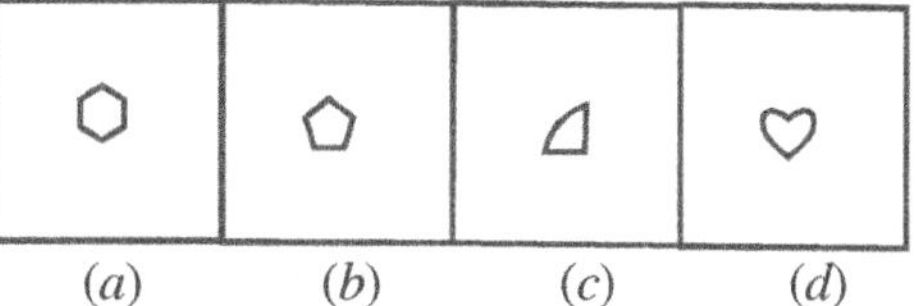

(*a*) (*b*) (*c*) (*d*)

44. Problem figure

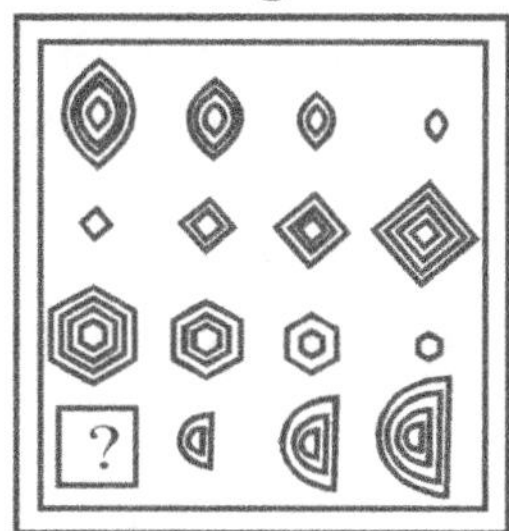

Answer figures

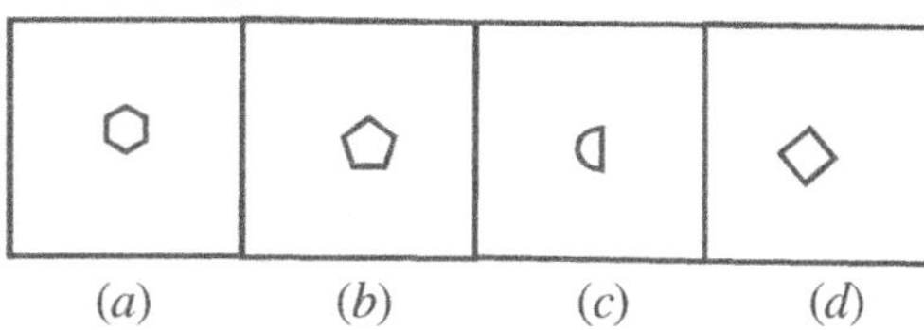

(*a*) (*b*) (*c*) (*d*)

45. Problem figure

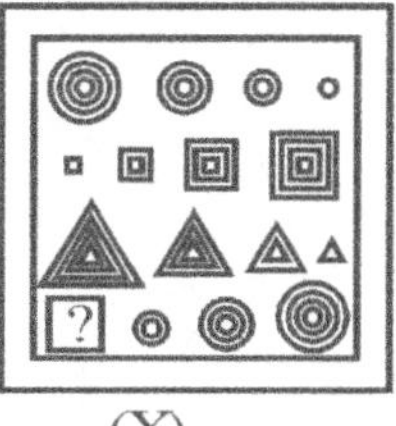

(X)

Answer figures

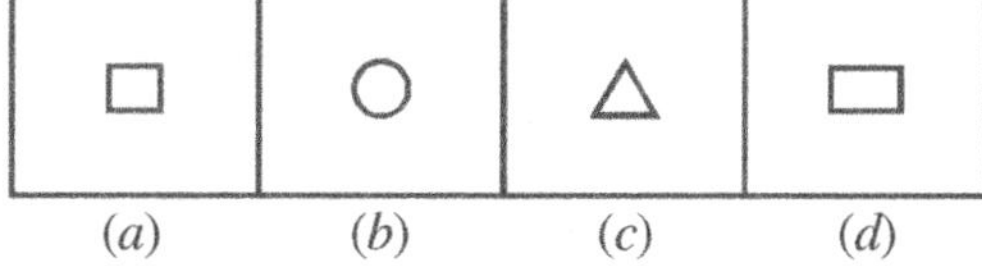

(*a*) (*b*) (*c*) (*d*)

46. Problem figure

Answer figures

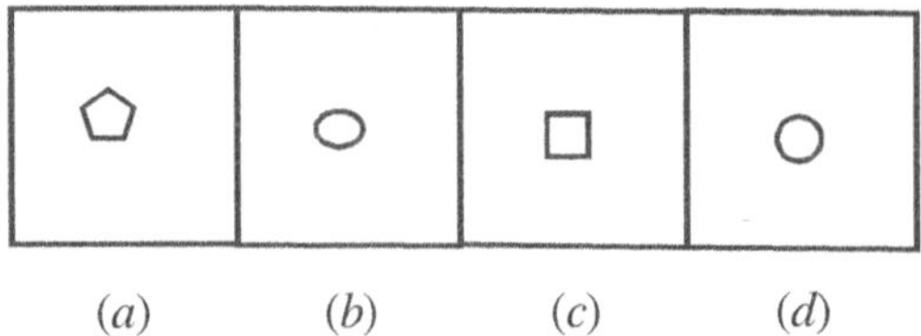

(a)　　　(b)　　　(c)　　　(d)

Directions (Q. 47 to 48): *In each of these questions in which of the answer figures the given figure X is hidden?*

47. Problem figure

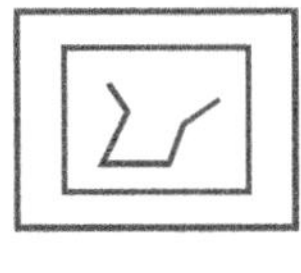

(X)

Answer figures

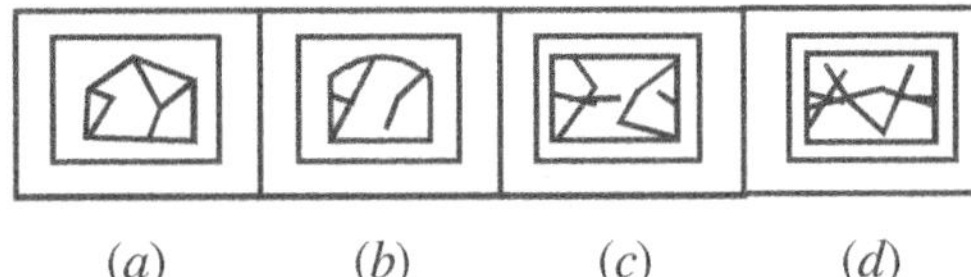

(a)　　　(b)　　　(c)　　　(d)

48. Problem figure

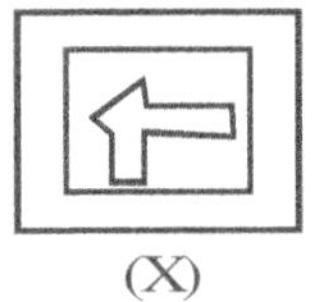

(X)

Answer figures

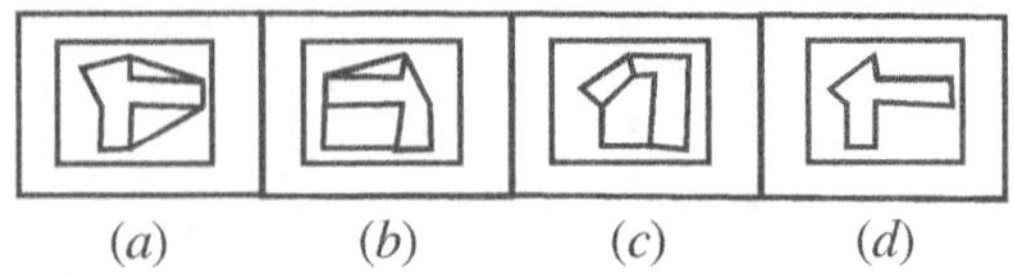

(a)　　　(b)　　　(c)　　　(d)

Directions (Q. 49 to 50): *In each of these questions which one of the answer figure is hidden in the figure X?*

49. Problem figure

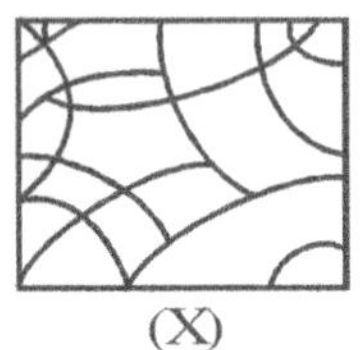

(X)

Answer figures

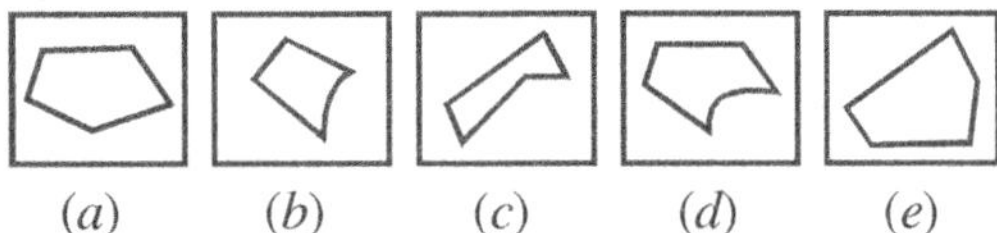

(a)　　　(b)　　　(c)　　　(d)　　　(e)

50. Problem figure

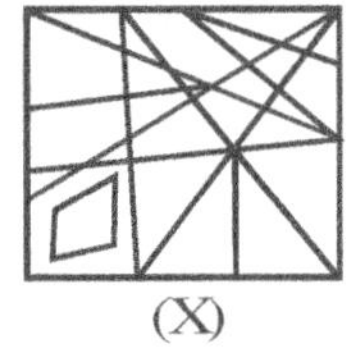

(X)

Answer figures

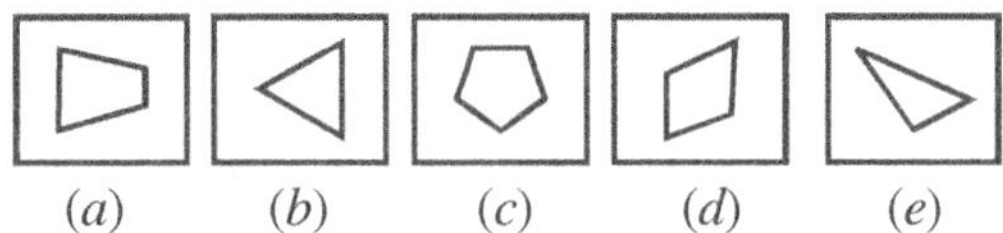

(a)　　　(b)　　　(c)　　　(d)　　　(e)

EXPLANATORY ANSWERS

1. Except (*a*), all the other options carry 3 letters and their places according to the alphabets respectively.

2. Only at-one end in (*c*) there are two Δ while in all the wings, there are circles.

3. Except (*c*), in all the other options, the number is divisible by 7.

4. Option (*c*) has one more solid triangle.

5. Except (*b*), others are opposite in meaning to one another.

6. Except (*e*), others have two wings in the lower parts.

7. Except (*c*), all the other numbers are complete cube.

8. Except (*c*), all the designs are complete.

9. Moving from X to Y, one design is increased in the same way moving from Z to (*a*) one design is increased.

10. (*a*) : From X to Y rectangle changes to square in the same way from Z to (*a*) rectangles are changing to squares.

11. (*b*) : Moving from X to Y the number of designs are doubled. In the same way from Z to (*b*) the number of designs are doubled.

12. (*c*) : Moving from X to Y the number of circle inside the design is increased by one and so from Z to (*c*) it is also doubled.

13. (*d*) : As 'Table' is made from 'Wood' in the same way 'Coat' is made from 'Cloth'.

14. (*b*) : The feminine of 'Boy' is 'Girl' in the same way the feminine of 'Nephew' is 'Niece'.

15. (*c*) : As fish swims in water and bird flies in air similarly submarine sails in water and aeroplane moves in air.

16. (*b*) : As the feminine of Uncle is 'Aunt' in the same way the feminine of 'Cock' is 'Hen'.

17. (*a*) : We find

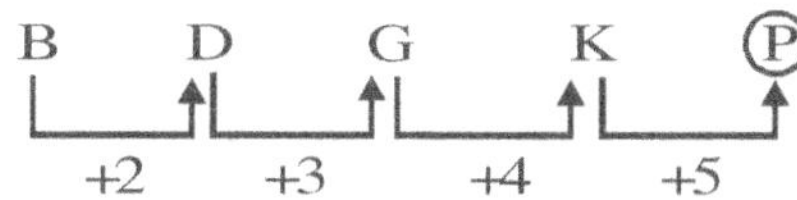

18. (*d*) : In each subsequent problem figure, one line is increased. In spite of this, the innerlines are changed from horizontal to vertical and vice versa.

19. (*a*) : We see that

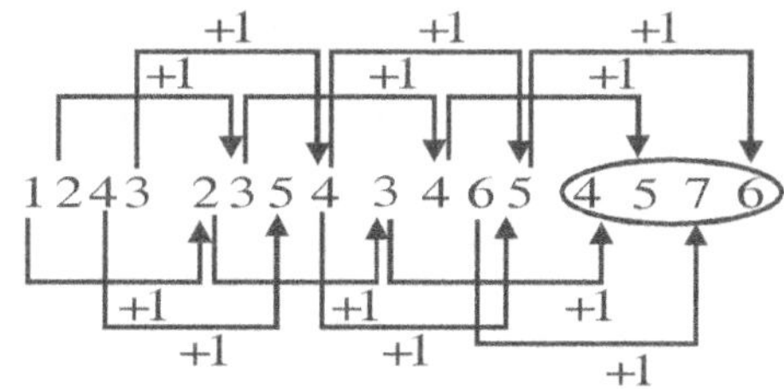

20. (*b*) : In each subsequent problem figure, two designs are increased.

21. (*b*) : We observe

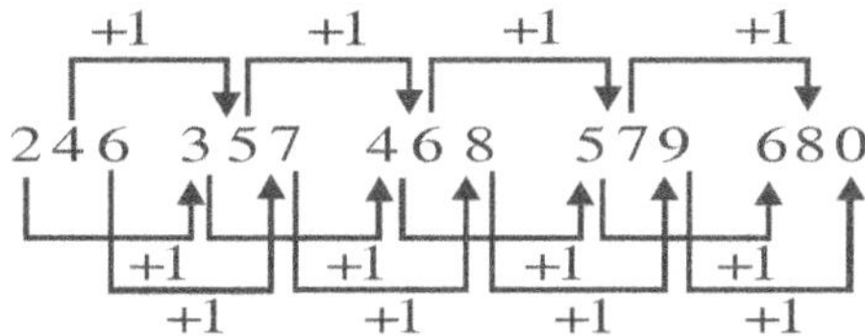

22. (*c*) : In each subsequent figure, a line comes at upper side first then lower side and in the third case both lines meet at one corner. So in the next figure one line comes at the upper side.

23. (*a*) : $A \xrightarrow{+2} C \xrightarrow{+2} E \xrightarrow{+2} (G)$

and $2 \xrightarrow{+2} 4 \xrightarrow{+2} 6 \xrightarrow{+2} (8)$

We find in each subsequent terms, the letters and digits are reversed.

24. (*a*) : From the problem figure (2), a new design takes place of black ▲ and to the left to ▲, a white △ is changed into black ▲.

25. (*b*) : After arranging the words according to dictionary: Dawn, Dear, **Decide**, Departure, Diagram.

26. (*c*) : After arranging the words according to dictionary: Bachelor, Balance, **Banana**, Barrister, Battalian.

27. ENKAL → ANKLE → 4th letter is L.

28. HCDNGRHAIA → CHANDIGARH → 4th letter is N.

29. HEPES → SHEEP → 4th letter is E.

30. NEGOAR → ORANGE → 4th letter is N.

31. ∵ $2 \times 8 = 16 = (4)^2$ and

$4 \times 9 = 36 = (6)^2$

In the same way,

$5 \times 5 = 25 = (5)^2$

∴ $5 \times 5 \to 5$.

32. (*d*) : $A + E \to 1 + 5 = 6$

∴ $A \times E \to 1 \times 5 = 5$.

33. He is in the room → second word → 'is'.

34. This is a sweet mango → second word → 'is'.

35. Code of ANKLE → CRANKLE *i.e.*, CR is added in the beginning. In the same way, code of OWN → CROWN.

36. (*d*) : Code of ARE → STARE *i.e.*, ST is added in the beginning, in the same way, code of ARCH → STARCH.

37. (*b*) : Q $\xrightarrow{-1}$ P in the same way, M $\xrightarrow{-1}$ L

B $\xrightarrow{-1}$ A   P $\xrightarrow{-1}$ O

S $\xrightarrow{-1}$ R   O $\xrightarrow{-1}$ N

J $\xrightarrow{-1}$ I   E $\xrightarrow{-1}$ D

T $\xrightarrow{-1}$ S   P $\xrightarrow{-1}$ O

O $\xrightarrow{-1}$ N

38. (*b*) : S $\xrightarrow{+1}$ T in the same way, S $\xrightarrow{+1}$ T

T $\xrightarrow{-1}$ S   L $\xrightarrow{-1}$ K

A $\xrightarrow{+1}$ B   E $\xrightarrow{+1}$ F

N $\xrightarrow{-1}$ M   E $\xrightarrow{-1}$ D

D $\xrightarrow{+1}$ E   P $\xrightarrow{+1}$ Q

39. (*c*)	**40.** (*d*)	**41.** (*a*)	**42.** (*b*)
43. (*c*)	**44.** (*c*)	**45.** (*b*)	**46.** (*a*)
47. (*c*)	**48.** (*d*)	**49.** (*a*)	**50.** (*d*)

Sainik School Entrance Exam, 2006
(CLASS VI)

PAPER-I : MATHEMATICS AND LANGUAGE

PART–A : MATHEMATICS

1. 12% of a certain sum of money is ₹ 43.50 P. find the sum.

2. Find the numbers for the blanks to continue the series:
   (*a*) 3, 8, 15, 24, ...   (*b*) 4, 10, 18, 28

3. Divide Rs. 1530 into three shares proportional to the numbers 2, 3, 4.

4. Find the prime factors of 999999.

5. Find the diagonal of a rectangle whose sides are 12 metres and 5 metres.

6. Subtract $13\dfrac{3}{5}$ from $21\dfrac{5}{8}$.

7. Express $\dfrac{37}{11}$ as mixed numbers.

8. What percentage is equivalent to $\dfrac{3}{8}$?

9. Simplify $\dfrac{\dfrac{1}{2}+\dfrac{2}{3}}{\dfrac{3}{4}-\dfrac{2}{9}}$.

10. Find the area of a triangle whose sides are 50 metres, 78 metres, 112 metres respectively.

11. Express a speed of 18 km per hour in metres per second.

12. In what time will ₹ 8500 amount to ₹ 15767.50 at $4\dfrac{1}{2}$ per cent per annum Simple Interest?

13. 'A' can do a piece of work in 5 days, and 'B' can do it in 6 days. How long will they take if both work together?

14. Find the sum of $-\dfrac{2}{5}$ and $\dfrac{3}{8}$.

15. (*a*) Area of rectangle = ? (*b*) Area of square = ?

16. Find the circumference of a circle whose radius is 42 metres.

17. A man buys a pen for ₹ 25 and sells it for ₹ 23. Find his loss per cent?

18. $\dfrac{1}{4}$ of a number subtracted from $\dfrac{1}{3}$ of the number gives 12. The number is—

19. State, True or false.
    (*a*) A parallelogram is a four-sided figure whose opposite sides are parallel.
    (*b*) A rhombus is a parallelogram all of whose sides are equal.

20. The population of four towns is 35560, 30000, 27500 and 25600 respectively. What is the average population of a town?

21. Find the reciprocal of $-\dfrac{125}{216}$.

22. Write the decimal form of $\dfrac{17}{5}$.

23. Simplify $\left(-\dfrac{1}{5}\right)^{3}\times\left(-\dfrac{1}{5}\right)^{2}$.

24. Name any four objects from your environment having the shape of a cuboid.

25. Piyush lost 20% by selling a bicycle for ₹ 1536. Find the cost price of the bicycle.

26. Find S.I. on ₹ 5000 at 12% per annum for 3 years.

27. If 23% of a number is 46, find the number.

28. Write True (T) or False (F) for the following statements:

(*a*) Every rational number can be represented on a number line

(*b*) Speed = $\dfrac{\text{Distance}}{\text{Time}}$.

29. Seven dozen oranges cost ₹ 91. Find the cost of 10 dozen oranges.

30. In $\triangle ABC$, $\angle A = 50°$, $\angle B = 50°$, and $\angle C = 80°$. Which two sides of this triangle are equal.

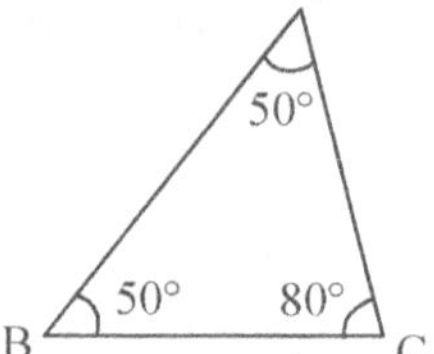

EXPLANATORY ANSWERS

1. Here, $\quad P = \dfrac{I \times 100}{r \times t}$

$$= \dfrac{43.50 \times 100}{12 \times 1} = \dfrac{4350}{12} = ₹\, 362.50$$

2. (*a*)

3	8	15	24	$\boxed{35}$
↓	↓	↓	↓	↓
$2^2 - 1$	$3^2 - 1$	$4^2 - 1$	$5^2 - 1$	$6^2 - 1$

(*b*) 4 10 18 28 $\boxed{40}$

$\quad\quad +6 \quad +8 \quad +10 \quad +12$

3. Here, sum of the ratios $= 2 + 3 + 4 = 9$

Hence, Ist share $= \dfrac{2}{9} \times 1530 = ₹\, 340$

2nd share $= \dfrac{3}{9} \times 1530 = ₹\, 510$

3rd share $= \dfrac{4}{9} \times 1530 = ₹\, 680.$

4.

3	999999
3	333333
3	111111
7	37037
11	5291
13	481
	37

$\therefore\ 999999 = 3 \times 3 \times 3 \times 7 \times 11 \times 13 \times 37.$

5. The length of the diagonal of a rectangle

$$= \sqrt{(12)^2 + (5)^2} = \sqrt{(144) + (25)}$$

$$= \sqrt{169} = 13 \text{ m.}$$

6. $21\dfrac{5}{8} - 13\dfrac{3}{5} = (21 - 13) + \left(\dfrac{5}{8} - \dfrac{3}{5}\right)$

$$= 8 + \dfrac{25 - 24}{40} = 8\dfrac{1}{40}.$$

7. $\dfrac{37}{11} = \dfrac{33}{11} + \dfrac{4}{11} = 3\dfrac{4}{11}.$

8. $\dfrac{3}{8} = \dfrac{\dfrac{3}{8} \times 100}{100}$

$$= \dfrac{75}{2} \times \dfrac{1}{100} = 37\dfrac{1}{2}\%.$$

9. $\dfrac{\dfrac{1}{2} + \dfrac{2}{3}}{\dfrac{3}{4} - \dfrac{2}{9}} = \dfrac{\dfrac{3+4}{6}}{\dfrac{27-8}{36}}$

$$= \dfrac{\dfrac{7}{6}}{\dfrac{19}{36}} = \dfrac{7}{6} \times \dfrac{36}{19} = \dfrac{42}{19} = 2\dfrac{4}{19}.$$

10. Here, $\quad a = 50 \text{ m},\ b = 78 \text{ m},\ c = 112 \text{ m}$

$\therefore \quad s = \dfrac{1}{2}(50 + 78 + 112) \text{ m}$

$$= \dfrac{1}{2} \times 240 \text{ m} = 120 \text{ m}$$

$\therefore$ Required Area of $\triangle$

$$= \sqrt{s(s - a)(s - b)(s - c)}$$

$$= \sqrt{120(120 - 50)(120 - 78)(120 - 112)}$$

$$= \sqrt{120 \times 70 \times 42 \times 8}$$

$$= \sqrt{2 \times 2 \times 2 \times 3 \times 5 \times 2 \times 5 \times 7 \times 2 \times 3 \times 7 \times 2 \times 2 \times 2}$$

$$= \sqrt{2^2 \times 2^2 \times 2^2 \times 2^2 \times 3^2 \times 5^2 \times 7^2}$$

$$= 2 \times 2 \times 2 \times 2 \times 3 \times 5 \times 7 = 1680 \text{ sq.m.}$$

11. $\quad 18 \text{ km/hr} = \dfrac{18 \times 1000}{60 \times 60} \text{ m/sec.} = 5 \text{ m/sec.}$

12. Here, S.I. = ₹ 15767.50 – ₹ 8500 = ₹ 7267.50

$$\therefore \quad \text{Time} = \frac{\text{S.I.} \times 100}{p \times r} = \frac{7267.50 \times 100}{8500 \times 4.5}$$

$$= \frac{726750}{850 \times 45} = 19 \text{ years.}$$

13. Here, 'A' and 'B' can do $\left(\dfrac{1}{5} + \dfrac{1}{6} \right) = \dfrac{11}{30}$ of the work in 1 day.

Hence 'A' and 'B' together can do the whole work in $\dfrac{30}{11} = 2\dfrac{8}{11}$ days.

14. $\quad -\dfrac{2}{5} + \dfrac{3}{8} = \dfrac{-16 + 15}{40} = -\dfrac{1}{40}.$

15. (*a*) Area of rectangle = Length × Breadth

(*b*) Area of square = (Side)^2 or Side × Side.

16. Here, $C = 2\pi r = 2 \times \dfrac{22}{7} \times 42 = 264 \text{ m.}$

17. $\quad \text{Loss \%} = \dfrac{\text{Loss}}{\text{CP}} \times 100 = \dfrac{25 - 23}{25} \times 100$

$$= \frac{2}{25} \times 100 = 8\%.$$

18. According to question, $\dfrac{x}{3} - \dfrac{x}{4} = 12$

$$\Rightarrow \frac{4x - 3x}{12} \Rightarrow \frac{1}{12} x = 12$$

$$\therefore \qquad x = 144.$$

19. (*a*) True   (*b*) True

20. Required average $= \dfrac{35560 + 30000 + 27500 + 25600}{4}$

$$= \frac{118660}{4} = 29665.$$

21. The Reciprocal of $-\dfrac{125}{216} = -\dfrac{216}{125}.$

22. $\quad 5)\,17\,(3.4$

$$\underline{15}$$
$$20$$
$$\underline{20}$$
$$\times$$

Hence, $\dfrac{17}{5} = 3.4.$

23. $\left(-\dfrac{1}{5} \right)^3 \times \left(-\dfrac{1}{5} \right)^2 = \dfrac{-1}{125} \times \dfrac{1}{25} = \dfrac{-1}{3125}.$

24. **Cuboid:** Instrument box; Lunch box; Chalk box; Breck.

25. Here S.P. = ₹ 1536,   Loss = 20%

$$\text{C.P.} = \frac{100}{100 - \text{Loss\%}} \times \text{SP} = \frac{100}{100 - 20} \times 1536$$

$$= \frac{100}{80} \times 1536 = 10 \times 192 = ₹ 1920.$$

26. Here, P = ₹ 5000,   R = 12% p.a., T = 3 years, S.I. = ?

$$\text{S.I.} = \frac{\text{P} \times \text{R} \times \text{T}}{100} = \frac{5000 \times 12 \times 3}{100} = ₹ 1800.$$

27. Let the number be x.

Here, 23% of $x = 46$

$$\Rightarrow \quad \frac{23}{100} \times x = 46$$

$$\Rightarrow \quad x = \frac{46 \times 100}{23}$$

$$\therefore \qquad x = 200$$

Hence, the number is 200.

28. (*a*) True   (*b*) True

29. Since it is a case of direct variation,

Hence, $\dfrac{7}{10} = \dfrac{91}{x}$

$$\therefore \qquad x = \frac{91 \times 10}{7} = 130$$

Hence, the cost of 10 dozen oranges will be ₹ 130.

30. Here, $\angle A = \angle B = 50°$

Hence, the sides of opposite of the equal angles must be equal.

The sides opposite of $\angle A$ and $\angle B$ are BC and AC respectively.

So, in $\triangle$ ABC, BC = AC.

PART–B : LANGUAGE

1. Write an essay on any one of the following—
   (*a*) Computer Revolution in India
   (*b*) India of 21st century
   (*c*) Terrorism

2. Read the following passage and answer the questions that follow—

The Taj Mahal is situated on the banks of Yamuna about six kilometres away from the city of Agra. It is one the most famous buildings in the world. Its beauty attracts thousands of travellers to our country. They come every year from all parts of the world to visit Agra and see the Taj. People plan their visit in such a way that they must be in Agra on full moon day. Under the clear cloudless sky, in the light of full moon, the Taj has a beauty that no one can forget and the still water of the pool before it, reflects building and adds to its beauty. Emperor Shah Jahan, the grandson of Akbar built the Taj. He built it in the loving memory of his queen Mumtaz Mahal. The building stands upon a large quadrangle. River Yamuna flows on one of its sides. On the other three sides there are high walls of red stone. Two exactly alike mosques face each other. The quadrangle is nine hundred and sixty feet long and three hundred and twenty nine feet wide. A large minar stands on each corner of the quadrangle. There are many flower plants and shady trees all around. There are many shops near the Taj. One can see many marble models of the Taj and beautiful articles of handicraft in these shops.
   (*a*) Which river flows by the Taj Mahal?
   (*b*) Why did Shah Jahan build the Taj?
   (*c*) Why are travellers eager to visit Agra?
   (*d*) On what day most of the people wish to see the Taj Mahal?
   (*e*) What is generally sold in the shop near the Taj?

3. Fill in the blanks by selecting the correct word—
   (*a*) The boy .... English fluently.
                        (speak, speaks)
   (*b*) My friends .... here daily. (comes, come)
   (*c*) My father .... to see you. (wish, wishes)
   (*d*) Sometimes it .... heavily. (rain, rains)
   (*e*) Pathan .... at least one bouncer in every over.   (bowls, bowl)

   (*f*) I do not .... many friends.
                        (have, has)
   (*g*) I .... like listening classical music.
                        (do not, does not)
   (*h*) Rabits .... short tails.   (have, has)
   (*i*) My sisters .... English.
                        (speak, speaks)
   (*j*) The lion ....   (roar, roars)

4. Make meaningful sentences from words written below—
   (*a*) Your, mind, business, own
   (*b*) truth, loved, Gandhiji, ahimsa, and
   (*c*) history, Ashoka, My, hero, is, in, the great favourite
   (*d*) now, India, country, is, free, a
   (*e*) four, for, I, have, been, ill, days

5. Make a sentence with the given word—
   (*a*) Fastest   (*b*) Honest
   (*c*) Crops   (*d*) Spend
   (*e*) Jump

6. Correct the following sentences—
   (*a*) I felt my hand to shake.
   (*b*) We compelled her in accepting the offer.
   (*c*) The terrorists were hanged.
   (*d*) My mother continually worries about my future.
   (*e*) Life can be compared to a stage.

7. Fill in the blanks with appropriate adjectives—
   (*a*) Is there .... money in your pocket.
                        (such, any)
   (*b*) I have to get up early .... day. (very, every)
   (*c*) How .... money do you need?
                        (many, much)
   (*d*) He read .... books he had.
                        (a few, many)
   (*e*) A .... knowledge is dangerous.
                        (much, little)

8. Do as directed—
   (*a*) Piyush saw an elephant.
                        (Change into Negative)
   (*b*) He did not go to school.
                        (Change into Affirmative)
   (*c*) Riya is as tall as Ghutghut.
                        (Change in comparative degree)

(*d*) He will never hurt you.
(Change into Passive)

(*e*) Animals are loved by Children.
(Change into Active)

9. Make sentences to bring out the difference between each pair of words in the following—

(*a*) Presume; Assume

(*b*) Regret; Sorrow

(*c*) Deny; Refuse

(*d*) Begin; Start

(*e*) Beautiful; Handsome

EXPLANATORY ANSWERS

1.   **TERRORISM**

Terrorism is perhaps the most hated word in the modern age. It is particularly an anathema to those who have had personal experience of its diabolical dimensions.

Of late, terrorism has become a world-wide phenomenon. India had been telling the world of the large-scale destruction being caused to life and property in Kashmir by the Pakistan sponsored terrorists. But most of the western world had turned a blind eye to India's pleadings. The west, particularly the USA, realized its taste when the (WTC) towers in America were levelled down through explosions caused by the sudden attacks by striking aeroplanes on them on 11th September, 2001 (9/11). Thus, the 9/11 event opened the eyes of the world.

As a result of this 9/11 incident, America took up the task of defending the world and getting it rid of the scourge of terrorism. Accordingly the American President in collaboration with the U.K. Prime Minister Tony Blair drew up a road map of controlling and eliminating terrorism. A number of terrorist organisations, Al Qaeda being the most conspicuous among them, were banned. A number of countries were declared as the Axis of Evil. Afghanistan was attacked and the regime of the Taliban was brought to an end. But the most wanted terrorist, Osama Bin Laden could not be killed or captured.

Later, America attacked Iraq declaring that the country possessed Weapons of Mass Destruction (WMD), although its dictatorial President Saddam Hussein denied it all along. The war was won. Later, two sons of Saddam Hussein were killed, though the President himself went underground. But, later in December 2003, he was captured in a dramatic manner in a hole under the earth.

In Kashmir, the terrorists have been playing havoc for about two decades. Thousands of terrorists themselves, members of security forces and innocent citizens, including men and women have been killed. Indian parliament had to face a terrorist attack on 13th December 2001. Fortunately, the Parliament which was in session was saved but a number of security guards lost their lives.

Terrorism had its heyday in Punjab in the 1980s and in early 1990s. In Andhra Pradesh we have Marxist terrorists (People's War Group PWG). In Assam and some other eastern State we have ULFA, Bodo and other terrorists. In December 2003 there was a crack-down on ULFA terrorists in Bhutan who operated against India from that land.

In order to overcome the menace of terrorism, all the States in India and all the countries in the world should join hands to form a concerted coordinated policy.

2. (*a*) Yamuna River flows by the Taj Mahal.

(*b*) Shah Jahan built the Taj in the loving memory of his queen Mumtaz.

(*c*) Travellers visit Agra for seeing the Taj.

(*d*) People want to see the Taj Mahal on a full moon day.

(*e*) Models of Taj and beautiful articles of handicrafts are sold in the shops near the Taj.

3. (*a*) speaks, (*b*) come, (*c*) wishes, (*d*) rains, (*e*) bowls, (*f*) have, (*g*) do not, (*h*) have, (*i*) speak, (*j*) roars

4. (*a*) Mind your own business.

(*b*) Gandhiji loved truth and ahimsa.

(*c*) My favourite hero in history is Ashoka, the great.

(*d*) India is now a free country.

(*e*) I have been ill for four days.

5. (*a*) Shatabdi Express is the fastest bus of U.P.

(*b*) Ram is an honest man.

(c) The flood has ruined the crops.

(d) We shall spend the whole money.

(e) Ram jumped the barrier.

6. (a) I felt my hand shaking.

(b) We compelled her to accept the offer.

(c) Terrorists were hanged.

(d) My mother always worries about my future.

(e) Life can be compared to a stage.

7. (a) any   (b) every

(c) much   (d) a few

(e) little

8. (a) Piyush never saw an elephant.

(b) He went to School.

(c) Riya is not taller than Ghutghut.

(d) You will never be hurt by him.

(e) Children love animals.

9. (a) **Presume**—I presume Ram is an honest man.

Assume—I assume my brother will send me money in time.

(b) **Regret**—I have suspended him to my great regret.

Sorrow—His mother's death has plunged him into deep sorrow.

(c) **Deny**—I deny my participation in the cocktail party.

Refuse—I refuse to give him money.

(d) **Begin**—Let us begin the work.

Start—Now the train starts.

(e) **Beautiful**—Radha is very beautiful girl.

Handsome—Ram is a handsome young man.

PAPER–II : INTELLIGENCE TEST

Directions: *In each of the following questions find the odd one.*

1. (a) Jesus   (b) Buddha

(c) Gandhi   (d) Mohammed

2. (a) Raincoat   (b) Umbrella

(c) Gun boats   (d) Sari

3. (a) Fox   (b) Wolf

(c) Deer   (d) Panther

4. (a) Barber   (b) Carpenter

(c) Blacksmith   (d) Tailor

5. (a) Gangtok   (b) Singhbhum

(c) Hyderabad   (d) Chennai

6. (a) Carrot   (b) Potato

(c) Spinach   (d) Turnip

7. (a) Coat   (b) Socks

(c) Shirts   (d) Jacket

8. (a) January   (b) March

(c) July   (d) September

9. (a) Bulb   (b) Fan

(c) Candle   (d) Sun

10. (a) Lungs   (b) Liver

(c) Heart   (d) Eyes

Directions: *In each of the following questions complete the series.*

11. U, O, I, E, ...

(a) B   (b) C

(c) A   (d) Z

12. A, C, F, H, ...

(a) I   (b) J

(c) K   (d) L

13. 3, 6, 18, 72, ...

(a) 144   (b) 288

(c) 350   (d) 360

14. 1, 2, 6, 24, ...

(a) 72   (b) 120

(c) 48   (d) 96

15. 5, 16, 49, 104, ...

(a) 133   (b) 144

(c) 180   (d) 181

16. 1, 4, 9, 16, 25, ...

(a) 35   (b) 36

(c) 49   (d) 64

17. 20, 19, 17, ...

(a) 12   (b) 13

(c) 14   (d) 15

18. 2, 3, 5, 7, 11, ...

(a) 12   (b) 13

(c) 14   (d) 15

19. 3, 9, 27, 81, ...

(a) 243   (b) 343

(c) 210   (d) 324

20. A, B, D, G, ...

(a) M   (b) L

(c) K   (d) H

Directions: *In a certain language CHARCOAL is codes as 45164913 and MORALE is coded as 296137, how are the following words coded in that language?*

21. ARCHER
(a) 164576   (b) 185476
(c) 197457   (d) 184576

22. MECHRALE
(a) 26756137   (b) 27456137
(c) 47956137   (d) 29456137

23. ROCHEL
(a) 695478   (b) 691387
(c) 994537   (d) 694573

24. LARCH
(a) 36145   (b) 31645
(c) 31546   (d) 31456

25. MARCH
(a) 24615   (b) 25416
(c) 21645   (d) 23456

26. COLLER
(a) 397758   (b) 497782
(c) 483359   (d) 493376

27. REAL
(a) 8519   (b) 6713
(c) 6513   (d) 6719

28. COACH
(a) 38137   (b) 49145
(c) 49451   (d) 85145

29. ALLOCHRE
(a) 17693935   (b) 15933653
(c) 13394567   (d) 13368957

30. HEARL
(a) 57361   (b) 57163
(c) 75613   (d) 57931

Directions: *In each of the following questions, four words have been given, out of which three are alike in some manner and the fourth one is different. Choose out the odd one.*

31. (a) Jasmine   (b) Coriander
    (c) Lotus   (d) Rose

32. (a) Diving   (b) Driving
    (c) Swimming   (d) Sailing

33. (a) Cochin   (b) Vishakhapatanam
    (c) Mysore   (d) Mumbai

34. (a) Charan Singh   (b) S.Radhakrishnan
    (c) Morarji Desai   (d) Chandrashekhar

35. (a) Potato   (b) Ginger
    (c) Carrot   (d) Cabbage

36. (a) Birbal   (b) Faiz Ahmed
    (c) Abul Fazal   (d) Tansen

37. (a) Lakshadweep   (b) Sikkim
    (c) Maharashtra   (d) Manipur

38. (a) Father   (b) Sister
    (c) Mother   (d) Friend

39. (a) Thin   (b) Tall
    (c) Sharp   (d) Small

40. (a) Man   (b) Lion
    (c) Elephant   (d) Deer

Directions: *In each of the following sets of figures, select the one that is different from the rest.*

41. 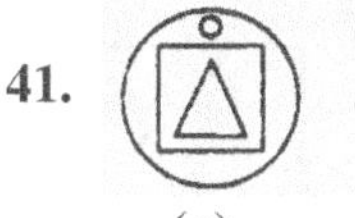  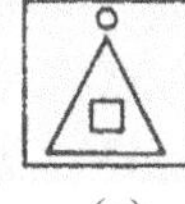 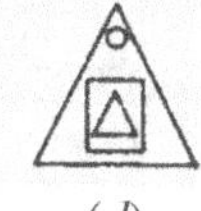
(a)   (b)   (c)   (d)

42.   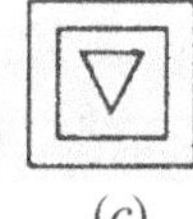 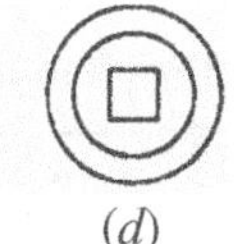
(a)   (b)   (c)   (d)

43. 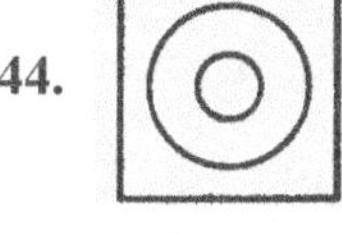 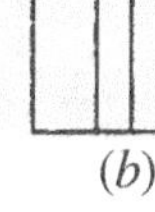 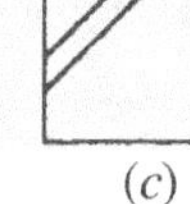 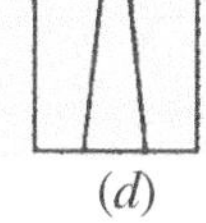
(a)   (b)   (c)   (d)

44.   
(a)   (b)   (c)   (d)

45. 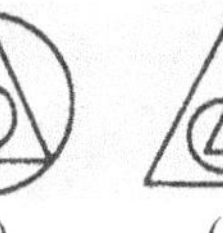 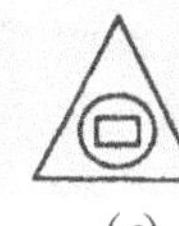 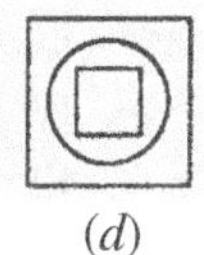
(a)   (b)   (c)   (d)

Directions: *Each of the following questions, consists of unmarked figures followed by four figures mark (a), (b), (c) and (d). Select a figure from the marked figures which will continue the series established by the unmarked figures.*

46. Problem Figures

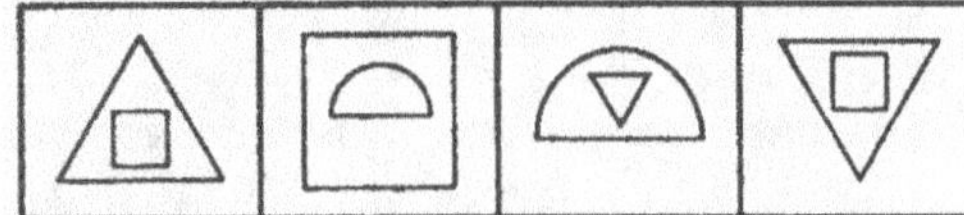

Answer Figures

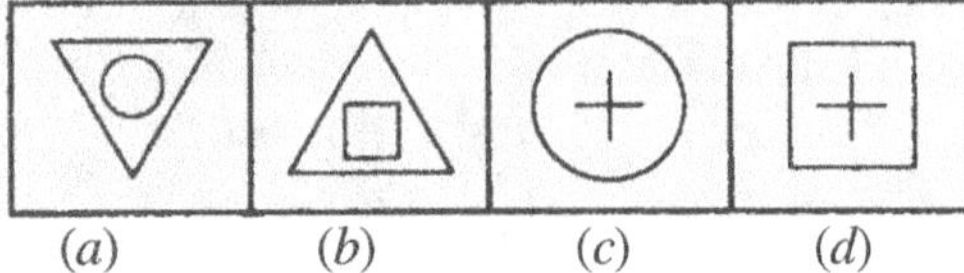

(a)   (b)   (c)   (d)

47. Problem Figures

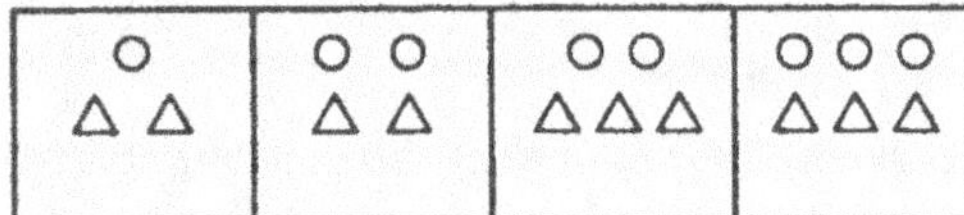

Answer Figures

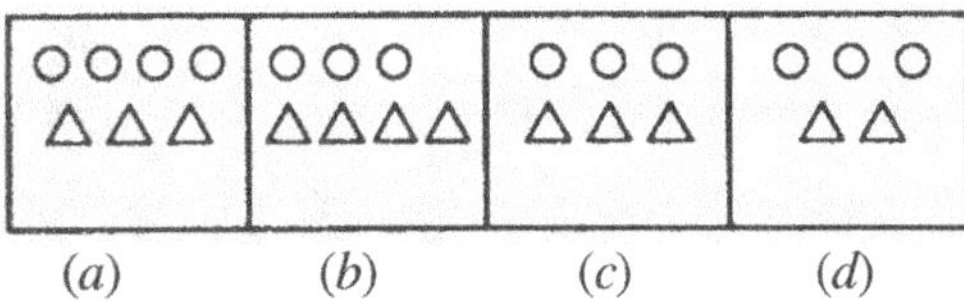

(a)   (b)   (c)   (d)

48. Problem Figures

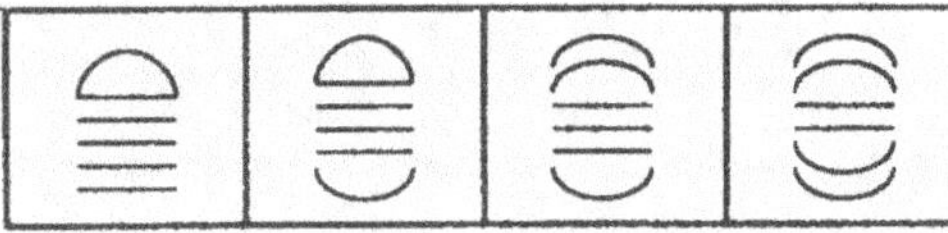

Answer Figures

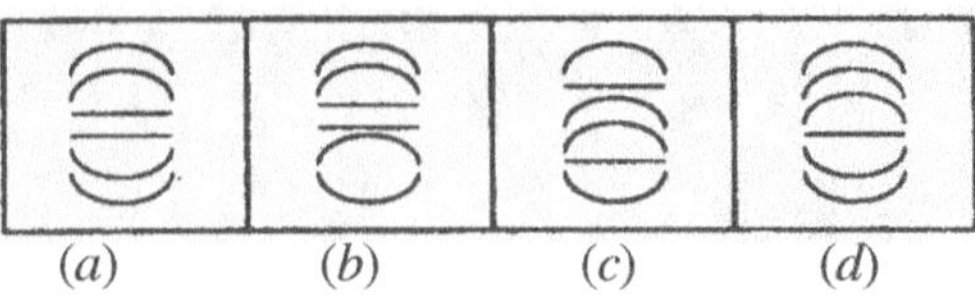

(a)   (b)   (c)   (d)

49. Problem Figures

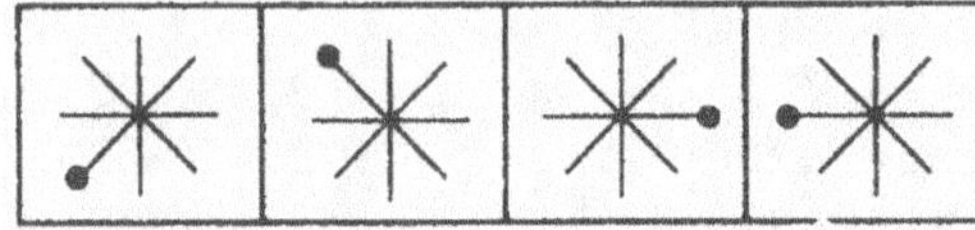

Answer Figures

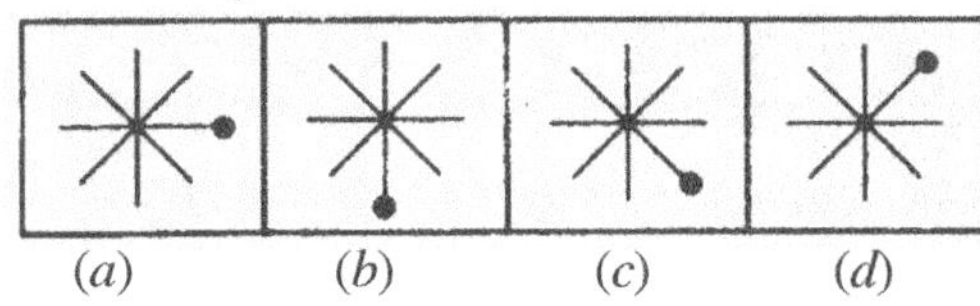

(a)   (b)   (c)   (d)

50. Problem Figures

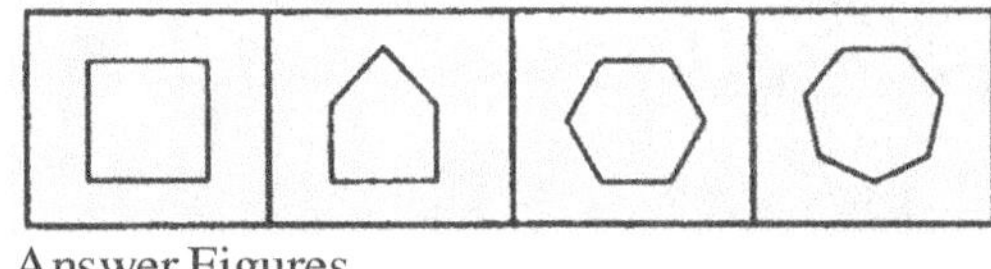

Answer Figures

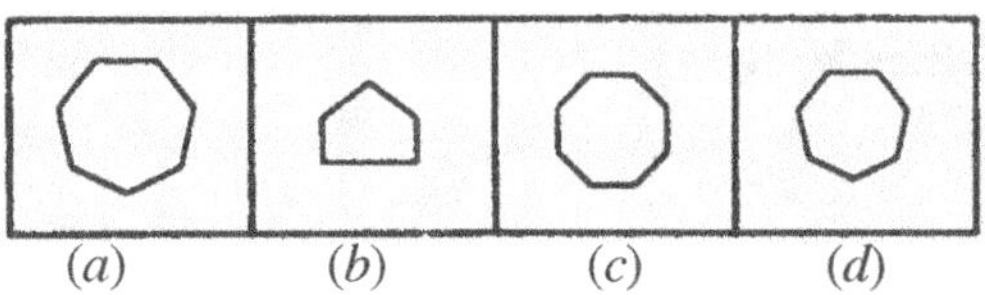

(a)   (b)   (c)   (d)

EXPLANATORY ANSWERS

1. Except (c) all others are founders of religion.
2. Except (d) all other items are used for protection form rain.
3. Except (c) all others are flesh eating animals.
4. Except (a) all others require raw material to work.
5. Except (b) all others are capitals of states of India.
6. Except (c) all other vegetables grow under the ground.
7. Only (b) are put on the leg.
8. Only (d) have 30 days.
9. Only (b) produces the air.
10. Except (b) all others are organs, but (b) is gland.
11. (c) The series has vowels in reverse order.

12. (c) A   C   F   H $\boxed{K}$
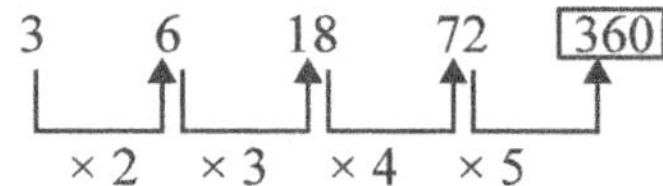
    + 2   + 3   + 2   + 3

13. (d) The given pattern is

3   6   18   72 $\boxed{360}$
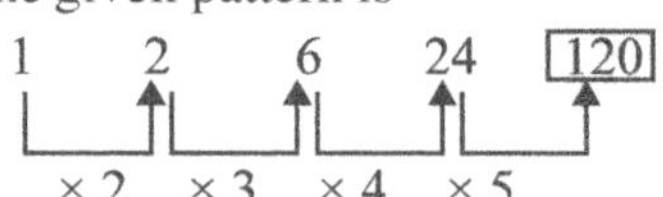
    × 2   × 3   × 4   × 5

14. (b) The given pattern is

1   2   6   24 $\boxed{120}$
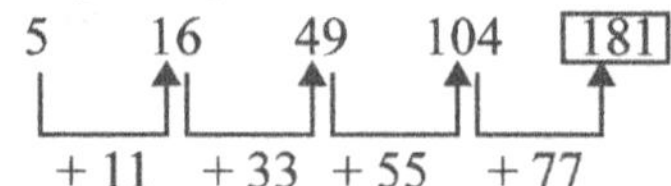
    × 2   × 3   × 4   × 5

15. (d) The given pattern is

5   16   49   104 $\boxed{181}$

    + 11   + 33   + 55   + 77

143

16. (*b*) The numbers are $1^2, 2^2, 3^2, 4^2, 5^2$

Hence, missing number = $6^2 = 36$

17. (*c*) The pattern is $-1, -2, \ldots\ldots$

Hence, missing number = $17 - 3 = 14$

18. (*b*) The given series consists of prime numbers starting from 2. The prime number after 11 is 13.

19. (*a*) Each term of the given series is obtained by multiplying its preceding term by 3.

Hence, next no. = $81 \times 3 = 243$.

20. (*c*)
```
A    B    D    G    [K]
|___↑|___↑|___↑|___↑
  +1   +2   +3   +4
```

21. (*a*)

A	R	C	H	E	R
↓	↓	↓	↓	↓	↓
1	6	4	5	7	6

22. (*c*)

M	E	C	H	R	A	L	E
↓	↓	↓	↓	↓	↓	↓	↓
2	7	4	5	6	1	3	7

23. (*c*)

R	O	C	H	E	L
↓	↓	↓	↓	↓	↓
6	9	4	5	7	3

24. (*c*)

L	A	R	C	H	Q
↓	↓	↓	↓	↓	
3	1	6	4	5	

25. (*c*)

M	A	R	C	H
↓	↓	↓	↓	↓
2	1	6	4	5

26. (*c*)

C	O	L	L	E	R
↓	↓	↓	↓	↓	↓
4	9	3	3	7	6

27. (*c*)

R	E	A	L
↓	↓	↓	↓
6	7	1	3

28. (*c*)

C	O	A	C	H
↓	↓	↓	↓	↓
4	9	1	4	5

29. (*c*)

A	L	L	O	C	H	R	E
↓	↓	↓	↓	↓	↓	↓	↓
1	3	3	9	4	5	6	7

30. (*c*)

H	E	A	R	L
↓	↓	↓	↓	↓
5	7	1	6	3

31. Except (*b*) all others are flowers.

32. Except (*b*) all others are activities performed in water.

33. Except (*c*) all others are harbours.

34. Except (*b*) all others were the Prime Minister of India.

35. Except (*d*) all others grow under ground.

36. Except (*b*) all others were among the nine gems in Akbar's court.

37. Except (*a*) all others are states of India.

38. Except (*d*) all others are denote blood relations.

39. Except (*c*) all others are related to dimension.

40. Except (*a*) all others are animals.

41. Except (*a*) in all others, the outer and inner figures are the same.

42. Except (*a*) in all others, the first two outer figures are same.

43. Except (*d*) all others have parallel lines inside.

44. Except (*c*) all others have similar figures inside as well as outside.

45. Except (*c*) in all others, the outer and inner figures are the same.

46. In each subsequent figure the inner figure becomes the outer one. The outer figure disappears and another figure comes inside. So, the answer figure (*d*) is obtained.

47. In every alternate figure the number of triangles and the number of circles increase. So the answer figure (*b*) is obtained.

48. (*d*) One line in each figure changes to a curve up and down alternately. Therefore, the required answer (*d*) is obtained.

49. (*c*) In a clockwise direction the dots move, two steps, three steps, four steps, five steps respectively.

50. (*c*) In each figure the number of sides increases by one in each step. So, figure will be containing eight sides.

SAINIK SCHOOL ENTRANCE EXAM, 2005

(CLASS VI)

PAPER-I : MATHEMATICS AND LANGUAGE

PART–A : MATHEMATICS

1. Area of a rectangle is 12 sq. cm and its length is 4 cm. Find its breadth.
2. Write the prime factor of 48.
3. The difference of two numbers is 190825308. If the greater number is 212122202. Find the smaller number.
4. Find the numbers for the blanks to continue the series:
   (a) 1, 9, 25, 49, ...   (b) 2, 5, 10, 17, ...
5. What is the circumference of a circle whose radius is 4.9 cm?
6. Convert into smallest fraction : 0.75 =
7. Find the square of 0.02.
8. Solve the sum and write the sum in decimals :

$$\frac{11}{50} + \frac{7}{25} =$$

9. $\dfrac{2}{3} + \dfrac{4}{5} + \dfrac{5}{7}$ of $2\dfrac{13}{25}$

10. Express $\dfrac{11}{200}$ in the percentage form.

11. A motor car starts from a city 'A' at 5.30 A.M. and reaches city 'B' 360 km. away at 11.30 A.M. Find the average speed of the motor car.

12. ABCD is a parallelogram. If $\angle A = 120°$, Find $\angle D$.

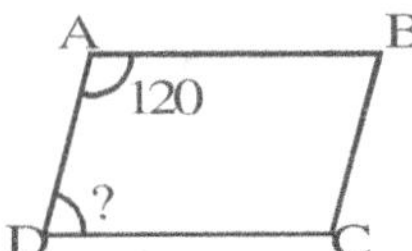

13. Simplify : $0.077 \div 7 - 0.005 \div 5$
14. Find the simple interest on an amount of ₹ 1250 for 4 years at 6% per annum.
15. A tank is 5m long, 4m wide and 3m high. How much water can it hold?

16. The radius of a circle is 7 cm. The length of its semicircle approximately is:
    (a) 14 cm   (b) 22 cm
    (c) 20 cm   (d) 36 cm
17. Arun buys an article for Rs. 500 and sells it to Ravi at a profit of 10%. Find the price paid by Ravi.
18. Which is greater $66\dfrac{2}{3}\%$ of 342 or 60% of 300?
19. State True or False:–
    (a) A line does not have a definite length.
    (b) A line has no end points.
    (c) We cannot draw a line on a paper but can represent it by a diagram.
20. A bag contains $86\frac{2}{3}$ kg of sugar. How much sugar do 10 such bags contain?
21. When a solid is immersed in water standing to a height of 20 cm in a vessel, the water level was raised $\frac{1}{5}$ of its level. What is the present height of water level? What is the percentage of increase in height?
22. Ramesh spends 15% of his salary on house rent and 20% of his salary on food, how much does he spend monthly for house rent and food together if his salary is ₹ 7000 per month.
23. Simplify: $\quad 5\dfrac{1}{2} - \left\{ \dfrac{2}{5} \text{ of } \dfrac{5}{6} + \left(7 \div 1\dfrac{3}{4} \right) \right\}$
24. Mohan got 120 marks out of 250, Neeta 140 out of 280, whose score is higher?
25. Find the area of the following figure:

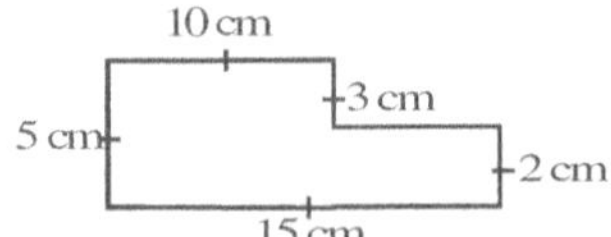

26. The capacity of two types of containers is 17½ litres and 15½ litres respectively. How much water will be required to fill 12 tins of first type and 15 tins of second type?

27. During a journey, a train covers 493 kms, in 5 hrs. 48 minutes. Find its average speed.

28. A cuboid is 4 cm long 3 cm broad and 2 cm high and a cube has an edge of 3 cm. Which one has a greater volume?

29. Write True or False:

(*a*) A quadrilateral ABCD is a trapezium if AB $\parallel$ CD

(*b*) Cost Price = Selling Price – Loss

(*c*) The average of three numbers is always one of the three numbers.

(*d*) An angle whose measure is greater than 90° is an obtuse angle.

(*e*) A triangle can have two right angles.

30. A watchmaker bought an old watch for ₹ 80. He spend ₹ 10 on its repair and sells it for ₹ 117. Find his gain or loss per cent.

EXPLANATORY ANSWERS

1. Breadth $= \dfrac{12 \text{ cm}^2}{4 \text{ cm}} = 3$ cm.

2.

$$
\begin{array}{r|l}
2 & 48 \\
2 & 24 \\
2 & 12 \\
2 & 6 \\
\hline
 & 3
\end{array}
\qquad 48 = 2 \times 2 \times 2 \times 2 \times 3 = 2^4 \times 3.
$$

3. The smaller number $= 212122202 - 190825308$
$$= 21296894.$$

4. (*a*) 81, (*b*) 26.

5. Circumference of the circle $= 2\pi r$.

$$= 2 \times \frac{22}{7} \times 4.9$$

$$= 44 \times 0.7 = 30.8 \text{ cm}.$$

6. $0.75 = \dfrac{75}{100} = \dfrac{3}{4}.$

7. $(0.02)^2 = 0.02 \times 0.02 = 0.0004.$

8. $\dfrac{11}{50} + \dfrac{7}{25} = \dfrac{11+14}{50} = \dfrac{25}{50}$

$$= \dfrac{25 \times 2}{50 \times 2} = \dfrac{50}{100} = 0.50.$$

9. $\dfrac{2}{3} + \dfrac{4}{5} + \dfrac{5}{7} \text{ of } 2\dfrac{13}{25}$

$$= \dfrac{2}{3} + \dfrac{4}{5} + \dfrac{5}{7} \times \dfrac{63}{25} = \dfrac{2}{3} + \dfrac{4}{5} + \dfrac{9}{5}$$

$$= \dfrac{10 + 12 + 27}{15} = \dfrac{49}{15} = 3\dfrac{4}{15}.$$

10. $\dfrac{11}{200} = \dfrac{11}{2} \times \dfrac{1}{100} = \dfrac{5.5}{100} = 5.5\%.$

11. Distance = 360 km

Time = 11.30 – 5.30 = 6 hours

$$\therefore \text{ Speed } = \dfrac{360}{6} = 60 \text{ km per hour}.$$

12. In given parallelogram
$$\angle D = 180° - 120° = 60°.$$

13. $0.077 \div 7 - 0.005 \div 5 = 0.077 \times \dfrac{1}{7} - 0.005 \times \dfrac{1}{5}$

$$= 0.011 - 0.001 = 0.01.$$

14. Simple Interest $= \dfrac{1250 \times 6 \times 4}{100}$

$$= 25 \times 12 = \text{Rs. } 300.$$

15. Volume of the tank $= l \times b \times h$
$$= 5 \times 4 \times 3 = 60 \text{ m}^3.$$

16. (*d*) Length of semicircle

$$= \dfrac{1}{2}(2\pi) \times \text{radius} + \text{diameter}$$

$$= \dfrac{1}{2} \times 2 \times \dfrac{22}{7} \times 7 + 2 \times 7 = 36 \text{ cm}.$$

17. S.P. of Article $= \dfrac{110}{100} \times 500 = ₹ 550.$

18. $66\dfrac{2}{3}\% \text{ of } 342 = \dfrac{200}{3 \times 100} \times 342 = \dfrac{2}{3} \times 342$

$$= 114 \times 2 = 228.$$

$60\% \text{ of } 300 = \dfrac{60}{100} \times 300 = 60 \times 3 = 180$

Hence, $66\dfrac{2}{3}\%$ of 342 is greater than 60% of 300.

19. (*a*) True   (*b*) True   (*c*) True

20. Required quantity of sugar $= 10 \times 86\dfrac{2}{3}\,\text{kg}$

$$= 10 \times \dfrac{260}{3} = \dfrac{2600}{3} = 866\dfrac{2}{3}\,\text{kg}.$$

21. Water level raised by immersing a solid

$$= 20 \times \dfrac{1}{5} = 4\,\text{cm}$$

Present height of the water column $= 20 + 4 = 24$ cm

Percentage increase $= \dfrac{4}{20} \times 100 = 20\%.$

22. The amount spends on house rent

$$= \dfrac{15}{100} \times 7000 = ₹\ 1050$$

The amount spends on food

$$= \dfrac{20}{100} \times 7000 = ₹\ 1400$$

Required expenditure $= 1050 + 1400$
$$= ₹\ 2450.$$

23. $5\dfrac{1}{2} - \left\{\dfrac{2}{5}\ \text{of}\ \dfrac{5}{6} + \left(7 \div 1\dfrac{3}{4}\right)\right\}$

$$= \dfrac{11}{2} - \left\{\dfrac{2}{5}\ \text{of}\ \dfrac{5}{6} + \left(7 \times \dfrac{4}{7}\right)\right\}$$

$$= \dfrac{11}{2} - \left\{\dfrac{2}{5}\ \text{of}\ \dfrac{5}{6} + 4\right\}$$

$$= \dfrac{11}{2} - \left\{\dfrac{2}{5} \times \dfrac{5}{6} + 4\right\} = \dfrac{11}{2} - \left\{\dfrac{1}{3} + 4\right\}$$

$$= \dfrac{11}{2} - \left(\dfrac{1+12}{3}\right) = \dfrac{11}{2} - \dfrac{13}{3} = \dfrac{33-26}{6} = \dfrac{7}{6} = 1\dfrac{1}{6}.$$

24. Percentage marks of Mohan $= \dfrac{120}{250} \times 100\%$

$$= 12 \times 4\% = 48\%$$

Percentage marks of Neeta $= \dfrac{140}{280} \times 100\%$

$$= \dfrac{1}{2} \times 100\% = 50\%$$

Hence, Neeta got more marks.

25. The area of the given figure
$$= 10 \times 3 + 15 \times 2$$
$$= 30 + 30 = 60\ \text{cm}^2.$$

26. Volume of water required

$$= 12 \times 17\dfrac{1}{2}l + 15 \times 15\dfrac{1}{2}l$$

$$= 12 \times \dfrac{35}{2}l + 15 \times \dfrac{31}{2}l = 6 \times 35l + \dfrac{465}{2}l$$

$$= 210\,l + 232.50\,l = 442.50\,l.$$

27. Distance $= 493$ km

Time $= 5$ hours 48 minutes

$$= \left(5 + \dfrac{48}{60}\right) = \left(5 + \dfrac{4}{5}\right) = \dfrac{25+4}{5}$$

$$= \dfrac{29}{5}\ \text{hours}$$

Speed $= \dfrac{493}{\dfrac{29}{5}} = \dfrac{493 \times 5}{29} = 85$ km. per hour.

28. Volume of cuboid $= l \times b \times h$
$$= 4 \times 3 \times 2\ \text{cm}^3 = 24\ \text{cm}^3$$
Volume of cube $= (\text{Length of the edge})^3$
$$= 3 \times 3 \times 3 = 27\ \text{cm}^3$$
Thus, Volume of the cube is greater than the volume of the cuboid.

29. (*a*) True
(*b*) False
(*c*) False
(*d*) True
(*e*) False

30. Net cost price $= ₹\ 80 + ₹\ 10 = ₹\ 90$
Selling price $= ₹\ 117$

$$\text{Profit\%} = \dfrac{117-90}{90} \times 100 = \dfrac{27}{90} \times 100$$
$$= 30\%.$$

PART–B : LANGUAGE

1. Write an essay on any one of the following—
   (*a*) What would I like to become on growing up?
   (*b*) A Rainy Day
   (*c*) Cottage Industry

2. Read the following passage and answer the questions that follow—

A man shot a crane and gave it to his servant. The servant roasted it and ate one of its legs. Then he put the roasted crane in a plate on the dinner table.

The master came and sat down for dinner. He turned the crane upside down and asked, "Where is the other leg?"

The servant replied, "A crane has one leg, Sir."

Next morning the master and the servant went together to the river bank. A crane was standing in the water on one leg. The master clapped his hands; the crane lowered its other leg and flew away.

The master turned to his servant and said, "Look at that crane. It has two legs."

The servant replied. "That is true, Sir. But you didn't clap your hands yesterday and so the crane on your plate didn't lower its other leg."

   (*a*) Why did the man give the crane to his servant?
   (*b*) What did the master notice about the roasted crane on his plate?
   (*c*) Why did the servant say that a crane has only one leg?
   (*d*) Why did the master clap his hands?
   (*e*) Was the servant a clever person? How can you say that?

3. Fill in the blanks by selecting the correct word—
   (*a*) There is .... dirt on this plate.   (some, a)
   (*b*) Mary wants .... doll with blue eyes.
                                                    (an, the)
   (*c*) We enjoyed .... very much at the dance.
                                                    (ourselves, us)
   (*d*) They knew all about my friend and ....
                                                    (I, me)
   (*e*) These mangoes are .... cheap that they cannot be good.   (so, too)

   (*f*) I haven't .... more information for you.
                                                    (some, any)
   (*g*) I want .... of these two things.
                                                    (none, neither)
   (*h*) He used to come here daily, ...
                                                    (didn't he ?, did he ?)
   (*i*) He .... a good speech yesterday.
                                                    (gave, made)
   (*j*) The coffee is .... hot to drink.   (too, enough)

4. In the following sentences some words are given in **bold.** Frame your own sentences by using these words—

One afternoon a big wolf **waited** in a **dark** forest. A little girl came along. She was the **daughter** of a woodcutter and she was **carrying** a **basket** of food to her grandmother.

5. Make meaningful sentences from words written below—
   (*a*) hot, was, the sun, burning
   (*b*) garden, a, our, has, school, beautiful
   (*c*) live, your, where, grandmother, does
   (*d*) water, were, flooded, soon, with, streets, the
   (*e*) work, he, any, kind, hated, of

6. Make sentences to bring out the difference between each pair of words in the following—
   (*a*) Act; Action   (*b*) Artful; Artificial
   (*c*) Fatal; Fatalist   (*d*) Human; Humane
   (*e*) Loudly; Aloud

7. Do as directed—
   (*a*) She wants some more tea.
                                      (Change into Negative)
   (*b*) Misha is as tall as Renu.
                              (Change into Comparative Degree)
   (*c*) She asked me some questions.
                                 (Change into Interrogative)
   (*d*) City is a big town.   (Change into Plural)
   (*e*) The Taj Mahal is a very beautiful building.
                          (Change into Exclamatory Sentence)

8. Correct the following sentences—
   (*a*) This chain is mine, not your.
   (*b*) She is a member of the woman's club.
   (*c*) If I were him I would not do it.

(*d*) She asked him that what your name is.

(*e*) She has a ugly face.

9. Match the following Adjectival words with the Proper Nouns—

(*a*) Happy   (*b*) Good

(*c*) Fresh   (*d*) Black

(*e*) Dense.

Fruits, Hair, Family, News, Forest.

EXPLANATORY ANSWERS

1. (*b*)   **A Rainy Day**

Rain is a blessing bestowed by God on mankind. If there were no rains, probably there would be no life on the earth.

Rain is usually welcomed after a spell of hot summer days, provided it is not given by the Almighty in an excessive dose.

Sometimes, it causes inconvenience, particularly to workers, office-goers, students and the poor people.

Yesterday was a rainy day. For the whole one week, people had been feeling tormented due to intense heat and had been praying to god Indra to be merciful. So, rain was quite welcome.

When I got up early in the morning, I felt the wafts of cool breeze which had sprung up.

I came out of my house. I was thrilled to find large heaps of woolen black and white clouds floating in the sky.

Soon, drizzling started. Not very late, there emerged a heavy down-pour. Some people had thought that drizzling would continue for some time more, were, as if taken unawares.

Many people were drenched. Soon the streets and ponds were flooded with water. The clouds thundered and the lightning flashed fiercely.

Children began to float paper-boats on water. Some houses began to leak. The wage-earners lost the day. There was thin attendance in offices, schools and colleges.

In the afternoon, rain stopped. I came out of my house. I found some people having folded umbrellas in their hands. The roads were slippery. Many persons stopped and fell down.

Frogs croaked in ponds. Trees looked greener and fresher. A beautiful rainbow appeared in the sky in the evening.

2. (*a*) The man gave the crane to his servant for roasting and then serve it for dinner.

(*b*) He saw that roasted crane had only one leg.

(*c*) Because he had already eaten the other leg of the roasted crane.

(*d*) Because he wanted to see whether crane had one leg or two legs.

(*e*) Yes the servant was a clever person. He already ate one of the legs of the roasted crane and also by his quick wit he succeeded in befooling the master.

3. (*a*) Some   (*b*) the

(*c*) ourselves   (*d*) me

(*e*) so   (*f*) any

(*g*) neither   (*h*) didn't he?

(*i*) made   (*j*) too

4. Waited — Ram waited for a bus at the bus stop.

Dark — The colour of his paint is dark-blue.

Daughter — Sita is only daughter of Shyam.

Carrying — Mohan was carrying a heavy load on his head.

Basket — There are so many fruits in his basket.

5. (*a*) The sun was burning hot.

(*b*) Our school has a beautiful garden.

(*c*) Where does your grandmother live?

(*d*) Soon the streets were flooded with water.

(*e*) He hated any kind of work.

6. (*a*) Act – I became very happy to see your act of kindness.

Action – To every action there is equal and opposite reaction.

(*b*) Artful – You could not achieve success by artful means.

Artificial – Aryabhatta is a artificial sattelite.

(*c*) Fatal – Mohan could not take care of fatal wound in his left leg.

Fatalist – Weak hearted persons are generally fatalist.

(*d*) Human – Casteism is a crime for humanbeings.

Humane – Poor should be treated under humane conditions.

(*e*) Loudly – They speak loudly.
  Aloud – Never speak in aloud voice.

7. (*a*) She does not want any more tea.
  (*b*) Renu is not taller than Misha.
  (*c*) Did she ask me any questions?
  (*d*) Cities are big towns.
  (*e*) What a beautiful building the Taj Mahal is!

8. (*a*) This chain is mine, not yours.
  (*b*) She is a member of the women's club.
  (*c*) If I were he I would not do it.
  (*d*) She asked him what his name was.
  (*e*) She has an ugly face.

9. (*a*) Happy family. (*b*) Good news.
  (*c*) Fresh fruits. (*d*) Black hair.
  (*e*) Dense forest.

PAPER–II : INTELLIGENCE TEST

Directions: *In each of the following questions complete the series.*

1. D, F, I, M, R, ...
  (*a*) Y (*b*) V
  (*c*) W (*d*) X
  (*e*) N

2. A, C, B, D, F, E, G, I, ...
  (*a*) J (*b*) H
  (*c*) F (*d*) E
  (*e*) R

3. A, C, F, J, O, ...
  (*a*) R (*b*) S
  (*c*) T (*d*) U
  (*e*) V

4. Z, A, D, E, H, I, N, O, ...
  (*a*) S (*b*) W
  (*c*) G (*d*) T
  (*e*) V

5. 24, 35, 48, 63, ...
  (*a*) 87 (*b*) 83
  (*c*) 80 (*d*) 79
  (*e*) 74

6. 3, 8, 18, 33, ...
  (*a*) 61 (*b*) 57
  (*c*) 53 (*d*) 47
  (*e*) 38

7. 4, 5, 9, 18, 34, ...
  (*a*) 59 (*b*) 58
  (*c*) 50 (*d*) 43
  (*e*) 39

8. $3, \dfrac{1}{3}, 14, \dfrac{1}{14}, 25, \dfrac{1}{25}, ...$
  (*a*) $\dfrac{1}{36}$ (*b*) $\dfrac{1}{34}$

  (*c*) 34 (*d*) 36
  (*e*) 42

9. 9, 19, 30, 42, 55, 69, ...
  (*a*) 89 (*b*) 85
  (*c*) 84 (*d*) 79
  (*e*) 76

10. 1, 3, 7, 13, 21, ...
  (*a*) 33 (*b*) 31
  (*c*) 29 (*d*) 27
  (*e*) 25

11. If the code of MOTHER is OQVJGT, then what is the code of SISTER?
  (*a*) CJUVGT (*b*) TJTUFS
  (*c*) TJTUES (*d*) UKUVGT

12. If the code of TELEPHONE is ENOHPELET, then what is the code of ALIGATOR ?
  (*a*) ROTAGILE (*b*) ROTAGILA
  (*c*) ROTEGILA (*d*) ROTAGIAL

13. If the code of TEACHER is VGCEJGT, then what is the code of CHILDREN?
  (*a*) EJKNFGTO (*b*) EJKNEGTP
  (*c*) EJKNFHTP (*d*) EJKNFTGP

Directions: *In each of the following questions fill the blanks.*

14. As Dhanush is related to arrow in the same way gun is related to ....
  (*a*) SOLDIER (*b*) BARREL
  (*c*) TRIGGER (*d*) BULLET
  (*e*) SHOT

15. Fish is related to Fin in the same way bird is related to ....
  (*a*) NEST (*b*) FLY
  (*c*) SKY (*d*) CHPP
  (*e*) FEATHER

Directions: *In each of the following questions find the odd one.*

16. (a) Brahmputra   (b) Kaveri
    (c) Ganga   (d) Kailash
    (e) Sutlej
17. (a) Crow   (b) Duck
    (c) Sparrow   (d) Parrot
    (e) Maina
18. (a) Earth   (b) Moon
    (c) Mercury   (d) Saturn
    (e) Venus
19. (a) Marathi   (b) Telgu
    (c) Kannar   (d) Gujarati
    (e) Sanskrit
20. (a) Litre   (b) Yard
    (c) Kilogram   (d) Weight
    (e) Inch
21. (a) Tiger   (b) Deer
    (c) Lion   (d) Wolf
    (e) Leopard
22. (a) Instructor   (b) Student
    (c) Teacher   (d) Director
    (e) Lecturer
23. (a) Neigh   (b) Voice
    (c) Bray   (d) Bark
    (e) Mew
24. (a) Taste   (b) Smell
    (c) Thumb   (d) Hear
    (e) Scene
25. (a) Finger   (b) Wrist
    (c) Palm   (d) Thumb
    (e) Thigh

Directions: *In each of the following questions which one is odd?*

26. (a) AabD   (b) cCDf
    (c) dDeG   (d) PpQS
    (e) pQrT
27. (a) ADG   (b) BEH
    (c) ZWT   (d) CFI
    (e) DGJ
28. (a) XYZ   (b) UVW
    (c) RST   (d) NOR
    (e) KLM
29. (a) BCE   (b) FGI
    (c) JKM   (d) NOQ
    (e) RST
30. (a) 1.5   (b) 3
    (c) 4.5   (d) 6
    (e) 7.25

31. (a) NOPM   (b) STUR
    (c) VWXU   (d) KJLM
    (e) CDEB
32. (a) 7   (b) 11
    (c) 13   (d) 17
    (e) 21
33. (a) 81   (b) 64
    (c) 50   (d) 36
    (e) 25
34. (a) 123   (b) 231
    (c) 312   (d) 132
    (e) 342
35. (a) 343   (b) 216
    (c) 120   (d) 64
    (e) 27

Directions: *In each of the following questions there is a series of 5 figures in which at 5th place a question mark is given. Choose one figure from the answer figures, which fit in the place of question mark.*

36. **Problem Figures**

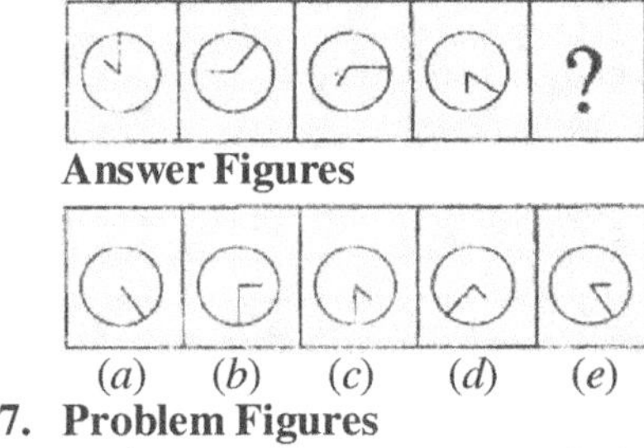

Answer Figures

37. **Problem Figures**

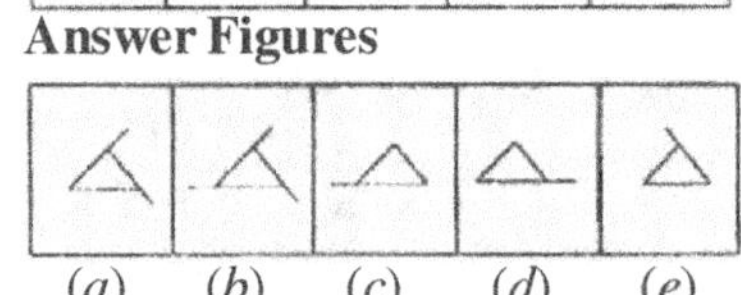

Answer Figures

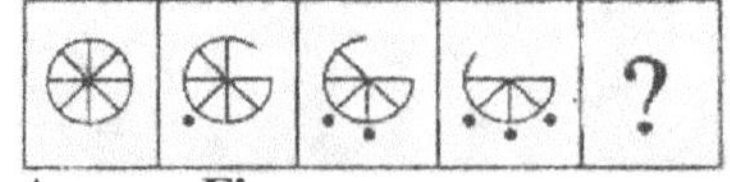

38. **Problem Figures**

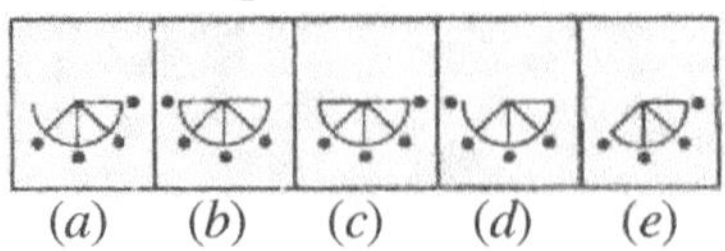

Answer Figures

151

39. Problem Figures

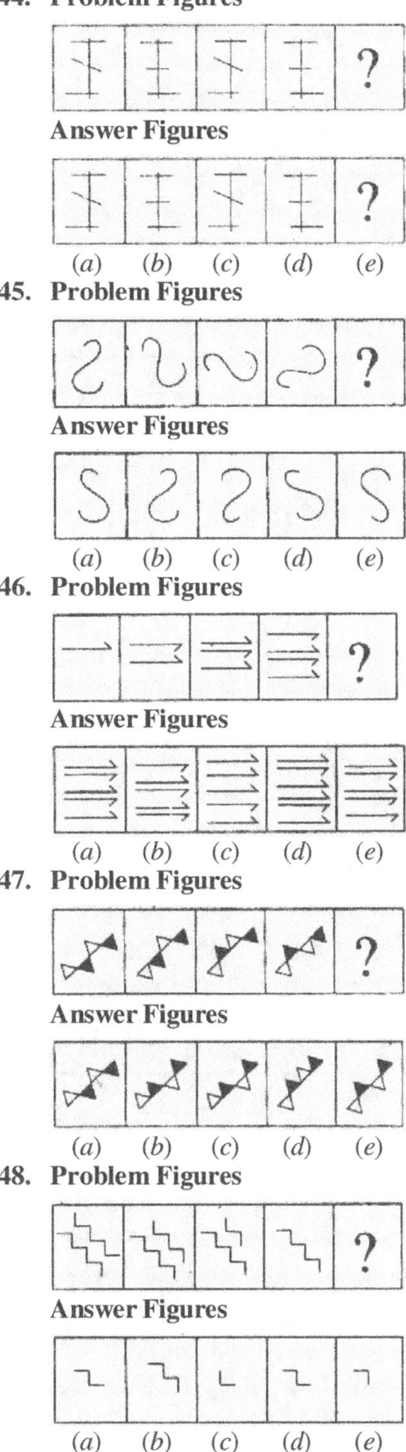

Answer Figures

(a) (b) (c) (d) (e)

40. Problem Figures

Answer Figures

(a) (b) (c) (d) (e)

41. Problem Figures

Answer Figures

(a) (b) (c) (d) (e)

42. Problem Figures

Answer Figures

(a) (b) (c) (d) (e)

43. Problem Figures

Answer Figures

(a) (b) (c) (d) (e)

44. Problem Figures

Answer Figures

(a) (b) (c) (d) (e)

45. Problem Figures

Answer Figures

(a) (b) (c) (d) (e)

46. Problem Figures

Answer Figures

(a) (b) (c) (d) (e)

47. Problem Figures

Answer Figures

(a) (b) (c) (d) (e)

48. Problem Figures

Answer Figures

(a) (b) (c) (d) (e)

49. Problem Figures

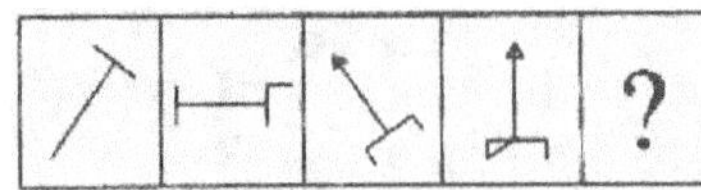

Answer Figures

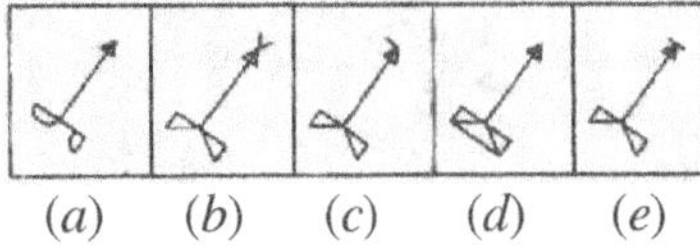

(*a*)   (*b*)   (*c*)   (*d*)   (*e*)

50. Problem Figures

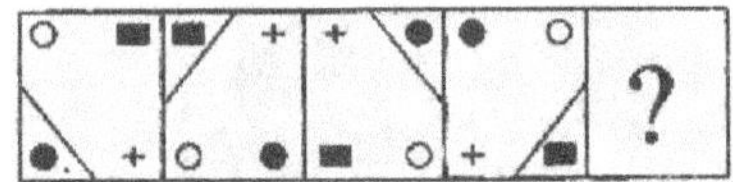

Answer Figures

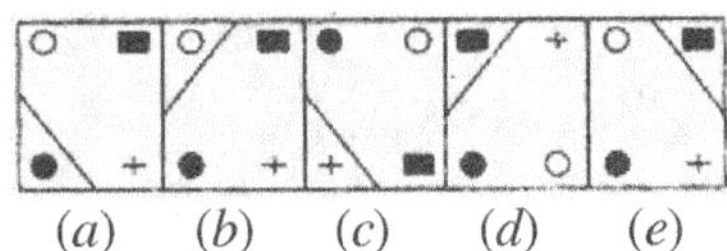

(*a*)   (*b*)   (*c*)   (*d*)   (*e*)

EXPLANATORY ANSWERS

1. (*d*):

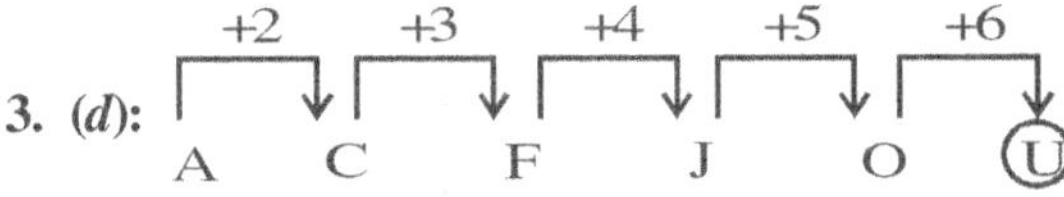

11. (*d*): As

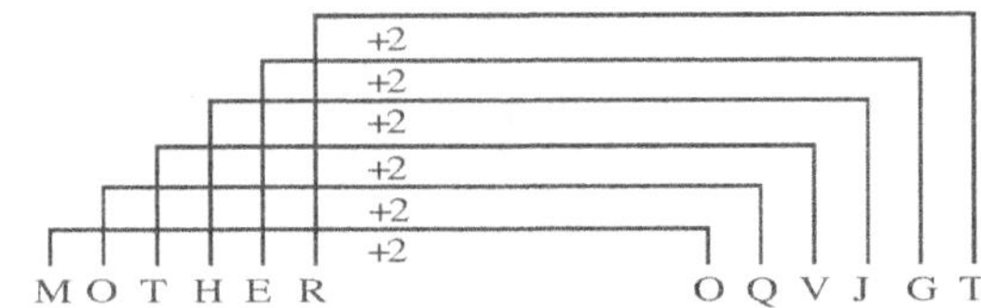

Similarly,

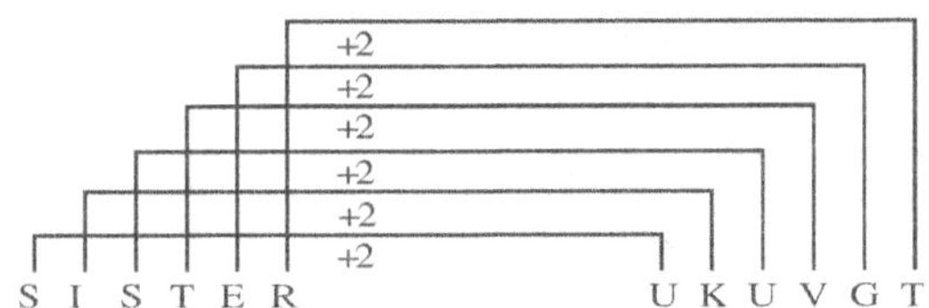

12. (*b*): On writing the letters of the original word in reversing order, Code is formed.

13. (*d*): As

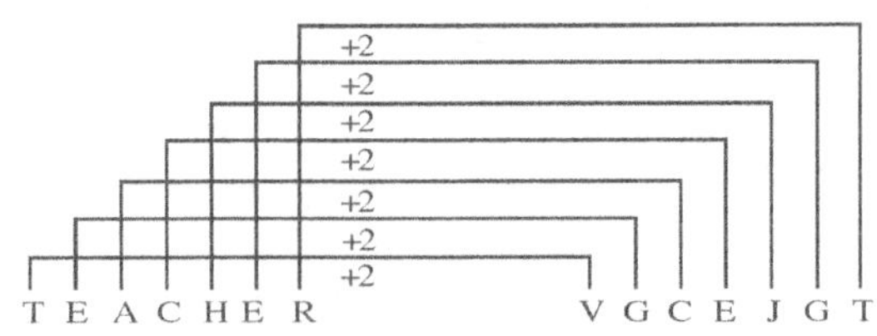

Similarly,

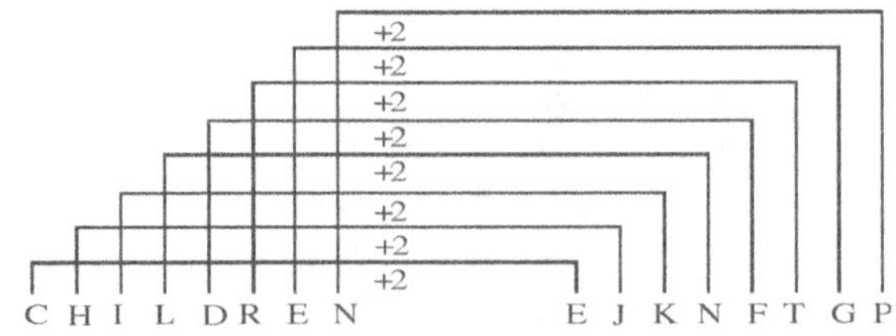

2. (*b*):

A C B   D F E   G I H

3. (*d*):

A   C   F   J   O   U

4. (*d*):

Z   A D   E H   I N   O T   U
vowel vowel vowel vowel vowel

5. (*c*):

24   35   48   63   80

6. (*c*):

3   8   18   33   53

7. (*a*):

4   5   9   18   34   59

8. (*d*):

3   1/3   14   1/14   25   1/25   36

9. (*c*):

9   19   30   42   55   69   84

10. (*b*):

1   3   7   13   21   31

14. (*d*): Here, shooting element from Dhanush is arrow. Similarly, shooting element from gun is BULLET.

15. (*e*): Here, The wings of a fish → Fins. Similarly, The wings of a bird → FEATHERS

16. (*d*): Kailash is not a river.

17. (*b*): Remaining can not swim in water.

18. (*b*): Remaining are planets of solar system.

19. (*e*): Remaining are regional languages.

20. (*d*): Remaining are unit of measurements.

21. (*b*): Remaining are flesh-eating animals.

22. (*b*): Remaining are teachers.

23. (*b*): Remaining are voices of different animals.

24. (*c*): Remaining are senses obtained from all the sense-organs.

25. (*e*): Remaining are different parts of hand.

26. (*e*):

+0 +2 / +1	+0 +2 / +1	+0 +2 / +1	+0 +2 / +1	+1 +2 / +1
A a b D	c C D F	d D e G	P p Q S	P Q r T

27. (*c*):

+3 +3	+3 +3	−3 −3	+3 +3	+3 +3
A D G	B E H	Z W T	C F I	D G J

28. (*d*):

+1 +1	+1 +1	+1 +1	+1 +3	+1 +1
X Y Z	U V W	R S T	N O R	K L M

29. (*e*):

+1 +2	+1 +2	+1 +2	+1 +2	+1 +1
B C E	F G I	J K M	N O Q	R S T

30. (*e*):

+1.5	+1.5	+1.5	+1.25	
1.5	3	4.5	6	7.25

31. (*d*):

+1 / +1 +1	+1 / +1 +1	+1 / +1 +1	−2 / −1 +2	+1 / +1 +1
NOPM	STUR	VWXU	KJLM	CDEB

32. (*e*): Only 21 is not prime number.

33. (*c*): Only 50 is not perfect square.

34. (*e*): Remaining numbers are formed by digit 1, 2 and 3.

35. (*c*): Only 120 is not perfect cube.

36. (*c*): Minute hand moves 10 minute ahead from problem figure (1) to (2) but hour hand shifts 5 minute back. This order is reversed from problem figure (2) to (3). The same changes continue onwards.

37. (*c*): One line is increasing in each figure upto problem figure (3) while from problem figure (4) one line is decreasing in each figure.

38. (*a*): One of the radii and 1/8 of circumference is decreased while one dot is increasing in each subsequent problem figure.

39. (*a*): A new design is increased in each subsequent problem figure and after problem figure (2) each design shifts one place anticlockwise direction.

40. (*b*): Either a line or a semicircle is increased and where the design ends, the new design is formed from that place in each subsequent problem figure.

41. (*c*): Black part shifts clockwise 1, 2, 3 and 4 parts respectively in each subsequent figure.

42. (*b*): The arrow shifts to next line clockwise from problem figure (1) to (3) and from (3) to (5) while it shifts to next line clockwise from problem figure (2) to (4).

43. (*d*): The central line is moving clockwise and arrow is changing his position from top to bottom in each subsequent figure.

44. (*b*): Problem figure (1), (3) and (5) will be same.

45. (*c*): The design is moving through 45° anti clockwise in each subsequent problem figure.

46. (*a*): Previous design shifts lower and a reversed design is increased at its place in each subsequent problem figure.

47. (*e*): From bottom, first, second, third and fourth design reverses respectively in each subsequent problem figure.

48. (*e*): One, two, three and four lines are decreased respectively in each subsequent problem figure.

49. (*b*): Here the design is moving through 45° clockwise and two and three lines are increased respectively in each subsequent problem figure.

50. (*a*): Here design at the corner shifts to next corner anti clockwise while line shifts to next corner clockwise in each subsequent problem figure.

Sainik School Entrance Exam, 2004

(CLASS VI)

PAPER-I : MATHEMATICS AND LANGUAGE

PART–A : MATHEMATICS

1. Simplify : $5\dfrac{7}{8} \div 3\dfrac{1}{4} \times 7\dfrac{5}{16} + \dfrac{7}{8}$ of 16

2. Fill in the blanks :
   (i) The number of sides in a quadrilateral is ....
   (ii) The diameter is the .... chord of a circle.

3. How many 250 gm of salt packets can be made out of 12.25 kg of salt?

4. Add the 'difference' and 'sum' of largest and smallest 6 digit number.

5. Write True or False :
   (i) When the selling price of an article is less than the cost price, then the seller is in loss.
   (ii) The difference between the place value of 6 and 4 in 868594327 is 59999996.

6. Find L.C.M. of the following :
   39, 52, 65

7. A tin contains 6.5 kg of oil. How many such tins will be required to hold 175 kg of oil?

8. Rakhi bought $8\dfrac{1}{3}$ metre of cloth at the rate of Rs. 9 per metre. How much money would Rakhi have to pay?

9. Which of the following cannot be the three angles of the same triangle?
   (a) $m\angle A = 90°, m\angle B = 90°, m\angle C = 20°$
   (b) $m\angle A = 68°, m\angle B = 12°, m\angle C = 100°$
   (c) $m\angle A = 45°, m\angle B = 110°, m\angle C = 25°$

10. Replace each * with same number.

	3	*	5	2
+	1	0	7	*
+	5	4	*	2
+	*	7	3	*
1	*	9	2	*

11. Find the volume of a cuboid whose length is 1 m, width 25 cm and height 75 cm.

12. Subtract the sum of 1.549 and 2.381 from the difference of 3.152 and 9.342.

13. Rita purchased a watch for ₹ 150 and sold it for Rs. 135. Find the percentage of loss made by her.

14. Shyam purchased 2 kg 400 gm Dal, 1 kg 500 gm salt, 3 kg 50 gm tomato and 2 kg 250 gm patato. How much weight is he carrying?

15. A bus travels 38 km in first hour, 35 km in second hour, 52 km in third hour and 35 km in last hour. Find the average speed of the bus per hour.

16. Which football ground is bigger?
    'A' measuring 125 m in length and 48 m in width or 'B' measuring 108 m in length and 72 m in width.

17. The air fare from Delhi to Mumbai is ₹ 7800 plus 8% service tax. Find the total fare including service tax.

18. Find the largest 4 digit number which is exactly divisible by 66.

19. Find the circumference of a circle whose diameter is 7 cm.

20. Ram is late for Raman's birthday party. He cycles at a speed of 200 m/minute. How long will he take to reach Raman's house which is 1.2 km away?

21. A boy gets ₹ 3 for every 2 correct aims and loses ₹ 0.50 for every aim he misses. In a game of 9 trials he missed 3 times. How much amount he will get?

22. (i) A lift can carry 28 children or 14 men. How many children can be taken with 10 men?
    (ii) An aeroplane travels 2848 km in 8 hours. How long will it take to fly 1683 km?

23. Ashok borrowed a sum of ₹ 1650 from Ramesh at the rate of 8% per annum. He returned the

money after 1 year and 6 months. How much has he paid to Ramesh?

24. Find the length of the side of a square whose area is equal to the area of a rectangle which has its length 48 m and width 12 m?

25. A shopkeeper purchased an old cycle for ₹ 1250 and spent 20% on its repair and sold it for ₹ 1650. Find the percentage gain or loss.

26. The length of a rectangular field is double of its width. Find the perimeter and area of the field if the width is 20 m.

27. Find the simple interest on ₹ 1400 for $5\frac{1}{2}$ years

at the rate of 9% per annum. Also find the total amount.

28. Two boxes are bought for ₹ 140 each and first box is sold at a loss of 10% and the other at 8% profit. Find the net loss or gain.

29. A person travels on a circular path and covers a distance of 44 m and returns to same point. How much distance he would have travelled if he passes through centre of the circular path and touches the opposite end?

30. Ram had ₹ 40 with him. He gave ₹ 16 to Lalit and ₹ 24 to Harish. In what ratio did he distributed the money?

EXPLANATORY ANSWERS

1. $5\dfrac{7}{8} \div 3\dfrac{1}{4} \times 7\dfrac{5}{16} + \dfrac{7}{8}$ of 16

$= \dfrac{47}{8} \div \dfrac{13}{4} \times \dfrac{117}{16} + \dfrac{7}{8} \times 16$

$= \dfrac{47}{8} \div \dfrac{13}{4} \times \dfrac{117}{16} + 14$

$= \dfrac{47}{8} \times \dfrac{4}{13} \times \dfrac{117}{16} + 14$

$= \dfrac{423}{32} + 14 = \dfrac{423 + 448}{32} = \dfrac{871}{32} = 27\dfrac{7}{32}$.

2. (i) Four (ii) Largest.

3. 12.25 kg = 12.25 × 1000 = 12250 gm

∴ Number of packets $= \dfrac{12250}{250} = 49$.

4. The difference of largest number and smallest number of six digits

```
  999999
- 100000
  899999
```

The sum of largest and smallest number of six digits

```
  999999
+ 100000
 1099999
```

Then the required sum

```
   899999
+ 1099999
  1999998
```

5. (i) True

(ii) False. The difference between the place value of 6 and 4 in 868594327.

```
  60000000
     - 4000
  59996000
```

6. 13 ⌐ 39, 52, 65
    3, 4, 5

$= 13 \times 3 \times 4 \times 5 = 780$

The L.C.M. of 39, 52 and 65 = 780.

7. Number of tins $= \dfrac{175}{6.5} = \dfrac{1750}{65} = 26\dfrac{12}{13}$

So, there will be need of 27 tins.

8. Rakhi have to pay $= ₹\, 9 \times \dfrac{25}{3} = ₹\, 75$.

9. A

10. 6.

11. Length = 1 m = 100 cm

Volume of the cuboid $= l \times b \times h$

$= 100 \times 25 \times 75$

$= 187500\ \text{cm}^3$.

12.
```
   1.549        9.342
 + 2.381      - 3.152
   3.930        6.190
```
```
   6.190
 - 3.930
   2.260
```

13. Loss $= 150 - 135 = ₹\ 15$

Loss % $= \dfrac{15 \times 100}{150} = 10\%.$

14.
$$
\begin{array}{rl}
& 2 \text{ kg } 400 \text{ gm} \\
+ & 1 \text{ kg } 500 \text{ gm} \\
+ & 3 \text{ kg } \ \ 50 \text{ gm} \\
+ & 2 \text{ kg } 250 \text{ gm} \\
\hline
& 9 \text{ kg } 200 \text{ gm}
\end{array}
$$

15. Average Speed $= \dfrac{38 + 35 + 52 + 35}{4} = \dfrac{160}{4}$

$= 40$ km/hr.

16. The area of ground "A" $= 125 \times 48$

$= 6000$ m^2

The area of ground "B" $= 108 \times 72$

$= 7776$ m^2

Therefore, football ground "B" is bigger.

17. The air fare between Delhi to Mumbai including 8% service tax =

$$= 7800 + \dfrac{8}{100} \times 7800$$

$$= 7800 + 624$$

$$= ₹\ 8424.$$

18.
$$
\begin{array}{r}
66)\ 9999\ (151 \\
\underline{66} \\
339 \\
\underline{330} \\
\times\times\ 99 \\
\underline{66} \\
33
\end{array}
$$

The required number $= 9999 - 33 = 9966.$

19. Diameter $= 7$ cm

The circumference of the circle $= \pi \times d$

$= \pi \times 7$

$= \dfrac{22}{7} \times 7$

$= 22$ cm

20. 1.2 km $= 1.2 \times 1000 = 1200$ m

The required time $= \dfrac{1200}{200} = 6$ min.

21. Number of correct aims $= 9 - 3 = 6$

The amount for 6 correct aims $= 6 \times \dfrac{3}{2} = ₹\ 9$

The amount deducted for 3 missed aims
$$= 3 \times 0.50 = ₹\ 1.50$$
Therefore, the amount he gets $= 9 - 1.50$
$$= ₹\ 7.50.$$

22. (*i*) 8 children

(*ii*) The average speed of aeroplane

$$= \dfrac{2848}{8} = 356 \text{ km/hr}$$

The required time $= \dfrac{1683}{356} = 4\dfrac{259}{356}$ hrs.

23. Time $= 1$ year 6 months $= 1\dfrac{6}{12} = 1\dfrac{1}{2} = \dfrac{3}{2}$ years

Simple Interest $= \dfrac{1650 \times 3 \times 8}{100 \times 2} = ₹\ 198$

The amount to be paid to Ramesh $= 1650 + 198$
$$= ₹\ 1848.$$

24. The area of rectangle $= 48 \times 12$

$= 576$ m^2

Therefore, area of the square will be 576 m^2

Now, length of the side of the square $= \sqrt{576}$

$= \sqrt{2^2 \times 2^2 \times 2^2 \times 3^2}$

$= 2 \times 2 \times 2 \times 3$

$= 24$ m.

25. The cost price of an old cycle $= ₹\ 1250$

Expenditure on its repair $= \dfrac{20}{100} \times 1250$

$= ₹\ 250$

The net cost price $= 1250 + 250$

$= ₹\ 1500$

Selling price $= ₹\ 1650$

Gain $= 1650 - 1500 = ₹\ 150$

Gain % $= \dfrac{150 \times 100}{1500} = 10\%.$

26. The width of the rectangular field $= 20$ m

The length will be $= 2 \times 20 = 40$ m

Then, Perimeter $= 2\,(40 + 20) = 2 \times 60 = 120$ m

The Area $= 40 \times 20 = 800$ m^2.

27. Simple Interest $= \dfrac{1400 \times 11 \times 9}{100 \times 2} = ₹\ 693$

Amount $= 1400 + 693 = ₹\ 2093$.

28. The C.P. of two boxes $= 140 + 140 = ₹\ 280$

S.P. of Ist box $= \dfrac{90}{100} \times 140 = ₹\ 126$

S.P. of another box $= \dfrac{108}{100} \times 140 = \dfrac{1512}{10}$

$\qquad\qquad = ₹\ 151.20$

The S.P. of two boxes $= 126 + 151.20$

$\qquad\qquad\qquad = ₹\ 277.20$

Net loss $\qquad\quad = 280 - 277.20$

$\qquad\qquad\qquad = ₹\ 2.80.$

29. The circumference of circular path

$\qquad = 2\pi r = 44$ m

$\therefore \qquad r = \dfrac{44}{2\pi} = \dfrac{44 \times 7}{2 \times 22} = 7\,\text{m}$

The required distance $= 2 \times 7\text{m} = 14\text{m}.$

30. The required ratio $= \dfrac{16}{24} = \dfrac{2}{3}$

$\qquad\qquad\qquad = 2 : 3.$

PART–B : LANGUAGE

1. Write 15 sentences on any one of the following topics :

(*a*) Children's Day

(*b*) My School

2. Prithvi Raj Chauhan was the last Rajput King who sat on the throne of Delhi. His cousin Jaichand was the king of Kannauj. Prithvi Raj was in love with Sanyogita, the daughter of Jaichand and the princess returned the love. But Jaichand was the deadly enemy of Prithvi Raj. He refused to give his daughter in marriage to him. Instead he ordered, "Let Sanyogita choose her husband at an open Swayamver !" All the princes except Prithvi Raj were invited to this grand Swayamvar.

(*a*) Who was Prithvi Raj Chauhan?

(*b*) What is Swayamvar?

(*c*) Whose daughter was Sanyogita?

(*d*) Why did Jaichand ordered for Swayamvar?

(*e*) Who was not invited for Swayamvar?

3. Re-write the following sentences by changing Genders and making other necessary changes, if needed:

(*a*) The king is sitting with his nephews.

(*b*) He did not marry and remained bechelor all his life.

(*c*) The poet was honoured for his great service to the nation.

(*d*) A shepherd rears sheep and goats and leads a hard life.

(*e*) The Jew was a miser and did not lend his money to anyone.

4. Re-arrange the group of words given below into meaningful sentences:

(*a*) Cage, the, escaped, from, parrot, the

(*b*) Apples, I, you, gave, my, sell, to

(*c*) No, I, interested, with, in, playing, you, am, longer

(*d*) Want, I play, to, football, him, with

(*e*) Babloo, in, his, succeeded, building, home

5. Use the following in sentences to show the difference.

(*a*) except, accept $\qquad$ (*b*) brought, bought

(*c*) peace, piece $\qquad\quad$ (*d*) male, mail

(*e*) week, weak

6. Write the corresponding Adjectives to the following words:

(*a*) Success $\qquad\qquad$ (*b*) Beauty

(*c*) Cheer $\qquad\qquad\quad$ (*d*) Comfort

(*e*) Excite $\qquad\qquad\quad$ (*f*) Dare

(*g*) Darkness $\qquad\qquad$ (*h*) Raise

(*i*) Hate $\qquad\qquad\qquad$ (*j*) Noise

7. Replace the following sentences by one word :

(*a*) One who does not eat meat ....

(*b*) A person-who stitches cloths ....

(*c*) A person who does not belong to the country ....

(*d*) A person who distributes the post ....

(*e*) Large area of land that is thickly covered with trees ....

8. Change the following sentences as directed :

(*a*) She is a good player (Make Interrogative)

(*b*) Were you a naughty boy? (Make Negative)

(*c*) Is your father not going to Agra? (Make Positive)

(*d*) Meera has a new book. (Make Interrogative)

(*e*) Hari reads the Ramayan. (Make Negative)

9. Fill in the blanks with the words opposite to that of given in brackets :

(*a*) How ..... flower it is? (ugly)

(*b*) You must maintain .... in the library. (noise)

(*c*) Every mother looks .... her children carefully. (before)

(*d*) He has a very .... voice. (sore)

(*e*) Did the police ...... the chief? (leave)

EXPLANATORY ANSWERS

1. (*b*) **My School**

I read in Gaur Senior Secondary School. It has a big building. It has about 45 class-rooms. It has three laboratories. It has a big and rich library. The library contains a large number of books, newspapers and magazines. All the rooms in our school are airy and spacious. Our school has a big dispensary. Our school-playground is very big. The students play hockey, cricket, football and volleyball in it. Our school is counted among good schools in Delhi. It is on the top in sports and studies. The school-staff is highly educated. Our school shows good result every year. Our Principal Sh. S.B. Sharma is very able and kind. All the teachers take pains in teaching the students. The school has good discipline. There is a rush in the school at the time of admission.

2. (*a*) Prithvi Raj Chauhan was the last Rajput King of Delhi.

(*b*) A ceremony in which of princess choose her husband is called a Swayamvar.

(*c*) Sanyogita was the daughter of Jaichand.

(*d*) Jaichand never wanted his daughter Sanyogita to marry Prithvi Raj Chauhan, so he ordered for Swayanvar.

(*e*) Prithvi Raj was not invited for Swayamvar.

3. (*a*) The queen is sitting with her niece.

(*b*) She did not marry and remained Virgin all her life.

(*c*) The poetess was honoured for her great service to the nation.

(*d*) A shepherdess rears ram and billy goats and leads a hard life.

(*e*) The Jewish was a miser and did not lend her money to anyone.

4. (*a*) The parrot escaped from the cage.

(*b*) I gave you my apples to sell.

(*c*) No longer I am interested in playing with you.

(*d*) I want to play football with him.

(*e*) Babloo succeeded in building his home.

5. (*a*) Except : All persons were present in the party except Mohan.

Accept : Ram said to Rohit accept my blessings for good future.

(*b*) Brought : Narendra brought some books from school library.

Bought : Mohan bought one kg. sweet from market.

(*c*) Peace : Mental peace is very important in life.

Piece : A cat was carrying a piece of meat.

(*d*) Male : Male are stronger than female.

Mail : The delivery of mail will be on time.

(*e*) Week : There are seven days in a week.

Weak : After fever she has become very weak.

6. (*a*) Success – successful

(*b*) Beauty – beautiful

(*c*) Cheer – cheerful

(*d*) Comfort – comfortable

(*e*) Excite – exciting

(*f*) Dare – daring
(*g*) Darkness – dark
(*h*) Raise – Rise
(*i*) Hate – hateful
(*j*) Noise – noisy

7. (*a*) Vegetarian   (*b*) Tailor
(*c*) Foreigner   (*d*) Postman
(*e*) Forest

8. (*a*) Is she a good player?
(*b*) You were not a naughty boy.
(*c*) Your father is going to Agra.
(*d*) Has Meera a new book?
(*e*) Hari does not read the Ramayan.

9. (*a*) Beautiful   (*b*) Silence
(*c*) After   (*d*) Sweet
(*e*) Catch

PAPER–II : INTELLIGENCE TEST

Directions (Qs. 1 to 9) : *Which of the given options will complete the series.*

1. O P I O P M O P R O P ?
(*a*) V   (*b*) Q
(*c*) W   (*d*) X

2. M M O P M M R S M M U ?
(*a*) W   (*b*) X
(*c*) M   (*d*) V

3. P Q O M N L J K I G ?
(*a*) E   (*b*) D
(*c*) H   (*d*) F

4. V U T E F G S R Q H I J P O ?
(*a*) N   (*b*) L
(*c*) M   (*d*) K

5. 90, 75, 60, 45, ?
(*a*) 30   (*b*) 35
(*c*) 20   (*d*) 25

6. 16, 27, 49, 93, ?
(*a*) 175   (*b*) 171
(*c*) 181   (*d*) 185

7. 4, 11, 32, 95, ?
(*a*) 284   (*b*) 184
(*c*) 174   (*d*) 274

8. 53, 44, 35, 26, ?
(*a*) 17   (*b*) 15
(*c*) 19   (*d*) 14

9. B C A Y Z X E F D ?
(*a*) V   (*b*) W
(*c*) U   (*d*) R

Directions (Qs. 10 to 14) : *Write the correct choice in the given empty box.*

10. Army is to soldier as Galaxy is to—
(*a*) Planets   (*b*) Satellites
(*c*) Stars   (*d*) Meteors

11. Infant is related to child as Girl is to—
(*a*) Mother   (*b*) Aunt
(*c*) Sister   (*d*) Woman

12. Hydrogen is a Gas as .... is a liquid.
(*a*) Diamond   (*b*) Nitrogen
(*c*) Mercury   (*d*) None

13. Rectangle is to square as Ellipse is to—
(*a*) Rhombus   (*b*) Circle
(*c*) Triangle   (*d*) Hexagon

14. Sri Lanka is to Colombo as India is to—
(*a*) Asia   (*b*) Neighbour
(*c*) Delhi   (*d*) Capital

Directions (Qs. 15 to 23) : *In the following question spot the odd-one out.*

15. (*a*) Gangtok   (*b*) Singhbhum
(*c*) Hyderabad   (*d*) Chennai
(*e*) Bhubaneshwar

16. (*a*) Sun   (*b*) Moon
(*c*) Star   (*d*) Mars
(*e*) Universe

17. (*a*) Diamond
(*b*) Heart
(*c*) Bridge (Game of Cards)
(*d*) Spade
(*e*) Club

18. (*a*) Metre   (*b*) Furlong
(*c*) Yard   (*d*) Mile
(*e*) Acre

19. (*a*) Curve   (*b*) Diagonal
(*c*) Tangent   (*d*) Radius
(*e*) Diameter

20. (*a*) Curd   (*b*) Butter
(*c*) Oil   (*d*) Cheese
(*e*) Cream

21. (*a*) Pistol   (*b*) Sword
(*c*) Gun   (*d*) Rifle
(*e*) Cannon

22. (*a*) Geometry   (*b*) Algebra
(*c*) Trignometry   (*d*) Mathematics
(*e*) Arithmetic

23. (*a*) Poland   (*b*) Greece
(*c*) Spain   (*d*) Italy
(*e*) Korea

Directions (Qs. 24 to 30) : *Write the choice of the correct code.*

24. If ATLAS is coded as ZGOZH, then NEW will be coded as—
(*a*) MDV   (*b*) MVD
(*c*) NDV   (*d*) DVM
(*e*) None

25. If NEARER is coded as AENRER and SYSTEM is coded as SYSMET, then MOTHER will be coded as—
(*a*) REHTOM   (*b*) OMHTRE
(*c*) TOMREH   (*d*) HTOMRE
(*e*) None

26. Numbers are given in the first line and letters are given in the second. Numbers are the code for letters and letters are codes for numbers.
Numbers   4   5   6   7   8   9
Letters   K   L   M   P   Q   R
Then KM57RQ will be coded as—
(*a*) 46LP98   (*b*) 64LP8
(*c*) 46PL98   (*d*) 64PL98
(*e*) None

27. If 1234 is coded as AbCd, then 5678 will be coded as—
(*a*) EFGH   (*b*) EFgH
(*c*) EfGh   (*d*) eEgH
(*e*) None

28. If COME is coded as DPNF, then HELLO will be coded as—
(*a*) IFKKN   (*b*) IFMMP
(*c*) IDKKN   (*d*) IFMMN
(*e*) None

29. If TEAM is coded as VGCO, then LIFE will be coded as—
(*a*) NJGE   (*b*) NKHH
(*c*) NKHG   (*d*) NLIH
(*e*) None

30. If 1234 is coded as BADC, then 5678 will be coded as—
(*a*) EFGH   (*b*) DGFI
(*c*) FEHG   (*d*) FGHI
(*e*) None

Directions (Qs. 31 to 36) : *Figure 'P' has some relationship with figure 'Q' figrue 'R' has the same relationship with one of the four choice figures (a), (b), (c) and (d). Choose the correct figure.*

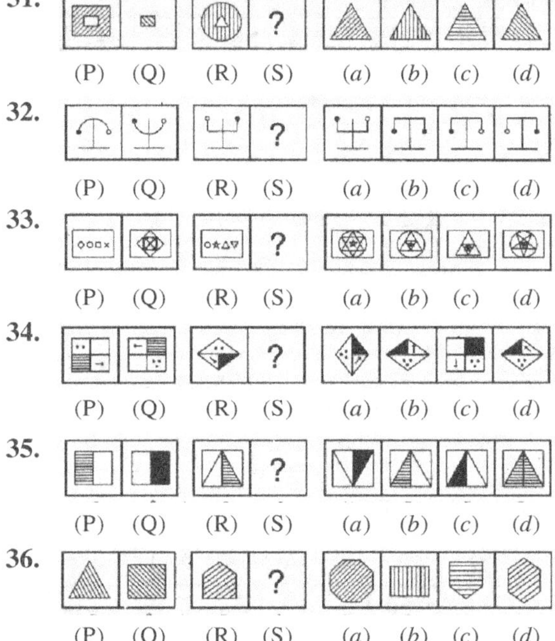

31. (P) (Q) (R) (S)   (*a*) (*b*) (*c*) (*d*)

32. (P) (Q) (R) (S)   (*a*) (*b*) (*c*) (*d*)

33. (P) (Q) (R) (S)   (*a*) (*b*) (*c*) (*d*)

34. (P) (Q) (R) (S)   (*a*) (*b*) (*c*) (*d*)

35. (P) (Q) (R) (S)   (*a*) (*b*) (*c*) (*d*)

36. (P) (Q) (R) (S)   (*a*) (*b*) (*c*) (*d*)

Directions (Qs. 37 to 44) : *Write the choice of the figure which will come next in the series.*

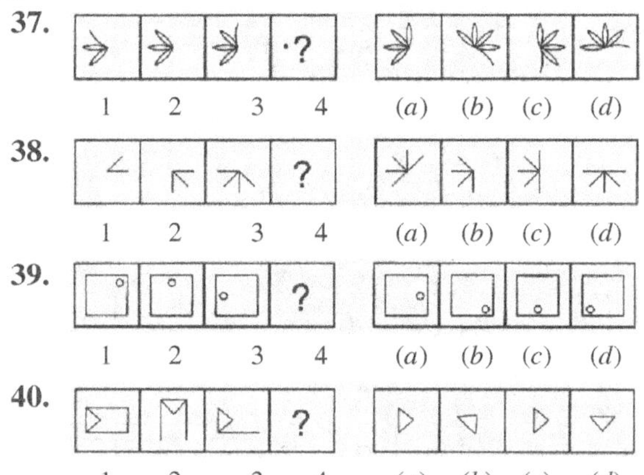

37. 1 2 3 4   (*a*) (*b*) (*c*) (*d*)

38. 1 2 3 4   (*a*) (*b*) (*c*) (*d*)

39. 1 2 3 4   (*a*) (*b*) (*c*) (*d*)

40. 1 2 3 4   (*a*) (*b*) (*c*) (*d*)

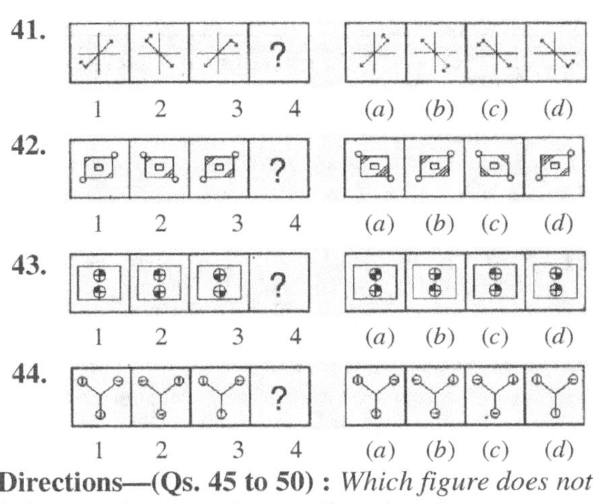

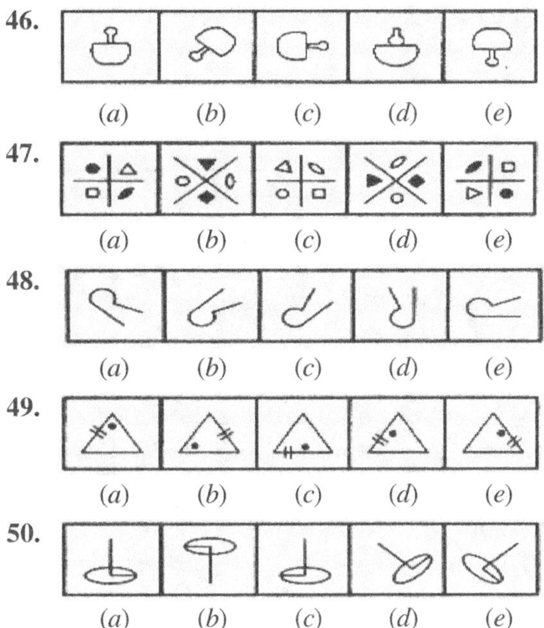

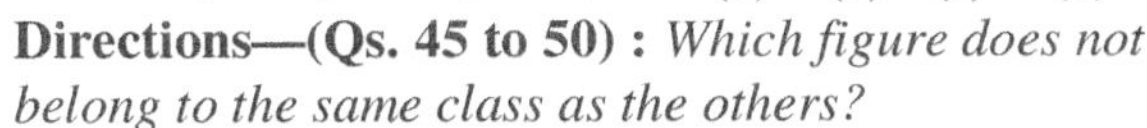

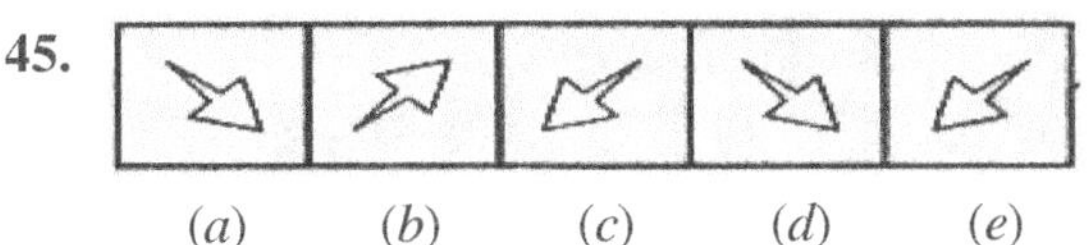

Directions—(Qs. 45 to 50) : *Which figure does not belong to the same class as the others?*

EXPLANATORY ANSWERS

1. (*d*)

2. (*d*)

3. (*c*): Here, 16 17 15 13 14 12 10 11 9 7 8 6
        P Q O M N L J K I G H F

4. (*a*):

5. (*a*): 90 —15→ 75 —15→ 60 —15→ 45 —15→ [30]

6. (*c*): 16 +11→ 27 +22→ 49 +44→ 93 +88→ [181]

7. (*a*): 4 +7→ 11 +21→ 32 +63→ 95 +189→ [284]

8. (*a*): 53 −9→ 44 −9→ 35 −9→ 26 −9→ [17]

9. (*a*):
```
           2   3   1        25  26  24
           B   C   A   →    Y   Z   X
Similarly, 5   6   4        22  23  21
           E   F   D   →    V   W   U
```

Therefore, lette 'V' will replace the question mark.

10. (*c*)

11. (*c*)

12. (*c*)

13. (*b*)

14. (*c*)

15. (*b*): Except Singhbum, all are capitals of different States.

16. (*e*)

17. (*c*)

18. (*e*): Except Acre, all are unit of Length.

19. (*a*)

20. (*c*): Except oil, all are made from milk.

21. (*b*): Except sword, all fire bullets.

22. (*d*): Mathematics is a subject, while all are its branches.

23. (*e*): Except Korea, all are situated in Europe continent.

24. (*b*)

25. (*c*)

26. (*a*)

27. (*c*)   1 2 3 4 → A b C d
Similarly, 5 6 7 8 → E f G h

28. (*b*)

29. (*c*):

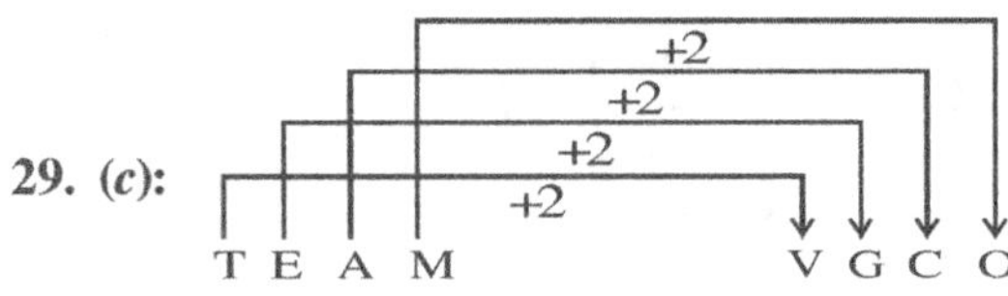

Similarly,

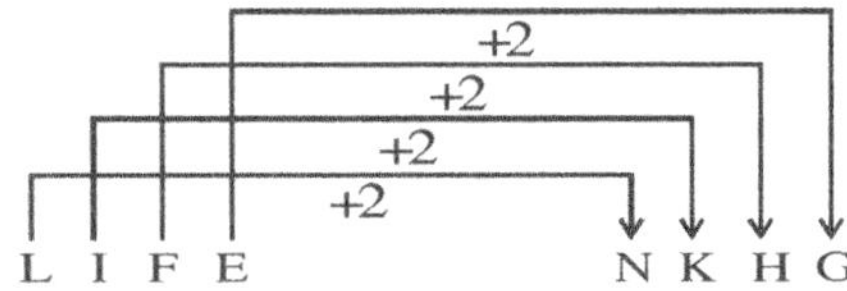

30. (*c*)

31. (*c*)

32. (*d*)

33. (*a*): As all designs of 'P' are available in 'Q', similarly all designs of 'R' are available in answer figure 'A'.

34. (*d*): Whole design rotates through 180° from problem figure P to Q and number of black dots increased by one.

35. (*c*)

36. (*d*)

37. (*a*)

38. (*c*): Whole design rotates through 90° clockwise in each successive problem figure and each time a new line is added to them.

39. (*b*)

40. (*d*)

41. (*b*): Whole design rotates through 90° clockwise in each successive problem figure.

42. (*a*): Outer small circles move one side in the clockwise direction and one more line is added in each successive problem figure.

43. (*d*)

44. (*c*)

45. (*b*): Only in figure (*b*), the arrow is upward direction.

46. (*d*): In figure (*d*), the smaller design is made in different way.

47. (*c*)

48. (*b*): Except (*b*), semicircle combined with the line is towards the bottom.

49. (*b*): Except (*b*), in all figure black dot is opposite to the small two parallel lines on the line of triangle.

50. (*b*): Only in figure (*b*), right angle is towards the bottom.

Sainik School Entrance Exam, 2003
(CLASS VI)
PAPER-I : MATHEMATICS AND LANGUAGE
PART–A : MATHEMATICS

1. Which one is bigger —
   25% of 144 or 19% of 200?

2. Find the gain or loss on an article whose cost price is ₹ 140 and selling price is ₹ 160.

3. Calculate the interest—
   (a) On ₹ 5000 at 8% p.a for 1 year.
   (b) On ₹ 900 at 7% p.a for 5 years

4. Simplify— $2\dfrac{1}{2}+3\dfrac{5}{7}\times\dfrac{7}{13}-\dfrac{1}{3}\times 3$

5. Divide 0.192 by 12.

6. (a) Can there be two right angles in a triangles.
   (b) Can there be two obtuse angles in a triangle.
   (c) Can there be one obtuse angle and one right angle is a triangle.

7. Find true or false in each of the following questions—
   (a) A line is not of a definite length.
   (b) A line has no end points.
   (c) A line cannot be drawn on a paper but it can be represented by a picture.

8. What should be added to 28910 so that the sum may be 47909?

9. Find the square root of 0.09.

10. Area of a circle is 154 sq. cm. Find its radius and circumference :

11. Convert $\dfrac{11}{200}$ into percentage—

12. Fill in the blanks—
    (a) Reciprocal of $\dfrac{11}{5}$ = ...
    (b) $\dfrac{2}{3}\div\dfrac{1}{2}$ = ...

13. If Kamla borrows ₹ 400 for 3 years at the rate of 8% per annum, how much total interest will she have to pay?

14. Volume of a cube is 512 Cu cm. What the length of its one edge?

15. The area of a rectangle 12 sq. cm. If its length is 4 cm, what is the breadth of the rectangle?

16. Vimla has 7.5 metres long ribbon. She wants to divided it into equal parts with Kamla. How much each will have?

17. A soapcake is 7 cm long 5 cm broad and 2.5 cm high. How many soapcakes can be kept in a card-board box of length 56 cm, breadth 49 cm and height 25 cm?

18. Ramesh spends 15% of his income on house rent and 20% on food. If his monthly incme is ₹ 7000, then how much total money does he spends on his house rent and food?

19. Rahim covers a distance of 108 km at a speed of 15 m/sec by car. How many hours will he take to cover this distance?

Directions (Qs. 20 to 22): *Fill in the blanks.*

20. (a) Half of circle is called .....
    (b) ..... is the largest chord of a circle.

21. (a) Angle which is less than 90° is called .....
    (b) Angle which is equal to 90° is called .....

(c) Angle which is more than 90° is called ....

22. (a) The space occupied by a solid is called .....

(b) Solid and hollow pipes of same size have ..... volumes.

23. What is the cost of carpet whose length is 5 m and breadth is 3 m, if its cost per square metre is ₹ 10?

24. If a train starting from New Delhi to Govindpuri, covers a distance of 440 km in 5 hrs and 30 mins, what is the speed of the train?

25. An alloy contains 15% Zinc, 25% brass and rest copper. How much copper is there is 75 kg of that alloy?

26. Kumar has bought following items from Rama Provision Store, New Delhi on 5.1.2000—

(a) 5 kg rice at ₹ 14 per kg

(b) 1 kg Moongdal at ₹ 29 per kg

(c) 3 kg mustard oil at ₹ 58 per kg

According to the informations given above prepare a bill.

How much total money will Kumar have to pay?

27. Convert the following celcius temperatures into Farenheit temperature—

(a) 30°C (b) 20°C

(c) 40°C (d) 100°C

28. In a school there are 29, 43, 38, 26 and 34 children respectively in classes from I to V. Each student of the school gives ₹ 10 for school function. How much total money will be collected?

29. Four buckets have milk 8 litre, 9 litre, 11 litres and 12 litres respectively. A milk man wants to distributes milk equally into 2 parts in a hotel without the help of a measuring utensil. How will he distribute it?

30. The length, breadth and height of a soapcake are 7 cm, 5 cm and 2.5 cm respectively. How many such soapcakes can be put in a card board box of length, breadth and height 56 cm, 40 cm and 25 cm respectively?

EXPLANATORY ANSWERS

1. 25% of 144 = $144 \times \dfrac{25}{100} = 36$

and 19% of 200 = $200 \times \dfrac{19}{100} = 38$

$\because$ 38 > 36 $\therefore$ 19% of 200 is bigger.

2. According to question,

C.P. = ₹ 140

and S.P. = ₹ 160

$\therefore$ Profit = S.P. – C.P.

$\therefore$ Profit = ₹ 160 – ₹ 140

= ₹ 20.

3. (a) Interest = $\dfrac{5000 \times 1 \times 8}{100}$ = ₹ 400.

(b) Interest = $\dfrac{900 \times 5 \times 7}{100}$ = ₹ 315.

4. $2\dfrac{1}{2} + 3\dfrac{5}{7} \times \dfrac{7}{13} - \dfrac{1}{3} \times 3$

$= \dfrac{5}{2} + \dfrac{26}{7} \times \dfrac{7}{13} - \dfrac{1}{3} \times 3 = \dfrac{5}{2} + 2 - 1$

$= \dfrac{5+4-2}{2} = \dfrac{9-2}{2} = \dfrac{7}{2} = 3\dfrac{1}{2}.$

5. 12) 0.192 (0.016

   12

   72

   72 $\therefore$ 0.192 ÷ 12 = 0.016.

   ×

6. (a) No

(b) No

(c) No

7. (a) True

(b) True

(c) True

8. Reqd. number = 47909 − 28910 = 18999.

9. $\sqrt{0.09} = \sqrt{0.3 \times 0.3} = \sqrt{(0.3)^2} = 0.3$.

10. Radius of the circle $= \sqrt{\dfrac{\text{Area}}{\pi}} = \sqrt{\dfrac{154}{\dfrac{22}{7}}}$

$$= \sqrt{154 \times \dfrac{7}{22}} = \sqrt{7 \times 7} = 7 \text{ cm.}$$

and circumference $= 2\,\pi\,r$

$$= 2 \times \dfrac{22}{7} \times 7 = 44 \text{ cm.}$$

11. $\dfrac{11}{200} = \dfrac{11}{200} \times 100\% = \dfrac{11}{2}\% = 5\dfrac{1}{2}\%$.

12. (*a*) Reciprocal of $\dfrac{11}{5} = \dfrac{5}{11}$

(*b*) $\dfrac{2}{3} \div \dfrac{1}{2} = \dfrac{2}{3} \times \dfrac{2}{1} = \dfrac{4}{3}$.

13. Principal = ₹ 400, Time = 3 years, Rate = 8% p.a.

$$\therefore \quad \text{Interest} = \dfrac{\text{Principal} \times \text{Time} \times \text{Rate}}{100}$$

$$= \dfrac{400 \times 3 \times 8}{100} = ₹ 96.$$

14. ∵ Volume of the cube = (edge)^3

∴ $\quad 2^3 \times 2^3 \times 2^3 = $ (edge)^3

∴ Length of one edge = 2 × 2 × 2 = 8 cm.

15. Breadth of the rectangle $= \dfrac{12}{4} = 3$ cm.

16. Length of each ribbon = 7.5 ÷ 2 = 3.75.

17. Reqd. number of soapcakes

$$= \dfrac{\text{Volume of the box of cardboards}}{\text{Volume of one soapcake}}$$

$$= \dfrac{56 \times 49 \times 25}{7 \times 5 \times 2.5} = 784.$$

18. Amount spent on rent = 15% of ₹ 7000

$$= \dfrac{15}{100} \times 7000$$

$$= ₹ 1050$$

and amount spent on food
$$= 20\% \text{ of } ₹ 7000$$

$$= \dfrac{20 \times 7000}{100}$$

$$= ₹ 1400$$

∴ Total amount spent = 1050 + 1400
$$= ₹ 2450.$$

19. Speed of Car = 15 m/sec

$$= 15 \times \dfrac{18}{5} \text{km / hr}$$

$$= 54 \text{ km/hr}$$

$$\therefore \quad \text{Time taken} = \dfrac{\text{Distance travelled}}{\text{Speed}}$$

$$= \dfrac{108}{54} = 2 \text{ hours.}$$

20. (*a*) Semicircle

(*b*) Diameter

21. (*a*) Acute angle

(*b*) Right angle

(*c*) Obtuse angle.

22. (*a*) Volume

(*b*) Unequal

23. Area of the carpet = 5 × 3 = 15 sq. m.

∴ Cost of the carpet = 15 × 10 = ₹ 150.

24. Distance = 440 km.

and time = 5 hrs, 30 mins $= \dfrac{11}{2}$ hours

$$\therefore \quad \text{Speed} = \dfrac{\text{Distance travelled}}{\text{Time taken}}$$

$$= \dfrac{440}{\dfrac{11}{2}} = \dfrac{440}{1} \times \dfrac{2}{11} = 80 \text{ km/hr.}$$

25. Percentage of copper in the alloy
$$= [100 - (15 + 25)]\%$$

$$= (100 - 40) = 60\%$$

∴ Quantity of copper in 75 kg of alloy

$$= \dfrac{60}{100} \times 75 = 45 \text{ kg.}$$

26. **Rama Provision Store, New Delhi**

Date 5.1.2000

S. No.	Name of item	Rate	Quantity	Total Cost
(a)	Rice	Rs. 14/kg	5 kg	70.00
(b)	Moong Dal	Rs. 29/kg	1 kg	29.00
(c)	Mustard Oil	Rs. 58/kg	3 kg	174.00
			Total	**273.00**

27. $\because \dfrac{C}{5} = \dfrac{F-32}{9} \Rightarrow F = \dfrac{9C}{5} + 32$

(a) $\therefore 30°C = \dfrac{9}{5} \times 30 + 32 = 54 + 32 = 86°F$

(b) $\therefore 20°C = \dfrac{9}{5} \times 20 + 32 = 36 + 32 = 68°F$

(c) $\therefore 40°C = \dfrac{9}{5} \times 40 + 32 = 72 + 32 = 104°F$

(d) $\therefore 100°C = \dfrac{9}{5} \times 100 + 32 = 180 + 32$
$$= 212°F.$$

28. Total number of students
$$= 29 + 43 + 38 + 26 + 34 = 170$$

$\therefore$ Total money collected
$$= ₹ 170 \times 10 = ₹ 1700.$$

29. Total quantity of milk in 4 buckets
$$= 8 + 9 + 11 + 12 = 40 \text{ litres}$$

$\therefore$ Half of the total milk $= \dfrac{1}{2} \times 40 = 20$ litres

Hence, he will give at one place the buckets of 8 litres and 12 litres milk.

30. Number of soapcakes

$$= \dfrac{\text{Volume of the box of cardboard}}{\text{Volume of 1 soapcake}}$$

$$= \dfrac{56 \times 40 \times 25}{7 \times 5 \times 2.5} = 640.$$

PART–B : LANGUAGE

Directions: *Read the following passage carefully and answer the questions that follows–*

1. Distance in large cities are long. All the people do not have their own means of transport. They have to depend upon the state or private buses. The number of bus users is very large. Every bus stop is therefore, crowded. The number of buses is not adequate. Thus people suffer the torture of long wait at the bus stop. Some bus stops are quite orderly. People form queues and get in the buses turn by turn. However, after this order is forgotten and confusion spreads when the bus comes and the law of jungle prevails.

(a) What happens when the people do not have their own means of transport?

(b) Why are the bus stops crowded?

(c) What happens when the bus comes at the bus stop?

(d) From the passage find and write opposite word of 'order'.

(e) What does the word 'adequate' mean in the passage? Tick (✓) the correct answer.
  (i) much   (ii) proper
  (iii) sufficient   (iv) just

2. Complete the sentences by giving correct word out of the words given below—
fox, block, galaxy, pile, wolf, mule, deer

(a) A .... of stones.

(b) A .... of stars.

(c) As stubborn as a ....

(*d*) As shy as a ....

(*e*) As hungry as a ....

3. Rewrite the following sentences changing the Gender of the Noun and making other changes if needed—

(*a*) The bull ran at a fast speed

(*b*) The dog is barking

(*c*) The king loves his white horse

(*d*) My nephew lives in London

(*e*) The male bird flew away

4. Pair each Adjective with the Noun it most suitably describes—

mountain, building, water, fix, fruit, light, person.

(*a*) quick .....

(*b*) humorous .....

(*c*) bright .....

(*d*) magnificent .....

(*e*) ice cold .....

5. Write 15 sentences on any one of the following topics—

(*a*) My Aim in Life

(*b*) Our National Flag

6. Rearrange the group of words given below into meaningful sentences—

(*a*) dress, he, about, his, keen, is, very,

(*b*) rubber, are, of, these, made, shoes,

(*c*) playing, fond, children, of, are

(*d*) the, knocking, who, at, door, is ?

(*e*) late, he, bus, the, reached, stop

7. Make your own sentences using the **bold** words in the following paragraph—

An **aimless** life is worthless life. A man who has no aim of life is **like** a ship **without** a destination. His life would be **meaningless** to him and useless to others. An aim in life gives **direction** to a man.

8. Fill in the blanks with such Adjectives as are opposite to those given in brackets—

(*a*) The man got the ..... of his house decorated (Interior)

(*b*) He came ..... in the class in Physics. (first)

(*c*) Do not cut fruit with a ..... knife. (sharp)

(*d*) Let us drink ..... water. (pure)

(*e*) There are two ..... boys in our class. (dull)

9. Fill in the blanks with the correct form of verb given in the brackets—

(*a*) I ...... a letter to you yesterday. (had written/ wrote)

(*b*) Did the police ..... the thief. (catch/caught)

(*c*) It ..... raining since 2 o'clock (is, has been)

(*d*) I ..... for Bombay tomorrow. (shall leave/ leaving)

(*e*) He ..... in Delhi for ten years. (lives/has lived)

10. Change each of the following sentences as directed—

(*a*) He got into the running bus. (make 'interrogative')

(*b*) He loves reading. (make 'negative')

(*c*) Shyam is not in the habit of smoking. (make 'positive')

(*d*) Radha has played the game. (make 'interrogative')

(*e*) Is he going to school today? (make 'negative')

EXPLANATORY ANSWERS

1. (*a*) When the people do not have their own means of transport they travel by state or private buses.

(*b*) The bus stops are crowded because the number of passengers is very large.

(*c*) When the bus comes at the bus-stand, people enter the bus one-by-one or sometimes they do not follow the rule.

(*d*) Disorder.

(*e*) Sufficient.

2. (*a*) A pile of stones

(*b*) A galaxy of stars

(*c*) As stubborn as a block

(*d*) As shy as a deer

(*e*) As hungry as a fox

3. (*a*) The cow ran at a fast speed.
 (*b*) The bitch is barking.
 (*c*) The queen loves her white mare.
 (*d*) My niece lives in London.
 (*e*) The female bird flew away.

4. (*a*) quick fix
 (*b*) humorous person
 (*c*) bright light
 (*d*) magnificient building
 (*e*) ice cold water

5. (*b*) **Our National Flag**
Our National Flag is a horizontal tricolour of deep saffron (Kesaria) at the top, white in the middle and dark green at the bottom in equal proportion. The ratio of width of the flag to its length is two to three. In the centre of the white band is a navy-blue wheel which represents the chakra. Its design is that of the wheel which appears on the abacus of the Sarnath Lion Capital of Ashoka. Its diameter approximates to the width of the white band and it has 24 spokes. The design of the National Flag was adopted by the constituent Assembly of India on 22 July, 1947. On our national festivals, Independence Day and Republic Day, tricolour flag is unfurled on every government building.

6. (*a*) He is very keen about his dress.
 (*b*) These shoes are made of rubber.
 (*c*) Children are fond of playing.
 (*d*) Who is knocking at the door?
 (*e*) He reached the bus stop late.

7. Aimless — Ram is an aimless wonderer.
 Without — Mohan can't read without spects.
 Like — Mohan walks like a sick person.
 Meaningless — Reading without aim is meaningless.
 Direction — Teacher gave proper direction to students.

8. (*a*) The man got the <u>exterior</u> of his house decorated.
 (*b*) He came <u>last</u> in the class in physics.
 (*c*) Do not cut fruit with a <u>blunt</u> kinfe.
 (*d*) Let us drink <u>impure</u> water.
 (*e*) There are two <u>brilliant</u> boys in our class.

9. (*a*) I <u>wrote</u> a letter to you yesterday.
 (*b*) Did the police <u>catch</u> the thief.
 (*c*) It <u>has been</u> raining since 2 o'clock.
 (*d*) I <u>shall leave</u> for Bombay tomorrow.
 (*e*) He <u>has lived</u> in Delhi for ten years.

10. (*a*) Did he get into running bus?
 (*b*) He does not love reading.
 (*c*) Shyam is in the habit of smoking.
 (*d*) Has Radha played the game?
 (*e*) Is he got going to school today?

PAPER–II : INTELLIGENCE TEST

Directions (Qs. 1–15): *Which one is the odd in each of the following questions?*

1. (*a*) Water (*b*) Lemon juice
 (*c*) Jelly (*d*) Coffee
 (*e*) Milk

2. (*a*) Tea (*b*) Coffee
 (*c*) Milk (*d*) Pizza
 (*e*) Coke

3. (*a*) Duck (*b*) Pigeon
 (*c*) Parrot (*d*) Crow
 (*e*) Owl

4. (*a*) Venus (*b*) Pluto
 (*c*) Moon (*d*) Mars
 (*e*) Earth

5. (*a*) Nose (*b*) Eye
 (*c*) Skin (*d*) Tongue
 (*e*) Tooth

6. (*a*) Nilgiri Hills (*b*) Aravali Hills
 (*c*) Satpura Hills (*d*) Rai Hills
 (*e*) Shivalik Hills

7. (*a*) Knee (*b*) Palm
 (*c*) Shoulder (*d*) Elbow
 (*e*) Molar Teeth

8.   (*a*) Novel   (*b*) Magazine
   (*c*) Comics   (*d*) Dictionary
   (*e*) Research papers

9.   (*a*) Swimming   (*b*) Running
   (*c*) Sitting   (*d*) Slipping
   (*e*) Flying

10. (*a*) Friend   (*b*) Mother
   (*c*) Brother   (*d*) Father
   (*e*) Sister

11. (*a*) Ginger   (*b*) Carrot
   (*c*) Spinach   (*d*) Beet
   (*e*) Potato

12. (*a*) Root   (*b*) Tree
   (*c*) Flower   (*d*) Fruit
   (*e*) Branch

13. (*a*) Polo   (*b*) Ludo
   (*c*) Chess   (*d*) Playing cards
   (*e*) Carrom

14. (*a*) Scooter   (*b*) Car
   (*c*) Transportation (*d*) Train
   (*e*) Truck

15. (*a*) Jaipur   (*b*) Lucknow
   (*c*) Mumbai   (*d*) Patna
   (*e*) Tripura

16. Z, X, V, T, R ....
   (*a*) O, K   (*b*) N, M
   (*c*) K, S   (*d*) M, N
   (*e*) P, N

17. C3, E5, G7, I9.....
   (*a*) X24, M21   (*b*) K14, M18
   (*c*) K11, M13   (*d*) M18, K14
   (*e*) K10, N13

18. AAZ, BBY, CC....
   (*a*) Y   (*b*) D
   (*c*) Z   (*d*) X
   (*e*) C

19. B, E, I, N, ...
   (*a*) S   (*b*) P
   (*c*) T   (*d*) X
   (*e*) Z

20. 6F, 7G, 9I, 12L, ...
   (*a*) 13M   (*b*) 16P
   (*c*) 17Q   (*d*) 14N
   (*e*) 15O

21. 1, 6, 12, 19, 27, ...
   (*a*) 38   (*b*) 36
   (*c*) 35   (*d*) 54
   (*e*) 34

22. 8, 48, 16, 96, 32, ...
   (*a*) 192   (*b*) 150
   (*c*) 64   (*d*) 288
   (*e*) 129

23. K....M K....LM KL....KK....MK
   (*a*) L, K, L, M   (*b*) L, K, M, K
   (*c*) L, K, M, M   (*d*) L, K, M, L
   (*e*) L, K, K, M

24. XW, DC, CB, ...
   (*a*) NM   (*b*) BC
   (*c*) PQ   (*d*) KL
   (*e*) ST

25. A, E, I, M, Q.....
   (*a*) T   (*b*) U
   (*c*) V   (*d*) W
   (*e*) X

Directions (Qs. 26 to 30): *Code-Decoding.*

26. If the code of 'BOMBAY' is 'CNNABX' then what will be code of 'DELHI'?
   (*a*) EDMGJ   (*b*) EGMGJ
   (*c*) FDMGH   (*d*) EDMIJ

27. If the code of 'CHAIR' is FKDLU' then what will be the code of 'TABLE'?
   (*a*) WDEOH   (*b*) WEDOH
   (*c*) VDEOH   (*d*) WDOEH

28. If the code of 'BAD' is 7. The code of 'HIS' is 36, then what will be the code of 'LOW'?
   (*a*) 50   (*b*) 8
   (*c*) 23   (*d*) 5

29. If the code of OUT is 7. 152120, then what is the code of 'IN'
   (*a*) 1015   (*b*) 819
   (*c*) 1813   (*d*) 5

30. In a code if JUNE is written as NXPF, then what will be the code of STAY?
   (*a*) WWCZ   (*b*) WVCZ
   (*c*) WWDB   (*d*) WWZC

Directions (Qs. No. 31 to 50): *Which figure does not belong to the same class as the others?*

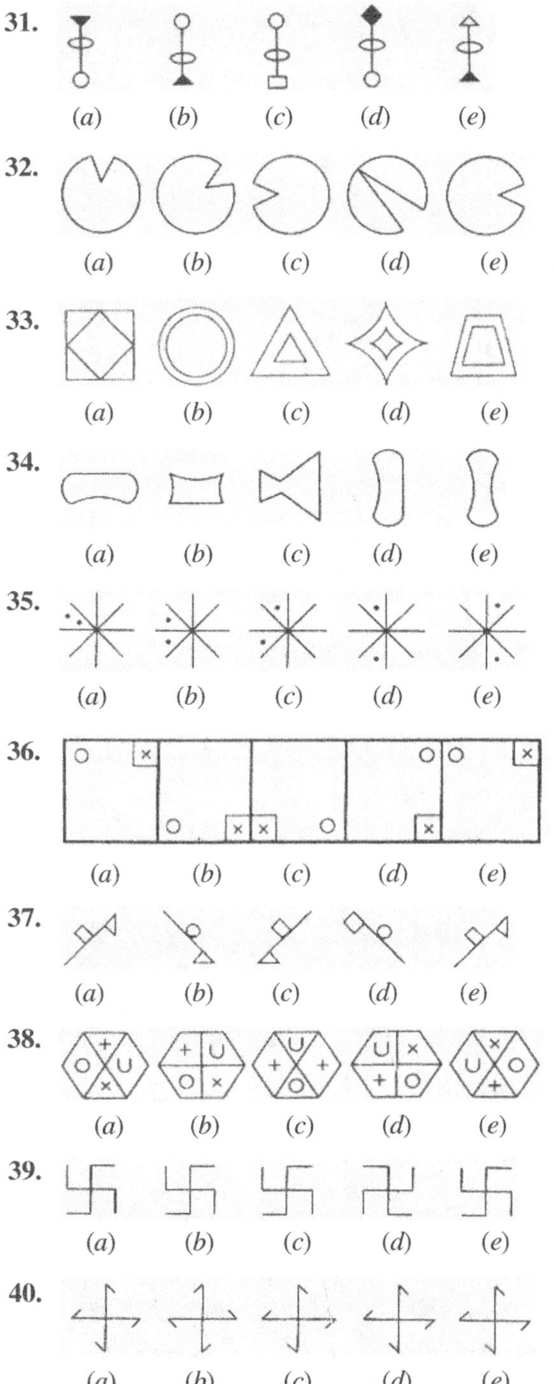

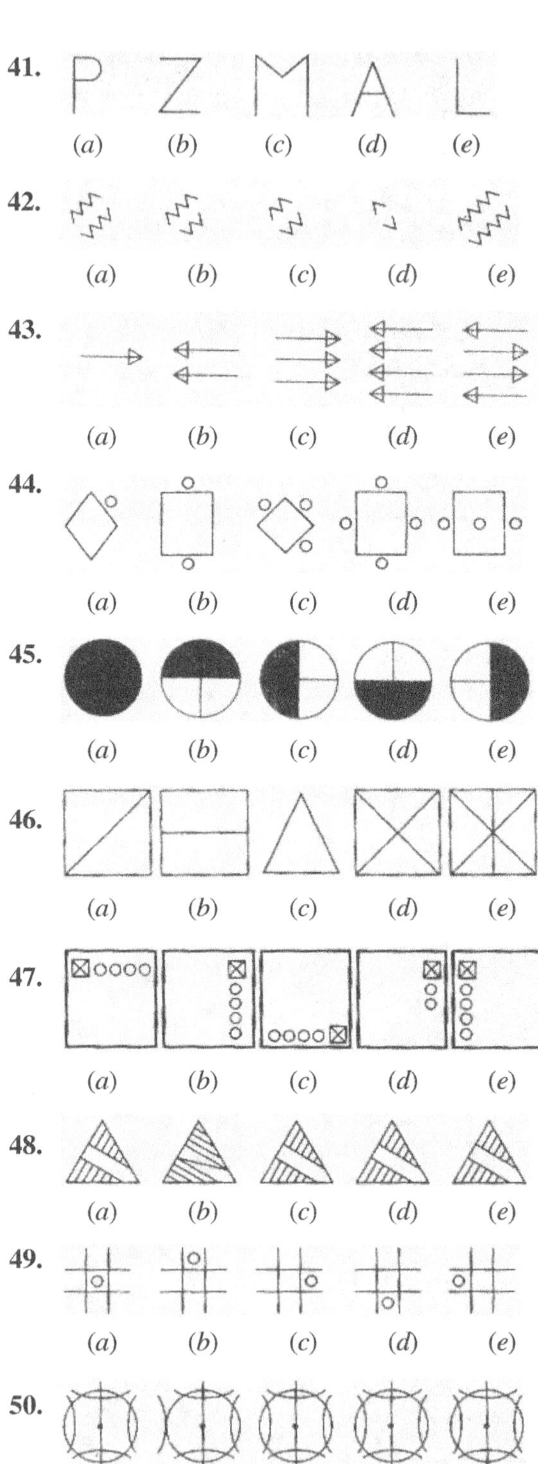

EXPLANATORY ANSWERS

1. (*c*): All others are drinking materials.

2. (*d*): All others are drinking materials.

3. (*a*): All others stay-flying birds.

4. (*c*): All others are planets.

5. (*e*): All others are sense-organs.

6. (*d*): All others are hills.

7. (*e*): All others are external parts of body.

8. (*e*): All others are different kinds of books.

9. (*c*): In all others is a change of place.

10. (*a*): All others are related to a family.

11. (*c*): All others grow under ground.

12. (*b*): All others are different parts of a tree.

13. (*a*): All others are indoor games.

14. (*c*): All others are means of transportation.

15. (*e*): All others are capitals of different states.

16. (*e*): 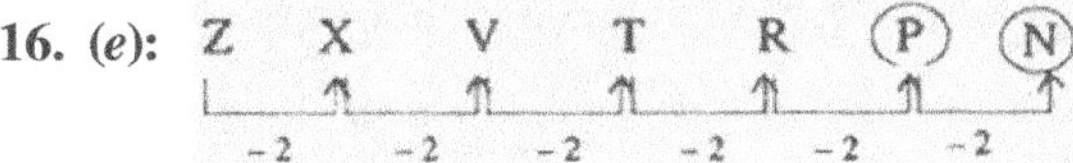

17. (*c*): 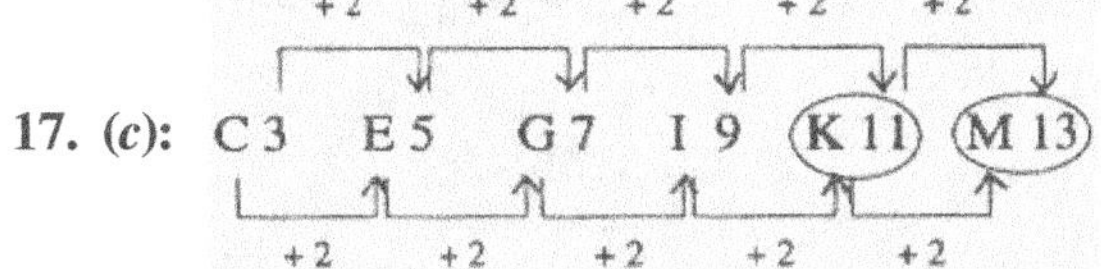

18. (*d*): 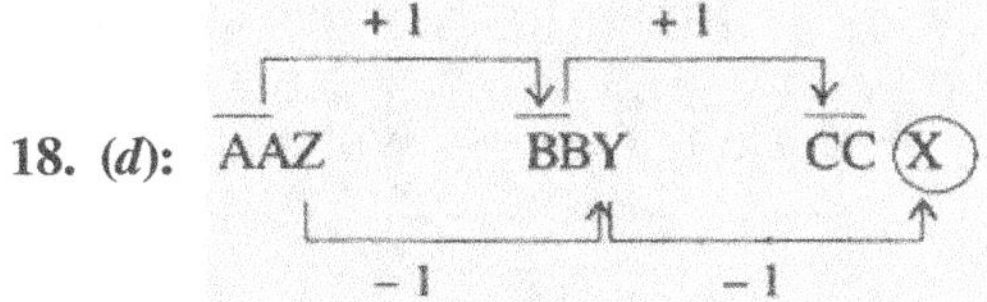

19. (*c*): 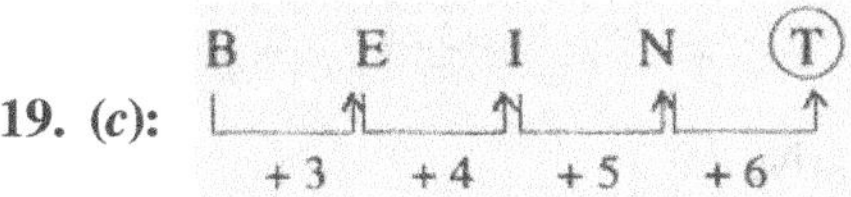

20. (*b*): 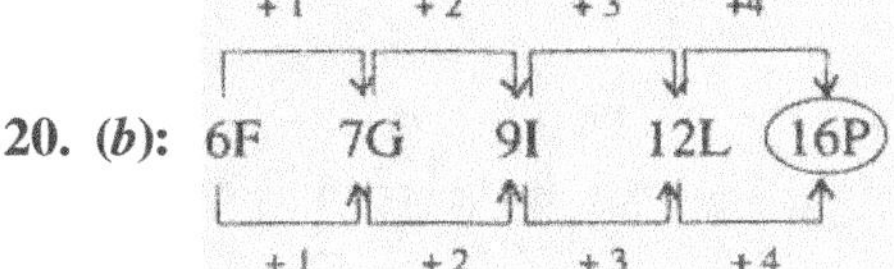

21. (*b*): 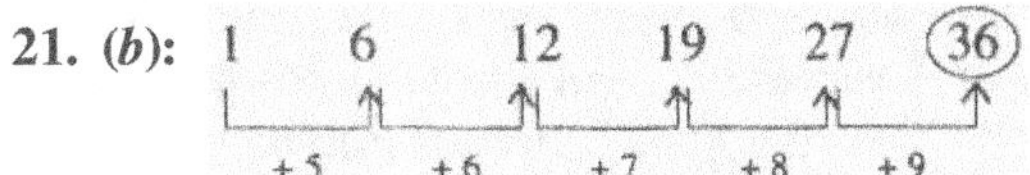

22. (*a*): 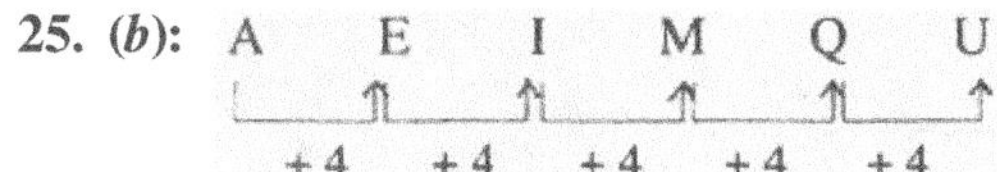

23. (*d*): K L M K K L M is repeated.

24. (*a*): 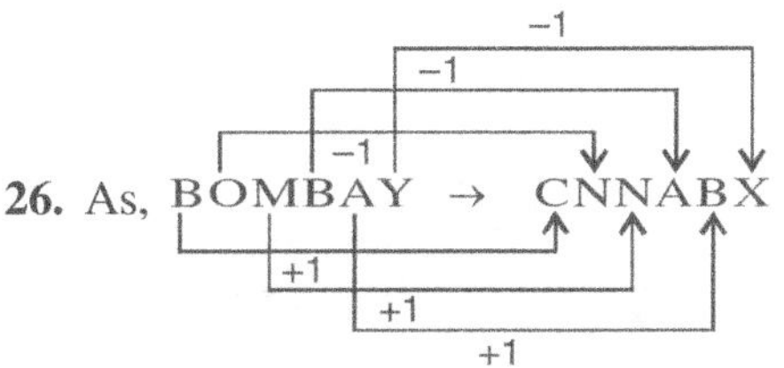

25. (*b*): 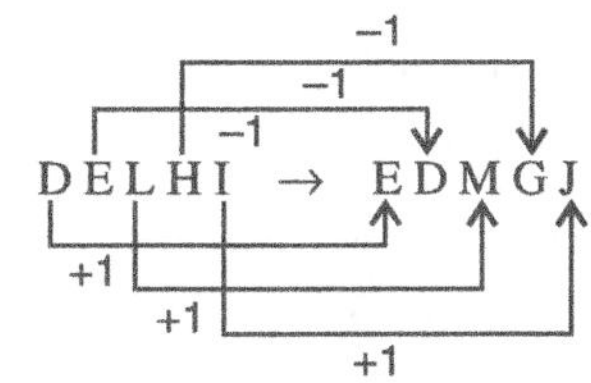

26. As, 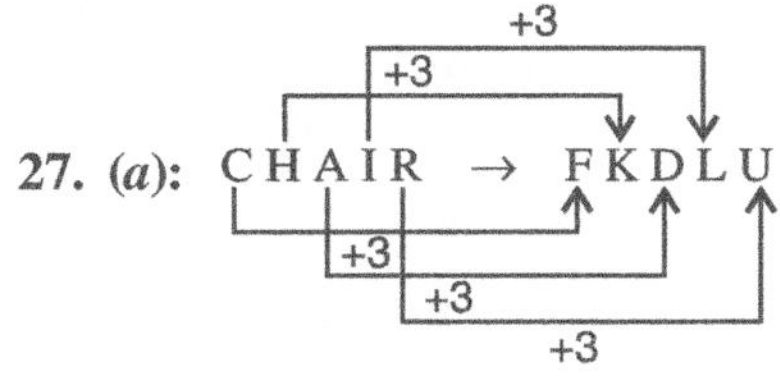

27. (*a*): 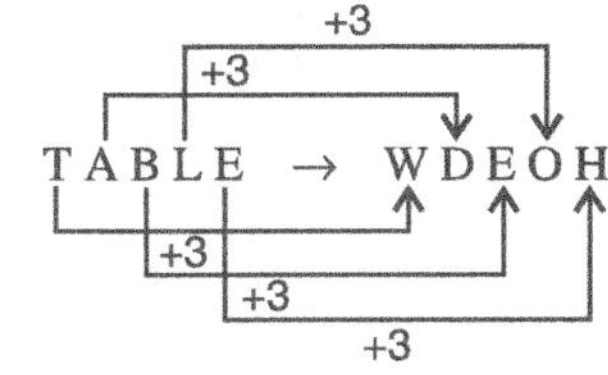

28. (*a*): The order of the letters B, A and D in English alphabets are 2, 1 and 4. Hence, the code of 'BAD' is 2 + 1 + 4 *i.e.*, 7. Similarly, the order of H, I, and S are 8, 9 and 19, so of the code of HIS is 8 + 9 + 19 *i.e.*, 36. In the same way the order of L, O and W are 12, 15 and 23 respectively. Hence, code of 'LOW' is 12 + 15 + 23 *i.e.*, 50.

29. (*d*): The code of 'OUT' is 15 21 20. Hence the order of O, U and T in English alphabets are 15, 21 and 20 respectively. Similarly the order of I and N in English alphabet are 9 and 14 respectively.

∴ Code of IN is 914.

30. (*a*): As, JUNE ⟶ NXPF

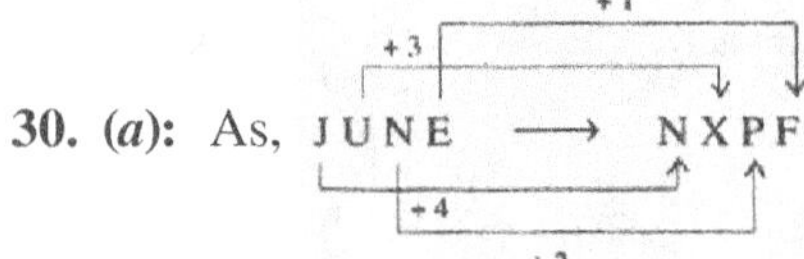

Similarly, STAY ⟶ WWCZ

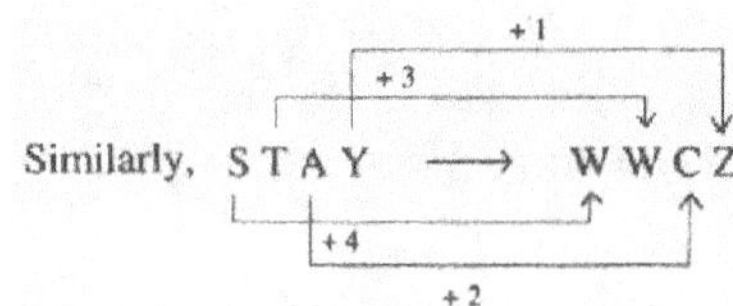

31. (*c*): In all other figures the one end of the design is black.

32. (*d*): All other figures are same.

33. (*a*): In all other figures two designs do not meet with one another.

34. (*c*): In all other figures, curved lines are used while figure (*c*) is made of straight lines.

35. (*a*): In all other figures both the dots are at different places while in Fig. (*a*) they are together.

36. (*b*): In all other figures the design X in clockwise direction is ahead one side of the design 'O'.

37. (*d*): In all other figures, the design at the vertex of each figure is same.

38. (*c*): In all other figures the inner designs in each figure are different *i.e.*, 0, +, U and X, While in Fig. (*c*) two designs are same.

39. (*d*): All other figures are same.

40. (*b*): All other figures are same.

41. (*a*): In all other figures the letters are made of straight lines.

42. (*b*): In all other figures both the designs are same.

43. (*e*): In all other figures the arrow or arrows are in the same direction.

44. (*e*): There is no inner circle in all other figures.

45. (*a*): In all other figures the circle is half-blackened.

46. (*c*): There is no inner line in the Fig. (*c*)

47. (*d*): It is different from the rest because it contains two circles while the rest have four circles.

48. (*b*): All other figures are same.

49. (*a*): In all other figures the design 'O' is not at the innermost place.

50. (*b*): All other figures are same.